Praise for *Kafka Connect*

Kafka Connect is the pillar for integrating Apache Kafka with the rest of the data ecosystem. This book tells you everything you need to know to connect external data sources and sinks with Kafka.

—*Jun Rao, cofounder, Confluent*

This comprehensive book covers everything from getting started to productionizing Kafka Connect at scale. It gives you the tools to build streaming data pipelines with Apache Kafka.

—*Ryanne Dolan, software engineer, LinkedIn*

An invaluable resource for both novice and seasoned professionals working with Kafka Connect. It offers comprehensive explanations and a wealth of practical tips.

—*Robin Moffatt, rmoff.net*

An invaluable resource for anyone looking to use Kafka alongside existing systems. I only wish I'd had access to this book when I first began using Kafka Connect!

—*Danica Fine, senior developer advocate, Confluent*

Kafka Connect
Build and Run Data Pipelines

Mickael Maison and Kate Stanley

Beijing · Boston · Farnham · Sebastopol · Tokyo

Kafka Connect

by Mickael Maison and Kate Stanley

Published by O'Reilly Media, Inc., 1005 Gravenstein Highway North, Sebastopol, CA 95472.

O'Reilly books may be purchased for educational, business, or sales promotional use. Online editions are also available for most titles (*http://oreilly.com*). For more information, contact our corporate/institutional sales department: 800-998-9938 or *corporate@oreilly.com*.

Acquisitions Editor: Jessica Haberman	**Indexer:** nSight, Inc.
Development Editor: Jeff Bleiel	**Interior Designer:** David Futato
Production Editor: Kristen Brown	**Cover Designer:** Karen Montgomery
Copyeditor: Liz Wheeler	**Illustrator:** Kate Dullea
Proofreader: Tove Innis	

September 2023:   First Edition

Revision History for the First Edition

2023-09-18:   First Release

See *http://oreilly.com/catalog/errata.csp?isbn=9781098126537* for release details.

978-1-098-12653-7

[LSI]

Table of Contents

Part II.   Developing Data Pipelines with Kafka Connect

Part III.   Running Kafka Connect in Production

Part IV.   Building Custom Connectors and Plug-Ins

Foreword

Consensus protocols, stream processing, distributed systems—in the midst of all the exciting ideas in the streaming world, it can be easy to overlook the role of the humble connector. But connectors solve the most fundamental problem in the streaming world—in a world of data at rest, how do you access streams at all? How do you plug your data-streaming platform into the rest of the business?

Kafka Connect's aim is to make that easier. Before the Kafka Connect framework existed, we saw many people build integrations with Apache Kafka and repeat the same mistakes. Reading data from one system and writing it to another seems simple enough, but the process can have a lot of hidden complexity. What happens if a machine fails? What happens when requests time out? How do you scale up your integration? Each unique Kafka integration had to solve these problems from scratch. Kafka Connect was designed to separate out the logic of reading and writing to a particular system from a general framework for building, operating, and scaling these integrations.

Kafka Connect is different from other integration or connector layers in a lot of important ways:

- It's designed for streaming first.
- It works with Kafka's semantics to enable exactly-once from systems that will allow it, and the strongest semantics possible for systems that don't.
- It lets you not just capture bytes, but also propagate some of the semantic structure of data.
- It solves a lot of the complex problems in partitioning, scaling, and fault tolerance.
- It lets you operate and monitor a pool of diverse connectors in a homogeneous way off a shared pool of hardware.

I think that these reasons are why Kafka Connect has proven so popular, why it has been embraced by Kafka users of all types, and why its ecosystem of connectors has grown to number in the hundreds.

Success with Kafka Connect lets you open up data from all across your company to your data-streaming platform, but before taking it to production, it's important to recognize that Kafka Connect is a sophisticated distributed system in its own right and to learn a little bit about how it works.

This book is an excellent way to learn how to use connectors, configure the Kafka Connect framework, monitor and operate it in production, and even develop your own source and sink connectors. I can't think of a better resource for those hoping to dive into this important topic and a faster way to get Kafka connected to the rest of your systems and applications.

— Jay Kreps
CEO, Confluent
August 2023

Preface

Kafka Connect is an awesome tool for building reliable and scalable data pipelines. It is part of the popular Apache Kafka streaming platform, and while it may not get as much attention as the brokers, clients, or Kafka Streams, Kafka Connect is a tool to be aware of. It allows you to easily get data into and out of your Kafka clusters and even mirror data between clusters. Its pluggable design makes it possible to build powerful pipelines without writing a single line of code.

We are both passionate about sharing knowledge, whether that is through presenting at conferences, writing blog posts, or just helping out fellow Kafka enthusiasts. As a result, we have spent a lot of time chatting about both Kafka and Kafka Connect to users and developers all around the world. As Kafka is a tremendously popular technology, there are a lot of great resources available such as books, blog posts, and tutorials. Many of these do cover Kafka Connect, but we see a lack of resources that go deeper into its various use cases, configurations, and operational processes. Although Kafka Connect is not hard to start using with basic knowledge, its flexibility and range of features mean that having a deeper understanding of how it works can really make a difference.

We have both given plenty of conference talks about Kafka Connect that go beyond the basics, but there's only so much you can fit into a 40-minute session. In writing this book, we have brought together all the knowledge we have shared over the past few years about Kafka Connect, plus everything that you can't fit into a conference session or a blog post! This includes our own individual experiences running it and the insights we've gained helping and advising customers. We have also taken the time to delve into every configuration setting, metric, and API to provide a thorough explanation of how Kafka Connect works. This has often involved writing custom plug-ins to try out code paths, poring over the code, and chatting with other Kafka contributors.

This book will give you all the knowledge needed to build reliable data pipelines for your use cases and run them in production. *Kafka: The Definitive Guide*[1] is the go-to text for Kafka (we both keep a copy on our desk) and we hope this book will be the same for Kafka Connect.

Who Should Read This Book

This book is written for all roles that interact with Kafka Connect environments. We have chosen to use the terms *data engineers*, *site reliability engineers*, and *developers* to distinguish between roles. Data engineers design and build pipelines to process and analyze data. This includes selecting the correct tools, designing the data flow, and testing the pipeline. Site reliability engineers are responsible for deploying and administering Kafka Connect environments. They may manage a single Kafka Connect cluster or many, and each cluster might be running multiple data pipelines. Finally, developers customize Kafka Connect by building custom plug-ins. This is an advanced use case, but much of the knowledge that is applicable to this role is also useful for data engineers to assess available tools.

In many organizations, it is likely the same engineers who perform all three roles, but in larger organizations it could be completely different teams. Although we split the book into multiple parts to cover these different roles, you will likely find it useful to understand them all.

You don't need any prior knowledge of Kafka or Kafka Connect to read this book. If you are already familiar with Kafka, feel free to skip Chapter 2, as this covers the Kafka basics you need to understand to use Kafka Connect. Equally, if you are already familiar with Kafka Connect, this book is still written with you in mind. Throughout the book we share best practices and advanced tips to help you develop your expertise further.

Kafka Versions

Kafka is a very active project, and each new version (released roughly every four months) brings new features and changes. At some point we had to stop revising and pick a version so we could get the book into the hands of readers. We settled on Kafka 3.5.0, released in June 2023, as the version of Kafka to refer to.

Any significant change to Kafka first needs to be voted on by the community. To facilitate this, Kafka uses Kafka Improvement Proposals (*https://oreil.ly/qg7qO*) (KIPs). A KIP is a document in the Kafka wiki that describes the motivation for the

---

[1] Gwen Shapira, Todd Palino, Rajini Sivaram, and Krit Petty, *Kafka: The Definitive Guide,* 2nd Ed. (O'Reilly, 2021); Neha Narkhede, Gwen Shapira, and Todd Palino, 1st Ed. (2017).

change as well as its technical details. Throughout the book, we mention KIPs that are relevant to the features and concepts we cover. If you're interested in a particular feature, we highly recommend checking out the related KIP to see the motivation and history behind the change. Be aware, though, that sometimes final implementations diverge from the original proposal.

Navigating This Book

This book is composed of twelve chapters grouped into four parts. Part I consists of two chapters and provides an introduction to Kafka Connect and Kafka in general. It is mostly aimed at engineers who are new to or just getting started with Kafka Connect.

Part II consists of four chapters and explains how to build data pipelines with Kafka Connect. It is particularly relevant for data engineers. Chapters 3 and 4 discuss the core Kafka Connect components and explain how to design resilient and efficient data pipelines by combining them. The other chapters in this part look in detail at some of the most popular connectors. Chapter 5 covers three connectors from the community: Confluent S3 sink, Confluent JDBC source, and Debezium MySQL source. Chapter 6 details how MirrorMaker, the mirroring tool which is part of Kafka, works. This includes the features and configurations of the Source, Checkpoint, and Heartbeat connectors.

Part III consists of four chapters and focuses on the operational aspects of running Kafka Connect. It is aimed at site reliability engineers. Chapter 7 shows how to deploy and operate Kafka Connect clusters in production environments. Chapter 8 goes over all the configuration settings Kafka Connect exposes, and provides some background and context to help you decide how and when to tune them. Chapter 9 describes how to use logs and metrics to continually monitor Kafka Connect clusters. Finally, Chapter 10 discusses the core considerations needed to run Kafka Connect clusters on Kubernetes. This includes a high-level introduction to Kubernetes and an explanation of the options available for deploying Kafka Connect on this type of infrastructure.

Part IV consists of two chapters and explains how to implement custom connectors and plug-ins for Kafka Connect. It goes into detail about the APIs and is aimed at developers looking to customize Kafka Connect for their use cases.

Conventions Used in This Book

The following typographical conventions are used in this book:

Italic
    Indicates new terms, URLs, email addresses, filenames, and file extensions.

Constant width

Used for program listings, as well as within paragraphs to refer to program elements such as variable or function names, databases, data types, environment variables, statements, and keywords.

Constant width bold

Shows commands or other text that should be typed literally by the user.

<REPLACE_ME>

Text within angle brackets should be replaced with user-supplied values or by values determined by context. For example, if running a file for a connector called my-source, the text might show /connectors/<CONNECTOR_NAME>/config, and you should update it to become /connectors/my-source/config.

This element signifies a tip or suggestion.

This element signifies a general note.

This element indicates a warning or caution.

O'Reilly Online Learning

 For more than 40 years, *O'Reilly Media* has provided technology and business training, knowledge, and insight to help companies succeed.

Our unique network of experts and innovators share their knowledge and expertise through books, articles, and our online learning platform. O'Reilly's online learning platform gives you on-demand access to live training courses, in-depth learning paths, interactive coding environments, and a vast collection of text and video from O'Reilly and 200+ other publishers. For more information, visit *https://oreilly.com*.

How to Contact Us

Please address comments and questions concerning this book to the publisher:

O'Reilly Media, Inc.
1005 Gravenstein Highway North
Sebastopol, CA 95472
800-889-8969 (in the United States or Canada)
707-829-7019 (international or local)
707-829-0104 (fax)
support@oreilly.com
https://www.oreilly.com/about/contact.html

We have a web page for this book, where we list errata, examples, and any additional information. You can access this page at *https://oreil.ly/KafkaConnect*.

For news and information about our books and courses, visit *https://oreilly.com*.

Find us on LinkedIn: *https://linkedin.com/company/oreilly-media*.

Follow us on Twitter: *https://twitter.com/oreillymedia*.

Watch us on YouTube: *https://youtube.com/oreillymedia*.

Acknowledgements

First, we would like to thank all the contributors and members of the Apache Kafka community. This vibrant and welcoming community is one of the reasons why Kafka is so popular and still growing and improving all the time. Special thanks to Jay Kreps, who took the time to provide the Foreword for this book.

We also thank the many reviewers who have provided feedback throughout the process of writing this book: Robin Moffatt, Randall Hauch, Chris Egerton, Ryanne Dolan, Dale Lane, Gerard Ryan, Jakub Scholz, Paolo Patierno, Federico Valeri, Andrew Schofield, and Chris Cranford. Your input really made a difference and greatly improved the quality of this book. Additionally, we thank the readers who submitted feedback to us after reading the early access version on the O'Reilly website.

Thanks to Eric Johnson and Jess Haberman for making this book a reality and to Aaron Black and Gregory Hyman from the O'Reilly team. We also thank our O'Reilly development editor Jeff Bleiel for all his help in getting the book written and for adjusting timelines to fit around our personal time constraints.

We want to thank all the members of the Kafka team at Red Hat for giving us the space to work on this book for many months.

Mickael wants to thank his family and friends for supporting him throughout this project. Writing a book takes a lot of time, and their help was very important to keep him focused and allow him to finish this book.

Kate would like to thank her husband, Russell, for his patience and support during the writing process. Without his help she wouldn't have been able to juggle completing a book and becoming a first-time mum. She also wants to thank her parents for their ongoing encouragement in all her pursuits. Finally, Kate thanks her mentors Holly and Erin for showing her what women in tech are capable of.

PART I

Introduction to Kafka Connect

The first part of this book gives a high-level introduction to Kafka Connect. It is aimed at data engineers, architects, and site reliability engineers who are unsure what Kafka Connect is or whether it is the right tool for them.

This part explains Kafka Connect's key features and why it is so popular. It covers the most common use cases and lists some alternatives. Finally, it provides a basic introduction to Apache Kafka to help you gain the minimum level of Kafka knowledge needed to fully use Kafka Connect. This includes key terms and concepts and how to set up a simple deployment.

CHAPTER 1

Meet Kafka Connect

Systems to handle data have existed since the early days of computers. However, the amount of data being generated and collected is growing at an exponential rate. In 2018, an estimated 2.5 quintillion bytes of data (*https://oreil.ly/_Ivp7*) were being created each day, and the International Data Corporation (IDC) expects (*https://oreil.ly/DMZe-*) that the total size of all existing data will double between 2022 and 2025.

For organizations to handle these large volumes of data, now called "big data," new classes of systems have been designed. There are now hundreds of different databases, data stores, and processing tools to cater to every conceivable big data use case. Today, a typical organization runs several of these systems. This may be because different systems have been inherited through acquisition, optimized for specific use cases, or managed by different teams. Or it could be that the preferred tools have changed over time and old applications have not been updated.

For most organizations, simply collecting and storing raw data is not enough to gain a competitive advantage or provide novel services. In order to extract insights, data must be refined by analyzing and combining it from multiple sources. For example, data from the marketing team can be used alongside data from sales to identify which campaigns perform the best. Sales and customer profile data can be combined to build personalized reward programs. The combination of tools that is used for data collection and aggregation is called a *data pipeline*.

Over the past ten years, Apache Kafka has emerged as the de facto standard for ingesting and processing large amounts of data in real time. Kafka is an open source data streaming platform and is designed to serve as the data backbone for organizations. It is now a key component in many data deployments, as it's used by over 80% of the Fortune 100 (*https://kafka.apache.org*). Many new applications are developed to work with Kafka so that their data is immediately highly available and can be easily reused and processed efficiently to drive real-time knowledge.

Most organizations already have a lot of data in existing systems. It may seem relatively easy at first sight to write an application to aggregate data from these systems because most of them have APIs. However, as the number of external systems you use increases, doing so can quickly become a large and costly burden in terms of maintenance and developer time. Systems have their own unique formats and APIs, and are often managed by different teams or departments. If you then add considerations around security and data privacy, such as the European Union's General Data Protection Regulation (GDPR) (*https://gdpr.eu*), writing an application can quickly turn into a challenging task.

To address these issues, a number of integration systems have been developed. An *integration system* is designed to connect to various systems and access data.

Kafka Connect is one of these integration systems. It is part of Apache Kafka and specializes in integrating other systems with Kafka so that data can be easily moved, reused, combined, or processed. For example, Kafka Connect can be used to stream changes out of a database and into Kafka, enabling other services to easily react in real time. Similarly, once data has been fully processed in Kafka, Kafka Connect can move it to a data store, where it can be kept for long durations.

Kafka Connect Features

Kafka Connect provides a runtime and framework to build and run robust data pipelines that include Kafka. It was first introduced in Kafka 0.10.0.0 in 2016 via KIP-26 (*https://oreil.ly/R5Ini*). Kafka Connect is battle-tested and known to be resilient under load and at huge scale. The Kafka Connect runtime also provides a single control plane to manage all your pipelines, and it often allows building pipelines without writing any code so that engineers can focus on their use cases instead of moving the data.

Kafka Connect distinguishes between *source pipelines*, where data is coming from an external system to Kafka, and *sink pipelines*, where data flows from Kafka to an external system. With Kafka Connect, one side of the pipeline has to be Kafka, so you can't directly connect two external systems together. That said, it is very common for data imported into Kafka via a source pipeline to end up in another external system via a sink pipeline once it has been processed.

For example, Figure 1-1 shows a source pipeline that imports data from a database into Kafka.

Figure 1-1. A basic source pipeline with Kafka Connect.

Let's take a closer look at the unique set of features and characteristics that make Kafka Connect a very popular platform for building data pipelines and integrating systems:

- Pluggable architecture
- Scalable and reliable
- Declarative pipeline definition
- Part of Apache Kafka

Pluggable Architecture

Kafka Connect provides common logic and clear APIs to get data into and out of Kafka in a resilient way. It uses *plug-ins* to encapsulate the logic specific to external systems. The Kafka community has created hundreds of plug-ins to interact with databases, storage systems, and various common protocols. This makes it quick and easy to get started with even complex data pipelines. If you have custom systems or none of the existing plug-ins satisfy your needs, Kafka Connect provides APIs so that you can implement your own.

Kafka Connect allows you to build complex data pipelines by combining plug-ins. The plug-ins used to define pipelines are called *connector plug-ins*. There are multiple types of connector plug-ins:

- Source connectors, which import data from an external system into Kafka
- Sink connectors, which export data from Kafka to an external system
- Converters, which convert data between Kafka Connect and external systems
- Transformations, which transform data as it flows through Kafka Connect
- Predicates, which conditionally apply transformations

A pipeline is composed of a single connector and a converter, and includes optional transformations and predicates. Kafka Connect supports both Extract-Load-Transform (ELT) and Extract-Transform-Load (ETL) pipelines. In ELT pipelines, Kafka Connect performs the extract and load steps, enabling you to use another system to perform transformations once the data reaches the target system. In ETL pipelines, Kafka Connect transformations update the data as it flows through Kafka Connect.

Figure 1-2 shows a simple ETL pipeline composed of a source connector, one transformation (a record filter), and a converter.

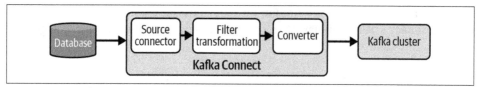

Figure 1-2. Kafka Connect plug-ins forming a source pipeline

Alongside connector plug-ins, there's another group of plug-ins that are used to customize Kafka Connect itself. These are called *worker plug-ins*:

- REST extensions customize the REST API.
- Configuration providers dynamically retrieve configurations at runtime.
- Connector client override policies police what configurations users can set for the Kafka clients used by connectors.

Scalability and Reliability

Kafka Connect runs independently from Kafka brokers and can either be deployed on a single host as a standalone application or on multiple hosts to form a distributed cluster. A host running Kafka Connect is named a *worker*.

These two deployment options allow Kafka Connect to handle a large spectrum of workloads. You can have workloads that scale from a single pipeline flowing just a few events to dozens of workers handling millions of events per second. You can also add workers to and remove workers from a Kafka Connect cluster at runtime, which allows you to adjust the capacity to match the required throughput.

When deployed as a cluster, workers cooperate and each one handles a share of the workload. This makes Kafka Connect very reliable and resilient to failures because if a worker crashes, the others can take over its workload.

Figure 1-3 shows a Kafka Connect cluster handling two data pipelines (from Database 1 to Kafka, and from Database 2 to Kafka), and the workload is distributed across the available workers.

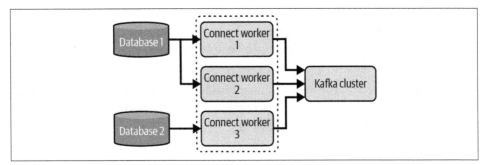

Figure 1-3. A Kafka Connect cluster composed of three workers handling two pipelines

Declarative Pipeline Definition

Kafka Connect allows you to declaratively define your pipelines. This means that by combining connector plug-ins, you can build powerful data pipelines without writing any code. Pipelines are defined using JSON (or properties files, in standalone configuration) that describes the plug-ins to use and their configurations. This allows data engineers to focus on their use cases and abstract the intricacies of the systems they are interacting with.

To define and operate pipelines, Kafka Connect exposes a REST API. This means you can easily start, stop, configure, and track the health and status of all your data pipelines.

Once a pipeline is created via the REST API, Kafka Connect automatically instantiates the necessary plug-ins on the available workers in the Connect cluster.

Part of Apache Kafka

Kafka Connect is part of the Apache Kafka project and is tailor-made to work with Kafka. Apache Kafka is an open source project, which means Kafka Connect benefits from a large and active community. As mentioned, there are hundreds of available plug-ins for Kafka Connect that have been created by the community. Kafka Connect receives improvements and new features with each Kafka release. These changes range from usability updates to alterations that allow Kafka Connect to take advantage of the latest Kafka features.

For developers and administrators who already use and know Kafka, Kafka Connect provides an integration option that doesn't require a new system and reuses many of the Kafka concepts and practices. Internally, Kafka Connect uses regular Kafka clients, so it has a lot of similar configuration settings and operation procedures.

Although it's recommended to always run the latest version of Kafka and Kafka Connect, you aren't required to do so. The Kafka community works hard to make sure that older clients are supported for as long as possible. This means you are always able to upgrade your Kafka and Kafka Connect clusters independently. Similarly, the Kafka Connect APIs are developed with backward compatibility in mind. This means you can use plug-ins that were developed against an older or newer version of the Kafka Connect API than the one you are running.

When Kafka Connect is run in distributed mode, it needs somewhere to store its configuration and status. Rather than requiring a separate storage system, Kafka Connect stores everything it needs in Kafka.

Now that you understand what Kafka Connect is, let's go over some of the use cases where it excels.

Use Cases

Kafka Connect can be used for a wide range of use cases that involve getting data into or out of Kafka. In this section we explore Kafka Connect's most common use cases and explain the benefits they provide for managing and processing data.

The use cases are:

- Capturing database changes
- Mirroring Kafka clusters
- Building data lakes
- Aggregating logs
- Modernizing legacy systems

Capturing Database Changes

A common requirement for data pipelines is for applications to track changes in a database in real time. This use case is called change data capture (CDC).

There are a number of connectors for Kafka Connect that can stream changes out of databases in real time. This means that instead of having many applications querying the database, you only have one; Kafka Connect. This reduces the load on the database and makes it much easier to evolve the schema of your tables over time. Kafka Connect can also transform the data by imposing a schema, validating data, or removing sensitive data before it is sent to Kafka. This gives you better control over other applications' views of the data.

There is a subset of connector plug-ins that remove the need to query the database at all. Instead of querying the database, they access the change log file that keeps a record of updates, which is a more reliable and less resource-intensive way to track changes.

The Debezium project provides connector plug-ins for many popular databases that use the change log file to generate events. In Chapter 5, we demonstrate two different ways to capture changes from a MySQL database: using a Debezium connector, and using a JDBC connector that performs query-based CDC.

Mirroring Kafka Clusters

Another popular use case of Kafka Connect is to copy data from one Kafka cluster to another. This is called *mirroring* and is a key requirement in many scenarios, such as building disaster recovery environments, migrating clusters, or doing geo-replication.

Although Kafka has built-in resiliency, in production-critical deployments it can be necessary to have a recovery plan in case your infrastructure is affected by a major outage. Mirroring allows you to synchronize multiple clusters to minimize the impact of failures.

You might also want your data available in different clusters for other reasons. For example, you might want to make it available to applications running in a different data center or region, or to have a copy with the sensitive information removed.

The Kafka project provides MirrorMaker to mirror data and metadata between clusters. MirrorMaker is a set of connectors that can be used in various combinations to fulfill your mirroring requirements. We cover how to correctly deploy and manage these in Chapter 6.

Building Data Lakes

You can use Kafka Connect to copy data into a purpose-built data lake or archive it to cost-effective storage like Amazon Simple Storage Service (Amazon S3). This is especially interesting if you need to keep large amounts of data or keep data for a long time (e.g., for auditing purposes). If the data is needed again in the future you can always import it back with Kafka Connect.

> The Kafka community is currently adding support for tiered storage to Kafka. This means that in a future version, you will be able to configure Kafka to store some of its data in longer-term storage system without affecting connected applications. However, creating a complete copy of the data will still require a tool like Kafka Connect.

Copying your event data from Kafka into a dedicated storage system can also be useful for machine learning (ML) and artificial intelligence (AI), both of which commonly use training data. The more realistic the training data, the better your system becomes. Rather than creating mock data, you can use Kafka Connect to copy your real events to a location that can be accessed by your ML or AI system.

In Chapter 5, we demonstrate how to use a connector to export data from Kafka topics to a bucket in Amazon S3.

Aggregating Logs

It is often useful to store and aggregate data such as logs, metrics, and events from all of your applications. It is much easier to analyze the data once it is in a single location. Also, with the rise of the cloud, containers, and Kubernetes, you must expect the infrastructure to completely remove your workloads and recreate them from scratch if it observes an error. This means it's essential to store data such as logs in a central place, rather than with the application, in order to avoid losing them. Kafka is a great fit for data aggregation, as it's able to handle large volumes of data with very low latency.

Kafka can be configured as an appender by logging libraries like Apache Log4j2 to send logs directly from applications to Kafka instead of writing them to log files on storage. However, this only works for applications that can use this kind of library. Without Kafka Connect, you would likely need to add Kafka clients to many applications and systems as well as skill up all of your teams to understand how to write, deploy, and run those clients. Once you overcome this initial hurdle, you then have multiple different places to update if you change your mind about the shape of the data being collected or where it should be sent.

Adding Kafka Connect to these sorts of use cases reduces the overhead for collecting the data. You can have a single team deploy and manage the Kafka Connect cluster, and—given the sheer number of connectors already out there—they can often do so without writing any code. Since the connectors and their configuration are all handled through Kafka Connect, you can change data formats and target topics in one place.

Modernizing Legacy Systems

Modern architectures have trended toward deploying many small applications rather than a singular monolith. This can cause problems for existing systems that weren't designed to handle the workload of communicating with so many applications. They are also often unable to support real-time processing. Since Kafka is a publish/subscribe messaging system, it creates a separation between the applications sending data to it and those reading data from it. This makes it a very useful tool to have as an intermediary buffer between different systems. You can use Kafka Connect to make the legacy data available in Kafka, then have your new applications connect to Kafka instead. Kafka applications don't need to be connected all the time or read the data in real time. This allows legacy applications to process data in batches, avoiding the need to rewrite them.

Alternatives to Kafka Connect

Since there are many different data systems, it's no surprise that there are many different integration systems too. Kafka Connect is not the only tool designed for building data pipelines, and many other tools also support Kafka. We won't go into detail about all of the alternatives to Kafka Connect, but we will list a few popular ones. Each tool has its own specificities and you should pick one based on your requirements, current expertise, and tools. Many of the alternatives available provide integration with Kafka. The Kafka project supports multiple client versions, so your chosen tool does not necessarily use the latest Kafka client. However, if you use these tools, you may not be able to take advantage of new Kafka features as quickly as you could if you were using Kafka Connect.

Here are some open source alternatives you might consider:

Apache Camel (https://camel.apache.org)
> An integration framework. It can be deployed standalone or embedded as part of an application server. Apache Camel includes a Kafka component that can get data into and out of Kafka.

Apache NiFi (https://nifi.apache.org)
> A system to process and distribute data that can be deployed in a cluster. Apache NiFi provides processors for sending data to and from Kafka.

Apache Flume (https://flume.apache.org/documentation.html)
> A system to collect, aggregate, and move large amounts of log data from applications to a central location.

LinkedIn Hoptimator (https://github.com/linkedin/Hoptimator)
> An SQL-based control plane for complex data pipelines. Hoptimator includes an adapter for Kafka.

> A number of vendors offer support or custom distributions for the open source systems listed earlier. Many companies have also developed proprietary integration systems and platforms to target specific use cases or industries.

Summary

This first chapter introduced the current data landscape and the problems many organizations are facing with handling their data. Data is often spread across many different systems, which can make it hard for organizations to use it to gain insights and provide innovative services to their customers. Integration systems such as Kafka

Connect are designed to solve these issues by providing easy, scalable, and reliable mechanisms to build data pipelines between various systems.

Kafka Connect has some key features that make it popular. It has a pluggable architecture that makes it easy to build complex pipelines with no code. It is scalable and reliable, with a useful REST management API that can be used to automate operations. Finally, it is part of the open source Apache Kafka project and benefits from the thriving Kafka community.

CHAPTER 2

Apache Kafka Basics

Connect is one of the components of the Apache Kafka project. In this chapter, we give a quick overview of how Kafka works and the concepts you should be familiar with in order to fully understand the rest of this book. We also discuss the different Kafka clients, including Kafka Streams, and show you how to run them against a local Kafka cluster. You will likely need to run Kafka and related clients in your development environment, even if you have someone else running your Kafka cluster in production.

If you already have a good understanding of Kafka, you can skip this chapter and go directly to Chapter 3. If you want a deeper dive into Apache Kafka, we recommend you take a look at *Kafka: The Definitive Guide* (O'Reilly), by Gwen Shapira et al.

A Distributed Event Streaming Platform

On the official website, Kafka is described as an "open-source distributed event streaming platform." While that's a technically accurate description, most people need more detail in order to understand what that means, what Kafka is, and what you can use it for. Let's look at each part of that description and explain what it means.

Open Source

Due to its openness, many third-party tools and integrations have been created by the ever-growing Kafka community.

The project was originally created at LinkedIn, where they needed a performant and flexible messaging system to process the very large amount of data generated by their users. It was released as an open source project in 2010, and it joined the Apache Software Foundation in 2011. This means all the code of Apache Kafka is publicly available (*https://github.com/apache/kafka*) and can be freely used and shared as long as the Apache License 2.0 (*https://oreil.ly/TEIA1*) is respected.

 The Apache Software Foundation (ASF) is a nonprofit corporation created in 1999 whose objective is to support open source projects. It provides infrastructure, tools, processes, and legal support to projects to help them develop and succeed. It is the world's largest open source foundation, and as of 2021, it supported over 300 projects totaling over 200 million lines of code.

In addition to the source code of Kafka being available, the protocols used by clients and servers are also documented (*https://kafka.apache.org/protocol*). This allows third parties to write their own compatible clients and tools. Many third-party tools and integrations have been created by the ever-growing Kafka community. It's also noteworthy that Kafka's development happens in the open. All discussions about new features, bugs, fixes, releases, etc., happen in public spaces such as mailing lists, GitHub, and Jira. The process for adding new features is well defined, and includes creating a Kafka Improvement Proposal (KIP) (*https://oreil.ly/SCKsX*) that must be discussed and voted on by the community before it is added to the project.

Open governance means that Apache Kafka is not controlled by a single company that can discontinue the project or change its terms of use. Instead, it is managed by an active group of diverse contributors. To date, Kafka has received contributions from over 1000 different individuals. Out of this large group, a small subset (~50) are committers who can accept contributions and merge them into the Kafka codebase. Finally, an even smaller group of people (~30), the project management committee (PMC), oversees governance. They elect new committers and PMC members, sets the technical direction of the project, and ensures that the community around the project stays healthy. You can find the current roster of committers and PMC members for Kafka on the website (*https://oreil.ly/zeX-4*).

Distributed

Kafka is designed to be deployed over multiple servers. A server running Kafka is called a *broker*, and interconnected brokers form a *cluster*. Kafka is a distributed system, with the system workload being shared across all the available brokers.

Distributed systems benefit from the recent shift toward using "off the shelf" servers—ones made with commodity hardware—that are cheaper and more easily replaceable. This trend is made apparent by the popularity of cloud infrastructure services that allow you to provision standardized servers within minutes whenever the need arises.

The distributed nature of Kafka means that brokers can be added to or removed from a cluster dynamically to increase or decrease its capacity. This horizontal scalability enables Kafka to offer high throughput while providing very low latencies. Small clusters with a handful of brokers can easily handle several hundred megabytes of data per second, and internet giants such as LinkedIn (*https://oreil.ly/UjWLV*) and Microsoft (*https://oreil.ly/olX81*) have large Kafka clusters handling several trillion events per day.

Finally, distributed systems are resilient to failures localized to part of the system. Kafka is able to detect when a broker leaves the cluster, whether due to an issue or for scheduled maintenance. With appropriate configuration, Kafka is able to remain fully functional during these events by automatically redistributing the workload and data to the remaining brokers.

Event Streaming

An *event* captures that something has happened. For example, it could be a customer buying a car, a plane landing, or a sensor triggering. An *event stream* is an unbounded sequence of these events. In most industries, businesses are reacting to events in real time to make decisions and perform actions. Event streaming systems provide mechanisms to process and distribute events in real time and store them for future review.

Although Kafka is described as an event streaming platform, it is not limited to handling "events" or "streams" of data. Any arbitrary data, unbounded or finite, can be handled by Kafka, including messages sent between applications or information from other systems, such as databases. Many types of data benefit from the processing and replay capabilities of Kafka.

Platform

Kafka is a platform because it provides all the building blocks to create event streaming systems.

As shown in Figure 2-1, the Apache Kafka project consists of the following components:

Cluster
    Brokers form a Kafka cluster and handle requests for Kafka clients.

Clients

  Producer
      Sends data to Kafka brokers.

Consumer
>   Receives data from Kafka brokers.

Admin
>   Performs administrative tasks on Kafka cluster resources.

Kafka Connect
>   Facilitates building data pipelines between Kafka and external systems. This is the topic of this book!

Kafka Streams
>   Continuously processes data in Kafka and optionally writes the output data back to Kafka.

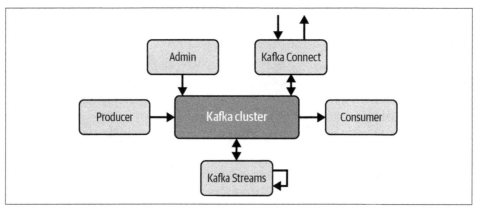

Figure 2-1. Components of the Kafka project

Putting all of these terms together, we see that Kafka is an *open source project* with open governance under the Apache Software Foundation. Because it is *distributed*, it is scalable, able to handle very high throughput, and provide high availability and low latency. Its unique characteristics make it ideal for handling *streams of events*. Finally, the components of the project create a robust and flexible *platform* for building data systems.

Kafka is a popular tool for many use cases. The most common ones fall into three categories:

Logs/metrics aggregation
>   Aggregating large volumes of data from applications in real time with very low latency.

Stream processing
>   Continuous processing and analyzing of events in real time to derive insights. This can drive automated actions or allow organizations to make decisions based on the latest data.

Messaging

Kafka provides a performant messaging solution that allows the sending and receiving applications to be decoupled.

Let's look at how Kafka handles event streams and makes them available to clients.

Kafka Concepts

While you don't need to be a Kafka expert to use Kafka Connect, it's useful to have a basic understanding of the main concepts in order to build reliable data pipelines.

Publish-Subscribe

Kafka uses the *Publish-Subscribe,* or *PubSub,* messaging pattern, which decouples senders and receivers. The utility of this pattern is easy to understand with a simple example. Imagine you have two applications that need to exchange data. An obvious way to connect them is to have each application send data directly to the other one. This method works for a small number of applications, but as the number of applications increases, so does the number of connections. This makes direct connections impractical, even if most applications only need to talk to a few others, as you can see in Figure 2-2.

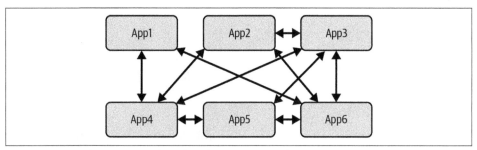

Figure 2-2. Applications sending data by connecting directly

Such tight coupling also makes it very hard to evolve applications, and a single failing application can bring the whole system down if others depend on it. PubSub introduces the concept of a system that acts as a buffer between senders and receivers. As shown in Figure 2-3, Kafka provides this buffer.

The PubSub model makes it easy to add or remove applications without affecting any of the others. For example, it is easy to add more receivers if a piece of data is relevant to multiple applications. In addition, if an application that is sending data goes offline for any reason, the receiving applications aren't affected; they just wait for more data to arrive in the buffer. In Kafka, applications sending data are called *producers* and applications receiving data are called *consumers*.

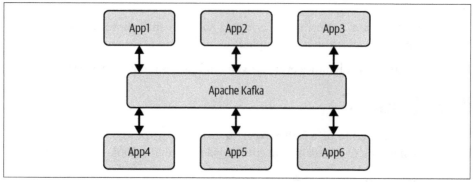

Figure 2-3. Apache Kafka provides a buffer between applications

Although there are many other technologies that use PubSub, very few are optimized for large numbers of consuming applications. Most messaging systems only allow a message or event to be read once, by a single consumer. If multiple consumers want access to the data, the messaging system creates a dedicated copy for each consumer. In contrast, Kafka does not remove data once it has been received by a particular consumer. Kafka applications can read a piece of data as many times as they like, and since it doesn't have to create new copies, adding new consuming applications introduces very little overhead.

Brokers and Records

As we noted earlier, a deployment of Apache Kafka—normally referred to as a Kafka *cluster*—is made up of one or more collaborating *brokers*. They store the data, and when a Kafka client wants to send or receive streams of data, it connects to one or more of these brokers.

To support the different Kafka use cases, the brokers need to be able to handle lots of different types of data, no matter what format it is in. Kafka does this using an abstraction known as *Kafka records*. A record is made up of a *key*, a *value*, a *timestamp*, and some *headers*.

The data in the key and value can be in any format that is needed for the use case. For example, it could be a string, a JSON document, or something more complex. Typically, the value is where you put the bulk of the data you want to send. The record key is optional and is often used to logically group records, and can inform routing. We look at how keys affect routing later in this chapter.

The headers are also optional. They are a list of key/value pairs that can be used to send additional information alongside the data. The timestamp is always present on a record, and can either be set by the application sending the record or added by the Kafka broker when it receives the record.

An example Kafka record could have:

- Record key: `test`
- Record value: `my first record`
- Record header: `customType=dev`
- Record timestamp: `2023-01-01T00:00:00+00:00`

The record abstraction is important, as it brings on a few specificities that make Kafka extremely performant. First, clients send records in the exact same binary format that brokers write to disk. Upon receiving records, brokers only need to perform some quick sanity checks, such as cyclic redundancy checks (CRC), before writing them to disk. This is particularly efficient, as it avoids making copies or allocating extra memory for each record. Another technique used to maximize performance is *batching*. This consists of grouping records together, resulting in a smaller total size sent over the network and stored on disk. Finally, to reduce sizes further, batches can be compressed using a variety of data compression libraries, such as gzip, LZ4, Snappy or zstd.

Now let's look at how records are stored in Kafka.

Topics and Partitions

Kafka doesn't store one single stream of data; it stores multiple streams, and each one is called a *topic*. When applications present records to Kafka, they decide which topic to send them to. To receive data from Kafka, applications choose one or more topics to consume records from.

There are many ways to decide what topics to create and how to assign your records to them, depending on how you want those records to be used. For example, suppose you are collecting temperature readings from sensors all over the world. If all applications need to see every reading, you could send all records to a single topic. However, if applications only want readings for specific countries, you could have a topic for each country. A *partition* is a subset of a particular topic. When you create the topic, you decide how many partitions you want, with a minimum of one. Partitions are numbered starting from zero.

Kafka is designed to handle a high volume of data, which it does by using partitions to spread the workload across the multiple brokers.

Figure 2-4 shows two topics spread across three brokers. The topic called `mytopic` has three partitions, and the topic called `othertopic` has two partitions.

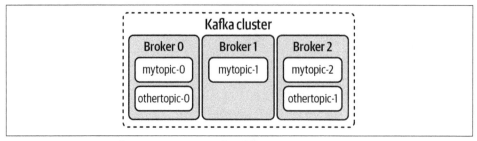

Figure 2-4. Topics and partitions in a Kafka cluster

If you only have one partition, every application that wants to send data to the topic has to connect to the same broker, which is a heavy load for a single broker. Creating more partitions allows Kafka to spread a topic across the brokers in the cluster. We talk more about how the partitions affect both producing and consuming applications in the section on Kafka clients, "Interacting with Kafka" on page 23.

Figure 2-5 shows records in a partition. Each record in a partition can be identified by its *offset*. The first record added to the partition gets an offset of 0, the second 1, etc. To uniquely identify a record in Kafka, you need a topic, a partition, and an offset.

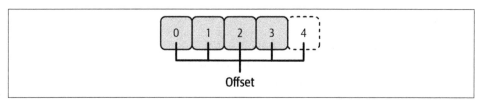

Figure 2-5. Records in a partition denoted by their offset

New records are always added to the end of the partition and are immutable. Kafka records are also ordered, meaning that Kafka guarantees that records are placed onto the partition in the order that it received them. This is a useful feature if you need to maintain the order of data in your stream. However, since the guarantee is only per partition, if you absolutely need all events in a topic to be kept in the order in which they were received, you are forced to use a single partition in your topic.

Replication

You should always be planning for component failure. In Kafka, brokers can go offline for many reasons, whether it's the underlying infrastructure failing or the broker being restarted to pick up a configuration change or perform an upgrade. Because it's a distributed system, Kafka is designed for high availability and can cope with a broker being unavailable. It does this using *replication*.

Kafka maintains copies of partitions, known as *replicas,* on a configurable number of brokers. This is useful because if one of the brokers goes down, replicas on other brokers in the cluster keep the partitions and data available. Applications can continue sending and receiving data by connecting to a different broker.

For each partition in a topic, one broker is the *leader* and the brokers containing other replicas are called *followers.* The leader is responsible for receiving records from producers, and followers are responsible for keeping their copies of the partition up to date. Followers that are up to date are called *in-sync replicas* (ISRs). Applications query Kafka to discover which broker is the leader for the topic partitions they are interested in, then communicate directly with those brokers. Consumers can connect to either the leader or an ISR to receive records from the partition. If the leader goes offline for some reason, Kafka performs a leader election and chooses one of the ISRs as the new leader. Kafka applications are designed to handle leadership changes and automatically reconnect to an available broker.

You configure the number of replicas for a topic by specifying the replication factor. If you have a replication factor of three, then Kafka will have one leader broker and two follower brokers for that topic partition. If there are multiple partitions in the topic, Kafka aims to spread out the leaders among the brokers.

Retention and Compaction

As mentioned earlier, Kafka topics handle unbounded streams of data. Since machine storage is limited, at some point Kafka needs to delete data to free up space.

When a topic is created, you can tell Kafka the minimum amount of time to wait, or the minimum amount of data to retain, before it can start deleting (also known as cleaning up) records. There are various configuration options you can use to control deletion, such as `log.retention.ms` and `log.retention.bytes`.

Kafka won't delete your records as soon as it hits the specified time or size. This is due to the way Kafka stores the records on disk. The records in a topic partition are stored in multiple, ordered files. Each file is called a *log segment.* Kafka only deletes a record when it can delete the entire log segment file. Log segments are built up sequentially, adding one record at a time, and you can control when Kafka starts writing to a new log segment using the `log.segment.ms` and `log.segment.bytes` settings.

Configuring retention based on time or size doesn't always make sense. For example, if you are dealing with orders, you might have multiple events that represent the status of the order (for example: placed, fulfilled, shipped, invoiced, closed) and only want to keep at least the last record for each order, no matter how old it is.

Kafka enables such use cases with a feature called *log compaction*. When enabled on a topic, Kafka can remove all previous records from a partition when a new record containing the same key has been produced. To enable log compaction, set the `cleanup.policy` to `compact` rather than the default, `delete`.

In order to delete all records with a specific key in a log compacted topic, you can send a record with `null` value, known as a *tombstone record*. When Kafka receives a tombstone record, it knows it can delete any previous records in that partition with the same key. The tombstone record stays on the partition for a configurable amount of time, but is also eventually deleted.

Compaction keeps the overall partition size proportional to the number of keys used, rather than the total number of records. This also makes it possible for applications to rebuild their state at startup by reprocessing the full topic.

Like record deletion, compaction doesn't happen immediately. Kafka only compacts records that are in non-active segment files. That means if the segment file is currently still having records sent to it, it won't be compacted.

KRaft and ZooKeeper

So far we have only talked about Kafka, but in order to function, Kafka needs a system to store its metadata and perform elections. Originally, Kafka relied on Apache ZooKeeper to perform that role. ZooKeeper is another open source project from the Apache Software Foundation that provides coordination to other services.

In 2019, as part of KIP-500 (*https://oreil.ly/s2VvE*), the community voted to replace ZooKeeper with a new built-in system. This proposal was made for several reasons:

- Running Kafka with ZooKeeper meant managing two distributed systems, each with different configurations, versions, and operations.
- The way metadata was stored in ZooKeeper limited scalability.

The new system is integrated in Kafka and internally uses the Raft consensus algorithm (*https://raft.github.io*), hence the name KRaft.

Since Kafka 3.3, KRaft mode is production-ready for new clusters. As of Kafka 3.5, a few features (*https://oreil.ly/xCkfp*) are still missing in KRaft mode compared to ZooKeeper mode. A migration process is available (in early access) as of Kafka 3.4 and allows moving a Kafka cluster that's using ZooKeeper over to KRaft. The Kafka project plans to remove support for ZooKeeper in Kafka 4.0.

Interacting with Kafka

To get data into and out of Kafka, you need a Kafka client. There are plenty of clients to choose from, or you can write your own. In this section, we introduce the Kafka clients that are included in the Kafka distribution. They are all Java clients and provide everything you need to get started with Kafka. We also look at the Kafka Streams library that you can use to perform stream processing.

The configuration options we cover are usually available within third-party clients as well. So even if you don't plan to use the included clients, the next few sections will help you understand how Kafka clients work. If you decide to use a third-party client, keep in mind that it can take some time for them to release a new version that supports the latest Kafka release.

Producers

Applications use producers to send records to topics. When producing records, you must specify the destination topic, and can optionally specify the partition. If your application does not specify a partition, then the Kafka client determines which partition to send your record to using a *partitioner*. Kafka provides several partitioners that fit most use cases, but you can also provide your own.

The default partitioner sends each record with the same key to the same partition. This is useful if you care about the ordering of specific records. For example, if you are tracking status updates to a specific entity, it makes sense to have these updates in the same partition so that you can take advantage of Kafka's ordering guarantees. For records without a key, the default partitioner spreads them out across the different partitions.

As shown in Figure 2-6, the default partitioner decides which partition the record should go to based on the key of the record and the number of partitions in the topic.

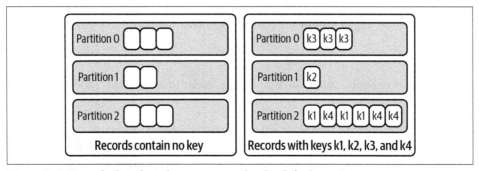

Figure 2-6. Records distributed on partitions by the default partitioner

There are a few different configuration options that you should be aware of when writing a producer application:

- `bootstrap.servers`
- `key.serializer`
- `value.serializer`
- `acks`
- `retries`
- `delivery.timeout.ms`
- `enable.idempotence`
- `transactional.id`

The `bootstrap.servers` configuration is a list of the broker endpoints that the application initially connects to. Once connected to a broker, clients automatically discover all other brokers in the cluster and subsequently connect to the necessary brokers. Including more than one broker in the `bootstrap.servers` list is recommended so that applications can still access the cluster even if a broker goes down.

The `key.serializer` and `value.serializer` configuration options specify how the client should convert records into bytes before sending them to Kafka. Kafka includes serializers for all of Java's primitive types and lists, such as `StringSerializer` and `ByteArraySerializer`.

You should configure `acks` and `retries` based on the messaging semantics you want for your specific use case. The `acks` configuration option controls whether the application should wait for confirmation from Kafka that a record has been received. There are three possible options:

0

Our producer application won't wait for confirmation that Kafka has received the record.

1

Your producer application will wait for the leader to acknowledge the record.

all *or* -1

This `acks` setting means the producer won't get acknowledgement back from the leader broker until all followers that are currently in-sync (have an up-to-date copy of the partition) have replicated the record. This is the default setting.

The `acks` configuration allows you to choose the delivery guarantees you want, from maximum throughput (0) to maximum reliability (all). If you have `acks` set to 1 or all, you can control how many times the producer retries on failure using the retries and delivery.timeout.ms settings. It is normally recommended to leave the retries setting as the default value and use the delivery.timeout.ms to set an upper bound for the time a producer takes trying to send a particular record. The retries setting determines how many times the producer tries to send the record if something goes wrong.

Using the acks and retries settings, you can configure producers to provide at-least-once or at-most-once semantics.

> To get maximum reliability from Kafka, you should carefully consider the value of the min.insync.replicas topic configuration when producing messages. When using acks=all, this specifies the minimum number of ISRs that must be present for Kafka to acknowledge the record.

Kafka also supports exactly-once semantics via the idempotent and transactional producers. You can enable the idempotent producer via the enable.idempotence setting, which is enabled by default from Kafka 3.0 onward. In this mode, a single producer instance sending records to a specific partition can guarantee that the records are stored in Kafka exactly once and in order. The transactional producer extends the capabilities of the idempotent producer. You enable the transactional producer using the transactional.id setting. In this mode, a producer can that guarantee a group of records are either all delivered exactly once to a set of partitions, or none of them are. While the idempotent producer does not require any code changes in order to be used, in transactional mode you need to explicitly start and end transactions in your application logic via calls to begin and commit or abort the transaction.

> If you don't use an idempotent or transactional producer, records may get reordered in case of failures. The behavior depends on two configuration settings: retries and max.in.flight.requests.per.connection. Kafka receives records in the order they are sent if either of the following are true:
>
> - retries are disabled
> - retries > 0 and max.in.flight.requests.per.connection is set to 1
>
> The idempotent and transactional producers allow setting max.in.flight.requests.per.connection up to 5 and enabling retries while keeping strict ordering.

Consumers

Consumer applications consume records from one or more Kafka topics. They can request data from specific partitions or use *consumer groups* to determine which partitions they receive data from.

Consumer groups are useful if you want to share the job of processing a topic's records among multiple instances of the same logical application. All consumers in a consumer group need to have the same `group.id` configuration. As shown in Figure 2-7, Kafka automatically assigns each partition within a topic to a particular consumer in the group.

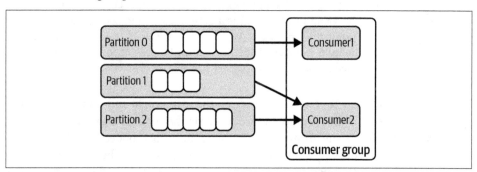

Figure 2-7. Consumers in a group consuming from different partitions

This means a single consumer in a consumer group can be assigned to multiple partitions, but a single partition has only one consumer processing it at a time. If a new consumer joins the group, or a consumer leaves the group, Kafka rebalances the group. During rebalancing, the remaining consumers in the group coordinate via Kafka to assign the partitions among themselves.

If you want more control over the partition assignments, you can assign them yourself in the application code. In Java applications, you can use the `assign` function to handle partition assignment manually or `subscribe` to let Kafka do it with a consumer group.

> For each group, one broker within a Kafka cluster takes on the role of *group coordinator*. This broker is responsible for triggering rebalances and relaying partition assignments to the consumers.

These are some of the configuration options you should be familiar with to write a consumer application:

- `bootstrap.servers`
- `group.id`
- `key.deserializer`
- `value.deserializer`
- `isolation.level`
- `enable.auto.commit`
- `auto.commit.interval.ms`

The `bootstrap.servers` configuration works identically to the matching configuration for producers. It is a list of one or more broker endpoints that the application can initially connect to. The `group.id` determines which consumer group the application joins.

Configure the `key.deserializer` and `value.deserializer` according to how the application should deserialize records from raw bytes when it receives them from Kafka. These settings need to be compatible with how the data was serialized by the producer application. For example, if the producer sent a string, you can't deserialize it as JSON. Kafka provides some default deserializers like `ByteArrayDeserializer` and `StringDeserializer`.

The setting `isolation.level` enables you to choose how consumers handle records sent by transactional producers. By default, this is set to `read_uncommitted`, which means consumers receive all records, including those from transactions that have not yet been committed by producers or have been aborted. Set it to `read_committed` if you want consumers to only see the records that are part of committed transactions. Regardless of how you set `isolation.level`, the consumers still receive all records that were not sent as part of a transaction.

The `enable.auto.commit` and `auto.commit.interval.ms` configuration options are related to how consumer applications know which record to read next. Kafka persists records even after a consumer has read them and allows consumers to consume the same record as many times as they want. This means it is up to the consumer to know which record it wants to read next and where to pick up from if it gets restarted. Consumers do this using offsets.

We mentioned that a record can be uniquely identified by its topic, partition, and offset. Kafka provides a built-in mechanism called *committing offsets* that lets consumers store their current position in a Kafka topic partition. Most consumer clients provide a mechanism for a consumer to automatically commit offsets to Kafka. In the Java client, this is the `enable.auto.commit` configuration option. When this is set to `true`, the consumer client automatically commits offsets based on the records it has read. It does this on a timer based on the `auto.commit.interval.ms` setting. Then, if the application is restarted, it first fetches the latest committed offsets from Kafka and uses them to pick up where it left off.

Alternatively, you can write logic into your application to tell the client when to commit an offset. The advantage of this approach is that you can wait until a record has finished being processed before committing offsets. Whichever approach you choose, it's up to you to decide how to best configure it for your use case.

If you choose not to use the built-in mechanism, you can write your own logic for storing offsets. Keeping track of consumer applications' offsets in memory is not recommended. If the application restarts for some reason, it will lose its place and have to start reading the topic from the beginning again or risk missing records. Instead, consumer applications should save their current position in the partition somewhere external to the application.

Kafka Streams

Kafka Streams is a Java library that gives you the building blocks to create powerful stream processing applications. Kafka Streams applications process data client-side, so you don't need to deploy a separate processing engine. As a key component of the Kafka project, it takes full advantage of Kafka topics to store intermediate data during complex processes. We give a brief overview of how it works here, but the Kafka website (*https://oreil.ly/wL1Tj*) goes into more detail if you want to do a deeper dive.

Kafka Streams applications follow the read-process-write pattern. One or more Kafka topics are used as the stream input, and as it receives records from Kafka, the application applies processing and emits results in real time to output topics. The easiest way to explain the architecture of a Kafka Streams application is through an example. Consider a partition containing records that match those in Figure 2-8. The top word is the key and the bottom is the value, so the first record has a key of choose_me and a value of Foo.

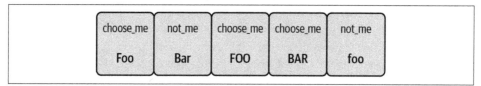

Figure 2-8. Records in a partition with a key and value

Imagine that you want to only keep the records with a key of choose_me, and you also want to convert each of the values to lowercase. You do this by constructing a *processor topology*, a graph where each node is a *stream processor* that performs an operation on the stream. So, for our example, we would need a topology that looks similar to Figure 2-9.

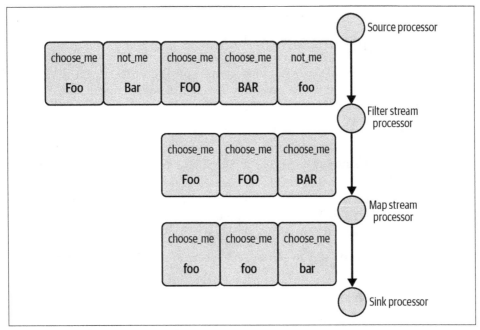

Figure 2-9. Kafka Streams topology

The first node reads from the input topic and is called a *source processor*. This passes the stream to the next node, which in our case is a filter that removes any record from the stream that doesn't have the key choose_me. The next node in the topology is a map that converts the record values to lowercase. The final node writes the resulting stream to an output topic and is called a *sink processor*.

To write our example in code, you would need something similar to the following:

```
KStream<String, String> source = builder.stream("input-topic")
    .filter((key, value) -> key.equals("choose_me"))
    .map((key, value) -> KeyValue.pair(key, value.toLowerCase()))
    .to("output-topic");
```

This example only uses stream processors that are part of the Kafka Streams domain-specific language (DSL). The DSL provides stream processors that are useful for many use cases, such as map, filter, and join. Using just the DSL, you can build very complex processor topologies. Kafka Streams also provides a lower-level processor API that developers can use to extend Kafka Streams with custom stream processors that are specific to their use case. Kafka Streams makes it easy to build processor topologies that contain many nodes and interact with many Kafka topics.

In addition to the basic stream processors used in the example, Kafka Streams also provides mechanisms to enable aggregating (combining) multiple records, windowing, and storing state.

Getting Started with Kafka

Now that you understand the main concepts of Kafka, it's time to get it running. First, you need to make sure you have Java installed in your environment. You can download it from java.com (*https://oreil.ly/FMds5*).

Then you need to download a Kafka distribution from the official Kafka website (*https://oreil.ly/zWLQz*). We recommend you grab the latest binary version. Note that different versions of Kafka may require different Java versions. The supported Java versions are listed in the Kafka documentation (*https://oreil.ly/rysd7*). Kafka releases are built for multiple versions of Scala; for example, Kafka 3.5.0 is built for Scala 2.12 and Scala 2.13. If you already use a specific Scala version, you should pick the matching Kafka binaries; otherwise, pick the latest.

Once you've downloaded the distribution, extract the archive. For example, for Kafka 3.5.0:

```
$ tar zxvf kafka_2.13-3.5.0.tgz
$ cd kafka_2.13-3.5.0
```

Scripts for Unix-based systems are in the bin folder and for Windows systems in bin/windows.

> We use the commands for Unix-based systems, but if you are using Windows, replace the script names with the Windows version. For example, ./bin/kafka-topics.sh would be .\bin\windows\kafka-topics.bat on Windows.

Starting Kafka

Kafka can currently run with KRaft or ZooKeeper. In this section, we cover both ways to start Kafka; you can follow one or the other. In both cases, we explain how to create a Kafka cluster with a single broker. This is fine for development, but not recommended for production systems, since Kafka requires multiple brokers in order to provide high availability.

Kafka in KRaft mode (without ZooKeeper)

In this mode, you can get a Kafka cluster running by starting a single Kafka broker.

You first need to generate a cluster ID:

```
$ ./bin/kafka-storage.sh random-uuid
RAtwS8XJRYywwDNBQNB-kg
```

Then you need to set up the Kafka storage directory. By default, the directory is /tmp/kraft-combined-logs, which can be changed to a different value by changing log.dirs in ./config/kraft/server.properties. To prepare the directory for KRraft, run the following command, replacing <CLUSTER_ID> with the value returned by the previous command:

```
$ ./bin/kafka-storage.sh format -t <CLUSTER_ID> \
    -c ./config/kraft/server.properties
Formatting /tmp/kraft-combined-logs
```

Now you can start a Kafka broker:

```
$ ./bin/kafka-server-start.sh ./config/kraft/server.properties
```

Look out for the following line to confirm the broker is running:

```
Kafka Server started (kafka.server.KafkaRaftServer)
```

Kafka with ZooKeeper

If you don't want to run in KRaft mode, you need to start ZooKeeper before starting Kafka. Fortunately, the ZooKeeper binaries are included in the Kafka distribution, so you don't need to download or install anything else. To start ZooKeeper, you run:

```
$ ./bin/zookeeper-server-start.sh ./config/zookeeper.properties
```

To confirm ZooKeeper is successfully started, look for the following line in the logs:

```
binding to port 0.0.0.0/0.0.0.0:2181
```

Then in another window, you can start Kafka:

```
$ ./bin/kafka-server-start.sh ./config/server.properties
```

You should see the following output in the Kafka logs:

```
[KafkaServer id=0] started (kafka.server.KafkaServer)
```

Sending and Receiving Records

Before exchanging records, you first need to create a topic. To do so, you can use the kafka-topics tool:

```
$ ./bin/kafka-topics.sh --bootstrap-server localhost:9092 \
--create --topic my-first-topic \
--partitions 1 \
--replication-factor 1
Created topic my-first-topic.
```

The `--partitions` flag indicates how many partitions the topic should have. The `--replication-factor` flag indicates how many replicas should be created for each partition. In this example, since we only started a single broker, we can only have a single replica.

Let's send a few records to your topic using the `kafka-console-producer` tool:

```
$ ./bin/kafka-console-producer.sh --bootstrap-server localhost:9092 \
--topic my-first-topic
>my first record
>another record
```

When you are done, you can stop the producer by pressing `Ctrl+C`.

You can now use the `kafka-console-consumer` tool to receive the records in the topic:

```
$ ./bin/kafka-console-consumer.sh --bootstrap-server localhost:9092 \
--topic my-first-topic \
--from-beginning
my first record
another record
```

Note that we added the `--from-beginning` flag to receive all existing records in the topic. By default, the consumer only receives new records.

When you are done, you can stop the consumer by pressing `Ctrl+C`.

Running a Kafka Streams Application

You can also run the example Kafka Streams application included in the Kafka distribution. This application, called `WordCountDemo`, consumes records from a topic and counts how many times each word appears. For each word, it produces the current count in a topic called `streams-wordcount-output`.

In order to run the application, you need to create the topic that it will use as its input:

```
$ ./bin/kafka-topics.sh --bootstrap-server localhost:9092 \
  --create --topic streams-plaintext-input \
  --partitions 1 \
  --replication-factor 1
Created topic streams-plaintext-input.
```

Once you've created the topic, start the Kafka Streams application:

```
$ ./bin/kafka-run-class.sh \
  org.apache.kafka.streams.examples.wordcount.WordCountDemo
```

Leave this running and open a new window to run the remaining commands.

In a new window, you can produce a few records to the input topic:

```
$ ./bin/kafka-console-producer.sh --bootstrap-server localhost:9092 \
  --topic streams-plaintext-input
>Running Kafka
>Learning about Kafka Connect
```

Again, press Ctrl+C to stop the producer once you're done.

Finally, you can see the output of the application by consuming the records on the streams-wordcount-output topic:

```
$ ./bin/kafka-console-consumer.sh --bootstrap-server localhost:9092 \
  --topic streams-wordcount-output \
  --from-beginning \
  --formatter kafka.tools.DefaultMessageFormatter \
  --property print.key=true \
  --property print.value=true \
  --property \
    key.deserializer=org.apache.kafka.common.serialization.StringDeserializer \
  --property \
    value.deserializer=org.apache.kafka.common.serialization.LongDeserializer
Running  1
Kafka    1
Learning 1
about    1
Kafka    2
Connect  1
```

For each word, the Kafka Streams application has emitted a record that has the lowercase word as the key and the current count as the value. For this reason, we configured the kafka-console-consumer command to have the appropriate deserializers for the key and value.

> You can find the source code for this Kafka Streams demo application in the Kafka GitHub mirror (*https://oreil.ly/wRT5i*).

Summary

In this chapter, we introduced the main concepts of Apache Kafka. You should now have a good understanding of the following key terms that we use throughout this book:

- Broker
- Record
- Partition

- Topic
- Offset

We also looked at the different components that interact with Kafka, from producers and consumers that write to and read from topics, to the Kafka Streams library that can process streams of data.

Finally, we walked through how to start Kafka, create a topic, produce and consume records, and run a Kafka Streams application. You can refer back to the steps in "Getting Started with Kafka" on page 30 as you progress through this book. You need Kafka running before you start Kafka Connect, and the producer and consumer sections can be used to either send test data for Kafka Connect to read, or check the data that Kafka Connect has put into Kafka.

PART II

Developing Data Pipelines with Kafka Connect

The second part of this book explains how to build data pipelines with Kafka Connect and is particularly relevant for data engineers. It describes in detail the roles of all the types of connector plug-ins and how to combine them.

It also covers the process of defining a pipeline, the main decision points to consider, and the best practices to follow. Finally, it explores the Capturing Database Changes, Building Data Lakes, and Mirroring Kafka Clusters use cases we introduced in Chapter 1 by demonstrating concrete examples with specific connectors.

CHAPTER 3

Components in a Kafka Connect Data Pipeline

A Kafka Connect pipeline involves one or more plug-ins and a Kafka Connect runtime that is responsible for executing them. Kafka Connect streams data between a Kafka cluster and one or more external systems. It is usual for a Kafka Connect pipeline to interact with a single Kafka cluster. For a single Kafka cluster, there is no limit to the number of Kafka Connect pipelines that it can be part of.

In this chapter, we take a closer look at the runtime and each of the Kafka Connect connector plug-ins: connectors, converters, transformations, and predicates. For each component, we explain its role in pipelines and how to use it. People often use the term "Connect" to refer to one component or the whole pipeline, so we introduce the correct terms for each component so you can differentiate them. By the end of this chapter, you will know how to build, configure and run a basic Kafka Connect pipeline using the official Kafka distribution.

Kafka Connect Runtime

At its core, Kafka Connect is a runtime that runs and manages data pipelines. You can easily run Kafka Connect on a laptop using the scripts, JAR files, and configuration files provided in the Kafka distribution. For example, Kafka 3.5.0 includes the following script in the bin directory for Unix-like operating systems:

```
connect-distributed.sh
```

The equivalent script for Windows operating systems is under bin/windows in the Kafka distribution:

```
connect-distributed.bat
```

The `libs` directory contains the Kafka Connect runtime JAR file, called `connect-runtime-3.5.0.jar`, as well as the Kafka Connect API JAR files and some plug-in JARs.

Finally, the `config` directory contains example properties files, including `connect-distributed.properties`, which you use to start Kafka Connect, and `connect-log4j.properties`, which contains the default logging configuration for Kafka Connect.

Running Kafka Connect

Before starting up Kafka Connect, make sure you have a Kafka cluster running. The Kafka Connect startup script requires a configuration file, so we will use the `connect-distributed.properties` file from the `config` directory of the Kafka distribution.

The configuration file must provide at least the following values:

`bootstrap.servers`
> A comma-separated list of addresses for Kafka Connect to use for Kafka

`group.id`
> A unique name for the Kafka Connect cluster, which is used by the Kafka Connect runtime to identify the workers in their cluster

`key.converter` *and* `value.converter`
> The default converter plug-ins to use for keys and values of records in a pipeline, unless otherwise specified

`offset.storage.topic`
> The topic Kafka Connect uses to store source connector offsets

`config.storage.topic`
> The topic Kafka Connect uses to store connector configurations

`status.storage.topic`
> The topic Kafka Connect uses to store the status of connectors

Kafka Connect is highly configurable and exposes many additional settings you can use to customize it. The default configuration file only includes a small subset of them; we cover the full list of settings in Chapter 8.

This configuration file assumes there is a Kafka broker accessible on `local host:9092`. If your environment is different, then you need to edit the `connect-distributed.properties` file before you use it.

Once your Kafka cluster has started, to start Kafka Connect, navigate to the directory containing the Kafka distribution and run the following command:

```
$ ./bin/connect-distributed.sh ./config/connect-distributed.properties
```

Your terminal will tail the Kafka Connect logs. Take a look at the logs and note that Kafka Connect prints out the configuration it's using. You can also make sure there are no errors. If you list the topics in your Kafka cluster, you can see the new topics created by Kafka Connect:

```
$ ./bin/kafka-topics.sh --bootstrap-server localhost:9092 --list
```

You will have one topic each for configs, offsets, and status:

```
connect-configs
connect-offsets
connect-status
```

Once you have started Kafka Connect, you can interact with it using the REST API.

Kafka Connect REST API

Kafka Connect exposes a REST API to allow you to manage and monitor your pipelines. By default, this endpoint is not secured and uses the HTTP protocol, but Kafka Connect can be configured to use HTTPS instead. You can also configure the port that Kafka Connect is listening on. The default value is 8083.

With Kafka Connect up and running, try the following `curl` command:

```
$ curl localhost:8083
```

It returns basic information about the Kafka Connect cluster:

```
{
  "version":"3.5.0",
  "commit":"c97b88d5db4de28d",
  "kafka_cluster_id":"SXu4poDjQZyzQ84eB4Asjg"
}
```

> You can pipe the REST API response to jq (*https://stedolan.git hub.io/jq/*) to print it in a more readable format. When doing so you can use the `-s` option to hide loading progress in the output:
>
> ```
> $ curl -s localhost:8083 | jq
> ```
>
> We omit the jq call from the `curl` commands in this book, but the output is displayed with jq formatting.

The REST API supports two different base paths: `/connectors` and `/connector-plugins`. For more details on how to use the REST API to manage connectors, see Chapter 7.

You can use the REST API with the `/connector-plugins` path to verify which connector plug-ins are currently installed into your Kafka Connect cluster:

```
$ curl localhost:8083/connector-plugins
```

By default, you have the MirrorMaker connectors available:

```
[
  {
    "class":"org.apache.kafka.connect.mirror.MirrorCheckpointConnector",
    "type":"source",
    "version":"3.5.0"
  },
  {
    "class":"org.apache.kafka.connect.mirror.MirrorHeartbeatConnector",
    "type":"source",
    "version":"3.5.0"
  },
  {
    "class":"org.apache.kafka.connect.mirror.MirrorSourceConnector",
    "type":"source",
    "version":"3.5.0"
  }
]
```

Installing Plug-Ins

The Kafka Connect runtime is the starting point for all Kafka Connect pipelines. Next you add additional plug-ins for your specific use cases. Connectors, converters, transformations, and predicates are all types of connector plug-ins you can load into Kafka Connect. Some plug-ins are included in the Kafka distribution and are already available on the Kafka Connect classpath. There are two ways to add new plug-ins: by using the `plugin.path` configuration option or by adding them to the Kafka Connect classpath. If possible, we recommend that you always use the `plugin.path` so that Kafka Connect only loads the libraries for the required plug-in. This properly isolates each plug-in and prevents classpath clashes between them.

Your `plugin.path` should be configured to point to a comma-separated list of one or more directories. Each directory can contain a combination of JAR files and directories that in turn contain the assets (JAR files or class files) for a single plug-in. For example, `plugin.path` could be set to `/opt/connect` if you have the following directory structure:

```
/opt/connect
+-- custom-plugin-1-uber.jar        ❶
+-- custom-plugin-2                  ❷
|      +-- custom-plugin-2-lib1.jar
|      +-- custom-plugin-2-lib2.jar
```

❶ An uber JAR for the plug-in and all its dependencies directly in the `plugin.path` directory

❷ A directory containing a set of JAR files, including the JAR file for the plug-in and the JAR files for all its dependencies

Whether you use the `plugin.path` approach or the classpath approach, when Kafka Connect starts up, it lists out the plug-ins it has loaded. For example:

```
INFO Added plugin 'org.apache.kafka.connect.converters.ByteArrayConverter'
INFO Added plugin 'org.apache.kafka.connect.mirror.MirrorCheckpointConnector'
INFO Added plugin 'org.apache.kafka.connect.transforms.TimestampRouter'
```

Deployment Modes

You can either deploy the runtime in "distributed" or "standalone" mode. The mode impacts the number of Kafka Connect workers (instances of the runtime) you can have in the cluster and determines how state is stored. You must decide which mode you want to use before starting Kafka Connect.

Distributed mode is generally the recommended deployment model for Kafka Connect. As shown in Figure 3-1, in this configuration you can have a single worker or many. Each one runs independently, and they coordinate with each other to spread out workload and store joint state in Kafka topics.

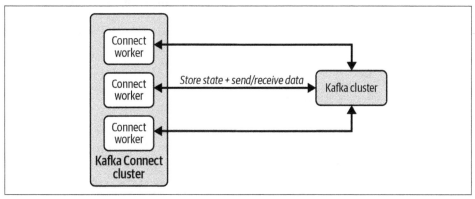

Figure 3-1. Kafka Connect runtime running in distributed mode

Having multiple workers means that Kafka Connect becomes fault-tolerant and that data will continue to flow even if a worker goes down. You can also add workers to or remove workers from the cluster as needed, so the system is resilient and scalable.

On the other hand, in standalone mode you can only run a single Kafka Connect worker and it stores some state directly on the filesystem, as shown in Figure 3-2.

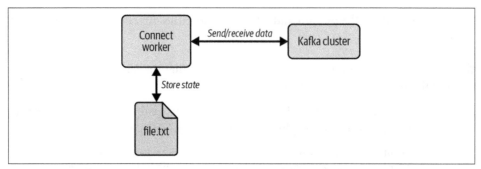

Figure 3-2. Kafka Connect runtime running in standalone mode

In this mode, there is no fault tolerance for the pipeline. If the standalone worker or its host machine fails, data will stop flowing in the pipeline. You can use this mode if you don't need the high-availability features that a cluster of workers gives. For example, if you have an application in a container that is emitting logs, you can run Kafka Connect in standalone mode alongside your application to stream the logs to your monitoring system.

 If you want to run more than one Kafka Connect cluster against the same Kafka cluster, make sure you consider where the state is stored. If running in distributed mode, make sure that the internal topics are uniquely named so that the different clusters don't inter-fere with each other, and also make sure that each Kafka Connect cluster has a unique `group.id` setting. If running Kafka Connect in standalone mode, make sure that each worker has its own file for storing state.

Source and Sink Connectors

Connectors serve as the interface between external systems and the Kafka Connect runtime, and encapsulate all logic specific to the external system. They allow the runtime to stay generic and not know any details of the connector's external system. A connector consists of one or more JAR files that implement the `Connector` API.

As shown in Figure 3-3, there are two types of connectors:

- *Sink connectors* consume records from Kafka and send them to external systems.
- *Source connectors* fetch data from external systems and produce it to Kafka as records.

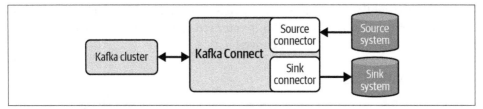

Figure 3-3. Example of a Kafka Connect runtime with both a source and a sink connector

A connector targets a single system or protocol. For example, you can have an Amazon S3 sink connector that is able to write records into Amazon S3, or a JDBC source connector that is able to retrieve records from a database via the Java API called Java Database Connectivity (JDBC). For some external systems, there are connectors available for both source and sink flows, but this is not always the case.

Connectors and Tasks

In a connector, the component that does the actual work of exchanging data with the external system is called a *task*. Multiple tasks can run in parallel, and they can also be spread across multiple workers when running in distributed mode.

This works like regular Kafka consumers in a group that distribute partitions among themselves. In Kafka Connect, if possible, the workload is split across tasks, and it can be dynamically rebalanced when resources change. This makes tasks the unit of scalability in Kafka Connect.

When a connector starts up, it computes how many tasks to start. This computation varies from connector to connector, but normally takes into account the value of the tasks.max connector configuration setting.

Configuring Connectors

In order to start a connector, you first need to define its configuration. Some configuration options are set in the worker properties that you provide when you start Kafka Connect and apply by default to all connectors; others are specified in the connector configuration. At the connector level, there are options specific to the particular connector, as well as common configuration options such as tasks.max, which is used in all connectors, and topics, which is used in all sink connectors. The connector-specific options depend on the connector's implementation, features, and on the system it's targeting. This means you can start multiple copies of the same connector with different configurations that run independently in parallel. For example, you can start two instances of the S3 sink connector to export different topics into different S3 buckets.

In a connector configuration, it is also possible to override the global configuration set at the worker level, which is useful if you need to adjust Kafka client configurations or change key, value, or header converters.

Running Connectors

Let's run our first connector. In addition to the built-in MirrorMaker connectors, Kafka also has a couple of example connectors: `FileStreamSourceConnector` and `FileStreamSinkConnector`. They allow streaming data between files and Kafka. They are not loaded by default, as they can read and write arbitrary files on the worker, so they can be a security issue in production. However, they are perfect for demonstration since they don't require an external system to interact with.

First we need to start a Kafka Connect worker with the `FileStream` connectors enabled:

```
$ CLASSPATH=./libs/connect-file-3.5.0.jar \
  ./bin/connect-distributed.sh ./config/connect-distributed.properties
```

If the connectors are correctly loaded, you should see the following output:

```
INFO Added plugin 'org.apache.kafka.connect.file.FileStreamSourceConnector'
INFO Added plugin 'org.apache.kafka.connect.file.FileStreamSinkConnector'
```

In our example, we use the `FileStreamSinkConnector` to stream the contents of a topic called `topic-to-export` to a file called */tmp/sink.out*. Create a file named `sink-config.json` that contains the desired configuration for the connector:

```
{
  "name": "file-sink", ❶
  "connector.class": "org.apache.kafka.connect.file.FileStreamSinkConnector",❷
  "tasks.max": "1", ❸
  "topics": "topic-to-export", ❹
  "file": "/tmp/sink.out", ❺
  "value.converter": "org.apache.kafka.connect.storage.StringConverter" ❻
}
```

❶ `name` specifies the name we're giving to this connector instance. When managing connectors or looking at logs, we use this name.

❷ `connector.class` is the fully qualified class name of the connector we want to run. You can also provide the short name, (`FileStreamSink` in this case).

❸ `tasks.max` defines the maximum number of tasks that can be run for this connector.

❹ `topics` specifies which topics this connector receives records from.

❺ `file` indicates where the connector writes Kafka records; you can change it to your preferred path. This configuration is specific to this connector.

❻ `value.converter` overrides the runtime's `value.converter` configuration. We use the `StringConverter` here so that Kafka Connect can read the raw text produced via the console producer.

Create a topic called `topic-to-export`:

```
$ ./bin/kafka-topics.sh --bootstrap-server localhost:9092 \
  --create --replication-factor 1 --partitions 1 --topic topic-to-export
```

Then use the Kafka Connect REST API to start the connector with the configuration you created:

```
$ curl -X PUT -H "Content-Type: application/json" \
  -d @sink-config.json \
  localhost:8083/connectors/file-sink/config
```

Once it has started, you can check the state of your connector via the Kafka Connect REST API:

```
$ curl localhost:8083/connectors/file-sink
 {
  "name": "file-sink",
  "config": {
    "connector.class": "org.apache.kafka.connect.file.FileStreamSinkConnector",
    "file": "/tmp/sink.out",
    "tasks.max": "1",
    "topics": "topic-to-export",
    "name": "file-sink",
    "value.converter": "org.apache.kafka.connect.storage.StringConverter"
  },
  "tasks": [
    {
        "connector": "file-sink",
        "task": 0
    }
  ],
  "type": "sink"
}
```

You can see that a `FileStreamSinkConnector` instance is running and that it has created one task.

The connector appends new records you produce to the */tmp/sink.out* file. Tail this file to wait for new data:

```
$ tail -f /tmp/sink.out
```

Let's insert some records into the `topic-to-export` topic. To do so, open a new terminal and use the console producer:

```
$ ./bin/kafka-console-producer.sh --bootstrap-server localhost:9092 \
  --topic topic-to-export
>First record
>Another record
>Third record
```

When you are done, you can stop the producer by pressing Ctrl+C.

The connector appends the records you produced to the file */tmp/sink.out*:

```
$ tail -f /tmp/sink.out
First record
Another record
Third record
```

Connectors do the actual work of moving data between Kafka and external systems, but the Kafka Connect runtime needs to know what format to use when sending the data to and from Kafka. That's where the next plug-in type, converters, comes in.

Converters

Converter plug-ins translate records between the format used by Kafka Connect and the one used by Kafka. Records are sent to and from Kafka as a stream of bytes. For source connectors, as shown in Figure 3-4, converters serialize the key, value, and headers from the records created by the connector before they are sent to Kafka.

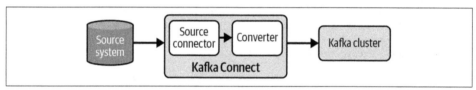

Figure 3-4. Source Kafka Connect pipeline

For sink connectors, converters deserialize the stream of bytes from Kafka before the record is passed to the connector, as shown in Figure 3-5.

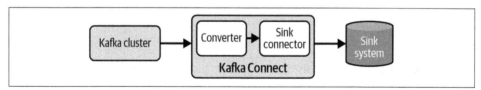

Figure 3-5. Sink Kafka Connect pipeline

Data Format and Schemas

To understand why converters are important, we need to consider the data that is flowing through the system. Kafka records are made up of a key, value, and headers. To support lots of different use cases, Kafka doesn't impose a required format for these parts. However, the format is very important when building pipelines. If the components in your pipeline don't agree on the data format, you will encounter deserialization exceptions. For sink pipelines, these deserialization exceptions will appear in Kafka Connect. For source pipelines, you will hit them when downstream applications try to deserialize the data from Kafka.

In a particular pipeline, the same converter is used to serialize or deserialize every record. For simple data types, the converter expects data to conform to that type in the same way every time. For example, `IntegerConverter` is able to write and read as an integer, and fails if asked to serialize anything except a Java `Integer` or `int`. For complex data types, the data can vary a lot more, so in order to manipulate it, converters need to know the exact schema the data is being put in.

In most cases, events are not single values, but complex types combining multiple values. It's best to use data formats that support *schemas* such as Apache Avro, Protobuf, or JSON. Schemas allow us to define complex types made of one of multiple nested values. For example, for the following JSON record:

```
{
  "title": "Kafka Connect",
  "publisher": "O'Reilly",
  "authors": ["Kate Stanley", "Mickael Maison"]
}
```

You could provide a schema using the JSON schema (*https://json-schema.org*) declarative language that looks like this:

```
{
  "type": "object",
  "properties": {
    "title": {"type": "string"},
    "publisher": {"type": "string"},
    "authors": {
      "type": "array",
      "items": {"type": "string"}
    }
  },
  "required": ["title"]
}
```

Although it is possible to include the schema as part of the record's payload for downstream applications, this adds unnecessary overhead to each record (consider the relative size of the earlier payload in comparison to its schema). Instead, it's common to use a *schema registry*. A schema registry allows you to store schemas in a central place and just include a reference to the schema with each record. Popular schema registries that work with Kafka are the Apicurio Registry (*https://oreil.ly/sJLFn*) and the Confluent Schema Registry (*https://oreil.ly/xZ-1H*).

Schema registries designed to be used with Kafka usually provide custom converters that you can use with Kafka Connect. The purpose of these custom converters is to perform the task of getting the schema from the schema registry and using it to correctly interpret the data. This includes storing the schema ID somewhere in the record before sending it to Kafka so that consuming applications can retrieve it when they read the message. If you are adding Kafka Connect to an existing system that already uses a schema registry, check whether that registry provides a converter that implements the Kafka Connect Converter API.

Configuring Converters

In Kafka Connect, there are two different types of converters: key/value convert‐ers and header converters. You specify the converter to use for the record key, record value, and headers by configuring the `key.converter`, `value.converter`, and `header.converter` settings, respectively. The `key.converter` and `value.converter` settings do not have a default value and must be configured when you start Kafka Connect. Since the header keys must be of type `String`, the `header.converter` configuration only impacts how header values are serialized and deserialized.

Kafka Connect comes with some built-in converters to save you needing to write your own. If you run Kafka Connect with the default classpath, you can use any of these converters without needing to install additional plug-ins. The following can be used as key, value, or header converters:

- `org.apache.kafka.connect.json.JsonConverter`
- `org.apache.kafka.connect.storage.StringConverter`
- `org.apache.kafka.connect.converters.ByteArrayConverter`
- `org.apache.kafka.connect.converters.DoubleConverter`
- `org.apache.kafka.connect.converters.FloatConverter`
- `org.apache.kafka.connect.converters.IntegerConverter`
- `org.apache.kafka.connect.converters.LongConverter`
- `org.apache.kafka.connect.converters.ShortConverter`

In addition, Kafka Connect also includes a header converter called `org.apache.kafka.connect.storage.SimpleHeaderConverter`, which is set as the default value of `header.converter`. This converter serializes header values as strings, then makes a best guess at what object to choose when deserializing them—for example, boolean, array, or map.

You can configure converters in two places: in the runtime configuration and in connector configuration. The converters that you specify as part of the runtime configuration are the default converters for every connector that the Kafka Connect runtime starts. Use this to set defaults that should apply to most of your pipelines, such as specifying a converter for your schema registry. You can override these defaults in your connector configuration if a particular pipeline has specific requirements.

Some converters have additional configuration options that you can apply to them. For example, let's consider the JSON converter that is included in Kafka Connect. The JSON converter serializes and deserializes to and from JSON, and it has a configuration option called `schemas.enable`. If you enable it, the converter will include a JSON schema inside the JSON it creates and look for a schema when it is deserializing data.

Let's say that you want to use the JSON converter and enable the schema for your record keys. You already have the configuration:

```
key.converter=org.apache.kafka.connect.JsonConverter
```

To enable a specific configuration option, you add a line to your properties that specifies the kind of converter you want to configure, followed by the configuration option you want to set. To set the `schemas.enable` configuration option to `true`, add the following:

```
key.converter.schemas.enable=true
```

 One of the most common mistakes when configuring converters is to look at Kafka Connect in isolation rather than considering the whole pipeline. In a source pipeline, you need to use a converter that will serialize the data in a way that downstream applications can consume. In a sink pipeline, your choice of converter is decided by the format of the data being produced into Kafka. In many cases, formats are chosen at the organization or department level so that all components in pipelines know which format to use. For example, an organization might choose to use Avro for formatting all of its data.

Using Converters

Let's see how using different converters can change the way data appears in an external system. We are going to start two copies of the `FileStreamSink` connector, one using the `StringConverter` and the other using the `JsonConverter`. Make sure you have Kafka Connect running in distributed mode and have created a new topic called `topic-to-export-with-converters`:

```
$ ./bin/kafka-topics.sh --bootstrap-server localhost:9092 \
  --create --replication-factor 1 --partitions 1 \
  --topic topic-to-export-with-converters
```

Create a file called *json-sink-config.json* with the following contents:

```
{
  "name": "file-json-sink",
  "connector.class": "org.apache.kafka.connect.file.FileStreamSinkConnector",
  "tasks.max": "1",
  "topics": "topic-to-export-with-converters",
  "file": "/tmp/json-sink.out",
  "value.converter": "org.apache.kafka.connect.json.JsonConverter",
  "value.converter.schemas.enable": "false"
}
```

Create a second file called *string-sink-config.json* that contains:

```
{
  "name": "file-string-sink",
  "connector.class": "org.apache.kafka.connect.file.FileStreamSinkConnector",
  "tasks.max": "1",
  "topics": "topic-to-export-with-converters",
  "file": "/tmp/string-sink.out",
  "value.converter": "org.apache.kafka.connect.storage.StringConverter"
}
```

Now run the following commands to start the two connectors:

```
$ curl -X PUT -H "Content-Type: application/json" \
  -d @json-sink-config.json \
  localhost:8083/connectors/file-json-sink/config

$ curl -X PUT -H "Content-Type: application/json" \
  -d @string-sink-config.json \
  localhost:8083/connectors/file-string-sink/config
```

Try sending some JSON messages to the `topic-to-export-with-converters` topic:

```
$ ./bin/kafka-console-producer.sh --bootstrap-server localhost:9092 \
  --topic topic-to-export-with-converters
>{"greeting":"hello"}
```

Compare the contents of the two files:

```
$ cat /tmp/json-sink.out
{greeting=hello}

$ cat /tmp/string-sink.out
{"greeting":"hello"}
```

Both connectors read the same message from Kafka; however, the one configured with the `JsonConverter` deserializes the record value into a structured Java object, in this case a `Map`. At first sight it seems the output of the example using `String Converter` is better, because it's valid JSON. However, it's important to understand that the example using `JsonConverter` actually parses the payload we sent into a data structure instead of just passing the bytes. Parsing the payload allows the connector (or, as we see in the next section, any transformations) to process the data more effectively. In the `JsonConverter` pipeline, the `FileStreamSink` connector has written the data into the file by iterating through the `Map` and printing `key=value`. Ultimately, `FileStreamSink` simply prints the value; however, other connectors are able to use the structured Java object (such as `Map`) created by the `JsonConverter` to send data structures in formats that make sense in the target system. When the `StringConverter` is used, the data is not interpreted by the connector; it is written out as-is.

Now try sending a message that isn't JSON; for example, you could send the string foo. The message only appears in the *string-sink.out* file, and if you look at the output in the terminal from the Kafka Connect worker that you started previously, you will see an exception from the `JsonConverter`:

```
Task threw an uncaught and unrecoverable exception.
Task is being killed and will not recover until manually restarted
[...]
Converting byte[] to Kafka Connect data failed due to serialization error
...
Caused by: com.fasterxml.jackson.core.JsonParseException:
  Unrecognized token 'foo'
...
```

The final plug-ins used in Kafka Connect pipelines are transformations and predicates.

Transformations and Predicates

Transformations, also referred to as single message transformations (SMT), are connector plug-ins that allow you to transform messages, one at a time, as they flow through Kafka Connect. This helps you get the data in the right shape for your use case before it gets to either Kafka or the external system, rather than needing to manipulate it later. A transformation is a class that implements the `Transformation` interface from the Kafka Connect API.

Unlike connectors and converters, transformations are optional components in a Kafka Connect pipeline. They are great for doing lightweight transformations on messages that would otherwise require additional stream processing applications. Examples of this kind of transformation include changing data types, adding field values, and modifying topic names.

While it's possible to perform complex logic in transformations, it's best to stick to fast and simple logic. As a rule of thumb, transformations should not store state nor interact with remote APIs. A slow or heavy transformation can significantly affect the performance of a Kafka Connect pipeline. If you find you are having to use many transformations together to fulfill your requirements, you should consider transforming the data via a dedicated stream processing tool instead, like Kafka Streams.

In a Kafka Connect pipeline, a transformation is always associated with a connector. For source connectors, as shown in Figure 3-6, transformations are invoked after the connector and before the converter.

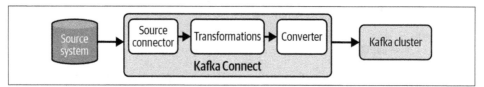

Figure 3-6. Source Kafka Connect pipeline with one or more transformations

For sink connectors, transformations are invoked after the converter and before the connector, as shown in Figure 3-7.

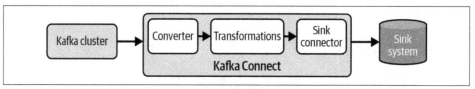

Figure 3-7. Sink Kafka Connect pipeline with one or more transformations

It's possible to chain multiple transformations together in a specific order to perform several modifications. To enable transformations, you need to declare them in the configuration of a connector so that the transformations are applied to the records that the connector handles. Different connectors running in the same Kafka Connect cluster can have different transformations associated with them.

Transformations were initially introduced in Kafka 0.10.2.0 via KIP-66 (*https://oreil.ly/bDPVK*) in February 2017. Transformations related to headers shipped with 2.4.0 via KIP-440 (*https://oreil.ly/ i3tQg*).

Transformation Use Cases

The main use cases for transformations are:

- Routing
- Sanitizing
- Formatting
- Enhancing

Note that while we've listed these categories to help you identify use cases, each transformation is not limited to performing a single modification. It's possible for a single transformation to perform several of them. Sometimes you can chain multiple single-purpose transformations together; in other cases, you may prefer using a single transformation that does multiple modifications.

For each category, we list the built-in transformations that enable the use case.

Routing

A routing transformation typically does not touch the key, value, or headers of a record but instead can change its topic and partition fields. This type of transformation is used to dynamically decide where each record will be written to.

This is useful when you want to split a stream of data into multiple streams or merge multiple streams together.

Kafka comes with the following built-in transformations that allow routing records:

- `RegexRouter` replaces the topic name with a configurable value if it matches a configurable regular expression (regex).
- `TimestampRouter` injects the record timestamp, with a configurable format, into the topic name.

Sanitizing

Sanitizing transformations allow you to remove data that you don't want to flow downstream in your Kafka Connect pipeline. This type of transformation involves directly altering the content of records or completely discarding them.

This is useful for removing sensitive data such as credentials, personally identifiable information (PII), and any data that is of no use to downstream applications.

The following sanitizing transformations come built-in with Kafka:

- `DropHeaders` removes headers whose keys match a configurable list.
- `ReplaceField` filters or renames one or more fields.

- `MaskField` replaces the value of a field in the content with its default `null` value or a configurable replacement.
- `Filter` drops the record.

Formatting

Formatting transformations allow you to change the structure and schema of records. It can be useful to move fields around or change the type of some fields to make the data easier to consume downstream. This can also be used to shape records into the format the converter is expecting.

For example, records may come using this JSON schema:

```
{
  "type": "struct",
  "fields": [
    {"type": "string","field": "item"},
    {"type": "string","field": "price"}
  ]
}
```

It would be preferable to have the `price` field as a number instead of as a string. In this case, you can use a transformation to change the type of this field.

The following formatting transformations are built into Kafka:

- `Cast` casts a field into a different configurable type.
- `ExtractField` extracts a configurable field and throws away the rest of the record.
- `Flatten` flattens the nested structure of the record and renames fields accordingly.
- `HeaderFrom` copies or moves a field from the record key or value to its headers.
- `HoistField` wraps the record's key or value with a new configurable field.
- `SetSchemaMetadata` sets the metadata for the key or value schema to configurable values.
- `ValueToKey` replaces the record's key with configurable fields from the record's value.

Enhancing

Enhancing transformations allow you to add fields and headers or improve data in some fields. In many cases, it is useful to inject additional data to records passing through a pipeline. This can be used for data lineage, tracing, or even debugging.

For example, you can use an enhancing transformation to inject a new field with the record timestamp. Even though Kafka records have a dedicated timestamp field, when they are exported to an external system, some sink connectors might not include it. To solve this issue, you can use `InsertField` to inject a field with the timestamp value.

The following enhancing transformations are built into Kafka:

- `InsertField` inserts fields with configurable values.
- `InsertHeader` inserts headers with configurable values.
- `TimestampConverter` converts timestamp fields using a configurable format.

To see the complete list of the Apache Kafka built-in transformations and their associated configuration options, see the Transformations section on the Kafka website (*https://oreil.ly/W1x03*).

Predicates

Predicates allow you to apply a transformation only when a configurable condition is met. They were introduced in Kafka 2.6.0 via KIP-585 (*https://oreil.ly/Hzug-*). Some transformations are always intended to be used with a predicate, such as `Filter`, which otherwise would apply to all records and result in all records being dropped. But predicates are also useful with many other transformations. For example, if a stream contains several types of events, you can apply transformations to certain types.

These are the built-in predicates in Kafka:

- `HasHeaderKey` is satisfied if the record has a header with a configurable name.
- `RecordIsTombstone` is satisfied if the record is a tombstone (i.e., if the value is `null`).
- `TopicNameMatches` is satisfied if the record's topic name matches a configurable regex.

 In Kafka, a record is called a tombstone if its value is `null`. The name comes from compacted topics where a record with a `null` value acts as a delete marker and causes all previous records with the same key to be deleted during the next compaction cycle.

Configuring Transformations and Predicates

You specify transformations and predicates as part of the connector configuration. The syntax to define them can seem a bit convoluted at first, so let's look over a simple example to see how it works.

To configure transformations, first you set the `transforms` field to be a comma-separated list of labels for the transformations. These labels are used to associate a configuration with the correct transformation. Although they can be chosen arbitrarily, you should choose a descriptive name to make the configuration easier to read. For example:

```
{
  "transforms": "renameTopic,filterTombstones"
}
```

Next, for each transformation in the list, you must specify the class you want Kafka Connect to use. Do this using the configuration `transforms.<LABEL>.type`:

```
{
  "transforms": "renameTopic,filterTombstones",
  "transforms.renameTopic.type":
    "org.apache.kafka.connect.transforms.RegexRouter",
  "transforms.filterTombstones.type":
    "org.apache.kafka.connect.transforms.Filter"
}
```

Finally, you can provide configurations specific to each individual transformation if needed. For example, the `RegexRouter` transformation has two configurations you can set:

```
{
  "transforms": "renameTopic",
  "transforms.renameTopic.type":
    "org.apache.kafka.connect.transforms.RegexRouter",
  "transforms.renameTopic.regex": "(.*)",
  "transforms.renameTopic.type": "$1-router"
}
```

To define a set of predicates, use the same mechanism: define a list of labels, configure the type for each label, then supply predicate-specific configuration. Each of these uses the `predicates` prefix, rather than `transforms`. In addition, you can specify that the predicate should apply to a specific transformation using the configuration `transforms.<LABEL>.predicate`.

Let's look at an example of using transformations and predicates together:

```
{
  [...]
  "transforms": "filterTombstones",
  "transforms.filterTombstones.type":
    "org.apache.kafka.connect.transforms.Filter",
  "transforms.filterTombstones.predicate": "isTombstone",

  "predicates": "isTombstone",
  "predicates.isTombstone.type":
    "org.apache.kafka.connect.transforms.predicates.RecordIsTombstone"
  [...]
}
```

This configuration sets up a pipeline with the Filter transformation that will drop any records that match the predicate. In this case, the predicate is checking if a record is a tombstone.

You can also negate a predicate if you want to test for the opposite condition. This allows using the same small set of predicates for both conditions. To do so, set the negate field on the predicate to true—for example:

```
{
  [...]
  "transforms": "keepMyTopic,dropMyTopic",
  "transforms.keepMyTopic.type": "Filter",
  "transforms.dropMyTopic.type": "Filter",

  "transforms.keepMyTopic.predicate": "topicMatch",
  "transforms.keepMyTopic.negate": "true",

  "transforms.dropMyTopic.predicate": "topicMatch",

  "predicates": "topicMatch",
  "predicates.topicMatch.type":
    "org.apache.kafka.connect.transforms.predicates.TopicNameMatches"
  "predicates.topicMatch.pattern": "mytopic.*",
  [...]
}
```

In this case, the keepMyTopic transformation is only applied if the topicMatch predicate is not satisfied (i.e., because the record topic name does not start with mytopic), whereas the dropMyTopic transformation is applied if the predicate is satisfied.

In Kafka, both the record's key and its value can contain arbitrary data. This means that many transformations can be applied to them. If that's the case, there are often two different classes: one that applies to the key, and one that applies to the value. Make sure that you specify the correct class in the `type` configuration of the transformation.

For example, the transformation `Cast` exposes two classes:

- `org.apache.kafka.connect.transforms.Cast$Key`: for casting a field in the key

- `org.apache.kafka.connect.transforms.Cast$Value`: for casting a field in the value

Using Transformations and Predicates

Let's enable some transformations in your Kafka Connect pipeline. Make sure you have Kafka Connect running in distributed mode and a new topic called `topic-to-export-with-transformations`.

```
$ ./bin/kafka-topics.sh --bootstrap-server localhost:9092 \
  --create --replication-factor 1 --partitions 1 \
  --topic topic-to-export-with-transformations
```

First, update the connector configuration in a file called *file-sink.json*:

```
{
    "connector.class": "org.apache.kafka.connect.file.FileStreamSinkConnector",
    "tasks.max": "1",
    "topics": "topic-to-export-with-transformations",
    "file": "/tmp/sink-transform.out",
    "value.converter": "org.apache.kafka.connect.json.JsonConverter",
    "value.converter.schemas.enable": "false",
    "transforms": "replaceSource,addTimestamp",               ❶
    "transforms.replaceSource.type":
        "org.apache.kafka.connect.transforms.ReplaceField$Value",  ❷
    "transforms.replaceSource.renames": "source:origin",      ❸
    "transforms.addTimestamp.type":
        "org.apache.kafka.connect.transforms.InsertField$Value",   ❹
    "transforms.addTimestamp.timestamp.field": "ts",          ❺
    "transforms.addTimestamp.predicate": "isTombstone",       ❻
    "transforms.addTimestamp.negate": "true",                 ❼
    "predicates": "isTombstone",
    "predicates.isTombstone.type":
        "org.apache.kafka.connect.transforms.predicates.RecordIsTombstone"
}
```

❶ You define two labels for transformations you want to apply: `replaceSource` and `addTimestamp`.

❷ The first label is associated with the transformation `ReplaceField`. Note that we specified the `ReplicaField$Value` class to apply the transformation on the value.

❸ The `source` field will be renamed to `origin`.

❹ The second transformation label, `addTimestamp`, is for `InsertField`, again on the value.

❺ It will insert the record's timestamp into a new field named `ts`.

❻ The transformation is configured with the predicate labeled `isTombstone`.

❼ The transformation is only applied to records that are not tombstones.

Then you produce another record to `topic-to-export`:

```
$ ./bin/kafka-console-producer.sh --bootstrap-server localhost:9092 \
    --topic topic-to-export-with-transformations
>{"source": "kafka-console-producer", "type": "event"}
```

Now start the connector:

```
$ curl -X PUT -H "Content-Type: application/json" \
    -d @file-sink.json \
    localhost:8083/connectors/file-sink/config
```

The connector processes that record and appends the following to your file:

```
$ cat /tmp/sink-transform.out
{origin=kafka-console-producer, type=event, ts=1647116995747}
```

Summary

In this chapter, we explored the main components of a Kafka Connect data pipeline and built a simple pipeline exporting records from a topic to a file.

We looked at the Kafka Connect runtime, including its REST API and modes of operation. To recap, the runtime can run in the following modes:

Distributed
> This mode is suitable for both development and production since it provides strong resiliency and scalability capabilities. It can be used with a single worker or many.

Standalone
> This mode supports only a single worker and therefore provides no resiliency and limited scalability capabilities.

We recommend that you use the distributed mode wherever possible, as it is easy to run on any system and allows you to work with the same mode in both development and production.

We then introduced connectors and described how they import and export data between Kafka and external systems. The two types of connectors are:

Sink
> Used to consume records from Kafka and send them to an external system

Source
> Used to fetch data from an external system and produce it to Kafka

We also covered converters and their role in translating data between formats and ensuring that data stays consistent for consuming applications.

Finally, we looked at transformations and predicates and explained how they can be used to fully control the content and format of data flowing through Kafka Connect.

CHAPTER 4

Designing Effective Data Pipelines

In this chapter, you will learn how to build resilient and effective data pipelines using Kafka Connect. We explain the key concepts and decision points that data engineers and architects have to understand when assembling the components we introduced in Chapter 3.

In the first half of this chapter, we look at how to choose connector plug-ins for your pipelines. You need a connector, a converter, and, optionally, some transformations and predicates. We discuss how to evaluate connectors and identify the one that satisfies your production requirements among the hundreds that are available in the community. Then we discuss how to model your data as it flows through the pipeline and the formatting options that you have available.

The second half of this chapter is focused on the resiliency characteristics of Kafka Connect. Before building your pipeline, you need to identify the semantics you require based on your use cases. For example, do you need to guarantee that every piece of data is delivered, or is it acceptable to lose some data in favor of increased throughput? We first dive into the inner workings of Kafka Connect, explaining why it is a robust environment that is able to handle failures. Then we look at the semantics that sink and source pipelines can achieve and the different configuration options and trade-offs available to target your specific use cases.

Choosing a Connector

When building a data pipeline that uses Kafka Connect, you first need to decide which connector to install. Since Kafka is a very popular technology, there are many existing connectors for you to choose from. Rather than reinventing the wheel, it is often better to use an existing connector, but only if it fulfills your requirements. Here are some things to consider when choosing whether to use a specific connector as part of your pipeline:

- Pipeline direction (source or sink)
- Licensing and support
- Connector features

Pipeline Direction

First, verify that the connector flows data in the right direction. Is it a source connector that produces data to Kafka or a sink connector that consumes from Kafka? Most connectors include this detail as part of the name, and it is usually clear from the documentation. If not, you can install the connector in a Kafka Connect environment and use the REST API to retrieve its type.

```
$ curl localhost:8083/connector-plugins
[
  {
    "class": "org.apache.kafka.connect.mirror.MirrorCheckpointConnector",
    "type": "source",
    "version": "3.5.0"
  },
  {
    "class": "org.apache.kafka.connect.mirror.MirrorHeartbeatConnector",
    "type": "source",
    "version": "3.5.0"
  },
  {
    "class": "org.apache.kafka.connect.mirror.MirrorSourceConnector",
    "type": "source",
    "version": "3.5.0"
  }
]
```

The type field indicates the type of the connector.

Some projects provide a single download that includes both a source and sink connector, but other projects may provide only one or the other.

Licensing and Support

Before using a connector, make sure to check what its license permits. Just because a connector's source code is public or freely available to download doesn't mean the license is permissive. You should also consider the level of maintenance and support you expect. The Kafka community works hard to make sure that older connectors are compatible with newer versions of the runtime; however, connectors are not all maintained or updated with the same regularity. Whatever connector you choose, whether it's open source or proprietary, make sure you know how often the connector is updated with the latest Kafka APIs and how the developers address security vulnerabilities.

The level of support you get for a particular connector varies greatly. Many companies offer paid-for support for connectors, whether proprietary or open source. This normally includes a dedicated communication channel if you have problems and access to industry experts for advice on configuration. That being said, many open source communities also respond to bug reports quickly and provide their own dedicated communication channels, which, depending on your use cases, may be an alternative to paid support.

 Since a single connector is often used for many different use cases, you may find there isn't one perfectly suited to your needs. If that is the case, instead of writing one from scratch, we would encourage you to see if there is an open source connector that you could contribute to. You still need to get your changes accepted, but most open source projects accept new contributors.

Connector Features

Once you have identified potential connectors for your pipelines, you need to take a closer look at the features offered by those connectors. To start with, does the connector support the type of connection you need? For example, your external system might require an encrypted connection, some form of authentication, or for the data to be in a specific format. You should also check if the connector is suitable for production use. For example, does it provide metrics for monitoring its status and logging to help you debug problems? Look over the documentation—and, for an open source connector, the code—to see how the connector works and assess the features it provides.

In Chapter 3, we introduced the common configuration options for all connectors: topics for sink connectors and tasks.max for both source and sink. Most connectors offer additional options to configure their specific features. For a particular connector, you can use the REST API to list all of the available configuration options and validate your configuration before starting the connector.

Using the REST API is especially useful if the code is not available, but be aware that this relies on the developer documenting their configuration correctly. Some fields might be incorrectly marked as optional or required. Similarly, the validation is useful for verifying the connector configuration will be accepted, but a successful validation request does not guarantee that your connector will work.

Use the `GET /connector-plugins/<CONNECTOR_PLUGIN>/config` endpoint to list the configuration options and the `PUT /connector-plugins/<CONNECTOR_PLUGIN>/config/validate` endpoint to validate a specific configuration.

We describe the REST API endpoints in detail in Chapter 7.

Defining Data Models

No two pipelines are identical. Even if they fulfill a similar use case or use the same components, the actual data and how that data evolves varies from pipeline to pipeline. When you are designing your pipeline, you need to consider when and how each individual data entry will change, as well as how the individual entries relate to each other. How you group or split (shard) your data will affect how well you can scale your pipeline as the amount of data it is processing increases. To examine these ideas in more detail, we first discuss when to apply data transformation in Kafka Connect using transformations and predicates, and then discuss techniques for mapping data between Kafka Connect and other systems.

Data Transformation

There are two common patterns that are used to evolve data as it flows through a pipeline: ETL (Extract-Transform-Load) and ELT (Extract-Load-Transform). In these patterns, the word "Transform" doesn't just refer to updating the format. Transformation could include cleaning the data to remove sensitive information, collating the data with other data streams, or performing more advanced analysis.

Both approaches have their advantages and disadvantages. In systems where storage is restricted, it is better to use the ETL approach and transform the data before loading it into storage. This makes it easy to query the data because it has already been prepared for analysis. However, it can be difficult to update the pipeline if a new use case that requires a different transformation is discovered. In contrast, ELT keeps the data as generic as possible for as long as possible, giving the opportunity for the data to be reused for other purposes. The ELT pattern has been gaining popularity and there are now many dedicated data processing and analysis tools that are built to support it. Some examples of these tools are Kafka Streams, Apache Spark, Apache Flink, Apache Druid and Apache Pinot.

So where do Kafka Connect transformations fit in this flow? In Kafka Connect, there is a rich set of transformations that you can perform on your data while it is in flight, which fits naturally into the ETL pattern. Using Kafka Connect for your transformations removes the need for a separate tool to transform the data before loading it. Since you choose the specific set of transformations to apply and Kafka Connect allows you to plug in custom ones, the possibilities are endless. However, Kafka Connect transformations do have their limitations, because they are applied to each piece of data independently. This means you can't perform more advanced processing, like merging two streams of data or aggregating data over time. Instead, you should use one of the dedicated stream processing technologies for these kinds of operations.

Even if you decide to use a dedicated technology for the bulk of your data processing and analysis, you can still make use of Kafka Connect transformations. Some particular transformations that you might want to consider are the ones that remove or rename fields and can drop records. These are very useful for ensuring that sensitive data isn't sent further down the pipeline and for removing data that could cause processing problems later. If you have multiple different sources that need to be aggregated in subsequent steps, you can also use Kafka Connect transformations to first align the data to have common fields. Figure 4-1 shows this sort of flow.

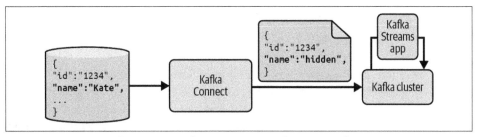

Figure 4-1. Data pipeline using Kafka Connect transformations for removing sensitive data and Kafka Streams to perform further processing

Mapping Data Between Systems

We have discussed how you can transform individual data entries, but what about the overall structure of your data as it is passed along the pipeline?

One of the hardest things to reason through when building a data pipeline is how to map data structures between different systems. More than just the format of individual entries, how the data should be grouped and stored, what ordering is required, and what happens when the pipeline needs to be scaled are all structural considerations. In Kafka Connect, a lot of these decisions are made for you by the developer who wrote the connector, but you should still be aware of the mechanisms that are available for connectors to use when mapping data between Kafka and other systems. If you understand these mechanisms, you are better equipped to assess a connector you want to use and configure it correctly for your use case.

To understand how connectors can group and map data, you need to consider the interaction between Kafka Connect tasks and Kafka partitions. In Chapter 3, we introduced tasks as the mechanism that Kafka Connect uses to do the actual work of transferring data from one place to another. In Chapter 2, we talked about partitions and highlighted the fact that Kafka provides ordering guarantees within a single partition. Both mechanisms provide a way to shard data.

Let's first look at the impact of tasks on source connectors. When a source connector reads data from an external system, each task is reading data in parallel. It is up to the connector to decide how to split this data among the available tasks to ensure there are no duplicates. A simple connector could run a single task and avoid the problem of sharding the data that's in the external system. This is actually how FileStreamSourceConnector, which is packaged with Kafka, works. See Figure 4-2 for an example.

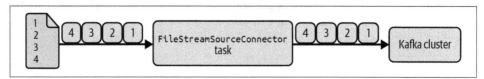

Figure 4-2. A single task in FileStreamSourceConnector reads the file line by line

Even if you increase the tasks.max setting, it still only runs a single task because it doesn't have a sensible mechanism to shard the data. Most connectors are more advanced than FileStreamSourceConnector and have built-in mechanisms to assign the data across the tasks. Figure 4-3 shows an example of such a connector that allows different tasks to read different lines of a table.

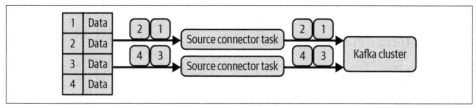

Figure 4-3. Multiple tasks that each read a subset of the data, preventing duplicates in Kafka

Let's consider partitions. An individual source connector can either choose which records should go to which partitions or rely on the configured partitioning strategy. Many connectors use keys to identify the data that needs to be sent to the same partitions. For example, status updates that apply to a particular entity might use the entity ID as the key. Figure 4-4 shows an example of tasks sending data to partitions.

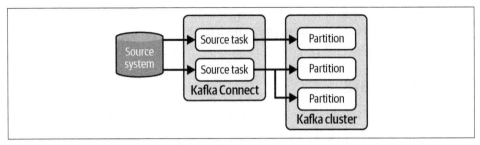

Figure 4-4. Source tasks can send their data to one or more partitions

How a source connector partitions its data affects the next stage of the pipeline, whether that next stage is a sink connector or just a Kafka consumer, due to the way that Kafka distributes partitions among both sink tasks and consumers from a group. Each partition can only be assigned to a single sink task of a particular sink connector, and likewise a single consumer within a particular group, so any data that needs to be read by a single task or consumer needs to be sent to the same partition by the source connector.

Now let's consider sink connectors. In sink connectors, tasks also run in parallel. This can affect the order in which data is sent to the external system. You can be sure that each task will write its own data in order, but there isn't any order coordination between tasks. The way that sink tasks interact with partitions also impacts the number of sink tasks you can run. If you have one partition and two tasks, only one task will receive any data, so when creating a data pipeline with a sink connector, make sure you are mindful about the number of partitions on the topics the connector is reading from. Figure 4-5 shows two sink tasks reading data from three partitions.

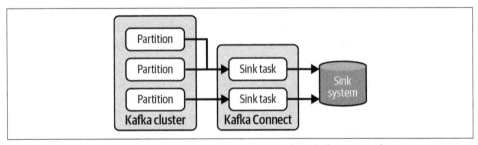

Figure 4-5. Each partition can only be read by one sink task for a specific connector

As you can imagine, the combination of tasks and partitions means that there are multiple ways that the data can be grouped and ordered as it flows through the system. When you are designing your Kafka Connect data pipeline, make sure you think about these options and don't leave the `tasks.max` and partitions configuration options as an afterthought.

Now that we have looked at how data at a high level can be transformed and mapped between systems, let's look at how you can control the specific format of data in a Kafka Connect pipeline.

Formatting Data

In Chapter 3, we talked about converters and how they serialize and deserialize data as it goes into and out of Kafka. We also briefly covered why you need to align your converters with the serializer and deserializer of the producers and consumers that are also interacting with the data. Here we discuss in more detail the differences among converters, transformations, and connectors, and how they impact the data format throughout the pipeline. We also look at how you can enforce this structure with schemas and a schema registry.

Data Formats

In a Kafka Connect pipeline, the format of the data and how it evolves depends on the connector, any configured transformations, and the converter. Let's look at each of these and how they affect the data format.

First, let's consider the connector. In a source flow, the connector runs first; it reads the data from the external system and creates a Java object called a `ConnectRecord`. The connector decides which parts of the record data should be kept and how to map them to the `ConnectRecord`. The specifics of this mapping can differ between connectors, even if they are for the same system, so make sure that the connector you choose keeps the parts of the data that are important to you.

In a sink flow, the connector runs last rather than first. It takes `ConnectRecord` objects and translates them into data objects that it can send to the external system. This means that a sink connector has the last say in what data makes it to the external system.

Now let's look at the difference between converters and transformations when it comes to their input and output:

- Transformations have `ConnectRecord` objects as both their input and output.
- Converters convert between `ConnectRecord` objects and the raw bytes that Kafka sends and receives. They run last in source pipelines and first in sink pipelines.

Figure 4-6 shows the different data types that are passed between connectors, transformations, and converters.

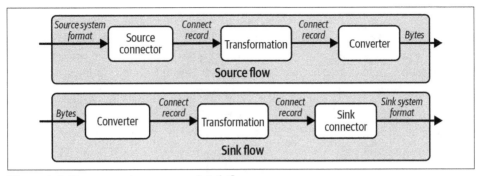

Figure 4-6. Data types in source and sink flows

Transformations and converters are separate steps to enable the composability that Kafka Connect offers. You could write a JSON converter that manipulates the contents of the record before sending it to Kafka. If you wanted a pipeline that manipulated the data in the same way but used a format like Avro, you would need a new converter. It would be better to create a transformation that manipulates the data and then use two converters, one for JSON and one for Avro.

Transformations can be chained, so rather than needing to write a custom transformation, you can run multiple simple transformations to fulfill your requirements. If you can't find transformations or converters that fit your requirements, you can write your own (see Chapter 12).

Now that you understand the roles of connectors, transformations, and converters, and the orders they can run in, you can make a better-informed decision about which libraries to use for your pipeline in order to get the exact data format you need at each stage. As with choosing connectors, make sure you take into account licensing and support requirements when choosing transformations and converters.

Schemas

A schema provides a blueprint for the shape of the data. For example, a schema can specify which fields are required and what types should be present. Using schemas is important when you are building a data pipeline because most data is complex and contains multiple fields of different types. Without schemas to give context to the data, it is very difficult for applications to reliably perform the steps to process and analyze it.

Almost all data management systems have a mechanism to define schemas. Your systems' specific schemas will vary, but here's how Kafka Connect pipelines generally make use of schemas. As we saw in the previous section, data transitions between two different formats while passing through Kafka Connect: the ConnectRecord and raw bytes. Each format has a different configuration mechanism.

Kafka Connect record schemas

A `ConnectRecord` contains an optional `Schema` object for both the key and the value. `Schema` is a Java class that is part of the Kafka Connect API and is used by connectors, transformations, and converters as the data travels through Kafka Connect. Let's look at how the `Schema` is used in both source and sink pipelines.

A source connector is responsible for constructing the initial `ConnectRecord` object and has control over the `Schema` that is added. How the `Schema` is defined depends on the connector. `FileStreamSourceConnector` always uses the `STRING_SCHEMA`, no matter what format the file is using. You can see this in the source code:

```
private static final Schema VALUE_SCHEMA = Schema.STRING_SCHEMA;

@Override
public List<SourceRecord> poll() throws InterruptedException {
    ...
    records.add(new SourceRecord(offsetKey(filename),
        offsetValue(streamOffset),
        topic,
        null,
        null,
        null,
        VALUE_SCHEMA,
        line,
        System.currentTimeMillis()));
    ...
}
```

Most connectors are more complex than `FileStreamSourceConnector` and make use of schemas provided by the system to construct the `Schema` object. For example, the Debezium connectors that read database change logs take note of database schema changes and use that information to construct the `ConnectRecord`. The `ConnectRecord` and included `Schema` objects are then passed to any transformations and to the converter. Transformations and converters can use the `Schema` to parse the `ConnectRecord` and do their respective work.

In a sink pipeline, it is the converter that constructs the `ConnectRecord`, and therefore the `Schema`; the transformations use this information to parse the contents. Sink connectors use the `ConnectRecord` to construct the object that is sent to the external system, which means that they can choose how to interpret the `Schema` that is included in the `ConnectRecord`. For example, `FileStreamSinkConnector` ignores the `Schema` completely, but that is only because it is writing to a file. Most sink connectors use the `Schema` information to construct the external system data.

Kafka record schemas

Kafka Connect pipelines can also use schemas to describe the data stored in Kafka. These schemas are used by converters to understand how to serialize and deserialize the data sent to and from Kafka. In a sink pipeline, the schema Kafka Connect uses to deserialize data is the same one that was used by the applications to produce that data. In a source pipeline, the schema Kafka Connect uses to serialize the data is also used by consuming applications or sink connectors to deserialize it further down the pipeline.

The ConnectRecord object has built-in support for schemas, but since records in Kafka are raw bytes, you need to decide on a mechanism to include the schema. The naïve approach is to put the schema alongside the payload in the value of the record. This is what the JsonConverter does by default.

If you run FileStreamSourceConnector with JsonConverter against a file with the following contents:

```
This is a string
Another string
A third string
The final string
```

The JsonConverter uses the String schema that the connector provides and constructs Kafka records with the values as:

```
{"schema":{"type":"string","optional":false},"payload":"This is a string"}
{"schema":{"type":"string","optional":false},"payload":"Another string"}
{"schema":{"type":"string","optional":false},"payload":"A third string"}
{"schema":{"type":"string","optional":false},"payload":"The final string"}
```

Although this makes it easy to pass a schema along for consumers, it means that every single record has to include the schema. The example here is simple, so the schema is small, but the more complex the schema, the bigger the overhead for each record.

A better approach is to only include a small identifier for the schema in each record and store the schemas elsewhere. This gives you the benefits of having schemas throughout your pipeline with only a negligible overhead. This is what most of the existing converter, serializer, and deserializer tools do, and they typically put the schema ID in one of two places: in a record header or at the beginning of the serialized value.

If you are building a source flow, make sure you choose a converter that will store the ID in a place that is expected by the downstream applications that will consume the record. Similarly, if you are building a sink flow, choose a converter that knows where in the record to look for the ID. It is relatively easy to build a system to store schemas that can be retrieved by your applications; otherwise, this is exactly what *schema registries* are built for.

A schema registry typically consists of two parts: a server that stores schemas and exposes APIs to retrieve and administer them, and serializer/deserializer/converter libraries to use in your clients. Schema registries often include additional features to help you manage your schemas. For example, many registries perform compatibility enforcement and allow you to control the lifecycle of your schemas. This is useful for applications, as it can prevent breaking changes from being introduced and allows administrators to inform application developers when a schema has been deprecated.

The two schema registries most commonly used with Kafka are the Confluent Schema Registry and the Apicurio Registry. Both allow you to use Kafka as the backing store for the registry, removing the need for a separate database or other storage system. They also both support the most common schema formats that are used with Kafka: Avro, JSON Schema, and Protobuf.

A detailed comparison of the available schema formats and schema registries for Kafka is outside the scope of this book, but we can give pointers. To choose a format, make sure you consider the tools and libraries that go along with each one. For example, do they support the language you want and provide code generation options? If using a schema registry, make sure your chosen converter and application serializer/deserializer are compatible with the registry. The Confluent schema registry will only work with Confluent libraries, whereas Apicurio Registry comes with a compatibility API, which means that you can use the dedicated Apicurio Registry libraries or the Confluent ones.

Exploring Kafka Connect Internals

In order to understand how Kafka Connect in distributed mode can withstand failures, you need to know how it stores its state with a mix of internal topics and group membership. Secondly, you should be familiar with the rebalance protocol Kafka Connect uses to spread tasks across workers and detect worker failures.

Internal Topics

As mentioned in Chapter 3, Kafka Connect in distributed mode uses topics to store state, which are:

- Configuration topic, specified via `config.storage.topic`
- Offset topic, specified via `offset.storage.topic`
- Status topic, specified via `status.storage.topic`

In the configuration topic, Kafka Connect stores the configuration of all the connectors and tasks that have been started by users. Each time users update the configuration of a connector or a connector requests a reconfiguration (for example, when it detects it can start more tasks), a record is emitted to this topic. This topic is compacted, so it always keeps the last state for each entity while ensuring that it does not use a lot of storage.

In the offset topic, Kafka Connect stores offsets of source connectors. (This topic is compacted for the same reasons.) By default, Kafka Connect creates this topic with several partitions, as each source task uses it regularly to write its position. Offsets for sink connectors are stored using regular Kafka consumer groups.

In the status topic, Kafka Connect stores the current state of connectors and tasks. This topic is the central place for the data queried by users of the REST API. It allows users to query any worker and get the status of all running plug-ins. It is also compacted and should also have multiple partitions.

At startup, Kafka Connect automatically creates these topics if they don't already exist. All workers in a Kafka Connect cluster must use the same topics, but if you are running multiple Kafka Connect clusters, each cluster needs its own separate topics. Data within all three topics is stored in JSON, so it can be viewed using a regular consumer.

For example, with the `kafka-console-consumer.sh` tool, here's how you can view the contents of the status topic:

```
$ ./bin/kafka-console-consumer.sh --bootstrap-server localhost:9092 \
  --topic connect-status \
  --from-beginning \
  --property print.key=true
status-connector-file-source {"state":"RUNNING","trace":null,
"worker_id":"192.168.1.12:8083","generation":5}
```

In this example, the runtime has `status.storage.topic` set to `connect-status`. Records in this topic show the status for a connector named `file-source` and Kafka Connect uses that name to derive the key, `status-connector-file-source`, for records related to the connector.

Group Membership

In addition to topics, Kafka Connect makes extensive use of Kafka's group membership API.

First, for each sink connector, the Kafka Connect runtime runs a regular consumer group that consumes records from Kafka to pass them to the connector. By default, the groups are named after the connector name; for example, for a connector named `file-sink`, the group is `connect-file-sink`. Each consumer in the group provides records to a single task. These groups and their offsets can be retrieved using regular consumer groups tools, such as `kafka-consumer-groups.sh`.

In addition, Kafka Connect uses the group membership API to assign connectors and tasks to workers and ensure each user partition is only consumed by a single sink task per connector. At startup, Kafka Connect creates a group using the `group.id` value from its configuration. This group is not directly visible by the consumer groups tools, as it's not a consumer group, but it works in essentially the same way. This is why all workers with the same `group.id` value become part of the same Kafka Connect cluster.

To be a member of a group, workers, just like regular consumers, have to *heartbeat* regularly. A heartbeat is a request that contains the group name, the member ID and a few more fields to identify the sender. It is sent at regular intervals (specified by `heartbeat.interval.ms`, with a default value of three seconds) by all workers to the group coordinator. If a worker stops sending heartbeats, the coordinator detects it, removes the worker from the group, and triggers a rebalance. During a rebalance, tasks are assigned to workers using a rebalance protocol.

Rebalance Protocols

The specifics of rebalance (or rebalancing) protocols are generally hard to comprehend. Thankfully, to use Kafka Connect effectively, it's enough to understand the high-level process described in this section.

Kafka Connect wants to ensure that all tasks are running, that each task is run by a single worker, and that tasks are spread evenly across all workers. The distribution of tasks has to be updated anytime the resources that are managed by Kafka Connect change, such as when a worker joins or leaves the group, or when tasks from a connector are added or removed. When resources change, Kafka Connect has to *rebalance* tasks across the workers.

The mechanism that Kafka Connect uses for rebalances has changed over time. Until Kafka 2.3, during a rebalance, Kafka Connect simply stopped all tasks and reassigned them all onto the available workers. This is called the `eager` rebalance protocol, also called "stop the world." The main issue with this protocol is that Kafka Connect can run a set of independent connectors, and each time one of these connectors decides to create or delete tasks, all connectors and tasks are stopped, then reassigned to workers, then restarted. In a busy Kafka Connect cluster, this can cause long and repetitive pauses in data processing. It also makes rolling restarts very expensive, as each worker causes two rebalances to happen: one when it shuts down and another one when it restarts.

In Kafka 2.3, Connect introduced an incremental cooperative rebalance protocol called `compatible`. The idea is to avoid stopping all connectors and tasks each time a rebalance happens and instead only rebalance the resources that need to be rebalanced (incrementally, if possible). For example, if a worker disappears, Kafka Connect waits a short duration before rebalancing anything. This is because workers usually don't experience destructive failures and will restart immediately. If a worker rejoins quickly, it keeps the tasks that it owned before and no rebalance is needed. If the worker does not rejoin quickly enough—the duration is specified via `scheduled.rebalance.max.delay.ms`, with a default of five minutes—then the tasks it used to run are reassigned to available workers.

Since Kafka 2.4, the default rebalance protocol is `sessioned`. In terms of rebalancing behavior, it works exactly the same way as `compatible`, but it also ensures that intra-cluster communications are secured. Like `compatible`, `sessioned` is only active if all workers support it; otherwise, it defaults to the common protocol shared by all workers.

The rebalance protocol used by Kafka Connect is specified by the `connect.protocol` configuration. Users should keep the default value for the version they use and only consider downgrading to `eager` if they rely on its specific behavior.

> For more details on the history behind each protocol, you can read the respective KIPs. The `compatible` rebalance protocol was introduced by KIP-415 (*https://oreil.ly/u7YeS*). The `sessioned` rebalance protocol was introduced by KIP-507 (*https://oreil.ly/qfa5P*).

Handling Failures in Kafka Connect

Now that you understand how Kafka Connect manages its state, let's take a look at the most common types of failures and how to handle them.

In order to build a resilient pipeline, it's key to understand how all components in your system handle failures. In this section, we focus on Kafka Connect and how it handles failures, ignoring other components such as the operating system, execution and deployment environment, or hardware.

We cover the following failures:

- Worker failure
- Connector/task failure
- Kafka/external systems failure

We also discuss how you can use dead letter queues to deal with unprocessable records.

Worker Failure

In distributed mode, Kafka Connect can run across multiple workers. We recommend using at least two workers to be resilient to worker failure.

For example, if we have three workers that are running two connectors (C1 and C2), the different tasks could be spread out like in Figure 4-7.

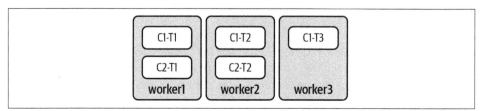

Figure 4-7. Example of a Kafka Connect cluster with three workers. Connector C1 has three tasks (T1, T2, T3) and C2 has two tasks (T1 and T2).

In this case, if worker2 is taken offline—either because it crashed or for maintenance—Kafka does not receive its heartbeat anymore. After a short interval, it automatically kicks worker2 out of the group, which forces Kafka Connect to rebalance all running tasks onto the remaining workers.

After the rebalance, the task assignment may look like Figure 4-8.

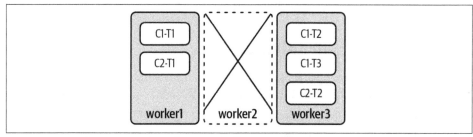

Figure 4-8. Kafka Connect has reassigned all tasks onto the remaining workers

While the rebalance is happening, the tasks that were on worker2 are not run. This mechanism triggers and completes within about five minutes. The actual time it takes depends mostly on the following configurations:

- `session.timeout.ms` is the maximum duration between two consecutive heartbeats from workers

- `rebalance.timeout.ms` is the maximum duration workers can take to rejoin the group when a rebalance happens

- `scheduled.rebalance.max.delay.ms` is the time to wait before re-allocating the connectors and tasks of workers that have fallen out of the group since the last rebalance

When a worker is not stopped cleanly, it's possible that its tasks did not commit offsets for all records they were processing. So, upon restarting, some tasks may reprocess some records. We discuss this problem later in this chapter.

In order for Kafka Connect to handle worker failures, you need to make sure that you have enough capacity to accommodate task redistribution. Kafka Connect has no mechanism to limit the number of tasks that can be assigned to a worker during a rebalance. If a worker is assigned too many tasks, its performance degrades and eventually tasks won't make any progress. At minimum, you should always have enough capacity to handle a single worker failure in order to reliably handle rolling worker restarts.

Connector/Task Failure

Another common type of failure is a crash of one of the connectors or one of its tasks. Until now, we've simplified what exactly happens when Kafka Connect runs a connector. In reality, it has to run one instance of the connector and zero or more task instances. Kafka Connect tracks the health of both and associates them with a state, which can be:

UNASSIGNED
A connector or task has not yet been assigned to a worker

RUNNING
A connector or task is correctly running on a worker

PAUSED
A connector or task has been paused by a user via the REST API

FAILED
A connector or task has encountered an error and crashed

RESTARTING
The connector/task is either actively restarting or is expected to restart soon

STOPPED
A connector has been stopped by a user via the REST API

The state of connectors and tasks can be retrieved via the REST API. Figure 4-9 depicts the most common transitions between the different states.

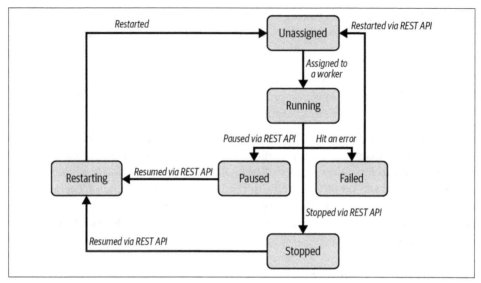

Figure 4-9. Most common state transitions for connectors and tasks

Kafka Connect emits detailed metrics tracking the time spent in each state by each connector. See Chapter 9 for details on how to retrieve and monitor metrics.

The statuses of the connector and tasks are determined independently. For example, some connectors may perform extra logic, such as connecting to their target system to discover resources when they start up. While this happens, the connector will be in RUNNING state, but no tasks will be created.

Each task can also encounter an error (and be marked FAILED) separately from the connector. By default, if a task has a problem, Kafka Connect lets it crash, marks it as FAILED, and does not attempt to restart it automatically. Kafka Connect emits metrics for the state of tasks, which administrators have to monitor to identify failures. A task failure does not trigger a rebalance.

In case of a one-off failure, administrators can restart tasks via the REST API. The REST API can also be used to retrieve the exception that crashed the task and its stack trace. In case of a systematic failure, such as a record that is impossible to process, Kafka Connect offers the option to skip it (and optionally emit a detailed log message) instead of failing the task. This can be configured per connector using the errors.tolerance configuration.

Kafka/External Systems Failure

As Kafka Connect flows data between Kafka and external systems, failures in either can impact Kafka Connect.

As detailed in Chapter 2, Kafka can be very resilient. To have a resilient production deployment, Kafka clusters must have multiple brokers and be configured to offer maximum availability. In addition, Kafka Connect must be configured to create its topics with multiple replicas so that it won't be negatively impacted by the failure of a single broker. This is important for topics that are either the source or sink for connectors, internal Kafka Connect topics, and __consumer_offsets and __transac tion_state topics.

On the other hand, an external system failure has to be handled by the connector. Depending on the system and the implementation of the connector, it may be handled automatically or it may crash tasks and require manual intervention to recover.

Before building a Kafka Connect pipeline, it's important to read the connector documentation and understand the failure modes of the external system to gauge the pipeline's resiliency. Sometimes there are multiple community implementations for the same connectors and you will need to pick the one that satisfies your needs. Then you need to perform resiliency testing to determine whether the connector provides the required resiliency for your use cases. Finally, it's important to monitor the appropriate metrics and logs from both the external system and the connector, which are described in Chapter 9.

Dead Letter Queues

When dealing with an unprocessable record, for sink connectors, Kafka Connect can use a *dead letter queue* rather than having to skip the record or fail. A dead letter queue, often abbreviated DLQ, is a concept from traditional messaging systems—basically a place to store records that can't be processed or delivered. In Kafka Connect, the dead letter queue is a topic (specified via errors.deadletter queue.topic.name in the connector configuration) where unprocessable records are written. Kafka Connect, however, does not provide a similar mechanism for source connectors, because it can't convert the undeliverable record from the external system into a Kafka record.

 Support for dead letter queues for sink connectors was first introduced via KIP-298 (*https://oreil.ly/iv_XJ*) and further improved in Kafka 2.6 via KIP-610 (*https://oreil.ly/_oU5D*).

Let's look at an example of using a dead letter queue. When running the Confluent S3 sink connector, the Kafka Connect runtime is reading records from a Kafka topic before passing them to the connector. As the topic is expected to contain Avro records, we configure the connector with an Avro converter. However, if a single record in the topic is not in the Avro format, the connector is not able to handle this record. Instead of failing the connector or losing this record, Kafka Connect can forward it to a dead letter queue and keep processing the other records in the topic. The connector configuration would contain the following settings:

```
{
  "connector.class": "io.confluent.connect.s3.S3SinkConnector",
  "value.converter": "io.confluent.connect.avro.AvroConverter",
  "errors.tolerance": "all",
  "errors.deadletterqueue.topic.name": "my-dlq"
}
```

This allows the contents of the dead letter queue topic to be processed by another mechanism, for example another connector or a consumer application.

Figure 4-10 shows an example of using a dead letter queue.

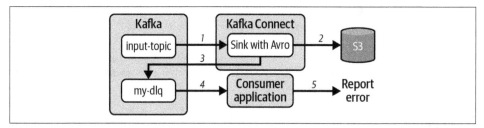

Figure 4-10. Unprocessable records are sent to a dead letter queue to be processed by another mechanism

The flow starts with the S3 sink connector configured with Avro receiving records from the input topic (1). Avro records are correctly processed and sent to S3 (2). If a record can't be processed due to failures in the converter, transformation, or sink task delivery phase, it is sent to the dead letter queue configured for the connector (3). In this example, another application receives records from the dead letter queue (4), processes them, and reports errors (5).

Understanding Processing Semantics

Processing semantics define the type of guarantees that are made when a message flows through a Kafka Connect pipeline. It can be one of these three types:

At-least-once
   A message entering the pipeline reaches the target system at least once as one or multiple copies. Extra copies of a message are called *duplicates*.

At-most-once

A message entering the pipeline may not arrive to the target system, and will never be duplicated.

Exactly-once

A message entering the pipeline is processed by downstream readers exactly once.

The exact semantics that a Kafka Connect pipeline provides depends on several aspects, including the connector being used, how it's configured, and the configuration of the runtime.

Let's look at each type of connector and see how to understand the semantics that can be provided.

Sink Connectors

To recap, these are the steps that constitute a sink pipeline:

1. The runtime consumes records from the Kafka topic
2. Records are passed to the configured converter
3. Records are passed to the configured transformations
4. Records are passed to the sink connector that writes them to the sink system

Figure 4-11 shows this flow.

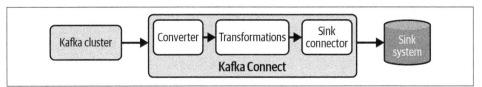

Figure 4-11. Steps in a sink pipeline

To determine the semantics of a sink pipeline, there are a few different elements to consider:

- The value of errors.tolerance
- Whether you are using a DLQ
- The behavior of the connector
- The characteristics of the target system

Let's first consider errors.tolerance. This configuration tells the Kafka Connect runtime what to do if the converter, transformations, or connector reports an error. The default value is none, which causes the task to fail. In this case, the task fails without committing offsets for the record that caused the error, so when it restarts, that record is consumed again by the task. This setup always provides at-least-once semantics; whether it provides exactly-once depends on the specific behavior of the connector (we discuss those considerations later in this section).

Sometimes it is unnecessary for the task to fail if it encounters an error. If a particular record is unprocessable (known as a *poison pill*), it can cause the task to fail repeatedly. Instead, you can set `errors.tolerance` to `all` so that the runtime skips records that cause failures. This is good for keeping your tasks running, but unhelpful if you are aiming for exactly-once or at-least-once semantics.

If you are using `errors.tolerance` set to `all` and you want exactly-once or at-least-once semantics, one option is to configure a dead letter queue. With a DLQ, if there is a failure, the runtime ensures no records are lost and it automatically forwards the affected records to the DLQ. This approach allows you to get at-least-once semantics in most cases, although it's worth noting that Kafka Connect does not retry when sending records to the DLQ.

Finally, you need to consider the connector itself in combination with the characteristics of the target system. The difference between at-least-once and exactly-once semantics often comes down to how data is sent to the target system. Because records in Kafka are immutable, if the same records are processed twice, the connector can emit the exact same records to the target system. In systems that offer *idempotent* writes—for example by storing records based on their key—they can remove duplicated records and only keep a single copy, effectively achieving exactly-once semantics.

The behavior of the connector also determines whether you have at-most-once or at-least-once semantics. Each time a task starts up, it restarts from the last committed offset. By default, the runtime only commits offsets for records that have been successfully passed to the connector and did not result in an error. This means if the connector writes data to the external system asynchronously, it must utilize the hooks provided to influence which offsets the runtime can commit. Otherwise, if the task were to crash before the connector successfully wrote the record and after the offset was committed, then this record would effectively be skipped when the task restarted.

To summarize, the `errors.tolerance` configuration is important when determining the semantics of a sink pipeline. If it is set to `all`, the runtime skips unprocessable records. If you want to avoid losing any records and maximize the availability of a sink pipeline, consider using a dead letter queue, but take into account the additional operational cost it requires. Also, while some steps may cause duplicates, some external systems are able to handle them and effectively provide end-to-end exactly-once semantics for sink pipelines.

Source Connectors

As a quick recap, these are the steps that constitute a source pipeline, as shown in Figure 4-12:

1. The connector consumes records from the external system

2. Records are passed to the configured transformations

3. Records are passed to the configured converter

4. Records are passed to the runtime that produces them to a Kafka topic

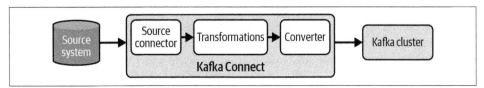

Figure 4-12. Steps in a source pipeline

To determine semantics for a source pipeline, you need to consider the following:

- Use of source connector offsets
- The value of errors.tolerance
- The behavior of the producer
- Whether exactly-once support is enabled

Similarly to the consumer fetching records in a sink pipeline, in a source pipeline the connector has to decide which data to retrieve from the external system. Not all external systems have a mechanism like offsets in Kafka that enables them to directly identify a record. For that reason, source connectors can associate an arbitrary mapping of keys to values—the sourceOffset field in SourceRecord objects—to express their current position. This arbitrary object can be retrieved by tasks as needed. It is the connector's responsibility to ensure that this object contains the appropriate information to correctly retrieve records from the external system. The Kafka Connect runtime automatically stores this object in the offset topic and it also provides a mechanism to let connectors know when it is committing offsets in case they want to do their own offset tracking in the target system. In most source connector pipelines, the offsets are committed after producing records to Kafka, so it's possible for a worker to successfully produce records to Kafka but fail before it's able to commit their offsets. Depending on how the connector works, this step may cause some record reprocessing, resulting in at-least-once semantics.

In case there are any errors in the transformations, converter steps, or in the producer used by the runtime, the value of the errors.tolerance setting determines whether the task is marked as FAILED or the failing record is skipped. Source tasks can't rely on dead letter queues, so tolerating errors makes these steps provide at-most-once semantics in case of errors.

Records in a source pipeline are pushed to Kafka via a producer from the runtime. As of Kafka 3.1.0, producers are configured to offer at-least-once by default, but this can be overridden in the connector configuration.

Support for exactly-once in source connectors was added via KIP-618 (*https://oreil.ly/ y7lxb*) in Kafka 3.3. When enabled, the runtime uses a transactional producer to commit offsets and produce to Kafka as part of a single transaction. In Chapter 8, we explain the worker and connector configurations required to enable this feature. Not all source connectors support exactly-once, so make sure you check the connector documentation. We also explain how to write a connector that supports exactly-once in Chapter 11. You can use this information to write your own connector or to evaluate the semantics of an existing one.

 Exactly-once semantics for source connectors is not available in standalone mode.

In summary, how source connectors handle offsets and how those are committed to Kafka are key factors in source pipeline semantics. As with sink pipelines, the errors.tolerance configuration also plays a role; however, unlike with sink pipelines, you cannot make use of dead letter queues to catch skipped records.

Summary

In this chapter, we looked at the different aspects that need to be considered in order to build resilient data pipelines with Kafka Connect.

We first looked at selecting the right connectors from the hundreds of connectors built by the Kafka community. You need to consider the pipeline direction, whether it fulfills your feature requirements, and whether it comes with an appropriate level of support.

Then we focused on data models and formats and the options you have for mapping data between systems. Whatever choice you make, you need to understand the structure of your data at each stage in the pipeline and make conscious transformation and formatting decisions. These decisions inform your choice of converter, transformations, and predicates. We also highlighted the benefits of using schemas and a schema registry to properly define, enforce, and manage the structure of the data.

We then examined the challenges in handling the many kinds of failures that can arise, from worker crashes to task errors. Although Kafka Connect is generally considered to be resilient, it cannot recover from all failures, so you should understand the levers we discussed and how to use them in response to failures.

Finally, we detailed how all the decisions taken regarding data models, error handling, runtime, and connector configurations directly impact the processing semantics that can be achieved by Kafka Connect pipelines. For sink pipelines, dead letter queues are a powerful feature to avoid losing data, and it's possible to achieve exactly-once semantics with capable downstream systems. Since Kafka 3.3, source pipelines can also achieve exactly-once with connectors that support this feature.

CHAPTER 5

Connectors in Action

After having covered how Kafka Connect works and how to use it, it's time to put your knowledge into practice! In this chapter we look at, and run, some of the most popular connectors: a sink connector for Amazon Simple Storage Service (S3), a JDBC source connector, and a MySQL source connector. We explain the use cases they target and their most important configurations, and demonstrate how to use them in various scenarios.

These three connectors address common use cases and appear in many pipelines across all industries, so having a good understanding of them is valuable. Even if you don't use these specific connectors, we expect many of the topics covered to be applicable to others.

All of the examples assume that you have a Kafka cluster running with a bootstrap server accessible at localhost:9092.

Confluent S3 Sink Connector

One of the most common use cases of Kafka Connect is to export data from Kafka into a storage system. Often, you need to keep data long after it has been processed; it could be for legal reasons, for preserving historical data, or simply for batch-oriented systems that only run periodically. While Kafka can store data indefinitely, if you handle very large amounts of data it can become costly to store it in Kafka forever.

Cloud storage systems like Amazon S3 are designed for storing large amounts of data for long durations at a low cost per gigabyte. In addition, storage services can be used as data lakes due to their integrations with data processing tools. Building a pipeline that copies data from Kafka into a storage service is common. If you want the data back in Kafka, you can import it with a source connector.

In this section we examine the Confluent S3 sink connector, which is available from the Confluent Hub website (*https://oreil.ly/IvosB*). The examples and configuration descriptions use version 10.5.1 of the connector. The community has built various S3 sink connectors that you can choose from; each has its own specificities and configuration settings, but overall they share similar functionalities. You can download a ZIP file containing all of the libraries for the Confluent connector from Confluent Hub. Once you've downloaded it, extract its contents and add the folder to your `plugin.path` for your Kafka Connect runtime.

Let's start by looking at the configuration that this connector exposes and the various ways you can run it.

Configuring the Connector

The Confluent S3 sink connector is very configurable and exposes over 50 settings to finely tune its behavior. Most of them have sensible defaults and most of the advanced settings are optional, so you typically only have to set a small number of configurations. In this section we cover the most important settings and explain how they enable common use cases. Once you understand the basics, we recommend taking a look at the full list of settings to see if your use cases can benefit from advanced tuning. Note that you can provide custom implementations for several settings that significantly alter how the connector works.

As a sink connector, the maximum number of tasks that can process data is equal to the number of partitions from topics listed in `topics` or `topics.regex`. If you set `tasks.max` to a larger value, the connector still starts that number of tasks, but the extra tasks don't process records and will needlessly use resources.

The configurations can be grouped into five categories:

- Connectivity and S3 details
- Object partitioning
- Object naming
- Object formats
- Object upload

Connectivity and S3 details

To connect the connector to your S3 instance, the first thing you need is your Amazon Web Services (AWS) credentials: the access key and secret key. There are multiple ways to provide your credentials to the connector. The first option is to set both `aws.access.key.id` and `aws.secret.access.key`. This allows you to use different credentials for each S3 connector you run. The other option is to use a credential provider to set the credentials in the Kafka Connect worker for all S3 connectors to use. By default, the connector has the `s3.credentials.provider.class` configuration set to `com.amazonaws.auth.DefaultAWSCredentialsProviderChain`, and this provider expects the credentials in specific places. It first checks environment variables—AWS_ACCESS_KEY_ID and AWS_SECRET_ACCESS_KEY—to retrieve credentials. If you can't use environment variables, this provider can use Java system properties (`aws.accessKeyId` and `aws.secretKey`), a credentials file (*~/.aws/credentials*), or various other methods that are documented in its Javadocs (*https://oreil.ly/AmTtD*).

Data in S3 is stored in *buckets*. You need to create a bucket in your S3 instance that the connector will write data into. You specify the bucket's name via the `s3.bucket.name` setting. This setting is required for starting the connector. The region the bucket is located in is specified using the `s3.region` setting, and it defaults to `us-west-2`.

By default, the connector does not handle tombstone records; if it receives a record with a `null` value, it will fail. As such records are relatively common, you should change the connector configuration `behavior.on.null.values` to `ignore` (default is `fail`) to skip these records.

When setting up the connection to the bucket, you can also provide more advanced configurations:

Server-side encryption
   You can configure S3 to automatically encrypt data as it's written to the bucket. Using `s3.ssea.name`, you can set the encryption algorithm to use either AES256 or `aws:kms` (unset by default). When set to AES256, you also need to provide an encryption key using `s3.sse.customer.key`. When set to `aws:kms`, the encryption key is retrieved from your AWS Key Management Service (KMS) service, and you specify the key name using `s3.sse.kms.key.id`.

Network proxy
   When connecting to S3 via a proxy, you can provide the proxy details via the `s3.proxy.url`, `s3.proxy.user`, and `s3.proxy.password` settings. Using a proxy can be helpful when connecting to S3 from a secured enterprise network.

Compression
   It's possible to compress data using Gzip as it's written to S3. In order to do so, set `s3.compression.type` to `gzip` (default is `none`). You can also configure the compression level by setting `s3.compression.level` to a number between `-1` and 9 where `-1` (the default) means using the system default compression level, 0 means no compression, and 9 is the best compression ratio. Enabling compression can reduce the size of objects written to S3, but it causes the connector to use additional CPU and memory.

Finally, while the connector is primarily targeting Amazon S3, it's also possible to use it with other S3-compatible storage systems. In order to do so, you need to set `store.url` to the URL of your storage system. For systems that are not fully compatible, you also need to provide an implementation of the `io.confluent.connect.stor age.Storage` (*https://oreil.ly/ZS3hX*) interface and pass it in the configuration using the `storage.class` setting.

Now that we understand how the connector connects to the S3 bucket, let's see how the connector partitions the data into objects.

Object partitioning

The connector needs to transform streams of records coming from each partition in Kafka into distinct objects in S3. This task is performed using a partitioner that is configured using the `partitioner.class` setting. This must be set to a class that implements the `io.confluent.connect.storage.partitioner.Partitioner` interface. By default, this is set to `io.confluent.connect.storage.partitioner.Default Partitioner`.

Out of the box, the connector provides five implementations:

- `io.confluent.connect.storage.partitioner.DefaultPartitioner`
- `io.confluent.connect.storage.partitioner.FieldPartitioner`
- `io.confluent.connect.storage.partitioner.TimeBasedPartitioner`
- `io.confluent.connect.storage.partitioner.DailyPartitioner`
- `io.confluent.connect.storage.partitioner.HourlyPartitioner`

`DefaultPartitioner` uses the Kafka partition that each `ConnectRecord` originates from to determine which object the record should be written into. With this partitioner, when using the default values for object naming, object names have this format: `topics/<topic>/partition=<partition>/<topic>+<partition>+<offset>.<suffix>`

`FieldPartitioner` uses one configurable field from each `ConnectRecord` to determine the object to write to. The field is configured using the `partition.field.name` setting. With this partitioner, object names have this format: `topics/<topic>/<field.name>=<field.value>/<topic>+<partition>+<offset>.<suffix>`

`TimeBasedPartitioner` uses the time to map records into objects. The time to use is specified with the `timestamp.extractor` setting. This can be set to:

- `Wallclock` to use the current time. This is the default.
- `Record` to use the timestamp from the `ConnectRecord`.

- `RecordField` to extract the timestamp from a field, specified via `time stamp.field`, of the `ConnectRecord`.

The extracted time appears in object names, so you can format it using the `path.format` setting. For example, if it is set to `'year'=YYYY/'month'= MM/'day'=dd/'hour'=HH`, object names have this format:

```
topics/<topic>/year=YYYY/month=MM/day=dd/hour=HH/<topic>+<partition>+
<offset>.<suffix>
```

`DailyPartitioner` and `HourlyPartitioner` work like `TimeBasedPartitioner`. They are shortcuts for grouping records daily and hourly, respectively.

In order to use `TimeBasedPartitioner`, `DailyPartitioner`, and `HourlyPartitioner`, you need to specify a timezone using the `timezone` setting. This can be set to short names such as `UTC`, `CET`, or `EST`, or long names such as `Europe/Paris` or `America/ New_York`. You also need to specify a locale via the `locale` setting, such as `en-GB` or `fr-FR`. The exact list of valid `timezone` and `locale` values depends on your Java virtual machine (JVM).

All built-in partitioners insert an offset in the last section of the object name. This is the Kafka offset of the first record that is contained in the object. The full object name mostly depends on how records are partitioned by the connector. However, you can further customize the naming using some other configurations.

Object naming

Objects in S3 are identified by their name, so it's crucial to understand the names that the connector generates for each object. In addition to the structure set by the partitioner, you can use the following settings to further customize the object name:

`topics.dir`
> This is added as a prefix to all objects. It defaults to `topics`, and we recommend customizing it if you want to differentiate objects coming from multiple connector instances.

`directory.delim`
> S3 uses a flat structure, but to simplify the process of organizing objects within a bucket, it treats parts of object names preceding a / as folders. This also makes browsing objects in buckets much easier. The setting defaults to / to use this feature.

`file.delim`
> With most partitioners, the last section of the object name typically contains a few values, such as the topic name, partition number, and offset. This setting specifies the delimiter used in between these values; it defaults to +.

`filename.offset.zero.pad.width`
> All built-in partitioners insert the start offset that each object contains into the object name. This setting allows you to introduce padding into the offset value in the form of zeros to keep objects ordered when sorting them lexicographically. This defaults to 10, meaning the offset includes 10 digits in total.

Now that we understand the names and organizations of our objects in S3, it's time to look at their actual content.

Object formats

The connector allows you to configure how the content of records is serialized when writing to S3. This is done via a *formatter*. The connector gets `ConnectRecord` objects that have been deserialized by the configured converter. When `ConnectRecord` objects include schemas, the formatter can use them to change the serialization format of the data and convert records—for example, from JSON to Parquet.

You need to carefully consider which format you write data in, because that determines the actual content of objects in S3. This impacts applications interacting with S3, but also determines the size used by objects in S3. Data serialized in JSON with schemas takes more space than the same data in the Avro format, for example.

The main setting to control this is `format.class`. This field is required, and it determines how the value of each `ConnectRecord` is converted before sending it to S3. It must be set to a class that implements the `io.confluent.connect.storage` `.format.Format` interface. The connector provides four implementations out of the box:

- `io.confluent.connect.s3.format.avro.AvroFormat`
- `io.confluent.connect.s3.format.bytearray.ByteArrayFormat`
- `io.confluent.connect.s3.format.json.JsonFormat`
- `io.confluent.connect.s3.format.parquet.ParquetFormat`

The object name suffix is determined by the configured `format.class` implementation. For example, `JsonFormat` adds `.json` to all objects. When using `ByteArray` `Format`, you can configure the object name suffix with the `format.bytearray.exten` `sion` setting; it defaults to `.bin`.

By default, the connector does not include the `ConnectRecord` key or headers in the S3 objects it generates. To include them, you need to set `store.kafka.keys` and `store.kafka.headers`, respectively, to `true`. This causes the connector to create separate objects for the keys and headers, with `.keys` and `.headers` added before the object name suffix respectively. Once included, their format classes can be set using `keys.format.class` and `headers.format.class`.

If you use the Avro or Parquet format, you can also specify the compression codec using `avro.codec` and `parquet.codec`, respectively. Avro supports the following codecs: `null` (the default), `bzip2`, `deflate`, and `snappy`. Parquet supports `snappy` (the default), `brotli`, `gzip`, `lzo`, `lz4`, `none`, and `zstd`.

Object upload

This last set of configurations determines when and how the connector uploads objects to S3. Objects in S3 can be up to 5TB in size, but in many cases it's preferable to have smaller objects to handle them more easily. You can configure how often new objects are created by the connector based on size and time.

Using the `flush.size` setting, you can control how many records an object can contain. This setting is required to start the connector and does not have a default value. For example, if it is set to 1, each S3 object will contain a single Kafka record. For performance reasons, we recommend using a larger value so that multiple Kafka records are written together in a single S3 object.

In order to create new objects based on time, you can use `rotate.schedule.inter val.ms` or `rotate.interval.ms`. With `rotate.schedule.interval.ms`, you specify how often a new object should be created. This works with the worker's clock, and as soon as the interval has passed, the current object is sent to S3 and a new object is started. On the other hand, `rotate.interval.ms` uses records' timestamps to manage the interval. When the first record is processed, its timestamp is extracted and serves as the beginning of the interval. When a record arrives, the connector checks if its timestamp fits within the current interval. If it does, the record is added to the current object; otherwise the current object is sent to S3 and a new object is started. Both of these settings cause new objects to be created, regardless of whether the existing object contains fewer records than the configured `flush.size`.

 When using `rotate.interval.ms`, objects are only sent to S3 once a record misses the current interval. If no new records arrive, then the current object is kept in memory. If you are expecting to handle bounded topics, you need to set `rotate.schedule.interval.ms` to a high enough value so that it never triggers while data is flowing, to ensure that all objects are eventually written to S3.

When uploading large objects, the connector uses *multipart requests*. This allows it to split requests into multiple parts that can be uploaded independently so that if a part fails, only that part needs to be sent again. By default, `s3.part.size` is set to 26214400 bytes (25 MB). If the connector fails to send a request, it retries up to `s3.part.retries` times (3 by default) before failing. The connector uses an exponential backoff in between retries that starts with `s3.retry.backoff.ms`.

In the next section, we'll see how you can configure the connector to provide exactly-once semantics.

Exactly-Once Semantics

As explained in Chapter 4, the achievable processing semantics for sink connectors depends on the target system. Luckily, S3 provides all the capabilities needed to support exactly-once semantics.

Exactly-once is possible because of two characteristics of S3:

- Support for multipart uploads
- Idempotent writes

We mentioned previously that the connector uses multipart requests to upload objects. S3 guarantees that an object is only written if all its parts have been uploaded successfully. Partially uploaded objects are never exposed to users. This allows the connector to retry sending parts in case of errors and prevents incomplete data from ever being exposed in case a crash or network loss causes the connector to disconnect abruptly.

The other S3 feature the connector relies on is idempotent writes. By default, if an object is uploaded twice to S3, the second write replaces the existing data. With the available settings, you can configure the connector to be deterministic so it always uploads the same objects when reading the same data from Kafka. This is possible because records in Kafka are immutable and partitions are append-only.

However, due to the many settings that you can use to control the connector behavior, there are some configurations that don't always produce exactly the same objects when processing the same data. Also, reconfiguring the connector to a different deterministic configuration may cause data loss or create duplicates. Let's look at the configurations that provide exactly-once semantics.

The partitioner is the main factor in terms of providing deterministic behavior. Both `DefaultPartitioner` and `FieldPartitioner` are always deterministic and offer exactly-once semantics, but when using a time-based partitioner, you need to carefully consider a few other settings.

In order for a time-based partitioner to be deterministic, it has to work using only data from the records the connector is processing; it must not use the time of the worker. Thus, you need to set `timestamp.extractor` to either `Record` or `Record Field`, so timestamps always come from records. Likewise, for deciding when to upload objects, we can only use `flush.size` and `rotate.interval.ms`.

Enough theory, now let's run the S3 sink connector!

Running the Connector

In order to run these examples, you need to create S3 buckets in AWS. You also need to create a user in AWS and grant it enough permissions so it can access your bucket. You should take a note of the user's access key and secret key and install the `aws` command-line tool to easily explore objects in your buckets.

 If you are using environment variables to provide the AWS credentials, be sure to export `AWS_ACCESS_KEY_ID` and `AWS_SECRET_ACCESS_KEY` before starting Kafka Connect.

Next, you need to create a Kafka topic called `orders` with five partitions using:

```
$ ./bin/kafka-topics.sh --bootstrap-server localhost:9092 \
  --create --topic orders \
  --partitions 5 --replication-factor 1
Created topic orders.
```

Then insert some records into the `orders` topic. Let's say that records in this topic track sales of books. The key is the book ID, and the value is in JSON and contains the book ID, name, and the quantity sold. You can use the `kafka-console-producer.sh` tool to send three records:

```
$ ./bin/kafka-console-producer.sh --bootstrap-server localhost:9092 \
  --topic orders --property parse.key=true
```

 We set the property `parse.key` to `true` in the console producer. This allows us to provide a payload using the format of first a key, followed by a TAB character and then a value. Without changing the `parse.key` property, the tool would use the entire payload as the value.

```
>1  {"schema": {"type": "struct", "fields": [{"type": "int64", "field": "id"},
{"type": "string", "field": "title"}, {"type": "int16", "field": "quantity"}],
"name": "order"}, "payload": {"id": 1, "title": "Kafka The Definitive Guide",
"quantity": 2}}
>2  {"schema": {"type": "struct", "fields": [{"type": "int64", "field": "id"},
{"type": "string", "field": "title"}, {"type": "int16", "field": "quantity"}],
"name": "order"}, "payload":{"id": 2, "title": "Mastering Kafka Streams and ks
qlDB", "quantity": 1}}
>3  {"schema": {"type": "struct", "fields": [{"type": "int64", "field": "id"},
{"type": "string", "field": "title"}, {"type": "int16", "field": "quantity"}],
"name": "order"}, "payload": {"id": 3, "title": "Kafka Connect", "quantity": 1
}}
```

```
>3  {"schema": {"type": "struct", "fields": [{"type": "int64", "field": "id"},
{"type": "string", "field": "title"}, {"type": "int16", "field": "quantity"}],
"name": "order"}, "payload": {"id": 3, "title": "Kafka Connect", "quantity": 2
}}
```

In Kafka, our records are spread across all partitions of the orders topic based on
their key, which is the book ID in this example. Since we are using the default
partitioner, records for the same book go to the same partition. In this example, we
end up with an event (key = 1) in partition 4 and the other three events (key = 2 and
key = 3) in partition 3.

Now that we have some data in Kafka, let's look at the first example connector
configuration.

Using the field partitioner

In this example, we use FieldPartitioner and configure the connector to give us
exactly-once semantics.

First, begin by creating a bucket and taking note of the region you select. Note that
bucket names must be globally unique.

Then create a file, *s3sink-field.json*, with the following contents, and make sure you
replace <BUCKET> with your bucket's name, <REGION> with your bucket's region and
<ACCESS_KEY_ID> and <SECRET_ACCESS_KEY> with your AWS credentials:

```
{
    "name": "s3sink-field",
    "connector.class": "io.confluent.connect.s3.S3SinkConnector",
    "tasks.max": "5",   ❶
    "topics": "orders",

    "key.converter": "org.apache.kafka.connect.converters.ByteArrayConverter",
    "value.converter": "org.apache.kafka.connect.json.JsonConverter",   ❷
    "value.converter.schemas.enable": "true",   ❷

    "s3.bucket.name": "<BUCKET>",
    "s3.region": "<REGION>",
    "storage.class": "io.confluent.connect.s3.storage.S3Storage",
    "aws.access.key.id": "<ACCESS_KEY_ID>",
    "aws.secret.access.key": "<SECRET_ACCESS_KEY>",

    "partitioner.class":
        "io.confluent.connect.storage.partitioner.FieldPartitioner",   ❸
    "partition.field.name": "id",   ❸
    "format.class": "io.confluent.connect.s3.format.json.JsonFormat",   ❹
    "flush.size": "3",   ❺
    "store.kafka.keys": "true",   ❻
    "keys.format.class":
        "io.confluent.connect.s3.format.bytearray.ByteArrayFormat"   ❻
}
```

❶ The topic has five partitions, so we set the maximum number of tasks accordingly.

❷ The value in our records is in the JSON format, so we use `JsonConverter` and enable `schemas.enable`, because our records include their schemas.

❸ In this example, we use `FieldPartitioner`. The `id` field is used to map the stream of records into objects.

❹ We keep our records formatted as JSON when they are stored in S3.

❺ The connector will commit the objects to S3 every three records. In a production system, this value will likely be higher (based on your use cases requirements on network traffic and lag time).

❻ The connector will create separate objects to store keys alongside the objects storing the record values. We use `ByteArrayFormat` to just write the raw keys.

Then you can start the connector using:

```
$ curl -X PUT -H "Content-Type: application/json" \
  -d @s3sink-field.json \
  localhost:8083/connectors/s3sink-field/config
```

You can now check what the connector created in the bucket using the `aws` CLI:

```
$ aws s3api list-objects --bucket <BUCKET> --query 'Contents[].{Key: Key}'
[
  {
    "Key": "topics/orders/id=2/orders+3+0000000000.json"
  },
  {
    "Key": "topics/orders/id=2/orders+3+0000000000.keys.bin"
  },
  {
    "Key": "topics/orders/id=3/orders+3+0000000001.json"
  },
  {
    "Key": "topics/orders/id=3/orders+3+0000000001.keys.bin"
  }
]
```

By using `FieldPartitioner`, we separate records for each book into different objects, so each object only contains records for a specific book. In this example, we see that objects containing books with IDs 2 and 3 have the following names:

- topics/orders/id=2/orders+3+0000000000.json
- topics/orders/id=3/orders+3+0000000001.json

We can tell which object is for which book based on the id=2 and id=3 in the name. You can see that they both have orders+3 in the object name, indicating that they were actually in the same Kafka topic-partition (orders-3). Because we enabled store.kafka.keys, we also have separate objects that contain the keys from our Kafka records.

Finally, as we've set flush.size to 3, only records from partition 3 have been sent to S3 so far. The other records are still held by the connector until the flush.size limit is reached. If you send another two records with the key set to 1, the matching objects will appear in S3.

Let's take a look at another example using a time-based partitioner.

Using the time-based partitioner

In this example, we use exactly the same input data from the orders topic, but we see how the objects created in S3 differ when we use the TimeBasedPartitioner instead of FieldPartitioner. This configuration uses rotate.schedule.interval.ms, so it does not provide exactly-once semantics.

First, begin by creating a bucket called orders-time and take note of the region you select.

Then create a new file, *s3sink-time.json,* with the following content and make sure you replace <REGION> with your bucket's region and <ACCESS_KEY_ID> and <SECRET_ACCESS_KEY> with your AWS credentials:

```
{
  "name": "s3sink-time",
  "connector.class": "io.confluent.connect.s3.S3SinkConnector",
  "tasks.max": "5",
  "topics": "orders",

  "key.converter": "org.apache.kafka.connect.converters.ByteArrayConverter",
  "value.converter": "org.apache.kafka.connect.json.JsonConverter",
  "value.converter.schemas.enable": "true",

  "s3.bucket.name": "orders-time",
  "s3.region": "<REGION>",
  "storage.class": "io.confluent.connect.s3.storage.S3Storage",
  "aws.access.key.id": "<ACCESS_KEY_ID>",
  "aws.secret.access.key": "<SECRET_ACCESS_KEY>",

  "partitioner.class":
        "io.confluent.connect.storage.partitioner.TimeBasedPartitioner", ❶
```

```
    "partition.duration.ms": "60000",
    "timestamp.extractor": "Record",  ❷
    "flush.size": "10",
    "rotate.schedule.interval.ms": "60000",  ❸
    "timezone": "UTC",  ❹
    "locale": "en-GB",
    "path.format": "'year'=YYYY/'month'=MM/'day'=dd/'hour'=HH",

    "format.class": "io.confluent.connect.s3.format.avro.AvroFormat"  ❺
}
```

❶ In this example, we use the TimeBasedPartitioner.

❷ Each record's timestamp is extracted from the ConnectRecord timestamp.

❸ Even if objects don't contain 10 records, new objects will be created each minute.

❹ The connector uses the UTC timezone to convert each timestamp to a date and
   time.

❺ Data is serialized in Avro using the schema retrieved from JSON.

Then, you can start the connector, using:

```
$ curl -X PUT -H "Content-Type: application/json" \
-d @s3sink-time.json \
localhost:8083/connectors/s3sink-time/config
```

You can now check what the connector created in the bucket using the aws command
line interface (CLI):

```
$ aws s3api list-objects --bucket orders-time --query 'Contents[].{Key: Key}'
[
  {
    "Key":
      "topics/orders/year=2023/month=06/day=08/hour=13/orders+3+0000000000.avro"
  },
  {
    "Key":
      "topics/orders/year=2023/month=06/day=08/hour=13/orders+4+0000000000.avro"
  }
]
```

This time, each object contains records that arrived during the same minute. Based
on the object names, we can deduce that some records were sent to partitions 3
and 4 between 13:00 and 14:00. In this example, even if the topic only contains the
initial four records, the connector ends up uploading all of them to S3 once the
rotate.schedule.interval.ms interval is reached.

Confluent JDBC Source Connector

Another common use case of Kafka Connect is to capture changes in databases and stream them to Kafka, where they can be processed by other services. This process is called change data capture (CDC) and it can be achieved using a Java Database Connectivity (JDBC) source connector. JDBC describes the API for Java applications to interact with databases. There are many different kinds of databases that support JDBC, from MySQL to PostgreSQL to MongoDB. Connectors that use JDBC perform query-based CDC, as they capture changes by repeatedly querying the database to compute changes.

In this section, we examine the Confluent JDBC source connector, which is available from the Confluent Hub website (*https://oreil.ly/8zfUU*). The examples and configuration descriptions use version 10.7.3 of the connector. As well as supporting query-based CDC, this connector provides an option to perform a bulk load of the contents of a database into Kafka. The community has built various JDBC source connectors that you can choose from. Each has its own specificities and configuration settings, but they share similar functionalities. You can download a ZIP file containing all the libraries for the connector from the website. Once you've downloaded it, extract its contents and add the folder to your `plugin.path` for your Connect runtime.

As well as adding the connector itself to your Kafka Connect runtime, you also need to add a JDBC driver for your database, which is normally available from your database provider. Place it in the same directory as the connector library JAR files. If the connector complains it can't find the driver, you can check it has loaded correctly by increasing the logging level of the Kafka Connect runtime to DEBUG using the REST API, as described in Chapter 7. Then, at start-up, if the driver has loaded correctly, you should see a log line similar to the following:

```
DEBUG Registered java.sql.Driver: com.mysql.cj.jdbc.Driver@7bbbb6a8 to
java.sql.DriverManager
```

Once you have Connect running, with both the JDBC connector plug-in and the JDBC driver for your database installed, you can create a new connector instance. We won't recap the configurations that apply to all source connectors, but we will talk about the configurations that are specific to the Confluent JDBC source connector.

Configuring the Connector

The configuration options for the JDBC source connector can be divided into the following categories:

- Connectivity
- Topic naming
- Table filtering

- Data collection mode
- Partitioning and parallelism

Let's look at each of these in turn.

Connectivity

The JDBC source connector has a set of configurations beginning with `connection.` that lets you configure how it talks to your database. The first of these is `connection.url`, where you provide the JDBC connection URL given to you by your database provider. For example, if you want to connect to a MySQL server that is hosting an endpoint at `localhost` with port `3306` and a database called `db_name`, you would use the URL `jdbc:mysql://localhost:3306/db_name`. To connect to a secure database, you then also supply the `connection.user` and `connection.pass word` configurations.

The connector does not contain any specific configurations for you to specify SSL settings. These are provided differently, depending on the JDBC driver, but are normally included in the connection URL. For example, for a MySQL database, your connection URL might be `jdbc:mysql://localhost:3306/db_name?verifyServer Certificate=false&useSSL=true&requireSSL=true`. If you want the connector to verify the server certificate and that certificate is not trusted by the default or system certificate authority, you also need to provide a truststore for it. You can add your own truststore to your Kafka Connect worker, giving its path in the connection URL, or add the certificate to the default JVM truststore. Check the documentation of your database, as each database has its own JDBC driver configuration options.

You can further configure the behavior of the connector during connection time using `connection.attempts` and `connection.backoff.ms`. These configure the number of attempts and the backoff time between attempts, respectively. By default, it retries three times, with 10,000 milliseconds between attempts, before moving into the `FAILED` state.

Topic naming

The JDBC source connector does not allow users to fully define the names of topics to produce to. By default, the connector sends data to a topic with the same name as the originating table. You can apply some customization by optionally specifying a prefix to be prepended using `topic.prefix`. For example, given a table called `orders` and a `topic.prefix` configuration of `jdbc-`, any records for that table would go to the `jdbc-orders` topic.

Table filtering

By default, the connector tries to read every table in the database at the chosen URL. This is often not recommended because there are likely to be default internal tables that the connector will struggle to read or tables you simply don't want to import into Kafka. You can influence the tables that are read using the following configurations:

- `catalog.pattern`
- `schema.pattern`
- `table.blacklist`
- `table.whitelist`
- `query`

The first two configurations, `catalog.pattern` and `schema.pattern`, let you select tables with a particular schema or catalog of schemas. In both cases, they are set to `null` by default, meaning that the database table schema won't be used for filtering down tables. If you set either configuration to `""`, the connector will specifically choose tables without a catalog or schema, respectively.

 If your database has a lot of tables, the settings `catalog.pattern` and `schema.pattern` are very important to make the connector's table-scanning query more efficient. Without these, you may find that the connector times out trying to find all the tables it should fetch data from.

The second way to select tables for your connector is to explicitly list table names to include or exclude. You can either set `table.blacklist` to ignore specific tables, or `table.whitelist` to select the specific tables you are interested in. Both of these are comma-separated lists of table names, and you can only set one at a time.

The final way to choose the specific tables and columns that are read by the connector is using the `query` configuration. This lets you influence the specific query the connector uses to get data from the database. When you start a connector, it logs the query it is using; for example:

```
INFO [mysql-source-bulk|task-0] Begin using SQL query: SELECT * FROM
    `books`.`kafka` (io.confluent.connect.jdbc.source.TableQuerier:179)
```

Overriding the query can be useful if, for example, you have a table with a lot of columns and only want to fetch a few of them, or you want the connector to run a JOIN and collect data from two different tables. As we described in Chapter 4 when we talked about building pipelines, you should be wary of over-optimizing your data collection, so use this setting with that in mind. Specifying a query does have limitations; for example, you can only specify a query with a WHERE clause if you are using the bulk mode that we talk about later in this section.

You may find it easier to use transformations or Kafka Streams applications to further manipulate the data, rather than trying to do it at the data load stage. If you run into problems with a custom query, check your connector configuration and the connector logs to confirm the query is what you expected.

Data collection mode

The JDBC source connector is designed to broadly support two different kinds of use cases. The first is to take the complete contents of a database at a point in time and copy it into a Kafka topic. The second is to provide a stream of events that represents updates to a database over time. To support these different use cases, the connector provides a mode configuration setting. You can set mode to one of the following:

- bulk
- incrementing
- timestamp
- timestamp+incrementing

The first option, bulk, allows you to load an entire database, while the other three allow you to track changes over time.

In bulk mode, for each table selected from the database, the connector reads it in its entirety and sends an event to Kafka for each row.

For example, if you have a database called shop that contains two tables, customers and orders, with three and four rows respectively, you would get three events to the topic customers and four to the topic orders. The connector then re-queries the database and sends a new set of events for the data after a set period of time. This time is configured using the connector configuration called poll.interval.ms, which defaults to 5000 (5 seconds). If you are using bulk mode, we recommend increasing the poll.interval.ms to suit your use case, as it is unlikely that you need to store a complete new copy of the database every five seconds.

Each of the modes, incrementing, timestamp, and timestamp+incrementing, provides a way to get events that represent changes or updates to the database, rather than a bulk load of everything. The name of the mode indicates the type of column that is used to recognize that the database has been updated.

If you set mode to incrementing, you must have a column in your tables that is strictly incrementing. Identify the incrementing column by setting the configuration option incrementing.column.name. Most databases allow you to specify a column that automatically increments when new rows are added. If you are using an auto-incrementing column, you can set `incrementing.column.name` to `""` and the connector automatically selects that column. In this mode, the connector sends a new event to the topic every time a higher increment appears in this selected column. This means you only get events for new rows, not changes to existing rows (where the ID is unchanged) or row deletions.

If you set `mode` to `timestamp`, you must have at least one column in your tables that is a timestamp. You specify the column using `timestamp.column.name`. This can actually be set to a comma-separated list of columns. The connector uses the COALESCE SQL function to select the first non-null timestamp from the provided columns. In this mode, the connector identifies new or modified rows by comparing the timestamp it finds to the largest timestamp it saw in the previous poll. The connector then sends an event to Kafka with the new, updated version of the row.

Although the `timestamp` mode does emit events when updates happen, there are quite a few limitations to be aware of. Like `incrementing` mode, it doesn't allow you to track row deletions, since there is no new timestamp to be returned. You also need to be careful about the timestamps that are used and how often the connector queries the database. Similarly to bulk mode, the frequency of queries is set by `poll.interval.ms`. If the connector queries the database, and a row is updated and then reverted before the next query, the connector will miss the changes. Also, for any changes that happen between polls, the connector is unable to determine what order they happened in.

The connector keeps track of the last timestamp it has seen. This can cause even permanent updates or additions to be missed. If a row is inserted or updated with an old timestamp, perhaps due to synchronization issues on the calling application, the connector might miss these updates. This can also be a problem during transactions, where a transaction that takes a long time can result in the connector storing new timestamps before the transaction is complete.

The final mode is the most reliable in terms of events for updates. As the name suggests, `timestamp+incrementing` requires you to specify both a strictly incrementing column and one or more timestamp columns. You must set both `incrementing.column.name` and `timestamp.column.name`. In this case, the connector stores both the timestamp and incrementing value, and uses this combination to resume. This gives the increased reliability of delivering updates even if the connector is restarted for some reason. However, similar to the `timestamp` and `incrementing` modes, it is not guaranteed to see all updates and it will still miss deletions.

Partitioning and parallelism

The Confluent JDBC source connector doesn't provide any specific configurations to let you influence the way data is partitioned and processed as it flows from the database to Kafka. However, you should be aware of its behavior when it comes to tasks, and the options for adding record keys.

As with all source connectors, you can configure the maximum number of tasks using `tasks.max`. If you are using the `query` configuration, the connector only starts a single task, even if `tasks.max` is set higher. This is because it has no way of distributing the query between tasks. If you are not using `query`, the connector creates the number of tasks equal to either the `tasks.max` or the number of tables, whichever is lower, and distributes the tables among the tasks. This means that each table is read by one task, but each task can fetch data from multiple tables.

By default, all the records sent to Kafka by the JDBC connector have a `null` key. This means if you have more than one partition, the records are spread across the partitions using the default partitioning strategy. If you want the records to use a key, you can use transformations to add one. For example, if you had a column called `id` in your database, you could use that as the key for Kafka records by making use of the `ValueToKey` and `ExtractField` transformations:

```
{
  ...
  "transforms": "valueToKey,extractField",
  "transforms.valueToKey.type":
    "org.apache.kafka.connect.transforms.ValueToKey",
  "transforms.valueToKey.fields": "id",
  "transforms.extractField.type":
    "org.apache.kafka.connect.transforms.ExtractField$Key",
  "transforms.extractField.field": "id"
  ...
}
```

Given a row in a database with the ID 1, Kafka Connect first uses the `ValueToKey` transformation to take the ID field from the value, then applies `ExtractField` to take just the number 1 as the key (rather than `id=1`). This is an approach that you can use with any source connector that doesn't provide key support.

Once you have decided what key to use, you can select the partitioner using client overrides, as described in Chapter 8.

Running the Connector

Let's look at two examples of running the JDBC connector, one using `bulk` mode and one using `timestamp+incrementing`. For these examples, we use a MySQL database. If you don't already have a MySQL database available, you can use an image from

DockerHub (*https://oreil.ly/hvmtv*) to run one in Docker on your machine. Remember to download and install the MySQL JDBC driver (*https://oreil.ly/u_NZb*) into your Kafka Connect runtimes.

Start by connecting to the MySQL server so you can execute commands using the `mysql` command line.

Now let's create a database and start using that database for our subsequent commands:

```
mysql> CREATE DATABASE inventory;
Query OK, 1 row affected (0.01 sec)

mysql> USE inventory;
Database changed
```

We create one table that contains books on Kafka:

```
mysql> CREATE table kafka_books
(
   id            INT unsigned NOT NULL AUTO_INCREMENT,
   title         VARCHAR(150) NOT NULL,
   subtitle      VARCHAR(150) NOT NULL,
   published     DATE NOT NULL,
   timestamp     DATETIME NOT NULL DEFAULT CURRENT_TIMESTAMP ON UPDATE
     CURRENT_TIMESTAMP,
   PRIMARY KEY   (id)
);
Query OK, 0 rows affected (0.02 sec)
```

Notice that we include both an `id` field and a `timestamp` field; we use these later to track updates to the table.

Now let's add some data:

```
mysql> INSERT INTO kafka_books ( title, subtitle, published) VALUES
   ( 'Kafka Connect', 'Build and Run Data Pipelines', '2023-10-01' ),
   ( 'Kafka The Definitive Guide',
     'Real-time Data and Stream Processing at Scale', '2017-07-07' );
Query OK, 2 rows affected (0.01 sec)
Records: 2  Duplicates: 0  Warnings: 0
```

Check the data is in the table as expected:

```
mysql> SELECT * FROM kafka_books;
+----+-----------------+-------------+------------+---------------------+
| id | title           | subtitle    | published  | timestamp           |
+----+-----------------+-------------+------------+---------------------+
|  1 | Kafka Connect   | Build and...| 2023-10-01 | 2023-08-31 07:31:38 |
|  2 | Kafka The Def...| Real-time...| 2017-07-07 | 2023-08-31 07:31:38 |
+----+-----------------+-------------+------------+---------------------+
2 rows in set (0.00 sec)
```

Using the bulk mode

Now let's first start a connector to do a bulk copy of the database. Create a file called *jdbc-source-bulk.json* with the following contents:

```
{
    "connector.class": "io.confluent.connect.jdbc.JdbcSourceConnector",
    "tasks.max": "1",

    "value.converter": "org.apache.kafka.connect.json.JsonConverter",
    "value.converter.schemas.enable": "true",

    "connection.url": "jdbc:mysql://localhost:3306/inventory",
    "connection.user": "<USER>",
    "connection.password": "<PASSWORD>",
    "topic.prefix": "mysql-bulk-",
    "mode": "bulk",
    "table.whitelist": "kafka_books"
}
```

Remember to replace the `connection.url`, `connection.user` and `connection.pass word` with your MySQL URL and credentials. Then start your connector:

```
$ curl -X PUT -H "Content-Type: application/json" \
  -d @jdbc-source-bulk.json \
  localhost:8083/connectors/mysql-source-bulk/config
{
  "name": "mysql-source-bulk",
  "config": {
    "connector.class": "io.confluent.connect.jdbc.JdbcSourceConnector",
    "connection.url": "jdbc:mysql://localhost:3306/inventory",
    "connection.user": "<USER>",
    "connection.password": "<PASSWORD>",
    "topic.prefix": "mysql-bulk-",
    "mode": "bulk",
    "table.whitelist": "kafka_books",
    "value.converter": "org.apache.kafka.connect.json.JsonConverter",
    "value.converter.schemas.enable": "true",
    "name": "mysql-source-bulk"
  },
  "tasks": [],
  "type": "source"
}
```

Your Kafka cluster should now include a topic called `mysql-bulk-kafka_books`:

```
$ ./bin/kafka-topics.sh --bootstrap-server localhost:9092 --list
...
mysql-bulk-kafka_books
```

Let's take a look at the contents:

```
$ ./bin/kafka-console-consumer.sh --bootstrap-server localhost:9092 \
  --topic mysql-bulk-kafka_books

{"schema":{"type":"struct","fields":[{"type":"int64","optional":false,"field":"id
"},{"type":"string","optional":false,"field":"title"},{"type":"string","optional"
:false,"field":"subtitle"},{"type":"int32","optional":false,"name":"org.apache.ka
fka.connect.data.Date","version":1,"field":"published"},{"type":"int64","optional
":true,"name":"org.apache.kafka.connect.data.Timestamp","version":1,"field":"time
stamp"}],"optional":false,"name":"kafka_books"},"payload":{"id":1,"title":"Kafka
Connect","subtitle":"Build and Run Data Pipelines","published":19631,"timestamp":
1656234290000}}
{"schema":{"type":"struct","fields":[{"type":"int64","optional":false,"field":"id
"},{"type":"string","optional":false,"field":"title"},{"type":"string","optional"
:false,"field":"subtitle"},{"type":"int32","optional":false,"name":"org.apache.ka
fka.connect.data.Date","version":1,"field":"published"},{"type":"int64","optional
":true,"name":"org.apache.kafka.connect.data.Timestamp","version":1,"field":"time
stamp"}],"optional":false,"name":"kafka_books"},"payload":{"id":2,"title":"Kafka
The Definitive Guide","subtitle":"Real-time Data and Stream Processing at Scale",
"published":17354,"timestamp":1656234290000}}
```

You can see that every five seconds the connector sends through an event for each row in the table. So in our example, every five seconds, we get two events, one for each book.

This gives us an opportunity to look at how fields in the resulting JSON events get formatted by the connector. Remember, the event is formatted with JSON using a schema due to the converter settings we are using. The published and timestamp fields are being converted into integers. For the timestamp this is ok, but if we want the published field to be more human-readable, we can add a transformation to our connector configuration. Add the following in *jdbc-source-bulk.json*:

```
{
  ...
  "transforms": "timestampConverter",
  "transforms.timestampConverter.type":
    "org.apache.kafka.connect.transforms.TimestampConverter$Value",
  "transforms.timestampConverter.field": "published",
  "transforms.timestampConverter.format": "yyyy-MM-dd",
  "transforms.timestampConverter.target.type": "string"
}
```

After you update the connector with the new configuration, the payload field of events in the topic looks like the following code, with a more human-readable published field:

```
"payload":{"id":2,"title":"Kafka The Definitive Guide","subtitle":"Real-time Data
and Stream Processing at Scale","published":"2022-06-23", "timestamp": 1656234290
000}
```

Using an incrementing mode

We can use the table that we've already created to see what happens with a new connector using the timestamp+incrementing mode. Create a file called *jdbc-source-inc.json* with the following contents, again replacing the connection. configurations with the values for your database:

```
{
    "connector.class": "io.confluent.connect.jdbc.JdbcSourceConnector",
    "tasks.max": "1",

    "value.converter": "org.apache.kafka.connect.json.JsonConverter",
    "value.converter.schemas.enable": "true",

    "connection.url": "jdbc:mysql://localhost:3306/inventory",
    "connection.user": "<USER>",
    "connection.password": "<PASSWORD>",
    "topic.prefix": "mysql-inc-",
    "mode": "timestamp+incrementing",
    "incrementing.column.name": "id",         ❶
    "timestamp.column.name": "timestamp",     ❷
    "table.whitelist": "kafka_books",

    "transforms": "timestampConverter",
    "transforms.timestampConverter.type":
        "org.apache.kafka.connect.transforms.TimestampConverter$Value",
    "transforms.timestampConverter.field": "published",
    "transforms.timestampConverter.format": "yyyy-MM-dd",
    "transforms.timestampConverter.target.type": "string"
}
```

The new connector instance uses the id column ❶ and timestamp columns ❷ to track updates. Before we start the connector, let's remind ourselves of the formats we used for these two update columns. The id column has INT unsigned NOT NULL AUTO_INCREMENT. The two important pieces are the NOT NULL and AUTO_INCREMENT. By default, the connector validates that both the incrementing.column.name ❶ and timestamp.column.name configurations ❷ point to columns that cannot be null. You can change this behavior by setting validate.non.null to false. The AUTO_INCRE MENT means that we don't need to configure the id when we add a new row; the database does it for us. If we update an existing row, the id remains the same, so we rely on the timestamp column to catch updates.

The timestamp column was created using the formatting DATETIME NOT NULL DEFAULT CURRENT_TIMESTAMP ON UPDATE CURRENT_TIMESTAMP. We set NOT NULL because otherwise the connector would complain. For the connector to notice updates, you need the timestamp to be updated when a row is updated. In MySQL you get this behavior by configuring the column with ON UPDATE CURRENT_TIME STAMP. If you don't include this in your column configuration, then changes to rows have to explicitly increase the `timestamp` column; otherwise the connector isn't informed of these updates.

Let's start a connector with this configuration:

```
$ curl -X PUT -H "Content-Type: application/json" \
-d @jdbc-source-inc.json \
localhost:8083/connectors/mysql-source-inc/config
```

Now you can run a consumer to see what events the connector has sent to the new `mysql-inc-kafka_books` topic. Make sure you use the flag `--from-beginning` so that you can see all events:

```
$ ./bin/kafka-console-consumer.sh --bootstrap-server localhost:9092 \
--topic mysql-inc-kafka_books --from-beginning
```

You should see two events in the topic, one for each row in the table. Let's leave the consumer running while we make some updates to get more data.

First, let's add a new row:

```
mysql> INSERT INTO kafka_books ( title, subtitle, published) VALUES
( 'Mastering Kafka Streams', 'Building real-time data systems by example',
'2021-02-26' );
```

You should see this new event returned by your consumer:

```
{"schema":{"type":"struct","fields":[{"type":"int64","optional":false,"field":"i
d"},{"type":"string","optional":false,"field":"title"},{"type":"string","optiona
l":false,"field":"subtitle"},{"type":"string","optional":false,"field":"publishe
d"},{"type":"int64","optional":false,"name":"org.apache.kafka.connect.data.Times
tamp","version":1,"field":"timestamp"}],"optional":false,"name":"kafka_books"},"
payload":{"id":3,"title":"Mastering Kafka Streams","subtitle":"Building real-tim
e data systems by example","published":"2021-02-26","timestamp":1656238142000}}
```

Now let's update one of the existing rows. There is a second edition of *Kafka: The Definitive Guide*, so we want to update the published column to put in a new date:

```
mysql> UPDATE kafka_books
SET
    published = '2022-09-23'
WHERE
    id = 2;
```

Your consumer receives the updated row with the new `published` value:

```
{"schema":{"type":"struct","fields":[{"type":"int64","optional":false,"field":"id
"},{"type":"string","optional":false,"field":"title"},{"type":"string","optional"
:false,"field":"subtitle"},{"type":"string","optional":false,"field":"published"}
,{"type":"int64","optional":false,"name":"org.apache.kafka.connect.data.Timestamp
","version":1,"field":"timestamp"}],"optional":false,"name":"kafka_books"},"paylo
ad":{"id":2,"title":"Kafka The Definitive Guide","subtitle":"Real-time Data and S
tream Processing at Scale","published":"2022-09-23","timestamp":1656240353000}}
```

As we have seen, the JDBC source connector provides a few options for getting data from a database and into Kafka. However, there are limitations, particularly when tracking updates using an incremental mode. To make use of the incremental mode, your tables must include specific columns that the connector can use to identify changes. Then there is a tradeoff to be made between the frequency of queries and changes captured. The connector will only capture the current value of each row, so if you don't poll frequently enough, you could miss intermediate updates. Finally, the connector does not create records for row deletions, which might be required for certain use cases.

In the next section, we look at a different connector that also provides change data capture events, but uses a different mechanism to track changes.

Debezium MySQL Source Connector

Most modern databases use a *transaction log* internally in order to capture changes as they are made. Having the history of changes for a database enables strong data guarantees, as changes can be rolled back or reapplied in case of a failure. The transaction log is also often used by databases to replicate data to multiple servers, as each server instance can just replay the history of changes to reproduce the same state.

The Debezium MySQL source connector relies on the transaction log of databases to capture changes. This is called *log-based change data capture* as opposed to the *query-based change data capture* used with the Confluent JDBC source connector.

Unlike query-based CDC, where near concurrent updates or deletes can be missed, log-based CDC allows you to reliably capture all changes made to the database. It is also more efficient, as the connector is notified of changes instead of always querying every table. There are drawbacks to this approach, however; JDBC is an industry standard that pretty much all existing databases support, but not all databases expose a mechanism for users to access their transaction log. Moreover, the databases that do all have their own formats and characteristics, so if you build a tool that works with MySQL, it won't be compatible with any other databases. Finally, the APIs that expose the transaction log typically require elevated privileges in the database server, and since this exposes all changes from all the resources, you should think carefully before granting this level of access.

Debezium (*https://debezium.io*) is an open source project that provides a platform for log-based change data capture. It provides source connectors for Cassandra, Db2, MongoDB, MySQL, Oracle, PostgreSQL, SQL Server, Vitess, and Spanner, and a JDBC sink connector. It also includes a number of transformations to modify records as they flow into Kafka. It exposes a user interface to manage connectors, metrics to ease the monitoring of connectors, and integrations with several industry standards, such as CloudEvents and OpenTracing.

In this section, we examine the Debezium MySQL source connector, which is available from the Debezium project website (*https://debezium.io/releases*). The examples and configuration descriptions use version 2.3 of the connector. You can download a ZIP file containing all the libraries for the connector from the website. Once you've downloaded it, extract its contents and add the folder to your `plugin.path` for your Kafka Connect runtime.

This section focuses on the MySQL connector, but many of the concepts covered are shared across all of the connectors. Nevertheless, each of the Debezium connectors has its own characteristics and specific configurations, so we recommend checking the Debezium documentation for the specific connectors you want to use.

 Several configuration settings changed names between the 1.x and 2.x releases of the Debezium MySQL source connector. If you choose to use a 1.x version of the connector, refer to the related documentation on the Debezium website for the correct configuration names.

Configuring the Connector

The Debezium MySQL connector is extremely configurable, exposing over 80 configurations. Only a handful of them are required to start the connector, and in most use cases, you only need to configure a small number of settings.

In this section, we only cover the most commonly used settings. For advanced use cases or very specific requirements, you should check the connector's documentation (*https://oreil.ly/g1rHy*) that details all of the settings.

The configurations we cover can be grouped into three categories:

- Connectivity
- Database and table filtering
- Snapshotting

The number of tasks you can use with a Debezium connector depends on the specific connector you are using, because different databases allow different mechanisms when reading updates. The MySQL Debezium connector always runs with a single task, even if you set `tasks.max` to a higher value, because of the way the connector interacts with MySQL's transaction log (the *binlog*). Other connectors, like the ones for MongoDB and SQL Server, make use of features specific to those databases which allow `tasks.max` to be set to a higher value. Check the documentation for the specific Debezium connector you are using before configuring `tasks.max`.

Connectivity

For the Debezium MySQL source connector to connect to a MySQL database, it needs to know things like the database address and user. To start the connector, you need to configure the following:

`database.hostname`
> IP address or resolvable hostname of the MySQL database you are using. This setting is required.

`database.port`
> Port number of the MySQL database server. This defaults to 3306.

`topic.prefix`
> This name is used as the prefix for Kafka topics that Debezium interacts with. As a result, it is important that this name is globally unique for all connectors that are connecting to the same Kafka instance. This setting is required.

`database.server.id`
> Unique ID of the connector. When a server connects to MySQL to read the transaction log, it must provide a unique server ID. It must be unique within all servers that are connecting to the MySQL server for replication, or to read the transaction log. Since this is a particular requirement of MySQL, other Debezium connectors do not have an equivalent configuration to this. This setting is required.

`database.user`
> The MySQL username to use to connect. This setting is required. All users should have a password, which you can specify via the `database.password` setting.

 Once you have deployed your connector, you must not change the `topic.prefix`. If you change this configuration after the connector has started up, it could result in unexpected behavior.

For the events the Debezium MySQL connector creates to contain the correct schema for the columns from the table, it must know the schema that was in place when that change was made. The connector monitors and stores schema changes in a Kafka topic so that it can re-read these changes if it is restarted. The topic it uses is referred to as the "database schema history topic" in the Debezium documentation.

The database schema history topic is not designed to be consumed by any application other than the Debezium connector itself. There are two configurations related to the schema history topic that are required to start the connector:

- `schema.history.internal.kafka.bootstrap.servers` is the list of brokers from the Kafka clusters.

- `schema.history.internal.kafka.topic` is the name of the database schema history topic.

 If the connection to Kafka is secured, you need to provide the required SSL (Secure Sockets Layer) and SASL (Simple Authentication and Security Layer) settings to enable Debezium to access its schema history topic. Debezium uses both a producer and consumer, so in order to configure these settings, you need to prefix them with the `schema.history.internal.producer.` and `schema.history.internal.consumer.` prefixes. For example, to use SSL as the security protocol, you need the following:

```
schema.history.internal.producer.security.protocol=SSL
schema.history.internal.consumer.security.protocol=SSL
```

In Kafka Connect, source connectors can only commit offsets when they send new events to Kafka. This can impact the MySQL connector if there are updates being added to the transaction log for tables that it is not creating events for. Since the connector isn't creating any events, it cannot store its updated location in the transaction log as an offset in the internal Kafka Connect offsets topic. This means if the connector restarts, it has to re-read transaction log messages it has already read—or if the transaction log has been cleaned up, the stored location might no longer be accessible.

To handle these scenarios, you can configure the connector to send heartbeat events to a topic in Kafka. If you set `heartbeat.interval.ms` to greater than 0 (the default), the connector sends events to a heartbeat topic, and at the same time commits the latest offset. You can configure the prefix for the topic using `topic.heartbeat.prefix`. The default prefix is `__debezium-heartbeat` and the topic name has the format `<HEARTBEAT_PREFIX>.<TOPIC_PREFIX>`, where `TOPIC_PREFIX` is the value of the configuration `topic.prefix`.

In addition to configuring the connector, it may be necessary to adjust some settings on your MySQL server as well. Obviously, the connector requires the binlog to be enabled, but there are a number of other settings, such as the binlog format, that you need to ensure are correctly configured before running the connector. Also, by default the binlog does not include the query that caused the change; you can change that by enabling `binlog_rows_query_log_events` in your MySQL configuration.

Debezium also requires a user with several permissions in order to function. To perform snapshots, it needs `SELECT`, `RELOAD,` and `SHOW DATABASES` permissions. In order to access the binlog, it requires both `REPLICATION SLAVE` and `REPLICATION CLIENT`.

Database and table filtering

Your MySQL server likely contains several databases and many tables. By default, Debezium picks all non-system tables from all databases; in most cases, you should instead precisely select the databases and tables it should capture changes from. Capturing changes you don't need wastes resources and may also expose sensitive data that should not be sent to Kafka and shared.

Use either `database.include.list` or `database.exclude.list` to specify the databases you are interested in. Then we recommend either using `table.include.list` or `table.exclude.list` to explicitly specify the tables you want using the `<DATA BASE_NAME>.<TABLE_NAME>` format, for example `inventory.customers` if the database is called `inventory` and the table is called `customers`. These four include/exclude settings accept a comma-separated list of values.

Debezium also allows you to filter columns to only see changes you are interested in. In order to do this, you can set either `column.include.list` or `column.exclude.list` to a comma-separated list of values. These two settings use the `<DATABASE_NAME>.<TABLE_NAME>.<COLUMN_NAME>` format, for example `inventory.customers.email` if the database is called `inventory`, the table is called `customers`, and the column is called `email`.

Finally, in cases where you want to know about changes in some columns but don't need the full values, or in cases where the values are sensitive, you can truncate or mask them. This is especially useful for columns containing personally identifiable information (PII) or secrets. In order to truncate values, you use `column.trun cate.to.<LENGTH>.chars` where `<LENGTH>` specifies the maximum allowed length before truncation. For masking values, you have two options: replacing with asterisk characters or hashing the values. To replace the value with asterisk characters, use `col umn.mask.with.<LENGTH>.chars`, where `<LENGTH>` is the number of * characters used to replace the actual values. To hash the values, you use `column.mask.hash.v2.<ALGO RITHM>.with.salt.<SALT>` where `<ALGORITHM>` is the name of the hashing algorithm, for example `SHA-256` and `<SALT>` is the salt to add when hashing values. All of these settings accept a comma-separated list of regexes for the columns and you can combine multiple of them if necessary.

Snapshotting

As we have mentioned, every change performed to the database is stored in the binlog. However, the binlog is not kept forever, and MySQL trims it at regular intervals. So if a database has existed for several days or weeks, depending on the server configuration, the binlog may not contain events for all the changes anymore.

This means that by reading the binlog, Debezium may only able to capture changes that happen after it started and shortly before. This can be problematic, as in many cases databases already contain a lot of data that would be useful to capture.

To address this, Debezium has the concept of *snapshots*. By default, when the MySQL connector starts for the first time, it captures the current state of all tables it is tracking and emits events for each existing row. While this is not the full history of the data, it allows the connector to start from a known state and track changes from that point onward.

You can configure this behavior via the `snapshot.mode` setting. This defaults to `initial`, which means a snapshot is only performed the first time the connector is started. There are a few other values this can be set to:

when_needed
: We've seen that MySQL regularly trims its binlog, so if the connector is stopped for a long duration and then restarted, it's possible that it missed some changes. With this mode, when the connector is restarting, it captures a new snapshot if it detects that it has missed some updates.

Never
: This mode disables snapshots.

initial_only
: In this mode, the connector captures a snapshot and immediately stops, so it does not read updates from the binlog.

schema_only
: In this mode, the connector only snapshots the tables' schemas and does not capture the tables' data.

schema_only_recovery
: This setting allows recovering the connector when its internal database schema history topic has been corrupted or lost.

Depending on the size of your database, snapshots can be expensive to compute and take hours to complete. While a snapshot is happening, the database can't accept any writes. Also, for a snapshot to be valid, it has to fully complete and include all databases and tables that the connector has been configured to track. These snapshots cannot partially run or be paused and resumed. To resolve these issues, since Debezium 1.7, MySQL supports *ad hoc incremental snapshots*.

Incremental snapshots are executed in small chunks and don't require the connector to lock the full database while they run. The connector can perform an ad hoc incremental snapshot in parallel with capturing changes via the binlog, and unlike regular snapshots, they can be paused and resumed as needed. This is particularly useful when adding new tables to `table.include.list`, as it allows the connector to only snapshot the newly added tables and not capture anything else. Ad hoc snapshots have to be explicitly triggered by users; this is done via a signaling table or a signaling topic.

A signaling table is a regular table you create in MySQL with a specific schema. You need to specify its name in the connector configuration using the `signal.data.col lection` setting. Then you can insert rows with specific values into that table to instruct the connector to perform actions. The table you specify is automatically added to the connector include list. Similarly, a signal topic is a regular Kafka topic where you can send specific events to trigger the connector to perform actions.

In order to use a signaling topic, you must configure the `signal.kafka.topic` setting. You must provide Kafka cluster connection details using the `signal.kafka.bootstrap.servers` setting, and any security configurations must be prefixed with `signal.consumer.`. For example:

```
signal.kafka.bootstrap.servers=localhost:9092

signal.kafka.topic=signaling_topic

signal.consumer.security.protocol=SSL
```

As of Debezium 2.0, all connectors apart from Vitess support snapshotting.

Event Formats

Kafka records created by Debezium connectors all have the same high-level format, but the specific contents vary from connector to connector. All records include a key to identify the row in the table that the record was created from. The value includes a field to identify the operation that was performed (create, update, delete), some data that describes the change, and a `source` field that includes details about how the record was created. The `source` field includes metadata about the change like the type of connector used, the table the change was in, and a timestamp of the change.

The types of the fields that are present in both the key and value are influenced by the schema of the table. Since this can evolve over time, we recommend that you persist these schemas when the records are sent to Kafka. If you are using the JsonConverter, you can include the schema as part of the Kafka record by setting schema.enable to true. The downside of this approach is that the schema adds a lot of bulk to your records, so alternatively you can make use of a schema registry to store the key and value schemas.

The Debezium documentation gives detailed information about the key and value for each connector, so here we only cover the most-used fields in records created by the MySQL connector.

The record's key contains a field for every column that makes up the PRIMARY KEY in the table. For example, say the database table in question has a single column called id, which is denoted as the PRIMARY KEY containing an integer; with the JsonConverter you would get a key that looks like:

```
{
  "schema": {
    "type": "struct",
    "name": "<CONNECTOR_NAME>.<DATABASE_NAME>.<TABLE_NAME>.Key",
    "optional": false,
    "fields": [
      {
        "field": "id",
        "type": "int32",
        "optional": false
      }
    ]
  },
  "payload": {
    "id": <ID>
  }
}
```

Instead of using the table's PRIMARY KEY, you can specify the columns you want the connector to use by configuring message.key.columns. This configuration uses the following format, <DATABASE_NAME>.<TABLE_NAME>:<COLUMN_NAME>, and you can specify multiple columns by providing a comma-separated list. If the table doesn't specify a PRIMARY KEY and you haven't configured message.key.columns, then the key is left empty and the schema will indicate that the value is optional.

If the columns selected for the key of a row changes, the connector creates two events: one indicating a delete with the old key, and one indicating a create with the new key.

The schema for the record value contains an envelope struct with multiple nested structs:

```
{
  "schema": {
    "type": "struct",
    "name": "<CONNECTOR_NAME>.<DATABASE_NAME>.<TABLE_NAME>.Envelope",
    "optional": false,
    "fields": [
      {
        "type": "string",
        "field": "op",          ❶
        "optional": false
      },
      {
        "type": "string",
        "field": "ts_ms",       ❷
        "optional": false
      },
      {
        "type": "struct",
        "name": "<CONNECTOR_NAME>.<DATABASE_NAME>.<TABLE_NAME>.Value",
        "field": "before",      ❸
        "optional": true,
        "fields": [...]
      },
      {
        "type": "struct",
        "name": "<CONNECTOR_NAME>.<DATABASE_NAME>.<TABLE_NAME>.Value",
        "field": "after",       ❹
        "optional": true,
        "fields": [...]
      },
      {
        "type": "struct",
        "name": "<CONNECTOR_NAME>.<DATABASE_NAME>.<TABLE_NAME>.Source",
        "field": "source",      ❺
        "optional": false,
        "fields": [...]
      }
    ]
  }
}
```

❶ The operation that was performed; this must be one of c, u, d, or r for CREATE, UPDATE, DELETE, or READ, respectively. READ is only used for snapshot events.

❷ The time the connector processed the event.

❸ The state of the row before the change was made; the specific fields present depend on the columns in the table. For a create event, this field is set to null.

❹ The state of the row after the change was made; the specific fields present depend on the columns in the table. For a delete event, this field is set to null.

❺ Additional metadata about the source of the event.

The record values created by the connector include the previous schema and a `payload` field.

The `source` field contains many fields. The following is a non-exhaustive list:

version
> The Debezium version of the connector.

connector
> The type of connector; the MySQL connector always puts `mysql` here.

name
> The name of the connector.

ts_ms
> The time the change was made in the database. You can compare this value with the top-level `ts_ms` to see the time taken for Debezium to see the update.

snapshot
> Refers to whether this event is part of a snapshot.

db
> The database the change was applied to.

table
> The table the change was applied to.

query
> The query that made the change. This is only included if `bin log_rows_query_log_events` has been set to `ON` in the MySQL database.

The record values created by the connector include the previous schema and a payload field.

Since all records include a key that identifies the row, Kafka can delete all earlier records for that row when compaction is enabled. In compacted topics, you can signify that all previous records with a key should be deleted using a tombstone record (where the value is `null`). If a row is deleted, the Debezium connector always creates a record that contains the `before` and `source` fields. However, it can additionally create a tombstone record with the key present and a `null` value. This is enabled by default, and you can disable this by setting `tombstones.on.delete` to `false`. If you have enabled this, then a delete record for a key change is also followed by a tombstone record.

Running the Connector

Let's run the connector and see how changes in a database are reflected as events in Kafka. In this example, we use a similar MySQL table as in "Confluent JDBC Source Connector" on page 100, to highlight the differences between these two connectors.

Start by connecting to the MySQL server so that you can execute commands using the `mysql` command line, create a database called `inventory`, and select it for subsequent commands:

```
mysql> CREATE DATABASE inventory;
Query OK, 1 row affected (0.01 sec)

mysql> USE inventory;
Database changed
```

Then create a table that contains books on Kafka:

```
mysql> CREATE table kafka_books
(
    id              INT unsigned NOT NULL AUTO_INCREMENT,
    title           VARCHAR(150) NOT NULL,
    subtitle        VARCHAR(150) NOT NULL,
    published       DATE NOT NULL,
    PRIMARY KEY     (id)
);
Query OK, 0 rows affected (0.02 sec)
```

Now let's add some data:

```
mysql> INSERT INTO kafka_books (title, subtitle, published) VALUES
    ('Kafka Connect', 'Build and Run Data Pipelines', '2023-10-01'),
    ('Kafka The Definitive Guide',
        'Real-time Data and Stream Processing at Scale', '2017-07-07');
Query OK, 2 rows affected (0.01 sec)
Records: 2  Duplicates: 0  Warnings: 0
```

Create a file called *mysql-debezium.json* with the following contents and make sure you replace <USER> and <PASSWORD> with your MySQL credentials:

```
{
    "connector.class": "io.debezium.connector.mysql.MySqlConnector",
    "tasks.max": "1",

    "key.converter": "org.apache.kafka.connect.json.JsonConverter",
    "key.converter.schemas.enable": "true",
    "value.converter": "org.apache.kafka.connect.json.JsonConverter",
    "value.converter.schemas.enable": "true",

    "database.hostname": "localhost",
    "database.port": "3306",
    "database.user": "<USER>",
    "database.password": "<PASSWORD>",
```

```
    "database.server.id": "10000",  ❶
    "topic.prefix": "dbserver1",

    "database.include.list": "inventory",
    "table.include.list": "inventory.kafka_books",  ❷

    "schema.history.internal.kafka.bootstrap.servers": "localhost:9092",
    "schema.history.internal.kafka.topic": "dbhistory.inventory",
    "include.schema.changes": "false"  ❸
}
```

❶ A unique ID to identify the connector with the database.

❷ A filter to only capture changes from the inventory.kafka_books table.

❸ By default, Debezium emits schema changes to a separate topic, but this feature is mostly useful in advanced use cases, so we disable it here.

Then, start the connector:

```
$ curl -X PUT  -H "Content-Type: application/json" \
  -d @mysql-debezium.json \
  localhost:8083/connectors/mysql-debezium/config
{
  "name": "inventory-connector",
  "config": {
    "connector.class": "io.debezium.connector.mysql.MySqlConnector",
    "tasks.max": "1",
    "key.converter": "org.apache.kafka.connect.converters.ByteArrayConverter",
    "key.converter.schemas.enable": "true",
    "value.converter": "org.apache.kafka.connect.json.JsonConverter",
    "value.converter.schemas.enable": "true",
    "database.hostname": "mysql",
    "database.port": "3306",
    "database.user": "<USER>",
    "database.password": "<PASSWORD>",
    "database.server.id": "184054",
    "topic.prefix": "dbserver1",
    "database.include.list": "inventory",
    "schema.history.internal.kafka.bootstrap.servers": "<BOOTSTRAP_SERVERS>",
    "schema.history.internal.kafka.topic": "dbhistory.inventory",
    "table.include.list": "inventory.kafka_books",
    "include.schema.changes": "false",
    "name": "inventory-connector"
  },
  "tasks": [],
  "type": "source"
}
```

At startup, Debezium automatically creates several topics in Kafka. We can see them by running:

```
$ ./bin/kafka-topics.sh  --bootstrap-server localhost:9092 --list | grep inventory
dbhistory.inventory   ❶
dbserver1.inventory.kafka_books ❷
```

❶ This is the database schema history topic that is used internally by Debezium.

❷ This topic contains events that describe all changes to the `inventory`
`.kafka_books` table.

When starting, the connector also took a snapshot of the existing rows in the kafka_books table and emitted events to the `inventory.kafka_books` topic. Here is its content:

```
$ ./bin/kafka-console-consumer.sh --bootstrap-server localhost:9092 \
  --topic dbserver1.inventory.kafka_books \
  --from-beginning --property print.key=true
{"schema":{"type":"struct","fields":[{"type":"int64","optional":false,"field":"id
"}],"optional":false,"name":"dbserver1.inventory.kafka_books.Key"},"payload":{"id
":1}}    {"schema":{...
{"schema":{"type":"struct","fields":[{"type":"int64","optional":false,"field":"id
"}],"optional":false,"name":"dbserver1.inventory.kafka_books.Key"},"payload":{"id
":2}}    {"schema":{...
```

We can see that it contains two records, one for each row in the table. The key for each record corresponds to the primary key of the table. For example, for the second record, the key is:

```
{"schema":{"type":"struct","fields":[{"type":"int64","optional":false,"field":"id
"}], "optional":false,"name":"dbserver1.inventory.kafka_books.Key"},"payload":{"i
d":2}}
```

as the value of the `id` column, the primary key, is equal to 2 for that record.

The value for each record contains the schema and the payload before and after the change, as well as some metadata describing the change (such as the date and position in the MySQL binlog). Since both of these events were emitted when these rows were added, both have the before payload set to `null`:

```
"payload": {
  "before": null,
  "after": {
    "id": 2,
    "title": "Kafka The Definitive Guide",
    "subtitle": "Real-time Data and Stream Processing at Scale",
    "published": 17354
  },
  ...
}
```

Also, we can see that both records come from the initial snapshot, as they have their snapshot field set to true (or last for the last event from the snapshot). Any new records retrieved from the MySQL binlog have the snapshot field set to false.

Let's update a row:

```
mysql> UPDATE kafka_books SET published = '2022-09-23' WHERE id = 2;
Query OK, 1 row affected (0.01 sec)
Rows matched: 1  Changed: 1  Warnings: 0
```

The new event is written to the topic and it contains the values from before and after the change:

```
"payload": {
  "before": {
    "id": 2,
    "title": "Kafka The Definitive Guide",
    "subtitle": "Real-time Data and Stream Processing at Scale",
    "published": 17354
  },
  "after": {
    "id": 2,
    "title": "Kafka The Definitive Guide",
    "subtitle": "Real-time Data and Stream Processing at Scale",
    "published": 19258
  },
  ...
}
```

Finally, let's look at the behavior when deleting a row.

```
mysql> DELETE FROM kafka_books WHERE id = 1;
Query OK, 1 row affected (0.01 sec)
```

In this case, two events are written on the topic. The first one is similar to the previous events, but in this case it's the after value that is set to null:

```
"payload": {
  "before": {
    "id": 1,
    "title": "Kafka Connect",
    "subtitle":"Build and Run Data Pipelines",
    "published":19631
  },
  "after": null,
  ...
}
```

The second event is a tombstone, because by default the `tombstones.on.delete` setting is set to `true`.

```
{"schema":{"type":"struct","fields":[{"type":"int64","optional":false,"field":"id
"}],"optional":false,"name":"dbserver1.inventory.kafka_books.Key"},"payload":{"id
":1}}    null
```

As we have seen, log-based change data capture connectors are capable of capturing all changes and they provide a lot more context and information about each change in comparison to connectors relying on querying only. This comes at the cost of being a bit more complicated to set up, so you should decide which type of connector to use based on your exact requirements.

Summary

In this chapter, we have looked at three of the most popular connectors that address use cases common to many industries. We've also demonstrated how to run them through basic scenarios.

We started with the Confluent S3 sink connector that enables copying data into Amazon S3. It is very configurable and can adapt to most common requirements. The most important settings are around object partitioning and naming, as they determine how the Kafka topic records are stored in the S3 bucket. We've also explained why using a configuration that generates deterministic objects allows the connector to offer exactly-once semantics.

Then we looked at the Confluent JDBC source connector that can import data from a database. This connector is very versatile, as you can use it to connect to a lot of different databases via JDBC. However, as it works by repeatedly querying the database, it's not able to capture all changes, regardless of the data collection mode you use.

Finally, we looked at the Debezium MySQL source connector. It is part of the Debezium project that provides connectors for several databases. This connector relies on MySQL's transaction log, so it's able to reliably capture all data changes as they happen in the database. It is extremely configurable and offers a lot of advanced features, such as snapshotting. The drawback of this connector is that it requires elevated access privileges to the database.

CHAPTER 6

Mirroring Clusters with MirrorMaker

The action of copying data between two Kafka clusters is called *mirroring*. This term is used to distinguish this process from the term "replication" that usually refers to the way data in Kafka is shared across brokers within the cluster. However, both terms are often used by the community when talking about copying data between clusters.

The idea of mirroring data between clusters is pretty much as old as Kafka itself. At Kafka's inception, mirroring was a feature of the broker, before it was then separated into its own tool in early 2012. The tool was a standalone application named Mirror-Maker, but due to its initial design, it had a number of limitations and was hard to operate. So in 2019, a new mirroring tool based on Kafka Connect was introduced via KIP-382 (*https://oreil.ly/YUGSj*) called MirrorMaker2. The initial MirrorMaker tool is now deprecated since Kafka 3.0 and will be removed in Kafka 4.0 (via KIP-720 (*https://oreil.ly/iGzg2*)); the new tool is now often simply called MirrorMaker or MM2.

In this chapter we only cover the new tool, and we refer to it as MirrorMaker. We introduce use cases that rely on mirroring, explain how the MirrorMaker connectors work, and finally demonstrate how to use them through some examples.

Introduction to Mirroring

Kafka scales very well, and it's possible to run a single cluster with an extremely large capacity. However, in many cases it's preferable to have multiple smaller clusters. This could be to better serve different geographies, but also for other reasons such as isolation or workload optimization. Whenever you have multiple Kafka clusters, it's common to want to mirror data between them.

Exploring Mirroring Use Cases

Mirroring data between clusters is interesting in a wide range of use cases. In this section, we explore four of the most common ones:

- Geo-replication
- Disaster recovery
- Migration
- Complex topologies

Geo-replication

While network throughput and latency across different geographies has improved dramatically in the last decade, the distance between machines still has an impact on performance. For this reason, in many cases it is beneficial to have Kafka clusters located near the Kafka clients, and it is therefore common for large enterprises to have one or more clusters in each region or market they serve. The process of mirroring data between Kafka clusters that are deployed in different geographies is called *geo-replication*.

One of the key aspects of geo-replication is that each application uses a Kafka cluster in its own region, and mirroring is used to flow data between regions. This could be to share data across all regions or to aggregate it all in a specific region. For example, in a *hub and spoke topology,* data from all regions is aggregated in one region (for example, the largest or where the company has its headquarters), where it is processed. Figure 6-1 shows a hub and spoke topology wherein the eu region is receiving data from all other regions.

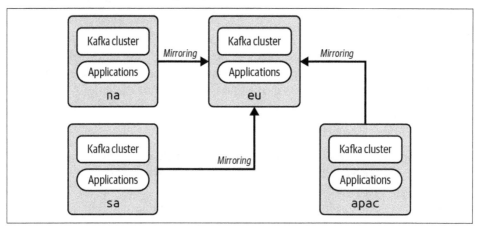

Figure 6-1. Example of a hub and spoke topology where applications only use their local Kafka cluster and data is aggregated to a single region, in this case eu

In geo-replication use cases, data can also flow bi-directionally between clusters. This is the case when all clusters broadcast some of their data to others. This can also be applicable in hub-and-spoke environments if the results of processing the aggregated data are fed back to individual clusters. Setups with a bi-directional flow of data are often called *active-active*.

Disaster recovery

As Kafka is adopted across many industries to run critical workloads, the availability and resiliency of clusters is crucial. With the right configurations and deployment, a Kafka cluster is able to sustain several types of failures, such as the failure of a single broker or even of the underlying data center. However, for highly sensitive workloads, it is necessary to be able to handle larger types of failures, such as the failure of a whole geographical region or the failures of multiple components at the same time.

To address these requirements, one option is to set up a backup cluster that acts as a copy of the main one. This backup cluster can be deployed on different hardware or in a different region to minimize the risk of it being affected by the same issue as the main cluster. If a major failure affects the main cluster, all the data is immediately available in the backup cluster and applications can be migrated to reduce the impact of the outage as much as possible.

In such a scenario, a mirroring tool is used to keep the backup cluster in sync at all times. Because applications have to be able to migrate seamlessly between clusters, it's crucial to mirror consumer offsets as well as the actual topic data. That way, applications can pick up where they left off once they switch to the backup cluster. The backup cluster receives mirroring traffic but is otherwise typically unused until an outage happens and applications failover, so this type of setup is called *active-standby* or *active-passive*. Figure 6-2 shows an example of an active-standby setup.

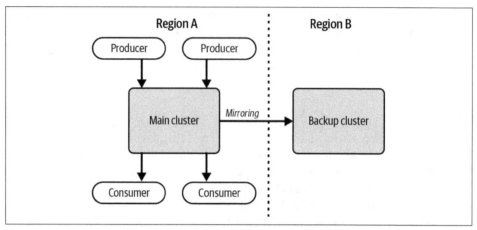

Figure 6-2. Example of a disaster recovery deployment where the cluster in region A is currently active while the cluster in region B acts as a standby, ready to be used if a failure impacts region A

Migration

There are two different use cases where mirroring might be used as a one-off action to fulfill a requirement; one is for new infrastructure, and the other is for upgrades.

Sometimes the infrastructure a Kafka cluster is deployed onto needs to be replaced. This could be because the platform is being decommissioned or its underlying hardware is not supported anymore, or simply because you are changing cloud providers. Replacing the platform below a deployment is not always possible, and even if possible, it often brings a lot of complexity. In these cases, it might be better to create a fresh Kafka cluster on the new infrastructure.

Another circumstance in which you might want to create a fresh Kafka cluster is when you are doing an upgrade. The Apache Kafka project publishes a new release every four months. There are generally very few large changes between two consecutive versions, and it's simple to find them all by using the release notes, so it's very easy and safe to upgrade up-to-date clusters. However, if administrators don't regularly upgrade their Kafka clusters, they can quickly become many versions behind. In this case, the risk of a breaking change going unnoticed before the upgrade is greatly increased. Kafka takes great care to ensure forward and backward compatibility between versions, but if the version gap is too large, an in-place upgrade could be considered risky for clusters handling critical workloads.

For these two use cases, mirroring can be used to migrate all the data from the existing cluster into a new cluster. Once all of the data—including consumer group offsets—has been mirrored, applications can start using the new cluster, and the old cluster can be decommissioned.

Complex topologies

Mirroring data between clusters provides a lot of flexibility. You can slice and dice data in many different ways and form complex mirroring topologies to perfectly match your requirements.

One example of this is a hybrid cloud scenario, where you might have an on-premises Kafka cluster and one deployed in the cloud. The on-premises cluster can be used for very sensitive data that needs to be kept in a controlled environment while it is processed. However, the result of this processing could be useful for other parts of your business, or even for your partners. In this case, it makes sense to copy the processing results to another Kafka cluster that is more widely accessible, or even one that is being managed for you in the cloud.

Another example of a complex topology is one designed for handling large numbers of client applications. Each client, producer, and consumer that is connected to a broker uses some resources. With several thousands of clients connected to a broker, it's not uncommon to have some resource contention, even if the throughput limit is not reached. A *fan-in* problem is when a broker is overwhelmed by producers; for consumers, this is called a *fan-out*.

To prevent clusters being overwhelmed by client connections, you can have a dedicated Kafka cluster for producers and a separate one for consumers. Then the clusters are linked together using mirroring so the data can flow from the producers to the consumers. This reduces fan-in/fan-out problems, because the process that mirrors data can use fewer resources. Figure 6-3 shows this type of topology.

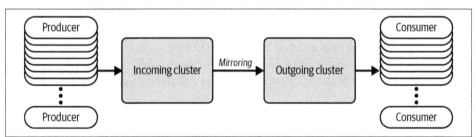

Figure 6-3. Example of a fan-in/fan-out topology where one cluster handles incoming traffic and another one handles outgoing traffic

Mirroring is a great way to unlock various use cases and satisfy complex enterprise requirements. Before we explore MirrorMaker in detail, let's look at what features are required in a mirroring tool for Kafka.

Mirroring in Practice

The requirements for a mirroring tool in Kafka may seem simple at first sight, since you just have to copy data from one cluster to another. In fact, this is pretty much what the original MirrorMaker tool did by linking a basic consumer, reading records from one cluster, to a producer, sending them to another cluster. However, this approach misses some key capabilities that are very often required in enterprise environments.

First, a Kafka cluster is more than just records inside topics. Topics also have configurations that should be mirrored, and users can add new partitions to existing topics that should be automatically created in the other cluster. In secured environments, it's common to have access control lists (ACLs) to finely control the authorizations of all users, so ACLs need to be mirrored too. Another important type of data inside a Kafka cluster is committed offsets. Without mirroring these offsets, consuming applications cannot seamlessly move between clusters. However, mirroring these offsets is not trivial.

In most cases, when records are mirrored between clusters they won't have exactly matching offsets for a few reasons. If a partition has existed for a while, its earliest offset is likely not 0, because retention policies delete old records. However, new partitions always start at offset 0, so if you start mirroring an old partition, the mirrored partition will start at offset 0 and never match the original partition. Another reason why offsets differ in different clusters is due to transactions. Transactions include *control records* that have offsets but are not visible to Kafka clients, so they also cause an offset skew. Finally, records in compacted topics often have non-consecutive offsets because only the last record for each key is retained.

Another aspect to take into account is that a mirroring solution needs to be easy to operate, scalable, and highly available. Administrators need metrics and APIs they can rely on to monitor both the mirroring process and the data gaps between clusters.

 For some scenarios, such as disaster recovery, a complete mirroring solution involves more than just the usage of a tool. It typically also relies on processes, automation, and cooperation between multiple teams. You should carefully consider these aspects and exercise any mirroring processes you put in place before depending on them for production systems.

Introduction to MirrorMaker

Mirroring typically underpins critical use cases, so MirrorMaker is designed to run 24/7 and handle high throughput with low latency to ensure the gaps between clusters stay as small as possible. MirrorMaker depends on Kafka Connect, which provides a lot of benefits for administrators. The Kafka Connect REST API offers a well-known control plane to manage mirroring routes. In addition, it provides logs and metrics that help operate MirrorMaker efficiently, and can be scaled easily by simply adding or removing workers. We cover the most common types of administrative operations in depth in Chapter 7.

In contrast to the previous tool that only copied topic data, MirrorMaker is able to copy topic configurations and keep the partition count of topics in sync. So if new partitions are added to the source cluster, MirrorMaker automatically creates them in the target cluster. In addition, it supports mirroring ACLs so that users keep similar permissions on both clusters. This is particularly useful in disaster recovery scenarios, when applications are expected to quickly switch from one cluster to another. Another major new feature is the ability to mirror consumer group offsets.

The final benefit of MirrorMaker is that it includes mechanisms to prevent creating *mirroring cycles*. A cycle happens when data is sent back into the cluster it originated from. When a cycle is created, it acts as a feedback loop; data is mirrored and mirrored again until it overwhelms your clusters. By preventing these cycles, MirrorMaker makes it easier to build complex mirroring topologies where data is flowing bi-directionally between clusters.

MirrorMaker is a set of three connectors made for copying data from one Kafka cluster to another. The connectors are:

MirrorSourceConnector
Mirrors topics data, configurations and ACLs

MirrorCheckpointConnector
Mirrors consumer group offsets

MirrorHeartbeatConnector
Monitors connectivity and latency between clusters

> KIP-382 (*https://oreil.ly/OKawn*), which introduced MirrorMaker, also described a sink connector called MirrorSinkConnector. It has not yet been implemented by the community.

MirrorMaker has been designed to fulfill all the requirements of a mirroring tool for Kafka. However, the community has built a number of third-party tools to also achieve mirroring. Each of these alternative tools provides a distinct set of features, and they each work differently:

uReplicator (https://github.com/uber/uReplicator)
> An open source mirroring tool developed by Uber. It uses Apache Helix to handle the definition of routes that each mirror data from one cluster to another.

Apache Brooklyn (https://brooklyn.apache.org)
> An open source tool for streaming data between systems. It is similar in concept to Kafka Connect but is wider in scope, as it does not necessarily have to interact with Kafka. It is able to stream data with Kafka, so it can be used to mirror clusters.

Confluent Replicator (https://oreil.ly/ewVja)
> A closed source connector that can be used with Kafka Connect to mirror data, including topic configurations, partitions, and consumer group offsets from one Kafka cluster to another.

Common Concepts

Before diving into each connector, let's introduce some common concepts that are important to understand in order to run MirrorMaker.

Local and remote topics

MirrorMaker has the concept of *remote topics*. A remote topic is a topic that has been mirrored from another cluster. For example, if you mirror a topic named `inventory` on the `eu` cluster to the `us` cluster, by default the data appears in the `us` cluster in a topic called `eu.inventory`. The `eu.inventory` topic on the `us` cluster is called a remote topic. The original topic on the `eu` cluster, `inventory`, is often referred to as a *local topic*.

In practice, you should avoid producing into remote topics and always prefer local topics instead. One reason is that MirrorMaker prevents you from mirroring a topic back into the cluster it came from, because that would create a cycle—so if you produce records into a remote topic, you are not able to mirror these records into the source cluster of the topic.

If you have consumer applications that need to be able to switch between clusters, you should ensure they are able to subscribe to both the local and remote topics. You can either list both names explicitly or use a wildcard subscription to match both.

Common configurations

All three connectors have a few configurations in common, the most important being the ones defining the clusters between which MirrorMaker mirrors data. This starts by defining aliases for both clusters using the `source.cluster.alias` and `target.cluster.alias` configurations. Along with these configurations, you also need to provide connection details for the clusters. Connectors usually only contain details about the external system they connect to, but as MirrorMaker connectors directly interact with both Kafka clusters, their connection details are needed in the connectors' configurations.

To provide the connection details, you use the normal client connection settings prefixed with either `source.cluster.` or `target.cluster.`. For example, the JSON configuration for a connector may contain:

```
{
    ...
    "source.cluster.alias": "eu",
    "target.cluster.alias": "us",

    "source.cluster.bootstrap.servers": "eu-kafka0:9092,eu-kafka1:9092",
    "source.cluster.security.protocol": "SASL_SSL",
    "source.cluster.sasl.mechanism": "PLAIN",

    "target.cluster.bootstrap.servers": "us-kafka0:9092,us-kafka1:9092",
    "target.cluster.security.protocol": "SSL",
    "target.cluster.ssl.truststore.location": "/tmp/server.truststore.jks",
    ...
}
```

The next common configuration is `enabled`. It defaults to `true`, so when deploying connectors in distributed mode, you don't typically have to set it.

> Due to their internal implementations, the MirrorMaker connectors still perform some actions when paused via the REST API. Since Kafka 3.5, you can use the PUT `/connectors/<CONNEC TOR_NAME>/stop` endpoint to fully stop a connector. In earlier versions, the `enabled` setting can be used to do so.

Some environments use centralized processes to perform administrative operations. For example, when using GitOps, users define topics and their configurations in a Git repository and a backend process creates them in the Kafka cluster. The `forwarding.admin.class` setting allows providing a custom class for performing administrative operations rather than using the Kafka admin client, which is the default value.

Finally, `admin.timeout.ms` can be used to configure the duration in milliseconds that the connectors wait when making requests, such as creating topics or listing consumer groups. The default value, 60000, works for most use cases.

Replication policies

Another key aspect of the MirrorMaker configuration is the replication policy. A replication policy determines how remote topics are named. MirrorMaker also uses the policy to find its internal topics and to detect mirroring cycles. The replication policy is pluggable and is configured by using the `replication.policy.class` setting, which must be set to a class that implements the `ReplicationPolicy` interface (*https://oreil.ly/5nl9E*). MirrorMaker comes with two built-in policies, `DefaultRepli cationPolicy` (the default) and `IdentityReplicationPolicy`.

`DefaultReplicationPolicy` prefixes remote topics with the alias of the cluster they originated from. For example, if you mirror a topic called `inventory` from a cluster aliased `eu`, the topic on the target cluster is called `eu.inventory`. You can use the `rep lication.policy.separator` setting to customize the separator between the cluster alias and the topic name, otherwise it defaults to `"."`.

`IdentityReplicationPolicy` keeps the original names of topics, so if you mirror a topic called `inventory`, it is still called `inventory` on the target cluster. This can be useful in disaster recovery scenarios to make the backup cluster as identical as possible to the main cluster. It also allows you to achieve the same behavior as the original MirrorMaker tool, which kept the topic names the same. One limitation of this policy is that it is not able to detect mirroring cycles because the origin of a topic can't be identified, so this policy should only be used when mirroring data in a simple topology, such as in a single direction between two clusters.

The last responsibility of the replication policy is to determine the names of the internal topics that MirrorMaker uses. MirrorMaker uses three internal topics, one for offset-syncs, one for checkpoints, and one of heartbeats. These are detailed in "MirrorMaker Connectors" on page 140.

Client overrides

The MirrorMaker connectors internally use producers, consumers, and admin client instances to function. You can tune these clients to satisfy your exact requirements; to do so, you need to provide client overrides in the connector configurations. You can override settings on all clients that connect to a cluster by using the `source.cluster.` or `target.cluster.` prefixes. It's also possible to override settings for a type of client by using the normal `producer.`, `consumer.`, or `admin.` prefixes. Finally, it's also possible to combine both prefixes to override configurations for a specific client connecting to a specific cluster. In that case, the `source.cluster.` or `target.cluster.` prefixes always go first: `source.cluster.producer.buffer.memory`.

For example, you could have the following client overrides in the configuration of a `MirrorSourceConnector` instance:

```
{
    ...
    "producer.linger.ms": "5",  ❶
    "source.consumer.auto.offset.reset": "latest",  ❷
    ...
}
```

❶ Any producer started by this connector should wait five milliseconds before sending a record to maximize batching.

❷ We want MirrorMaker to start mirroring new records only.

Note that you can also override the configuration of clients used internally by Kafka Connect. We cover how to do so in Chapter 8.

Deployment Modes

Like all other connectors, you can run the MirrorMaker connectors with Kafka Connect in distributed or standalone mode. In these modes, you explicitly run Kafka Connect runtimes and configure and start the connectors you require for your topology individually. This gives you the maximum flexibility and allows you to reuse all existing tools, automations, or processes that you already have for Kafka Connect. However, MirrorMaker can also run as a dedicated cluster. This mode is often also called *driver mode*.

In dedicated mode, you don't interact with the Kafka Connect REST API to start connectors; instead, you use a single configuration properties file to define clusters and mirroring routes. This file allows you to define multiple mirroring routes and contains the configurations for all three MirrorMaker connectors.

For example, a configuration file may contain:

```
clusters = eu, us  ❶

❷
eu.bootstrap.servers = eu-kafka0:9092, eu-kafka1:9092, eu-kafka2:9092
us.bootstrap.servers = us-kafka0:9092, us-kafka1:9092, us-kafka2:9092

❸
eu->us.enabled = true
eu->us.topics = .*

❹
us->eu.enabled = true
us->eu.topics = inventory
```

❶ We start by defining the aliases of our Kafka clusters. Here we have two clusters, and we name them eu and us.

❷ For each cluster, we provide its connection details. We can use all the regular connection configurations, including all the SASL and SSL settings, but we need to prefix them with the alias of the cluster they correspond to. In this case the cluster with the alias eu has three bootstrap servers, eu-kafka0:9092, eu-kafka1:9092, eu-kafka2:9092.

❸ We define a mirroring route from cluster eu to cluster us. This is done using the arrow notation (->) between the two cluster aliases. Routes are always defined with the arrow pointed to the right, and data will flow from the cluster on the left side to the cluster on the right side of the arrow. All the configurations for a specific route have this same arrow prefix. We can append any of the connector settings to fully configure the route. In this example, we have set the topics settings for MirrorSourceConnector to .*, which means all topics from cluster eu are mirrored to us.

❹ We define a second route from cluster us to eu. As we already have a route in the other direction, this results in a bi-directional mirroring deployment. This time we indicate that only the inventory topic should be mirrored from cluster us to eu.

To start MirrorMaker in dedicated mode, you use the `bin/connect-mirror-maker.sh` tool from the Kafka distribution:

```
$ ./bin/connect-mirror-maker.sh <CONFIGURATION_FILE>
```

Running this with the example configuration file would result in starting the topology shown in Figure 6-4.

It's easy to see the advantages that this mode provides over deploying every single connector by hand. The preceding example describes two mirroring routes, so it results in running two Kafka Connect runtimes and six connectors (MirrorSource Connector, MirrorCheckpointConnector and MirrorHeartbeatConnector in each direction). In distributed mode you would need to start all of these explicitly, whereas here we have done it with a single command.

However, this mode has a few limitations that currently greatly reduce its usability. The biggest issues are due to the fact that runtimes started in dedicated mode don't expose the REST API, a key interface for administrators managing Kafka Connect environments, whether it's for reconfiguring connectors at runtime or monitoring the state of pipelines. So to update mirroring routes, you need to change the properties file and restart the MirrorMaker instances. The REST API is also used by workers to communicate and handle dynamic changes in the external system, for example, to detect the creation of new topics in the source cluster. Since Kafka 3.5 and KIP-710 (*https://oreil.ly/YrE8K*), MirrorMaker in dedicated mode does start the necessary REST API endpoints for workers to communicate. This was not the case in earlier versions, so if you start multiple dedicated instances using Kafka 3.4 or below, the worker running the connector can spot the change but it can't be rolled out to the other workers running the tasks. We detail how Kafka Connect workers communicate in Chapter 7.

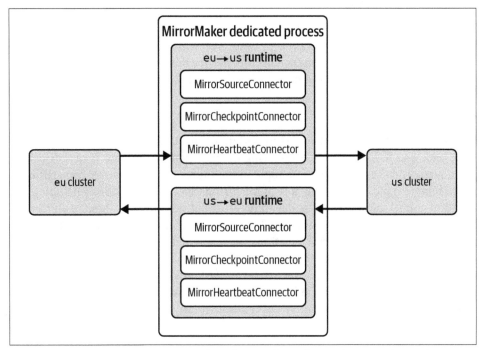

Figure 6-4. Mirroring topology with data flowing from the eu cluster to the us cluster, and from the us cluster to the eu cluster

The last disadvantage is that when you define multiple mirroring routes, the Kafka Connect runtimes will not always be optimally placed. Ideally, the preference is to deploy the runtime near the target cluster, where the runtime stores its state via its internal topics. If the runtime is far from its target cluster, it may experience some latency when accessing its topics, which can have a negative impact on its operations. In dedicated mode, all runtimes are run as part of the same process, so if you have a bi-directional topology, you can't place them optimally. For example, starting MirrorMaker near the us cluster is optimal for the eu to us route but it is not for the other route.

To work around this, you can use the `--clusters` flag when running `bin/connect-mirror-maker.sh` to specify which clusters are nearby and select the routes to enable. You can list multiple clusters separated by spaces. This allows you to keep a single file with all routes and start only the appropriate routes in each region. For example, with the configuration file described earlier in this section, you can run the following command in the eu region:

```
$ ./bin/connect-mirror-maker.sh <CONFIGURATION_FILE> --clusters eu
```

MirrorMaker Connectors

In this section, we look at the three MirrorMaker connectors. For each connector, we cover its features and configuration options. We also list the ACLs they require in both the source and target clusters, and the metrics they emit at runtime to monitor them. We give a full overview of monitoring Connect pipelines in Chapter 9.

MirrorSourceConnector

MirrorSourceConnector is the most important connector. Its first feature is to mirror topic data, and it does so while preserving the partition each record is in. For example, if a record is in partition 2 in a topic in the source cluster, it is sent to partition 2 in the remote topic. It is also capable of mirroring topic configurations (including the partition count) and ACLs. In order to do so, it periodically lists these resources on the source cluster and creates the matching resources on the target cluster. However, the connector does not mirror deletions, so if you delete a topic, the remote topic is not deleted. This is done primarily for two reasons. First, Kafka does not track who created a resource, so the connector cannot know if a topic is a remote topic it created or a regular topic created by a user. Also, in use cases like disaster recovery, the target cluster acts as a backup to cover administrative mishaps, so it's important to not mirror deletion.

The connector also builds mappings, called *offset-syncs*, between offsets from the source and target clusters that are used by MirrorCheckpointConnector to mirror offsets. Records in the offset-syncs topic are serialized as bytes. MirrorMaker provides a formatter to deserialize them, as it can be useful to see them when debugging issues. For example, to browse offset-syncs, you can use the following command:

```
$ ./bin/kafka-console-consumer.sh --bootstrap-server eu-kafka0:9092 \
  --topic mm2-offset-syncs.us.internal \
  --formatter org.apache.kafka.connect.mirror.formatters.OffsetSyncFormatter \
  --from-beginning
OffsetSync{topicPartition=heartbeat-0, upstreamOffset=0, downstreamOffset=0}
```

By default, the offset-syncs topic is located in the source cluster and it contains the alias of the target cluster it maps to (in our example, us). The offset-sync record has topicPartition set to the local topic-partition name, in this case heartbeat-0. The upstreamOffset field indicates the record offset on the source cluster. Finally, downstreamOffset indicates the offset of the matching record on the target cluster. Figure 6-5 shows the different topics used by MirrorSourceConnector in source and target clusters.

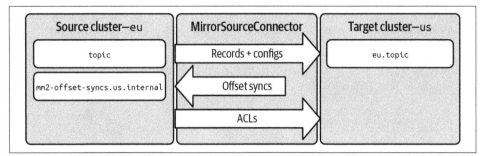

Figure 6-5. Architecture diagram showing data that MirrorSourceConnector mirrors between clusters

Since Kafka 3.5, this connector supports exactly-once semantics. See Chapter 8 for details on how to enable exactly-once for source connectors.

Now that we understand how MirrorSourceConnector works, let's look at its configurations.

Configurations

Due to its many responsibilities, this connector exposes a number of configurations.

Topic configurations. The first group of configurations determines the topics to mirror. The simplest setting is topics, which accepts a list of topic names and regular expressions. This defaults to .*, which means all topics from the source cluster are mirrored. By default, this excludes topics that are considered internal, which are topics starting with __ or ., for example __consumer_offsets, and topics that have the .internal or .replica suffix. You can also exclude specific topics using the topics.exclude setting. This also accepts a list of topic names and regular expressions. If you need more complex rules, you can use the topic.fil ter.class setting, which accepts a class that implements the org.apache.kafka.con nect.mirror.TopicFilter interface.

 Instead of always mirroring everything, you should very carefully select the topics to mirror. Every extra topic that you mirror adds some load onto Kafka Connect and may delay data from important topics. For example, Kafka Streams intermediate topics or internal topics from Kafka Connect are not usable on the target cluster, so you should filter them out.

You can also configure how often MirrorMaker will detect new topics and partitions on the source cluster by using the refresh.topics.interval.seconds setting. This defaults to 600, which means that MirrorMaker refreshes the list of topics and partitions from the source cluster every 10 minutes. You can disable this behavior by either setting this interval to -1 or by setting `refresh.topics.enabled` to `false`.

By default, MirrorMaker synchronizes all topic configurations between the local and remote topics except for the ones listed next. These configurations are either temporary or they depend on other cluster configurations:

- `follower.replication.throttled.replicas`
- `leader.replication.throttled.replicas`
- `message.timestamp.difference.max.ms`
- `message.timestamp.type`
- `unclean.leader.election.enable`
- `min.insync.replicas`

You can specify the topic configurations that shouldn't be mirrored by using `config.properties.exclude`, which takes a list of topic configurations and regular expressions. For even more control, you can also use `config.prop erty.filter.class` and provide a class that implements `org.apache.kafka .connect.mirror.ConfigPropertyFilter`.

Up to Kafka 3.4, MirrorMaker always used the `AlterConfigs` API when mirroring topic configurations. This API is not very flexible; it fully replaces the topic configurations on the target cluster and prevents having additional settings. It has been deprecated since Kafka 2.3. From Kafka 3.5, you can set `use.incremen tal.alter.configs` to instead use the `IncrementalAlterConfigs` API, which is a lot more granular and only mirrors the configurations explicitly set on the source cluster. When set to `requested`, the connector attempts to use the new API but reverts to the old behavior in case the Kafka cluster does not support it. You can also set it to `required` to force MirrorMaker to use the new API and fail if it is not supported. Up to Kafka 4.0, it is possible to keep the previous behavior by setting `use.incremental.alter.configs` to `never`. From 4.0 onward, the connector will always use the `IncrementalAlterConfigs` API.

The interval at which topic configurations are mirrored is controllable with the `sync.topic.configs.interval.seconds` setting, which defaults to `600`. To disable this feature, set the interval to -1 or set `sync.topic.configs.enabled` to `false`.

The replication factor of remote topics does not have to necessarily match the value from the source cluster. MirrorMaker can enforce a new value via the `repli cation.factor` setting. This defaults to 2, but it's often preferable to set it to -1 to instead use the default replication factor of the target cluster.

You can configure the timeout used for polling data from topics by using the `con sumer.poll.timeout.ms` setting. This determines the maximum duration, in milliseconds, the call to `poll()` can block in order to retrieve records to mirror, and it defaults to `1000`.

Offset-syncs configurations. Offset-syncs are stored in a compacted topic with a single partition. By default, the topic is created in the source cluster. However, in some environments, it is preferable to only grant MirrorMaker read access to the source cluster. To allow this, you can move the offset-syncs topic to the target cluster by setting the `offset-syncs.topic.location` setting to `target` (it defaults to `source`).

You can also configure the replication factor of the offset-syncs topic by using the `offset-syncs.topic.replication.factor` setting, which defaults to 3. Set this to `-1` to use the cluster default replication factor.

The name of the offset-syncs topic is determined by the replication policy. By default, it is `mm2-offset-syncs.<ALIAS>.internal`, where `<ALIAS>` is the alias of the target cluster by default, or of the source cluster if `offset-syncs.topic.location` is set to `target`.

In order to save space, the connector does not emit offset-syncs for each record it mirrors. Instead, it only emits offsets when the gap between the source and target offsets changes. You can also set a maximum allowed offset lag by using the `offset.lag.max` setting, which defaults to `100`. If the offset on the target cluster jumps by this value between two records, it will force the connector to emit another offset-sync.

ACLs configurations. The connector refreshes ACLs at a fixed interval that is configurable via `sync.topic.acls.interval.seconds`. Setting it to `-1` or setting `sync.topic.acls.enabled` to `false` disables this feature. When enabled, the connector creates ACLs that match ACLs from the source cluster on the target cluster. The only exception are ACLs with the permissions set to `ALLOW` for all (`ALL`) operations, as these are downgraded to `ALLOW` on `READ` only.

Metrics configurations. Since Kafka 3.5, you can use the `add.source.alias.to.met rics` configuration to include the source cluster alias in the metrics of this connector. It currently defaults to `false`, but from Kafka 4.0 onward, this configuration will be deleted and the source cluster alias will always be included.

Permissions

In order to function, the connector and the Kafka Connect runtime need to perform many operations on both the source and target clusters, so you need to ensure that they are given the required authorizations on both clusters.

Source cluster ACLs.   On the source cluster, you need to grant the following ACLs:

- READ on each topic to mirror
- DESCRIBE on each topic to mirror
- DESCRIBE_CONFIGS on each topic to mirror

If you keep the default value (source) for offset-syncs.topic.location, you also need to set:

- CREATE on the offset-syncs topic or CREATE on the cluster
- DESCRIBE on the offset-syncs topic
- WRITE on the offset-syncs topic

If you keep sync.topic.acls.enable enabled, you also need:

- DESCRIBE on the cluster

Target cluster ACLs.   On the target cluster, you need to grant the following ACLs:

- DESCRIBE on each mirrored topic
- WRITE on each mirrored topic
- CREATE on each mirrored topic or CREATE on the cluster
- ALTER on each mirrored topic
- ALTER_CONFIGS on each mirrored topic

If you set offset-syncs.topic.location to target, you need to set the following ACLs:

- CREATE on the offset-syncs topic or CREATE on the cluster
- DESCRIBE on the offset-syncs topic
- WRITE on the offset-syncs topic

If you keep sync.topic.acls.enable enabled, you also need:

- ALTER on the cluster

Metrics

`MirrorSourceConnector` emits metrics with the following name and labels:

```
kafka.connect.mirror:type=MirrorSourceConnector,source=<SOURCE_ALIAS>,
target=<TARGET_ALIAS>,topic=<TOPIC>,partition=<PARTITION>
```

where:

- `SOURCE_ALIAS` is the alias of the source cluster. This label is only available from Kafka 3.5 onward if `add.source.alias.to.metrics` is set to `true`. From Kafka 4.0 onward, it will always be present.

- `TARGET_ALIAS` is the alias of the target cluster.

- `TOPIC` is the remote topic name.

- `PARTITION` is the partition number.

You should monitor the following attributes:

`record-count` *and* `record-rate`
: The number and rate per second of records the connector has mirrored from the source cluster to the target cluster for this topic partition.

`byte-count` *and* `byte-rate`
: The number and rate per second of bytes the connector has mirrored from the source cluster to the target cluster for this topic partition.

`record-age-ms`
: The age of records when they are mirrored, in milliseconds. This is computed by subtracting the record timestamp from the timestamp when the connector handles it. This is useful to estimate the gap between the clusters. However, if records are using arbitrary timestamps or timestamps in the past, this metric loses some of its value. You can also find the minimum, maximum, and average values by respectively using `record-age-ms-min`, `record-age-ms-max` and `record-age-ms-avg`.

`replication-latency-ms`
: This metric works like `record-age-ms` but is computed by subtracting the record timestamp from the timestamp when the record has been committed to the target cluster. You can also find the minimum, maximum, and average values by respectively using `replication-latency-ms-min`, `replication-latency-ms-max`, and `replication-latency-ms-avg`.

It's often interesting to compute the duration it takes for MirrorMaker to mirror records; you can do so by subtracting the `record-age-ms` metric from the `replication-latency-ms` metric.

Let's now look at the next connector, MirrorCheckpointConnector.

MirrorCheckpointConnector

This connector enables you to mirror consumer group offsets from a source cluster to a target cluster. This is important in use cases where consumer applications are expected to switch from one cluster to another, for example, in disaster recovery or migration scenarios.

At runtime, the connector lists consumer groups on the source cluster and retrieves their committed offsets. As mentioned, the offsets between clusters rarely match, so the connector can't just reuse the offsets on the target cluster. Instead, MirrorCheckpointConnector uses the offset-syncs topic, populated by MirrorSourceConnector, to translate the offsets from the source cluster into their correct value in the target cluster. It stores the translated offsets as checkpoints in a compacted topic with a single partition in the target cluster. A *checkpoint* is a record that contains the consumer group name, the remote topic and partition, the committed offset on the source cluster, and the matching offset on the target cluster.

Records in the checkpoint topic are serialized as bytes. MirrorMaker provides a formatter to deserialize them, as it can be useful to see them when debugging. For example, to browse checkpoints, you can use the following command:

```
$ ./bin/kafka-console-consumer.sh --bootstrap-server us-kafka0:9092 \
    --topic eu.checkpoints.internal \
    --formatter org.apache.kafka.connect.mirror.formatters.CheckpointFormatter \
    --from-beginning
Checkpoint{consumerGroupId=my-group, topicPartition=eu.heartbeat-0,
    upstreamOffset=351, downstreamOffset=42, metadata=}
```

With the default replication policy, the checkpoints topic is named <SOURCE_ALIAS>.checkpoints.internal. In this example, MirrorCheckpointConnector has emitted a checkpoint for a group called my-group on partition heartbeat-0. The record contains the topic partition with the remote topic name eu.heartbeat-0, upstreamOffset indicates the offset on the source cluster (here, 351), and downstreamOffset is the offset on the target cluster (42). The metadata field is set to the metadata that was provided when the group committed its offsets in the source cluster; in this case, it was empty.

Since Kafka 2.7, MirrorCheckpointConnector can also directly commit the offsets into the target cluster. If you are expecting to move applications between clusters, you should enable this feature, as it simplifies the process. Otherwise, your applications need to process checkpoint records to find their positions when they connect to a new cluster. In JVM-based consumer applications, you can rely on the Remote ClusterUtils utility to process checkpoint records instead of directly interacting with the checkpoints topic, for example:

```
Map<String, Object> configs = new HashMap<>();
configs.put("bootstrap.servers", "us-kafka0:9092"); ❶

Map<TopicPartition, OffsetAndMetadata> offsets =
    RemoteClusterUtils.translateOffsets(configs,
                                        "us",
                                        "my-group",
                                        Duration.ofSeconds(5L)); ❷
```

❶ We construct a `Map` object with the connection details of the target cluster where the checkpoints topic is located.

❷ We call the `translateOffsets()` method. It takes four arguments:

- The `Map` object we created with the connection details
- The alias of the target cluster
- The consumer group whose offsets we want to retrieve
- The timeout for the operation as a `Duration` object

This method returns a `Map` in which the keys are the remote names of `Topic Partition` objects that this consumer group has committed offsets for, and the values are the matching offsets on the target cluster.

Applications based on third-party clients have to consume and process the checkpoints topic directly to compute their positions. Figure 6-6 shows the topics used when `MirrorCheckpointConnector` is enabled with a Kafka version of 2.7 or higher.

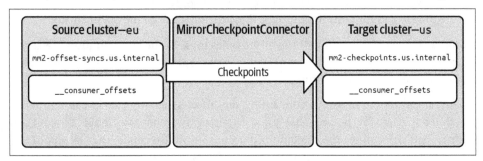

Figure 6-6. Architecture diagram showing the topics `MirrorCheckpointConnector` uses to mirror consumer group offsets between clusters

This connector is optional, so if you don't need to move consuming applications from one cluster to another, you don't need to run it.

Now that we understand how `MirrorCheckpointConnector` works, let's look at its configurations.

Configurations

This connector exposes several configurations. First, you can select the consumer groups that the connector mirrors with the groups setting. It takes a list of groups and regular expressions. It defaults to .*, which means all consumer groups except groups with the following prefixes: console-consumer-, connect-, and __. You can use groups.exclude to exclude different groups, and you can use group.fil ter.class to provide a class that implements the org.apache.kafka.connect.mir ror.GroupFilter interface to programmatically select groups to mirror.

To configure how often the connector detects new consumer groups in the source cluster, you can use refresh.groups.interval.seconds. It defaults to 600 and you can disable this feature by either setting it to -1 or by setting refresh.groups.enabled to false.

The interval at which checkpoints are emitted is configurable too. To do so, use the emit.checkpoints.interval.seconds setting, which defaults to 60. You can disable emitting checkpoints by setting it to -1 or by setting emit.checkpoints.enabled to false. You can configure the replication factor of the topic by using check points.topic.replication.factor. It defaults to 3, and you can set it to -1 to use the broker default replication factor.

The connector can also take responsibility for committing consumer group offsets to the target cluster. This is disabled by default, so to enable it, you must set sync.group.offsets.enabled to true. The interval used to commit offsets is con figurable via sync.group.offsets.interval.seconds, which defaults to 60. This feature only works for consumer groups that are not active in the target cluster.

If you've changed the location of the offset-syncs topic in the configuration of Mirror SourceConnector, you need to set offset-syncs.topic.location to the same value in the configuration of this connector too.

Finally, since the connector is consuming the offset-syncs topic, you can configure the timeout used for polling that topic by using the consumer.poll.timeout.ms setting. This determines the maximum duration, in milliseconds, the call to poll() can block in order to retrieve records, and it defaults to 1000.

Permissions

This connector and the Kafka Connect runtime require a few permissions on both the source and target cluster to operate correctly.

Source cluster ACLs.   On the source cluster, you need to grant the following ACLs:

- DESCRIBE on the cluster
- DESCRIBE on each group to mirror

If you keep the default value (source) for offset-syncs.topic.location, you also need to set:

- DESCRIBE on the offset-syncs topic
- READ on the offset-syncs topic

Target cluster ACLs.   On the target cluster, you need to grant the following ACLs:

- DESCRIBE on the cluster
- CREATE on the checkpoints topic or CREATE on the cluster
- DESCRIBE on the checkpoints topic
- WRITE on the checkpoints topic

If you set offset-syncs.topic.location to target, you need to set the following ACLs:

- DESCRIBE on the offset-syncs topic
- READ on the offset-syncs topic

If you set sync.group.offsets.enable to true, you also need these ACLs:

- READ on each mirrored group
- DESCRIBE on each mirrored group
- READ on each topic with offsets for each mirrored group

Metrics

MirrorCheckpointConnector emits metrics with the following name and labels:

```
kafka.connect.mirror:type=MirrorCheckpointConnector,source=<SOURCE_ALIAS>,
target=<TARGET_ALIAS>,group=<GROUP_ID>,topic=<TOPIC>,partition=<PARTITION>
```

where

- SOURCE_ALIAS is the alias of the source cluster
- TARGET_ALIAS is the alias of the target cluster
- GROUP_ID is the consumer group name

- TOPIC is the remote topic name
- PARTITION is the partition number

You should monitor the `checkpoint-latency-ms` attribute, which is the duration it takes in milliseconds for the connector to emit checkpoints to the target cluster. You can also find the minimum, maximum, and average values by respectively using `checkpoint-latency-ms-min`, `checkpoint-latency-ms-max` and `checkpoint-latency-ms-avg`.

There is one last connector to look at: `MirrorHeartbeatConnector`.

MirrorHeartbeatConnector

`MirrorHeartbeatConnector` is much simpler than the other two. Its role is to periodically emit *heartbeats*. Heartbeats are small records that contain the source and target cluster alias as the record key, and the current timestamp as the record value. By default, these heartbeats go to a topic called `heartbeats`, which has a single partition and is compacted.

Unlike the other connectors that emit data to the target cluster, `MirrorHeartbeatConnector` should be deployed into a Kafka Connect runtime that points to the source cluster. Heartbeats can be mirrored by `MirrorSourceConnector` from the source cluster to target clusters, and then you can use them to estimate the mirroring latency by comparing the timestamp in a heartbeat with the current wall-clock when you consume them in a target cluster. Another benefit of this connector is that the presence of new heartbeats can be used to validate that a mirroring pipeline is still working, even if there is no other traffic.

Records in the `heartbeats` topic are serialized as bytes. MirrorMaker provides a formatter to deserialize them, because it can be useful to see them when debugging issues. For example, to browse heartbeats you can use the following command:

```
$ ./bin/kafka-console-consumer.sh --bootstrap-server us-kafka0:9092 \
  --topic eu.heartbeats \
  --formatter org.apache.kafka.connect.mirror.formatters.HeartbeatFormatter \
  --from-beginning
Heartbeat{sourceClusterAlias=eu, targetClusterAlias=us, timestamp=1665592609324}
```

In this example, we're consuming a heartbeat from the us cluster. We can see that the heartbeat was first emitted by the connector into the eu cluster with the `source ClusterAlias` field. The `timestamp` field indicates the time it was emitted by the connector.

As demonstrated in Figure 6-7, at a high level `MirrorHeartbeatConnector` generates heartbeats in a Connect runtime connected to the source cluster.

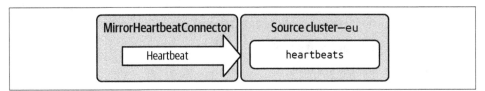

Figure 6-7. Architecture diagram showing `MirrorHeartbeatConnector` *sending heartbeats to the source cluster*

This connector is optional and does not necessarily need to be run as part of a mirroring solution. As explained earlier, MirrorMaker exposes latency metrics, and in many scenarios there are records constantly flowing, so heartbeats have only marginal value.

 `MirrorHeartbeatConnector` should send records to the source cluster, so it must be deployed in a different Kafka Connect runtime than those of the other two connectors that send records to the target cluster. If you don't already have a Kafka Connect runtime in the source cluster, you should consider whether the benefits of this connector are worth the cost of having an additional runtime. Client overrides make it possible to have the connector interact with the source cluster, even if it's deployed in a Kafka Connect runtime attached to the target cluster. However, if the two Kafka clusters are not very close, this is likely to impact the latency and reduce the value of heartbeats.

Now that we understand how `MirrorHeartbeatConnector` works, let's look at its configurations.

Configurations

This connector only exposes three settings.

The `heartbeats.topic.replication.factor` setting determines the replication factor of the `heartbeats` topic. It defaults to 3, but you can set it to `-1` to use the broker default replication factor.

You can also configure the interval in seconds between heartbeats by using the `emit.heartbeats.interval.seconds` setting, which defaults to 1. To disable emitting heartbeats, you can set it to `-1` or set `emit.heartbeats.enabled` to `false`.

Permissions

You only need to grant three ACLs on the source cluster for this connector to work:

- CREATE on the heartbeats topic or CREATE on the cluster
- DESCRIBE on the heartbeats topic
- WRITE on the heartbeats topic

MirrorHeartbeatConnector does not emit any metrics.

We have now covered all three MirrorMaker connectors, so it's time to get them running.

Running MirrorMaker

The best way to get started with MirrorMaker is to try deploying the connectors with a particular use case in mind. In this section, we walk through two examples to demonstrate the disaster recovery and geo-replication use cases.

For these examples, we need to start two Kafka clusters. To easily identify them, let's call them east-kafka and west-kafka. In order to run two Kafka clusters on a machine, you need to make sure that your brokers are configured correctly. In KRaft mode, you need to use different quorum voter lists (controller.quo rum.voters) for each cluster. In ZooKeeper mode, both clusters either need to use different ZooKeeper ensembles or use different ZooKeeper chroot paths (for example, zookeeper.connect=localhost:2181/east-kafka and zookeeper.con nect=localhost:2181/west-kafka). In our examples, the bootstrap addresses for east-kafka and west-kafka are east-kafka0:9092 and west-kafka0:9092, respectively. When running the commands yourself, make sure to use the correct bootstrap address for your setup.

Disaster Recovery Example

In this example, we start by using the east-kafka cluster as the main cluster. We will set up mirroring from east-kafka to west-kafka with MirrorSourceConnector and use MirrorCheckpointConnector to mirror consumer group offsets. We don't deploy MirrorHeartbeatConnector, as it would require starting another Kafka Connect runtime next to the source cluster, for limited benefits. We will also demonstrate how to migrate applications to west-kafka in case an issue affects east-kafka.

We first need to start a Kafka Connect runtime connected to west-kafka; let's call it west-connect. To do so, you can use the bin/connect-distributed.sh script and a properties file.

Once we have a Kafka Connect runtime, we can deploy `MirrorSourceConnector` to mirror the topic data. Create a file, *east-to-west-source.json*, with the following content:

```
{
    "name": "east-to-west-source",
    "connector.class": "org.apache.kafka.connect.mirror.MirrorSourceConnector",
    "tasks.max": "10",
    "key.converter": "org.apache.kafka.connect.converters.ByteArrayConverter",
    "value.converter": "org.apache.kafka.connect.converters.ByteArrayConverter",

    ❶
    "source.cluster.alias": "east-kafka",
    "target.cluster.alias": "west-kafka",
    "source.cluster.bootstrap.servers": "east-kafka0:9092",
    "target.cluster.bootstrap.servers": "west-kafka0:9092",

    "replication.factor": "-1",
    "offset-syncs.topic.replication.factor": "-1",

    ❷
    "refresh.topics.interval.seconds": "10",
    "sync.topic.configs.interval.seconds": "10",
    "sync.topic.acls.enabled": "false", ❸
    "replication.policy.class":
        "org.apache.kafka.connect.mirror.IdentityReplicationPolicy", ❹

    ❺
    "topics": ".*"
}
```

❶ After the usual connector settings, we define the aliases and connection details of both the Kafka clusters. Update these to match your Kafka clusters.

❷ To make the example simpler, we set low intervals so that changes in the source cluster are quickly applied to the target cluster. Setting such a short interval causes some extra load in both Kafka Connect and Kafka. In most real use cases, you can use intervals of several minutes; the defaults are 10 minutes.

❸ Many disaster recovery scenarios rely on mirroring ACLs. However, for this example, we disable ACL mirroring, as it would require setting up an Authorizer and ACLs in both Kafka clusters.

❹ We use the identity replication policy, so topics have the same name in both clusters. This simplifies the migration process for applications.

❺ Finally, we configure the topics we want to mirror. Disaster recovery use cases often require mirroring most topics. In production environments, you should carefully review all available topics on the source cluster and avoid mirroring topics that have no value on the target topics, such as intermediate topics from Kafka Streams applications.

Then you can start the connector:

```
$ curl -X PUT -H "Content-Type: application/json" \
  -d @east-to-west-source.json \
  west-connect:8083/connectors/east-to-west-source/config
```

Let's see what happens if we create topics and send records in the main cluster. Start by creating a topic called inventory in east-kafka:

```
$ ./bin/kafka-topics.sh --bootstrap-server east-kafka0:9092 \
    --create --topic inventory \
    --partitions 5 --replication-factor 1
```

Within a few seconds, the matching remote topic, inventory, appears in west-kafka:

```
$ ./bin/kafka-topics.sh --bootstrap-server west-kafka0:9092 \
    --list
connect-configs
connect-offsets
connect-status
inventory
```

We can send some records into inventory in east-kafka:

```
$ ./bin/kafka-console-producer.sh --bootstrap-server east-kafka0:9092 \
    --topic inventory
>a
>b
>c
```

These records are mirrored to west-kafka, into the remote topic:

```
$ ./bin/kafka-console-consumer.sh --bootstrap-server west-kafka0:9092 \
    --topic inventory \
    --from-beginning
a
b
c
```

If we look at the connector configuration via the REST API using the GET /connectors/east-to-west-source/ endpoint, we can see that it is running five tasks. The only topic being mirrored has five partitions, so it created one task per partition. Once the number of partitions to mirror goes beyond tasks.max, some tasks will be assigned multiple partitions. You can use the GET /connectors/east-to-west-source/tasks REST API endpoint to see the individual partitions assigned to each task with the task.assigned.partitions field:

```
[
  {
    "id": {
      "connector": "east-to-west-source",
      "task": 0
    },
    "config": {
      ...
      "task.assigned.partitions": "inventory-0",
      ...
    }
  },
  {
    "id": {
      "connector": "east-to-west-source",
      "task": 1
    },
    "config": {
      ...
      "task.assigned.partitions": "inventory-1",
      ...
    }
  },
  ...
]
```

This can be useful when debugging issues or identifying the impact caused when a task crashes.

To be able to migrate consumer applications, we need to run `MirrorCheckpoint` `Connector`. To do so, create a file, *east-to-west-checkpoint.json*, with the following contents:

```
{
    "name": "east-to-west-checkpoint",
    "connector.class":
        "org.apache.kafka.connect.mirror.MirrorCheckpointConnector",
    "tasks.max": "10",
    "key.converter": "org.apache.kafka.connect.converters.ByteArrayConverter",
    "value.converter": "org.apache.kafka.connect.converters.ByteArrayConverter",

    "source.cluster.alias": "east-kafka",
    "target.cluster.alias": "west-kafka",
    "source.cluster.bootstrap.servers": "east-kafka0:9092",
    "target.cluster.bootstrap.servers": "west-kafka0:9092",

    "checkpoints.topic.replication.factor": "-1",

    "refresh.groups.interval.seconds": "10", ❶

    "groups": ".*", ❷
    "sync.group.offsets.enabled": "true", ❸
```

```
"replication.policy.class":
    "org.apache.kafka.connect.mirror.IdentityReplicationPolicy" ❹
}
```

This connector is configured similarly to MirrorSourceConnector.

❶ We use a short interval, so groups are quickly mirrored to the target cluster.

❷ We configure the connector to mirror all groups from the source cluster.

❸ We enable automatic syncing of groups, so in addition to checkpoints, the connector also automatically commits offsets in the target cluster if possible.

❹ We need to use the same replication policy across the connectors.

Then start the connector:

```
$ curl -X PUT -H "Content-Type: application/json" \
 -d @east-to-west-checkpoint.json \
 west-connect:8083/connectors/east-to-west-checkpoint/config
```

Now create a group in east-kafka using the console consumer:

```
$ ./bin/kafka-console-consumer.sh --bootstrap-server east-kafka0:9092 \
 --topic inventory --from-beginning \
 --group my-group
```

At this point, we see that the connector has created a checkpoints topic, east-kafka.checkpoints.internal, with a single partition in west-kafka. Consumer group offsets can be retrieved from that topic using the RemoteClusterUtils class. For example, you can use the following logic to translate offsets for my-group:

```
public static void main(String[] args) throws Exception {
    Map<String, Object> configs = new HashMap<>();
    configs.put("bootstrap.servers", "west-kafka0:9092");
    configs.put("replication.policy.class",
      "org.apache.kafka.connect.mirror.IdentityReplicationPolicy");
    Map<TopicPartition, OffsetAndMetadata> offsets =
      RemoteClusterUtils.translateOffsets(configs,
                                          "east-kafka",
                                          "my-group",
                                          Duration.ofSeconds(5L));
    for (Map.Entry<TopicPartition, OffsetAndMetadata> o : offsets.entrySet()) {
        System.out.println(o.getKey() + " : " + o.getValue().offset());
    }
}
```

If you run this code, its output looks like:

```
inventory-2 : 1
inventory-3 : 0
inventory-4 : 3
```

```
inventory-0 : 8
inventory-1 : 0
```

Since we enabled group syncing, the group is automatically created in west-kafka
with committed offsets:

```
$ ./bin/kafka-consumer-groups.sh --bootstrap-server west-kafka0:9092 \
  --describe --group my-group

Consumer group 'my-group' has no active members.

GROUP      TOPIC       PARTITION  CURRENT-OFFSET  LOG-END-OFFSET  LAG ...
my-group   inventory   3          0               0               0   ...
my-group   inventory   4          3               3               0   ...
my-group   inventory   2          1               1               0   ...
my-group   inventory   0          8               8               0   ...
my-group   inventory   1          0               0               0   ...
```

The outputs from both the Java code and the kafka-consumer-groups script should
match and indicate the offsets that consumers using my-group should use to carry
on consuming from west-kafka. Syncing groups simplifies the process of migrating
consumers, as they can find their group and automatically restart from the matching
position they last committed in the source cluster. Otherwise, you would need to
embed the RemoteClusterUtils logic shown previously in your consumer applications and use the consumer seek() API to explicitly move their position to the
translated offsets.

While running such a topology, you should monitor the latency metrics of both
connectors. In practice, the target cluster is always slightly lagging behind the source
cluster, and those metrics help you understand the gap between both clusters. It also
helps quantify the amount of data you would lose if the source cluster was to fail,
forcing you to migrate applications to the target cluster.

Because we used the identity replication policy and enabled automatically syncing
consumer groups, in order to migrate applications, we just need to update their
connection details to point to the target cluster and restart them.

After stopping the applications in the source cluster, we can start new instances in the
target cluster:

```
$ ./bin/kafka-console-consumer.sh --bootstrap-server west-kafka0:9092 \
  --topic inventory --group my-group
```

Geo-Replication Example

In this example we mirror data bi-directionally between two Kafka clusters, so we
need to start two Kafka Connect runtimes. One runtime should connect to the
east-kafka Kafka cluster and the other to the west-kafka cluster. Let's call the Kafka
Connect runtimes east-connect and west-connect. In order to run two runtimes

on a machine, they need to use different REST API ports. In our example, the east-connect cluster has its REST API accessible on the host east-connect and port 8083, and the west-connect cluster is accessible on west-connect:8083.

In geo-replication use cases, applications typically don't have to move from one cluster to another, so in this example we don't use MirrorCheckpointConnector. We deploy MirrorHeartbeatConnector, since we have two runtimes and can benefit from its features with little overhead.

In order to create our first mirroring route, we need to deploy MirrorSourceConnector. Create a file, *east-to-west-source.json*, with the following content:

```
{
    "name": "east-to-west-source",
    "connector.class": "org.apache.kafka.connect.mirror.MirrorSourceConnector",
    "tasks.max": "10",
    "key.converter": "org.apache.kafka.connect.converters.ByteArrayConverter",
    "value.converter": "org.apache.kafka.connect.converters.ByteArrayConverter",

    ❶
    "source.cluster.alias": "east-kafka",
    "target.cluster.alias": "west-kafka",
    "source.cluster.bootstrap.servers": "east-kafka0:9092",
    "target.cluster.bootstrap.servers": "west-kafka0:9092",

    "replication.factor": "-1",
    "offset-syncs.topic.replication.factor": "-1",

    ❷
    "refresh.topics.interval.seconds": "10",
    "sync.topic.configs.interval.seconds": "10",
    "sync.topic.acls.enabled": "false",

    ❸
    "topics": "inventory,sales"
}
```

❶ After the usual connector settings, we define the aliases and connection details of both the Kafka clusters. Update these to match your Kafka clusters.

❷ Again, to make the example simpler, we set low intervals, so changes in the source cluster are quickly applied to the target cluster. Setting such a short interval causes some extra load in both Kafka Connect and Kafka. In most real use cases, you can use intervals of several minutes; the defaults are 10 minutes.

❸ In geo-replication use cases, you typically only want to mirror a specific set of topics. In this case we only mirror two topics, inventory and sales.

Then you can start the connector in west-connect:

```
$ curl -X PUT -H "Content-Type: application/json" \
  -d @east-to-west-source.json \
  west-connect:8083/connectors/east-to-west-source/config
```

Let's now start another MirrorSourceConnector in east-connect to mirror some data in the other direction. Create a file, *west-to-east-source.json,* with the following content:

```
{
    "name": "west-to-east-source",
    "connector.class": "org.apache.kafka.connect.mirror.MirrorSourceConnector",
    "tasks.max": "10",
    "key.converter": "org.apache.kafka.connect.converters.ByteArrayConverter",
    "value.converter": "org.apache.kafka.connect.converters.ByteArrayConverter",

    ❶
    "source.cluster.alias": "west-kafka",
    "target.cluster.alias": "east-kafka",
    "source.cluster.bootstrap.servers": "west-kafka0:9092",
    "target.cluster.bootstrap.servers": "east-kafka0:9092",

    "replication.factor": "-1",
    "offset-syncs.topic.replication.factor": "-1",

    "refresh.topics.interval.seconds": "10",
    "sync.topic.configs.interval.seconds": "10",
    "sync.topic.acls.enabled": "false",

    ❷
    "topics": "inventory"
}
```

The configuration is very similar to east-to-west-source.

❶ Compared to east-to-west-source, the cluster aliases are inverted, as this connector flows data in the other direction.

❷ In geo-replication use cases, each mirroring route may mirror a different set of topics; it depends on the exact requirements of the processing applications.

You can start the connector using the REST API:

```
$ curl -X PUT -H "Content-Type: application/json" \
  -d @west-to-east-source.json \
  east-connect:8083/connectors/west-to-east-source/config
```

Let's now see what happens if we create a topic called sales in the east-kafka cluster:

```
$ ./bin/kafka-topics.sh --bootstrap-server east-kafka0:9092 \
  --create --topic sales \
  --partitions 5 --replication-factor 1
```

Within a few seconds, the matching remote topic, `east-kafka.sales`, appears in `west-kafka`:

```
$ ./bin/kafka-topics.sh --bootstrap-server west-kafka0:9092 \
  --list
connect-configs
connect-offsets
connect-status
east-kafka.sales
```

Similarly, if we create a topic called `inventory` in the `west-kafka` cluster, the remote topic `west-kafka.inventory` is created automatically by MirrorMaker in `east-kafka`.

If we also have a local topic, `inventory`, in `east-kafka`, applications wanting to connect to `east-kafka` and consume all inventory events should subscribe to both `inventory` and `west-kafka.inventory`. This can be done by explicitly listing all topics in the call to `subscribe()` or by using a wildcard subscription, for example:

```
Pattern pattern = Pattern.compile("(.+\\.)?inventory");
consumer.subscribe(pattern);
```

We can now deploy an instance of `MirrorHeartbeatConnector` in each runtime. Starting in `east-connect`, create a file, *east-heartbeat.json*, with the following content:

```
{
    "name": "east-heartbeat",
    "connector.class":
        "org.apache.kafka.connect.mirror.MirrorHeartbeatConnector",
    "tasks.max": "1",  ❶
    "key.converter": "org.apache.kafka.connect.converters.ByteArrayConverter",
    "value.converter": "org.apache.kafka.connect.converters.ByteArrayConverter",

    ❷
    "source.cluster.alias": "east-kafka",
    "target.cluster.alias": "west-kafka",

    ❸
    "target.cluster.bootstrap.servers": "east-kafka0:9092",

    "heartbeats.topic.replication.factor": "-1"
}
```

❶ This connector can only use a single task, so set `tasks.max` to 1.

❷ Even though this connector is going to be running on the `east-connect` runtime, as heartbeats will be mirrored, `east-kafka` is still considered the source alias.

❸ This connector only needs to connect to its local Kafka cluster, `east-kafka`, to create the `heartbeats` topic. The connection details, however, have to be provided with the `target.cluster.` prefix. This is counterintuitive, but it's how the connector is currently implemented.

Then start the connector on the `east-connect` runtime:

```
$ curl -X PUT -H "Content-Type: application/json" \
  -d @east-heartbeat.json \
  east-connect:8083/connectors/east-heartbeat/config
```

You can follow the exact same steps to deploy a `MirrorHeartbeatConnector` instance in `west-connect`; you just need to make sure to invert the aliases and the target cluster connection details.

The connector deployed in `east-connect` creates the `heartbeats` topic in `east-kafka`, which is mirrored as `east-kafka.heartbeats` into `west-kafka`. We can see the heartbeat records using the console consumer with the heartbeat formatter:

```
$ ./bin/kafka-console-consumer.sh --bootstrap-server west-kafka0:9092 \
  --topic east-kafka.heartbeats \
  --formatter org.apache.kafka.connect.mirror.formatters.HeartbeatFormatter
Heartbeat{sourceClusterAlias=east-kafka, targetClusterAlias=west-kafka,
  timestamp=1666368851384}
Heartbeat{sourceClusterAlias=east-kafka, targetClusterAlias=west-kafka,
  timestamp=1666368852386}}
```

Another use of `MirrorHeartbeatConnector` is to map the mirroring topology. Heartbeats topics are used by `RemoteClusterUtils` to list all interconnected clusters and identify the numbers of hops between them. For example, if you run this logic:

```
public static void main(String[] args) throws Exception {
    Map<String, Object> configs = new HashMap<>();
    configs.put("bootstrap.servers", "west-kafka0:9092");

    Set<String> clusters = RemoteClusterUtils.upstreamClusters(configs);
    System.out.println(clusters);

    int hops = RemoteClusterUtils.replicationHops(configs, "east-kafka");
    System.out.println("hops to east-kafka: " + hops);
}
```

It prints the following:

```
[east-kafka]  ❶
hops to east-kafka: 1  ❷
```

❶ The only other cluster in this example deployment is `east-kafka`.

❷ As both clusters are directly connected with MirrorMaker, there is a single hop between them.

Summary

In this chapter, we looked at the concept of mirroring by first covering the most common use cases it enables. We explained the requirements for geo-replication, disaster recovery, migration, and more complex topologies, and the value that such environments can bring to businesses. The uses for mirroring vary widely, which is why the possible topologies you might want to deploy also vary.

We then introduced MirrorMaker, the mirroring tool that is part of Apache Kafka. It consists of three connectors:

- `MirrorSourceConnector` to mirror topics and their data
- `MirrorCheckpointConnector` to mirror consumer group offsets
- `MirrorHeartbeatConnector` to send heartbeats to clusters

`MirrorSourceConnector` is used in all mirroring topologies, while `MirrorCheckpoint` `Connector` and `MirrorHeartbeatConnector` should only be used as needed. When you deploy these connectors, make sure you understand the role the connector is playing, as well as the configuration options, the permissions they require to run, and the metrics they emit that you should monitor.

Finally, we demonstrated how to use MirrorMaker by covering a disaster recovery and a geo-replication scenario. We saw that for disaster recovery, `MirrorSourceCon` `nector` and `MirrorCheckpointConnector` could be run on a single Kafka Connect cluster. Then for geo-replication, we deployed two Kafka Connect clusters, each running both `MirrorSourceConnector` and `MirrorHeartbeatConnector`. Take special care when deploying `MirrorHeartbeatConnector`; unlike the other connectors, it should run on the Kafka Connect cluster nearest to the source Kafka cluster, not the target.

PART III

Running Kafka Connect in Production

The third part of this book focuses on running and operating Kafka Connect clusters. It is aimed at site reliability engineers (SREs) whose role is to keep data pipelines working. It describes the main concepts to understand when setting up Kafka Connect clusters, and the worker plug-ins you can use to customize them.

It covers topics such as scalability, common operation procedures, and the management REST API. It also details all the configuration options available, and the methods and best practices for monitoring pipelines via logs and metrics. Finally, it explores the considerations required to effectively run Kafka Connect clusters on Kubernetes.

CHAPTER 7

Deploying and Operating Kafka Connect Clusters

In this chapter, we focus on how to deploy and operate Kafka Connect clusters. Starting with deployment, we look at how to build a Kafka Connect environment, customize it using connector and worker plug-ins, and determine the network and permissions requirements. We also discuss how to size a cluster efficiently to handle the workload for your use cases. Then, moving into operation, we look at the most common operations that administrators perform on a running Kafka Connect cluster, such as adding and removing workers, applying upgrades, restarting failed tasks and resetting offsets. Finally, we give an overview of the Kafka Connect REST API and explain how to use each of the available endpoints to manage and monitor clusters.

After reading this chapter, you will be able to deploy and maintain a production Kafka Connect cluster.

Preparing the Kafka Connect Environment

In Chapter 3, we talked about the difference between standalone and distributed mode when you deploy Kafka Connect. Distributed mode comes with more operating steps but is recommended for production deployments due to the added resiliency it provides. For this chapter, we assume you are deploying Kafka Connect in distributed mode.

If you do choose to use standalone mode, keep the following in mind as you read this chapter:

- In standalone mode, you only deploy a single, independent worker and cannot automatically scale with new workers.

- In standalone mode, workers store state in the filesystem. Keep this in mind when considering sizing and capacity planning.

Before deciding how to configure your Kafka Connect cluster, you must first choose the environment to deploy it in. Like Kafka, Kafka Connect is a Java-based project. This means as long as you have the Kafka Connect libraries, you can run it on any Java environment. Make sure you use the Java version that is recommended on the Kafka website (*https://oreil.ly/xvQmF*).

Kafka Connect workers and Kafka brokers can run on the same physical nodes or separated ones. Separating them provides more resilience to failures, but in smaller environments it's common to collocate them. Regardless of how you place them, Kafka Connect workers should be deployed, configured, and upgraded independently of the brokers in the related Kafka cluster. Although workers and brokers require a similar environment, they have different lifecycles and need to be scaled independently.

The most common place to deploy Kafka Connect is on the same infrastructure as the Kafka cluster that it will be interacting with. Doing so provides benefits in two areas: operating processes and network traffic. The processes for operating Kafka and Kafka Connect are similar. They both require a Java environment, and they are distributed workloads that can be scaled and monitored in a similar way. This means that whether you deploy them on bare metal or on a platform like Kubernetes, it's easier to use the same infrastructure for both rather than having to adopt or create tools for multiple environments. Kafka Connect uses Kafka for storing state and coordinating between workers. If the clusters are close to each other, the latency for this kind of traffic is lower.

There are some scenarios where it is preferable to run Kafka Connect alongside the external system, rather than alongside the Kafka cluster. This depends on the external system and the connector. For example, the message queuing system IBM MQ includes two connection options: bindings mode and client mode. Both are supported by the IBM MQ connectors, but for MQ installations that only allow bindings connections, both the Kafka Connect cluster and the connectors must be running in the same environment as the IBM MQ system for the connection to be successful.

Let's look at the steps you need to take to prepare your chosen environment for your Kafka Connect cluster.

Building a Kafka Connect Environment

The Kafka distribution contains the Kafka Connect scripts and JAR files needed to start a Kafka Connect cluster. These files are:

- The Kafka Connect JAR files in the `libs` folder of the Kafka distribution. This includes the runtime JAR file, but also files it depends on, like the Kafka clients' JAR.

- The `connect-distributed.sh` script in the `bin` folder of the Kafka distribution (or `connect-distributed.bat` from `bin/windows` if running on Windows operating system).

- The `kafka-run-class.sh` script in the `bin` folder of the Kafka distribution (or `kafka-run-class.bat` from `bin/windows` if running on Windows operating system), since this is invoked by the `connect-distributed` script.

In addition to these files, you also need available in your Kafka Connect environment:

- A configuration file for each Kafka Connect worker using the properties format. The `config` folder of the Kafka distribution includes an example called *connect-distributed.properties*.

- A configuration file for the logging for each Kafka Connect worker using the properties format. The `config` folder of the Kafka distribution includes an example called *connect-log4j.properties*.

- The JAR files for the connector and worker plug-ins you want to use (see the next section for more on worker plug-ins).

 A *properties file* is a plain-text file that maps keys to values. Each line is a single mapping between a key and a value. The most common format is to use an equal sign (`key=value`), but you can also use a colon (`key:value`). For example, the following file has the keys `group.id` and `bootstrap.servers` set to `test-group` and `localhost:9092`, respectively:

```
group.id=test-group

bootstrap.servers=localhost:9092
```

Many developers choose to deploy Kafka Connect workers as containerized applications on platforms like Kubernetes. If you want to run your Kafka Connect workers as containers, you can either create the container image yourself, use one from the community, or purchase proprietary software that provides one.

Here is an example of a Dockerfile for a Kafka Connect worker using a well-known Java image as the base:

```
FROM eclipse-temurin:17

RUN mkdir -p /opt/kafka/bin /opt/kafka/libs /opt/kafka/config /opt/kafka/logs
COPY ./kafka/bin /opt/kafka/bin/
COPY ./kafka/libs /opt/kafka/libs/
COPY ./kafka/config/connect-distributed.properties /opt/kafka/config/
COPY ./kafka/config/connect-log4j.properties /opt/kafka/config/
RUN mkdir -p /opt/kafka/connectors
COPY <CONNECTOR_JARS> /opt/kafka/connectors
WORKDIR /opt/kafka
EXPOSE 8083

ENTRYPOINT ["./bin/connect-distributed.sh",
    "config/connect-distributed.properties"]
```

This example Dockerfile is not meant to be used as-is. It assumes that your Kafka distribution is downloaded to */opt/kafka* and the *connect-distributed.properties* file has set the plugin.path to be */opt/kafka/connectors/*.

There are plenty of open source projects that also provide images for you to use. These are often available on public container registries such as DockerHub (*https://hub.docker.com*) and Quay (*http://quay.io*). Two such projects are Strimzi and Debezium.

Strimzi (*https://strimzi.io*) is an open source project that provides tools for deploying Kafka Connect clusters onto Kubernetes. The operator provides a mechanism to let you build a custom Kafka Connect Docker image that includes the connector plug-ins you need. In Chapter 10, we explore more options for deploying Kafka Connect on Kubernetes and see Strimzi in action. Debezium (*https://debezium.io*) provides pre-built Docker images on DockerHub and Quay that already include all of the Debezium Kafka Connect plug-ins.

Finally, if you need a Kafka Connect container image that is fully supported, you can look to products such as Red Hat AMQ Streams, Confluent Platform or IBM Event Streams.

Now let's look at how you can add plug-ins for your use case to your Kafka Connect installation.

Installing Plug-Ins

You must make sure that you add all plug-ins to your environment before starting your Kafka Connect workers. Connector plug-ins (connectors, converters, transformations and predicates) are used to build pipelines, while worker plug-ins (which we discuss later in this chapter) customize the Kafka Connect workers. Workers load all plug-ins at startup and will not notice plug-ins that are added at runtime. There are some default plug-ins that are already added to the classpath of Kafka Connect. These can be found in the `libs` directory of the Kafka distribution.

There are some subtleties to how Kafka Connect loads plug-ins that impact the way you install them. At startup, Kafka Connect workers scan their classpath for plug-ins. However, the plug-ins that are loaded from the classpath aren't loaded in isolation, which means there is a risk of dependency conflicts between plug-ins. We recommend using the `plugin.path` worker configuration to add plug-ins. This option provides classpath isolation, but it can cause confusion for users as it does require the plug-ins to be stored in a specific directory structure. Let's look at how to correctly use the `plugin.path` configuration.

The `plugin.path` configuration expects a comma-separated list of directories. There is no limit to the number of directories you can include. The files for a plug-in must include all dependencies. This means the structure of your `plugin.path` directories depends on the way your plug-in is packaged. If you have multiple JAR files that together provide the plug-in and all the dependencies, you must put them together in a subdirectory of the `plugin.path` directory. However, if you have a single "uber" JAR file that contains the plug-in and dependencies all packaged together, you can place this directly in the top level of the `plugin.path`.

For example, consider the following structure:

```
/opt/connect
+-- custom-plugin-1-uber.jar        ❶
+-- custom-plugin-2                  ❷
|       +-- custom-plugin-2-lib1.jar
|       +-- custom-plugin-2-lib2.jar
```

❶ A single uber JAR file containing the plug-in and all its dependencies

❷ A directory containing a set of JAR files that include the JAR file for the plug-in and the JAR files for all its dependencies

If you didn't have the `custom-plugin-2` directory and instead placed those files next to `custom-plugin-1-uber.jar`, when you tried to use `custom-plugin-2` you would see `ClassNotFound` exceptions for any classes in the `custom-plugin-2-lib2.jar` file.

Kafka Connect is only able to handle one layer of subdirectories inside the `plugin.path` directory. For example, given a directory structure of:

```
/opt/connect/plugins
+-- custom-plugin1-uber.jar
+-- custom-plugin-2
|      +-- custom-plugin-2-lib1.jar
|      +-- custom-plugin-2-lib2.jar
```

The path /opt/connect/plugins is a valid `plugin.path` configuration, but /opt/connect is not.

Once you have decided which plug-ins to add, make sure you can see them being loaded correctly in the startup logs for Kafka Connect:

```
INFO Added plugin 'org.apache.kafka.connect.converters.ByteArrayConverter'
INFO Added plugin 'org.apache.kafka.connect.file.FileStreamSourceConnector'
INFO Added plugin 'org.apache.kafka.connect.transforms.TimestampRouter'
```

Once you've decided where to deploy Kafka Connect and added your plug-ins, you also need to consider the networking and permission requirements.

Networking and Permissions

To deploy Kafka Connect into a production environment, you need to make sure the workers are granted the correct permissions to receive and send requests. This should include restricting which endpoints are accessible from which components, which is important to reduce the opportunity for bad actors to disrupt your pipeline. There are four kinds of network traffic you should consider, which are shown in Figure 7-1:

- Connections in between Kafka Connect workers
- Connections between Kafka Connect workers and Kafka brokers
- Connections between Kafka Connect workers and external systems
- Connections from REST clients to the administrative endpoint

Each connection requires different permission and network considerations. We will go through each in turn.

Let's first look at connections between workers (connection 1 in Figure 7-1). Kafka Connect workers communicate directly with each other via the REST API, for example, if a task needs to be restarted when a connector has been reconfigured. As an operator of Kafka Connect, you must make sure that the Kafka Connect workers can talk to each other via the configured REST API port.

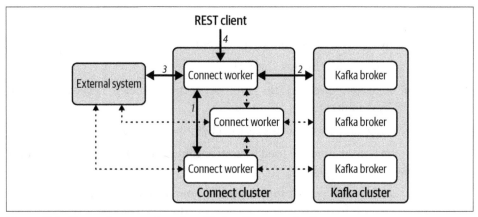

Figure 7-1. Network connections in a Kafka Connect pipeline

The second connection type is between the Kafka Connect workers and the brokers in the Kafka cluster (connection 2 in Figure 7-1). In a production system, it is likely that the Kafka cluster that Kafka Connect uses requires clients to authenticate and restricts which operations a specific user can perform. If your Kafka cluster is secured in this way, you must make sure the Kafka Connect user is granted all the permissions it needs. The operations that Kafka Connect needs to perform fall into two categories: operations required by a Kafka Connect worker, and operations for a specific connector.

To act as part of the Kafka Connect cluster successfully, Kafka Connect workers must have access to the correct topics, groups, and transaction IDs so that they can coordinate. Specifically, they must have the following ACLs:

- READ on the group listed as the group.id in the worker configuration
- CREATE on the configuration topic or CREATE on the cluster
- READ and WRITE on the configuration topic
- CREATE on the offset topic or CREATE on the cluster
- READ and WRITE on the offset topic
- CREATE on the status topic or CREATE on the cluster
- READ and WRITE on the status topic
- WRITE on the transactional ID used by the worker, if exactly-once source support is enabled

You can pre-create the configuration, offset, and status topics, and if you do that, Kafka Connect only needs READ and WRITE permissions, not CREATE.

Depending on which connectors you want to run, you also need:

- WRITE on any topics used by source connectors
- READ on any topics used by sink connectors
- READ on the group used by the sink connectors (named connect-<CONNEC
  TOR_NAME> by default)
- WRITE on any dead letter queue topics used by sink connectors
- WRITE on the transactional ID used by source connectors (if exactly-once support
  is enabled on the worker)
- READ and WRITE on the offset topics used by source connectors (if exactly-once
  support is enabled for the worker)

In addition, if you aren't pre-creating the topics for source connectors or the dead letter queue topics for sink connectors, you also need CREATE on those topics or CREATE on the cluster.

The third connection type in Figure 7-1 is between connectors and the external system. The connector must have the appropriate permissions on the external system. This normally requires the connector to be configured with some form of credentials. Exactly how you configure these depends on the connector, but most connectors provide configuration settings for them. Both for connections to the external system and connections to Kafka, consider using configuration providers (which we cover later in this chapter) that can help pull credentials from a variety of places and make it safer to configure them.

Finally, you need to configure your system so that you can perform administrative tasks such as starting and stopping connectors and tasks (connection 4 in Figure 7-1). This is normally done through the REST API, so consider whether this endpoint can be exposed to all users or if it also needs to be secured in some way.

In Chapter 8, we go into more detail about securing Kafka Connect, including providing user credentials to workers and connectors and how to secure the REST API.

Worker Plug-Ins

Connectors, converters, transformations, and predicates are all commonly referred to as *connector plug-ins* because they control the behavior of connectors. Kafka Connect also supports a few other plug-in types that administrators can use to customize the Kafka Connect runtime. These other plug-ins are called *worker plug-ins*. There are three types of worker plug-ins:

- Configuration providers
- REST extensions
- Connector client configuration override policies

Let's look at each of the worker plug-ins and what they do.

Configuration Providers

Configuration providers enable Kafka Connect to dynamically retrieve configurations at runtime instead of hardcoding values. They are classes that implement the `ConfigProvider` interface from the Kafka Connect API. You can specify them when configuring the Kafka Connect runtime and for individual connectors. The configuration provider mechanism was introduced in Kafka 2.0.0 via KIP-297 (*https://oreil.ly/it2wX*).

Configuration providers are useful when handling sensitive values like passwords or security keys, as they let you put a placeholder value in the configuration instead of the actual value. When the Kafka Connect runtime starts or when a connector is started, it automatically replaces the placeholders with the values generated by the configured configuration providers. This is safer, because when a user accesses the connector configuration via the REST API, the password is not exposed, and instead it shows the placeholder; otherwise, by default, anybody with access to the REST API can see the full configuration of all connectors. Another benefit of configuration providers is that you can have one configuration template that can be applied to multiple environments. Then, at runtime, each environment uses its own specific values.

In order to be used, configuration providers have to be enabled in the runtime configuration and present in either the classpath or in `plugin.path`.

Kafka comes with three built-in configuration providers:

`FileConfigProvider`
For retrieving configuration values from a properties file on the worker filesystem.

`DirectoryConfigProvider`
For retrieving configuration values from a directory containing files. For example, this works well with Kubernetes secrets where a single file cannot be provided. This provider was added via KIP-632 (*https://oreil.ly/PBpEO*) in Kafka 2.7.0.

`EnvVarConfigProvider`
For retrieving configuration values from environment variables. This provider was added via KIP-887 (*https://oreil.ly/R27NV*) in Kafka 3.5.0.

Let's see an example of how to use a configuration provider in practice. We want to run the MirrorMaker source connector and configure it to connect to the source Kafka cluster over TLS (Transport Layer Security). To do so, we need to specify values for a few SSL settings, including passwords for our truststore. Let's look at how we can use `FileConfigProvider` to avoid putting the password in clear text in our connector creation request.

First, the Kafka Connect runtime needs to have `FileConfigProvider` enabled. You do this by adding the following to *connect-distributed.properties*:

```
config.providers=file
config.providers.file.class=org.apache.kafka.common.config.provider.FileConfigPro
vider
```

The first line gives labels to the providers we are going to use. Here it says we're defining a single configuration provider that is called `file`. On the second line, we specify which specific implementation we want to use for the `file` label.

Then the runtime needs to have a properties file on its filesystem that contains the password. For example, we can create a file, */tmp/ssl.properties*, that contains the following:

```
password=secret-password
```

Once the runtime has the configurations shown earlier, we can create a connector that uses the configuration provider to retrieve the password value. In the connector JSON configuration, instead of using:

```
{
  ...
  "ssl.truststore.password": "secret-password",
  ...
}
```

We can have:

```
{
  ...
    "ssl.truststore.password": "${file:/tmp/ssl.properties:password}",
  ...
}
```

In this example, `file` is the label of the configuration provider set in the runtime, */tmp/ssl.properties* is the file on the runtime that contains the mappings, and password is the key we want to get the value from.

While it appears we just moved the password from one place to another, a file on the worker's filesystem can easily be secured. There are also other configuration providers that support supplying the credentials from, for example, an identity and secret management system such as Vault (*https://www.vaultproject.io*).

Another category of worker plug-ins is REST extensions.

REST Extensions

REST extensions allow you to customize the Kafka Connect REST API. For example, you can use them to add user authentication and fine-grained authorizations or validation logic for connector changes via the REST API. A *REST extension* is a class that implements the `ConnectRestExtension` interface from the Kafka Connect API. As with configuration providers, in order to use REST extensions, they have to be enabled in the runtime configuration via `rest.extension.classes` as a comma-separated list, and present in either the classpath or in `plugin.path`.

JAX-RS is a Jakarta EE API for defining web services. Using REST extensions, you can register JAX-RS plug-ins and make use of any functionality they provide.

By default, Kafka Connect includes a single built-in REST extension, `BasicAuth SecurityRestExtension`, that lets you secure the REST API with HTTP basic authentication.

Let's look at an example using `BasicAuthSecurityRestExtension` to enforce authentication to access the REST API. First, enable the plug-in in the Kafka Connect runtime configuration by adding the following to *connect-distributed.properties*:

```
rest.extension.classes=org.apache.kafka.connect.rest.basic.auth.extension.BasicAu
thSecurityRestExtension
```

Then we need a Java Authentication and Authorization Service (JAAS) file that is used to specify the mechanism to verify credentials. A JAAS file contains a `LoginMod ule`, which is a generic way to provide authentication in the JVM. In production environments, a `LoginModule` may interact with an external authentication system such as Kerberos or LDAP. For this scenario, we use `PropertyFileLoginModule`, which is an example built-in `LoginModule` that stores credentials in a properties file.

This example is not safe for production use because `PropertyFile LoginModule` requires its credentials to be present in clear text on the filesystem of the Kafka Connect worker. Also note that the REST API is accessed using HTTP, which means the credentials are sent over the network in clear text. When using authentication schemes that rely on sending secrets, like basic authentication, the REST API should be accessed via HTTPS.

Create a new file, */tmp/connect-jaas.conf*, with the following content:

```
KafkaConnect {
    org.apache.kafka.connect.rest.basic.auth.extension.PropertyFileLoginModule re
quired
    file="/tmp/credentials.properties";
};
```

We also need the file, */tmp/credentials.properties*, that stores the credentials for accessing the REST API with the following content:

```
mickael=p4ss
kate=w0rd
```

The syntax of this file is <USERNAME>=<PASSWORD>. The preceding example creates two credentials, one called `mickael` with `p4ss` as the password and one called `kate` with `w0rd` as the password.

Before starting Kafka Connect, we need to tell the JVM to load our JAAS file. We can do that by setting KAFKA_OPTS in the Kafka Connect environment:

```
$ export KAFKA_OPTS="-Djava.security.auth.login.config=/tmp/connect-jaas.conf"
```

KAFKA_OPTS is a specific environment variable that is automatically picked up by all Kafka tools.

Now start Kafka Connect and, once started, try to access the REST API without credentials. The request is rejected:

```
$ curl localhost:8083
User cannot access the resource.
```

To access the REST API, we need to provide one of the credentials we created. The `curl` command accepts basic authentication credentials using the `-u` flag and expects the username and the password to be separated by a colon. For example:

```
$ curl -u mickael:p4ss localhost:8083
{
    "version":"3.5.0",
    "commit":"c97b88d5db4de28d",
    "kafka_cluster_id":"xbuOyGSLTXyVsME9qLDgZg"
}
```

 REST extensions, including `BasicAuthSecurityRestExtension`, were added via KIP-285 (*https://oreil.ly/VSlUU*) in Kafka 2.0 in July 2018.

Finally, let's look at the last type of worker plug-in, connector client configuration override policies.

Connector Client Configuration Override Policies

In the configuration of connectors, you can include settings for the producers, consumers, and admin clients that the Kafka Connect runtime uses internally. Connector client configuration override policies allow administrators to define the client configurations that connectors are allowed to override. An override policy is a class that implements the `ConnectorClientConfigOverridePolicy` interface. You use the `connector.client.config.override.policy` setting in the runtime configuration to specify the policy to apply. The chosen policy applies to all connectors started on this runtime. This plug-in was introduced by KIP-458 (*https://oreil.ly/Zx3L5*) in Kafka 2.3.0.

Kafka comes with three built-in override policies:

- `AllConnectorClientConfigOverridePolicy` is the default policy; it allows connectors to override all client configurations. It has the `All` alias.

- `NoneConnectorClientConfigOverridePolicy` prevents connectors from overriding any client configurations. It has the `None` alias.

- `PrincipalConnectorClientConfigOverridePolicy` only allows overriding the following client configurations: `sasl.jaas.config`, `sasl.mechanism`, `security.protocol`. It has the `Principal` alias.

We describe how connectors can set client overrides in the next chapter.

Let's look at an example with this plug-in in action. This example assumes you have the `FileStreamSink` connector available in your Kafka Connect runtime. We first need to specify the override policy to use in the runtime configuration—for example, `Principal`—by adding the following in *connect-distributed.properties*:

```
connector.client.config.override.policy=Principal
```

Then start your Kafka Connect cluster. Next, let's deploy a test connector and try setting a client override. To set a consumer configuration, you have to prefix it with `consumer.override.`, for example, `consumer.override.fetch.min.bytes`. For this scenario, put the following configuration in a file called *file-sink.json*:

```
{
    "name": "file-sink",
    "connector.class": "org.apache.kafka.connect.file.FileStreamSinkConnector",
    "tasks.max": "1",
    "topics": "test",
    "file": "/tmp/sink.out",
    "value.converter": "org.apache.kafka.connect.storage.StringConverter",
    "consumer.override.fetch.min.bytes": "123"
}
```

Then attempt to start the connector with the following command:

```
$ curl -X PUT -H "Content-Type: application/json" \
-d @./config/file-sink.json \
localhost:8083/connectors/file-sink/config
```

This command fails and returns:

```
{
  "error_code": 400,
  "message": "Connector configuration is invalid and contains the following 1 err
or(s):\nThe 'Principal' policy does not allow 'fetch.min.bytes' to be overridden
in the connector configuration.\nYou can also find the above list of errors at th
e endpoint `/connector-plugins/{connectorType}/config/validate`"
}
```

We can see that the `Principal` client override policy rejected the connector configuration because it overrides a disallowed client setting, `fetch.min.bytes`.

If we replace `"consumer.override.fetch.min.bytes": "123"` with `"consumer.override.security.protocol": "PLAINTEXT"` in the connector configuration and try to start it again, it works:

```
$ curl -X PUT -H "Content-Type: application/json" \
-d @./config/file-sink.json \
localhost:8083/connectors/file-sink/config
{
  "name": "file-sink",
  "config": {
    "name": "file-sink",
    "connector.class": "org.apache.kafka.connect.file.FileStreamSinkConnector",
    "tasks.max": "1",
    "topics": "test",
    "file": "/tmp/sink.out",
    "value.converter": "org.apache.kafka.connect.storage.StringConverter",
    "consumer.override.security.protocol": "PLAINTEXT"
  },
  "tasks": [
    {
      "connector": "file-sink",
      "task": 0
    }
  ],
  "type": "sink"
}
```

As you can see, this is a useful way to provide tighter control over how different connectors on the same runtime can be configured.

Sizing and Planning Capacity

In order to effectively provision and allocate resources for setting up a Kafka Connect cluster, it's important to keep in mind how Kafka Connect spreads the workload across workers and tasks.

Tasks are the units that perform the work for connectors. Each task is basically composed of a Kafka client and a producer for source tasks or a consumer for sink tasks, combined with a client for an external system. The Kafka Connect runtime dynamically spreads tasks onto the available workers, so to make sure your cluster can support your workload, you need to make sure the workers have enough capacity to run these tasks. A Kafka Connect cluster can be scaled in two dimensions. It can be *scaled up* if administrators increase the capacity of the workers. It can also be *scaled out* if administrators increase the number of workers.

In this section we look at the resources that Kafka Connect uses, how to decide the number of tasks and workers you need, and how to combine these to inform sizing and planning decisions. We also discuss running a single Kafka Connect cluster versus multiple clusters.

Understanding Kafka Connect Resource Utilization

Kafka Connect does not require a minimum hardware configuration for workers, and it can start and run on a wide variety of hardware and virtual environments. In practice, however, and especially for production environments, it's useful to understand how Kafka Connect uses hardware resources to maximize its capacity and reliability while keeping costs at a minimum.

In distributed mode, Kafka Connect does not store any state locally on workers. Instead, all data is stored in its three internal topics in Kafka; this means that in order to deploy Kafka Connect, you only need just enough storage to store its logs and debugging artifacts, like verbose garbage collection (GC) logs and thread/heap dumps.

For the other main resources—CPU, memory, and network—as is the case most of the time with performance and sizing, the optimal configuration depends on your exact use cases. Let's look at the main factors that influence resource usage and performance:

Number of connectors and tasks
    Each connector and task uses resources, so the more you start, the more resources Kafka Connect will use.

Types of connectors
    Some connectors are more resource intensive than others. Resource consumption depends mostly on how connectors interact with the external system.

Enabled converters and transformations

Converters have to constantly serialize and deserialize data as it flows through Kafka Connect. Simple converters like `ByteArrayConverter` don't use a lot of resources because they effectively just forward raw bytes. On the other hand, converters that construct complex types, such as `AvroConverter`, use more CPU and memory. Each transformation that you add to your pipelines uses resources, mainly CPU in most cases.

Compression

Compressing messages uses CPU but allows you to reduce network usage. Compression can significantly improve throughput, but note that downstream systems will have to decompress data (and also use CPU) in order to use it.

Client configuration

Many client settings can impact performance. For example, if you have clients (for both Kafka and the external systems) that use TLS to encrypt data, you will be using extra CPU and memory.

There is often an important difference in the resource usage when a connector starts tasks, for example when starting up or rebalancing, compared to when it's running steadily. At startup, a connector might discover a huge backlog of records to flow through Kafka Connect and start processing them as fast as possible. For example, when you are sinking a topic that contains hundreds of gigabytes of data, the connector may have a much higher throughput than the regular incoming throughput. Only once the initial backlog is processed will Kafka Connect's throughput match the incoming throughput of the source.

Finally, in terms of capacity planning, you also need to consider the extra load that your Kafka Connect clusters add to both your Kafka cluster and external systems. This is especially important when sinking data out of Kafka. Kafka scales horizontally very well; for example, if you have a topic with 50 partitions, you can have up to 50 Kafka Connect sink tasks exporting data from it, each creating a client and connecting to the external system. For some systems, this can lead to a lot of contention if all tasks end up accessing the same entities in that system, such as a table in a database.

How Many Workers and Tasks?

In order to start sizing a use case, you need to estimate how much network throughput is required, in bytes per second. This is easy for sink connectors because the required throughput is the combined incoming byte rate of the input topics. For source connectors, the byte rate depends on the external system. Most systems expose metrics describing the rate of change on their resources; you can also use a test system to get a rough idea. (If you do this, use a test system that is as close as possible to what you intend to deploy in production.)

Once you have estimated network throughput for all the use cases you want to run on Kafka Connect, you can start thinking about the number of workers to have in the cluster. Regardless of capacity, in order to be resilient to worker failures and permit basic operations, you should always have at least two workers.

You need to compare your network throughput estimate with the worker capacity. For example, if you estimate that your use cases require 300 MB/s and each worker has 1 Gb/s network cards—hence 128 MB/s—you need a minimum of three workers. You should provision enough capacity to sustain this workload with a worker down or failing. This means you should either provision four workers or scale up and use workers with more network capacity; for example, if you upgraded to 2 Gb/s (256 MB/s) network cards, then three workers would be enough.

It's common for use cases to evolve and new use cases to appear, so you need to regularly review the capacity and number of workers in your clusters and monitor their resource usage via metrics. This enables you to notice when a worker approaches its capacity, then either increase its resources or add new workers to share the load. Kafka Connect emits a lot of metrics that enable you to gauge how each connector and task performs. We cover all these metrics in detail in Chapter 9.

With the worker count and specification sorted, you need to decide how many tasks each connector will run. Tasks enable splitting the workload into smaller chunks. With many connectors, it's possible to use a single task and have it handle the whole workload, but a single task can only run on a single worker. By increasing the number of tasks, we make the workload more granular so that it can be spread efficiently across more workers. In addition, with multiple tasks, the failure of a single task limits the failure's scope to only the resources that task is handling. However, more tasks also means more overhead, as each task has its own clients, each with their own connections and associated memory usage. You only control the maximum number of tasks, via `tasks.max`; connectors are free to start less based on their implementation.

First, for each connector you are running, you can work out the highest value you can set `tasks.max` to for that connector. For sink connectors, this corresponds to the number of partitions from the input topics—for example, when sinking data from three topics of 20 partitions each, a connector should only be configured with up to 60 tasks. For source connectors, it depends how the connector and external system work, so you should check their documentation.

The actual value you set `tasks.max` to is between 1 and the highest value possible for that connector. You should choose this by considering every connector that you want to run and making sure that each gets enough resources. One method to estimate a good value for `tasks.max` is to start with all connectors using a small value, then closely monitor the CPU, memory, and network usage of the worker. If all of these resources have spare capacity, you can bump `tasks.max` on one or more connectors and repeat the process.

Single cluster versus separate clusters

When scaling to handle larger or additional workloads, the first option is to add workers to an existing Kafka Connect cluster. This is a good starting point, and for many types of use cases, centralizing all data pipelines onto a single Kafka Connect cluster is the easiest and best solution. If the workload is fairly small, a single cluster with a few workers can easily handle it.

However, there are cases when you should consider splitting your workloads across multiple Kafka Connect clusters. Let's look at a few of the factors that you need to take into account when making this decision.

Maintainability

Any processes or tools you use have to connect and operate on all your clusters. This includes performing upgrades, applying security patches, and maintaining configuration, and scaling, but also includes all the monitoring via logs and metrics that enable site reliability engineers to operate the clusters. Having only a single cluster to maintain is easier.

Simplifying and reducing the number of maintenance operations also lowers the cost of ownership. Less hours are spent keeping clusters running and can be directed to improving or building new cases.

Isolation

Workloads on different clusters are better isolated because they can't directly interact with each other. This was very important when Kafka Connect only had the `eager` rebalance protocol, which triggers a rebalance of all connectors and tasks every time a connector is reconfigured. In clusters using `eager`, a single misbehaving connector can stop all workloads indefinitely. Now, with `sessioned` and `compatible` protocols, reconfigurations only affect the connector being reconfigured, keeping workloads a bit more isolated by default.

If you are running a set of connectors belonging to different teams, it may be preferable to run them on different clusters. Kafka Connect does not have a mechanism for allocating resources to a particular connector, so all connectors effectively contend to use them. In most cases, the operating system gives a fair share to each task (each task is executed in a thread), but depending on the configuration and the connectors used, that may not always be true.

The blast radius in a system indicates the number of affected workloads when a failure happens in that system. If you have a single Kafka Connect cluster and it goes offline, all of your workloads are affected. By having workloads spread across several environments, we can reduce the blast radius in case of failures.

Security

Another use case for having separate clusters is if a workload needs a specific security configuration (for example, for handling regulated data like medical or financial records). Such use cases usually require you to secure the REST API and access to the workers, and introduce some sort of auditing capabilities. If another team using this same cluster does not need these security measures, it may be annoying for them to follow these rules.

Use case optimization

Finally, some use cases benefit from a very specific configuration for performance, regulatory, or just functionality reasons. By default, with `connector.client.con` `fig.override.policy` set to `all`, the runtime enables users to provide specific client configurations to optimize connector behavior, so it's possible to run connectors with different settings—but this often makes tasks from different connectors behave very differently. While Kafka Connect automatically spreads tasks onto workers, it assumes all tasks are similar; when this is not the case, automatic task distribution can lead to very uneven loads on the workers. So for connectors requiring bespoke configurations, it may be preferable to run them in a purpose-built cluster.

Now that we have discussed the options for deploying a Kafka Connect cluster, let's look at what you need to do once it is running.

Operating Kafka Connect Clusters

To run a Kafka Connect cluster in production, you need to consider not only how to deploy it but also how to handle its ongoing operation. Although Kafka Connect can move tasks between workers, it does not include any logic to automatically scale workers or restart failed connectors. You need to create processes for these operational requirements as part of your system.

Since Kafka Connect is a very popular technology, there are plenty of tools available, so you needn't design your system from scratch. Rather than covering specific tools here, we walk you through the administrative steps. That way you can understand what steps you need to automate, or what actions a particular tool is taking in your cluster to achieve a specific goal.

To automate these processes yourself, you can use the Kafka Connect REST API or a dedicated command-line interface (CLI) tool like kcctl (*https://github.com/kcctl/kcctl*). Alternatively, if you are deploying on Kubernetes, you can make use of an operator to do the hard work for you. We discuss Kubernetes operators for Kafka Connect more in Chapter 10.

Let's look at the following actions that you might need to perform:

- Adding workers
- Removing workers
- Upgrading and applying maintenance to workers
- Restarting failed tasks and connectors
- Resetting offsets of connectors

Adding Workers

Whether you use a single cluster or multiple, one of the first tasks administrators perform is to start multiple workers and have them work together. You may want multiple workers to improve resiliency, or to increase the capacity of the cluster.

For a worker to join a Kafka Connect cluster, it needs to be able to connect to the following:

- The same Kafka cluster as the other workers
- All of the other workers on the host and port they expose via their advertised listener (which can be set using the `rest.advertised.listener`, `rest.adver tised.host`, and/or `rest.advertised.port` properties, and defaults to the value of the `listeners` setting if unset)
- All the external systems you want to connect to

Once you have a suitable environment, the runtime on this new worker needs to have some specific settings that match the other existing workers' runtimes:

- `group.id`
- `config.storage.topic`
- `offset.storage.topic`
- `status.storage.topic`
- `bootstrap.servers`

You should also ensure that any settings that affect the behavior of the runtime, such as timeouts and security, are configured the same way on all workers. Otherwise this could cause the whole cluster to behave erratically or even completely fail.

Once you have built a matching configuration, you can start the Kafka Connect runtime on the new worker:

```
$ ./bin/connect-distributed.sh ./config/connect-distributed.properties
```

If you have one or more connectors started—and assuming there are at least as many tasks as running workers—within a few minutes, some tasks should be assigned to this worker. You don't need to change the connector configuration to trigger this rebalance of workload. If you don't have any connectors, or there are fewer tasks than workers, the worker sits idle until it is needed. Once the worker is started, ensure your monitoring is picking it up and you are getting both metrics and logs.

Removing Workers

In case the workload decreases (or you move some of it to a separate cluster), you can also remove workers from a cluster. The process is extremely simple; you just need to shut down the Kafka Connect runtime on that worker. Kafka Connect automatically rebalances the tasks this worker was running onto other workers.

To stop the Kafka Connect process cleanly, you can send it a SIGQUIT signal. For example, once on the worker, find the Kafka Connect process:

```
$ ps -ef | grep ConnectDistributed
7152 ttys005    0:54.26 ... org.apache.kafka.connect.cli.ConnectDistributed ./con
fig/connect-distributed.properties
```

Then shut it down by sending SIGQUIT to the process ID:

```
$ kill -3 7152
```

Kafka Connect waits up to scheduled.rebalance.max.delay.ms milliseconds (by default, five minutes) before rebalancing the tasks this worker was running. Once all tasks have been reassigned to the remaining workers, this operation is complete.

Upgrading and Applying Maintenance to Workers

Once a cluster is running, the proper way for administrators to apply maintenance onto workers is via *rolling restarts*. A rolling restart means restarting a single worker at a time, and each time waiting for it to return before moving onto the next one. This allows you to keep disruption to a minimum. At the end of a rolling restart, all workers have been restarted once.

Administrators need to follow this process in order to upgrade the Kafka Connect runtime, plug-in JAR files, and any environment dependencies such as the JVM or the operating system. When upgrading the runtime, you should check the notable changes list from the upgrade section (*https://oreil.ly/wMqVM*) on the Kafka website. Kafka tries to maintain compatibility between releases, and this section mentions any changes that could affect your workload, as well as any new features. For each connector, you should check its documentation to verify whether new versions are compatible.

Before getting started, you need to identify the steps to perform while Kafka Connect is stopped in order to minimize downtime. You also need to estimate how long these steps will take you. If it takes longer than `scheduled.rebalance.max.delay.ms` (by default, five minutes), then Kafka Connect will reassign all tasks currently on this worker onto other workers. Kafka Connect automatically handles the reassignment, so this is not problematic, but it can significantly lengthen the overall duration of the operation, as you must wait for all tasks in the cluster to be reassigned to workers and restart before moving onto the next worker. If you need just a bit longer than the default `scheduled.rebalance.max.delay.ms` value, it may be worth slightly increasing this setting to avoid extra rebalances.

First, ensure that your Kafka Connect cluster is healthy and all tasks are running as expected. To do so, you can check the task metrics as described in Chapter 9 or check the status of all connectors via the REST API:

```
$ curl "localhost:8083/connectors?expand=status"
{
    "file-sink": {
    "status": {
        "name": "file-sink",
        "connector": {
            "state": "RUNNING",
            "worker_id": "192.168.1.12:8083"
        },
        "tasks": [{
            "id": 0,
            "state": "RUNNING",
            "worker_id": "192.168.1.12:8083"
        }],
        "type": "sink"
    }
    }
}
```

If everything is running, you can shut down the Kafka Connect process by sending it a `SIGQUIT` signal, like for removing a worker. Then you can perform the maintenance tasks you want. Once done, restart the Kafka Connect runtime:

```
$ ./bin/connect-distributed.sh ./config/connect-distributed.properties
```

Before moving onto the next worker, ensure that everything is running again.

Restarting Failed Tasks and Connectors

Like in every system, things can go wrong in Kafka Connect. If a task or a connector hits an unrecoverable error, it is stopped and put in the FAILED state. In that case, the administrator is responsible for investigating the failure and restarting any FAILED tasks and connectors.

Since the connector and tasks are separate threads, one might fail without affecting the others. For example, a task might fail because it can't access the external system, but the connector status is still RUNNING. This means you can't rely on the connector status alone to understand the health of your pipeline; you must also monitor the state of all the related tasks.

Kafka Connect emits metrics to track the state of all components, so you should rely on them to identify if any tasks or connectors have failed (we cover this in Chapter 9). If this happens, you can use the REST API to get detailed statuses for the relevant connector or tasks. For example, for a connector called file-source:

```
$ curl localhost:8083/connectors/file-source/status
{
  "name": "file-source",
  "connector": {
    "state": "RUNNING",
    "worker_id": "192.168.1.12:8083"
  },
  "tasks": [
    {
      "id": 0,
      "state": "FAILED",
      "worker_id": "192.168.1.12:8083",
      "trace": "org.apache.kafka.connect.errors.ConnectException: java.nio.file.A
ccessDeniedException: /tmp/source\n\tat
      ...
      java.base/java.util.concurrent.ThreadPoolExecutor$Worker.run(ThreadPoolExec
utor.java:635)\n\tat java.base/java.lang.Thread.run(Thread.java:833)\nCaused by:
java.nio.file.AccessDeniedException: /tmp/source\n\tat
      ...
      org.apache.kafka.connect.file.FileStreamSourceTask.poll(FileStreamSourceTas
k.java:91)\n\t... 9 more\n"
    }
  ],
  "type": "source"
}
```

In this example, the task with id=0 has failed and needs to be restarted. The trace field indicates the reason for the failure. In this case, the Kafka Connect runtime does not have permissions to access the file (AccessDeniedException). In most cases, you first need to address the root cause of the failure; if you simply restart the task, it will likely immediately hit the same issue and return to the FAILED state.

Once the cause of the failure has been identified and resolved, you can use the REST API to restart the task. Since Kafka 3.0.0, you can directly restart all failed components (connector and tasks) of a connector using the `POST /connectors/<NAME>/restart` endpoint:

```
$ curl -X POST \
  "localhost:8083/connectors/file-source/restart?includeTasks=true&onlyFailed=true"
```

This endpoint accepts two parameters:

`includeTasks`
> Defaults to `false`. When enabled, both the connector and its tasks are restarted.

`onlyFailed`
> Also defaults to `false`. When enabled, only components that are in the `FAILED` state are restarted.

Once restarted, recheck the detailed status of the connector to ensure that everything actually restarted correctly.

> Before Kafka 3.0.0, administrators had to restart connectors via `POST /connectors/<NAME>/restart` (without any parameters), and tasks one by one using the `POST /connectors/<NAME>/tasks/<TASK_ID>/restart` endpoint.

Resetting Offsets of Connectors

Connectors use the concept of offsets to identify their position in the data they are flowing through Kafka Connect. For sink connectors, the offsets are literally the offsets in the partitions it is consuming, and these are stored in a regular consumer group. For source connectors, the offsets are arbitrary mappings of keys and values generated by the connector, and these are stored in the topic specified via `offset.storage.topic`.

When a connector is deleted, the offsets it stored are not deleted. This is useful if you want to restart the connector later and have it carry on where it was, but it can cause problems if you want to restart the connector from scratch or if you don't plan to use this connector anymore. To prevent unexpected behavior when starting new connectors, you should manually delete the offsets. This allows you to safely reuse connector names. Before deleting any offsets, ensure the matching connector has been deleted using the REST API.

With KIP-875 (*https://oreil.ly/PWn-W*), the community added REST API endpoints to manage the offsets of connectors. Kafka 3.5.0 has an endpoint to list offsets of connectors. Endpoints to delete and reset offsets will be added in a later release. Until this is implemented, you need to follow the workarounds we describe in the next sections to reset offsets.

Sink connector offsets

Sink connector offsets can be deleted like any other committed offsets in Kafka by using the kafka-consumer-groups.sh tool to delete the related consumer group. The group name defaults to the connector name, prefixed with connect-.

For example, let's say we have a sink connector called file-sink and want to restart it from scratch. The consumer group for this connector is called connect-file-sink.

First, ensure the connector is deleted:

```
$ curl -X DELETE localhost:8083/connectors/file-sink
```

Then check the offsets committed for that group by running the following command and ensuring it shows that the group has no active members; otherwise, you will not be able to reset the offsets:

```
$ ./bin/kafka-consumer-groups.sh --bootstrap-server localhost:9092 \
  --describe \
  --group connect-file-sink

Consumer group 'connect-file-sink' has no active members.

GROUP              TOPIC            PARTITION  CURRENT-OFFSET  LOG-END-OFFSET ...
connect-file-sink  topic-to-export  0          210             210             ...
```

You can now delete the consumer group:

```
$ ./bin/kafka-consumer-groups.sh --bootstrap-server localhost:9092 \
  --group connect-file-sink \
  --delete \
  --execute
Deletion of requested consumer groups ('connect-file-sink') was successful.
```

Note that we can also adjust the offset by using kafka-consumer-groups.sh to commit a new value. For example, to reset the offset to 100:

```
$ ./bin/kafka-consumer-groups.sh --bootstrap-server localhost:9092 \
  --group connect-file-sink \
  --reset-offsets \
  --to-offset 100 \
  --topic topic-to-export \
  --execute
```

```
GROUP                  TOPIC                  PARTITION  NEW-OFFSET
connect-file-sink      topic-to-export        0          100
```

Finally, we can recreate our connector:

```
$ curl -X PUT -H "Content-Type: application/json" \
  -d "@file-sink.json" \
  localhost:8083/connectors/file-sink/config
```

Source connector offsets

Deleting source connector offsets is a bit more difficult, as we can't use Kafka consumer groups tools and instead need to directly interact with the offset topic from the Connect runtime.

Let's say we have a source connector running called `file-source`. First ensure the connector is deleted by running:

```
$ curl -X DELETE localhost:8083/connectors/file-source
```

We need to find which key Kafka Connect used for the offsets of our connector. To do so, we can use the `kafka-console-consumer.sh` tool:

```
$ ./bin/kafka-console-consumer.sh --bootstrap-server localhost:9092 \
  --topic connect-offsets \
  --from-beginning \
  --property print.key=true | grep file-source
["file-source",{"filename":"/tmp/source"}]    {"position":24}
["file-source",{"filename":"/tmp/source"}]    {"position":124}
```

Here, `connect-offsets` is the name of the offset topic specified in the Kafka Connect configuration using `offset.storage.topic`.

In addition to the connection settings, we use a few flags to display all the information we need:

`--property print.key=true`
> Prints the key of each record. The key contains the connector name and allows us to filter the specific connector we are interested in with `grep`.

`--from-beginning`
> Makes the consumer start from the beginning of the topic. Once our connector is stopped, it's not emitting new offsets, so we need to consume existing offset records.

Looking at the output, we are only interested in the last entry. It contains:

`["file-source",{"filename":"/tmp/source"}]`
> The record key. Take note of its value; we will need it to delete the offsets.

```
{"position":124}
```
The last offset our connector saved.

 The exact structure of the records in the offset topic depends on the connector. If you are using a different connector than the one in this example, it's likely that the key won't have the format you see here. Also, in this example, the connector always has a single task, and therefore a single key in the offset topic; other connectors might have multiple entries with different keys. If this is the case, you must reset each one.

The offset topic is a compacted topic, so in order to clear our offsets we need to send a tombstone record with the same key. Since Kafka 3.2.0, we can use the `kafka-console-producer.sh` tool to do so:

```
$ ./bin/kafka-console-producer.sh --bootstrap-server localhost:9092 \
  --topic connect-offsets \
  --property parse.key=true \
  --property null.marker=NULL \
  --property key.separator=#
>["file-source",{"filename":"/tmp/source"}]#NULL
```

Again, we use a few flags to get the desired behavior:

`--property parse.key=true`
Allows us to include a key in the message we produce.

`--property null.marker=NULL`
Defines the marker that will represent a `null` value in our message.

`--property key.separator=#`
Defines how the message key and value are separated.

The message we entered, `["file-source",{"filename":"/tmp/source"}]#NULL`, is a concatenation of the key we retrieved via the `kafka-console-consumer.sh` tool, the key separator, and the marker for `null`.

Note that we can also adjust the offset by producing a record with `{"position":<OFF SET>}` as the value, where `<OFFSET>` is the desired new offset. For example, to reset the offset to `100`:

```
>["file-source",{"filename":"/tmp/source"}]#{"position":100}
```

Finally, we can restart our connector:

```
$ curl -X PUT -H "Content-Type: application/json" \
  -d "@file-source.json" \
  localhost:8083/connectors/file-source/config
```

Before Kafka 3.2.0 (KIP-810 (*https://oreil.ly/ZJwY1*)), kafka-console-producer.sh was not able to produce tombstones, so you either needed to write a small program or use a third-party tool like kcat (*https://github.com/edenhill/kcat*) to reset offsets for source connectors.

Administering Kafka Connect Using the REST API

If you are administering a Kafka Connect pipeline, it's likely that you will want to use the REST API at some point. The REST API is primarily designed for managing the connectors and tasks that are running on the Kafka Connect cluster, although there are a few endpoints for more general purposes.

By default, the REST API is available on port 8083 and is not secured. In Chapter 8, we explain how to change the port and further configure the endpoint, e.g., to require authentication. The REST API expects all request bodies to use the content type application/json, and it sends all responses using that content type as well.

There isn't necessarily a clear separation between the owner of the Kafka Connect cluster and the owners of the individual connectors. This is noticeable when you look at the different endpoints offered. The REST API can be used by the administrator of the pipeline to control logging levels or see an overview of the status, or by individual data engineers who are responsible for just a single connector. This makes it even more important to secure your REST endpoint properly and control who can access it.

The Kafka documentation provides a reference guide (*https://oreil.ly/MVjuW*) that covers every endpoint. There is also an OpenAPI specification (*https://oreil.ly/rZyR-*) that describes all the return codes, as well as all the request and response schemas. To put each endpoint into context, let's discuss some operational scenarios that you will likely encounter while using Kafka Connect:

- Creating and deleting a connector
- Connector configuration
- Controlling the lifecycle of a connector
- Listing connector offsets
- Debugging issues

First, let's look at the API endpoints that you are most likely to need when first getting started with Kafka Connect, by examining how to create and delete a connector.

Creating and Deleting a Connector

Before starting any connector, you should check the version of your Kafka Connect cluster. This determines the features and options you are able to use and access. You can retrieve the version using the GET / endpoint:

```
$ curl localhost:8083
{
  "version": "3.5.0",
  "commit": "c97b88d5db4de28d",
  "kafka_cluster_id": "PSCn87RpRoqhfjAs9KYtuw"
}
```

Next, check what connector plug-ins are available in the Kafka Connect cluster. For that, use the GET /connector-plugins endpoint:

```
$ curl localhost:8083/connector-plugins
[{
    "class": "org.apache.kafka.connect.mirror.MirrorCheckpointConnector",
    "type": "source",
    "version": "3.5.0"
}, {
    "class": "org.apache.kafka.connect.mirror.MirrorHeartbeatConnector",
    "type": "source",
    "version": "3.5.0"
}, {
    "class": "org.apache.kafka.connect.mirror.MirrorSourceConnector",
    "type": "source",
    "version": "3.5.0"
}]
```

By default, this only lists the source and sink connector plug-ins that are installed in the Kafka Connect cluster. To discover other kinds of plug-ins—such as transformations, converters, and predicates that are installed—you can set the connectorsOnly query parameter to false:

```
$ curl "localhost:8083/connector-plugins?connectorsOnly=false"
```

 The connectorsOnly flag was added to Kafka in version 3.2 as part of KIP-769 (*https://oreil.ly/6yH6G*).

Now let's look at the endpoints for creating a connector. After Kafka Connect has started up, you can use the GET /connectors endpoint to see that no connectors are running yet:

```
$ curl localhost:8083/connectors
[]
```

To create your connector, you have two options: use a POST request to this /connec
tors endpoint, or use a PUT request using the connector name in the path. The body
of the request is slightly different for each endpoint, but both have the same effect.
The two code snippets that follow both result in a new FileStreamSink connector
called file-sink that reads records from the topic-to-export topic and writes them
to a file called */tmp/sink.out.*

Example PUT request:

```
$ curl -X PUT -H "Content-Type: application/json" \
  -d "@sink-config.json" \
  localhost:8083/connectors/file-sink/config
{
  "name":"file-sink",
  "config":{
    "connector.class":"org.apache.kafka.connect.file.FileStreamSinkConnector",
    "tasks.max":"1",
    "topics":"topic-to-export",
    "file":"/tmp/sink.out",
    "value.converter":"org.apache.kafka.connect.storage.StringConverter",
    "name":"file-sink"
  },
  "tasks":[],"type":"sink"
}
```

Where *sink-config.json* contains:

```
{
  "connector.class":"org.apache.kafka.connect.file.FileStreamSinkConnector",
  "tasks.max": "1",
  "topics": "topic-to-export",
  "file": "/tmp/sink.out",
  "value.converter": "org.apache.kafka.connect.storage.StringConverter"
}
```

Example POST request:

```
$ curl -X POST -H "Content-Type: application/json" \
  -d "@sink-config.json" \
  localhost:8083/connectors
```

Where *sink-config.json* contains:

```
{
  "name": "file-sink",
  "config": {
    "connector.class":"org.apache.kafka.connect.file.FileStreamSinkConnector",
    "tasks.max": "1",
    "topics": "topic-to-export",
    "file": "/tmp/sink.out",
    "value.converter": "org.apache.kafka.connect.storage.StringConverter"
  }
}
```

The output matches the one returned by the PUT request.

As you can see, an advantage of using the PUT request is that the configuration file is simpler as the config section isn't nested. You can also reuse the PUT request to update an existing connector.

Whichever option you choose, once you've created the connector you should now see the connector running:

```
$ curl localhost:8083/connectors
["file-sink"]
```

The GET /connectors endpoint lists only the names of the connectors in the cluster. To see more information about the connectors and their current status, you can use two query parameters. Calling GET /connectors?expand=info lists things like the configuration and any tasks, while GET /connectors?expand=status shows the status of the connector and related tasks.

You can also use these query parameters together:

```
$ curl "localhost:8083/connectors?expand=status&expand=info"
{
  "file-sink": {
    "status": {
      "name": "file-sink",
      "connector": {
        "state": "RUNNING",
        "worker_id": "192.168.1.110:8083"
      },
      "tasks": [
        {
          "id": 0,
          "state": "RUNNING",
          "worker_id": "192.168.1.110:8083"
        }
      ],
      "type": "sink"
    },
    "info": {
      "name": "file-sink",
      "config": {
        "connector.class":
          "org.apache.kafka.connect.file.FileStreamSinkConnector",
        "file": "/tmp/sink.out",
        "tasks.max": "1",
        "topics": "topic-to-export",
        "name": "file-sink",
        "value.converter": "org.apache.kafka.connect.storage.StringConverter"
      },
      "tasks": [
        {
          "connector": "file-sink",
```

```
          "task": 0
        }
      ],
      "type": "sink"
    }
  }
}
```

If you want to find out the status of a specific connector rather than all connectors at once, there are a few different endpoints available for you to use. These are:

GET /connectors/<CONNECTOR>/status
: To see the status for a specific connector

GET /connectors/<CONNECTOR>/tasks
: To see tasks for a specific connector

GET /connectors/<CONNECTOR>/tasks/<TASK_ID>/status
: To see status of a task for a specific connector

You can see these in action for the connector we just created:

```
$ curl localhost:8083/connectors/file-sink/status
{
  "name": "file-sink",
  "connector": {
    "state": "RUNNING",
    "worker_id": "192.168.1.110:8083"
  },
  "tasks": [
    {
      "id": 0,
      "state": "RUNNING",
      "worker_id": "192.168.1.110:8083"
    }
  ],
  "type": "sink"
}
$ curl localhost:8083/connectors/file-sink/tasks
[
  {
    "id": {
      "connector": "file-sink",
      "task": 0
    },
    "config": {
      "file": "/tmp/sink.out",
      "task.class": "org.apache.kafka.connect.file.FileStreamSinkTask",
      "topics": "topic-to-export"
    }
  }
]
```

```
$ curl localhost:8083/connectors/file-sink/tasks/0/status
{
  "id": 0,
  "state": "RUNNING",
  "worker_id": "192.168.1.110:8083"
}
```

As an administrator of a Kafka Connect pipeline, it can be useful to understand which topics a particular connector has interacted with. For sink connectors, the topic is listed in the configuration, but you can use regular expressions such as sink-.*, which makes it harder to get an exact list. For source connectors, this problem is even greater, since the topics they interact with vary from connector to connector. Some source connectors expect you to specify a topic, while others choose one based on the name of resources in the external system.

To help with this, Kafka Connect provides a mechanism to allow you to discover every topic that a connector has interacted with: GET /connectors/<CONNECTOR>/top ics. For example, for the file-sink connector we just created, you can see the single topic it has interacted with:

```
$ curl localhost:8083/connectors/file-sink/topics
{
  "file-sink": {
    "topics": [
      "topic-to-export"
    ]
  }
}
```

You can reset this list so that Kafka Connect will "forget" previous interactions using the PUT /connectors/<CONNECTOR>/topics/reset endpoint:

```
$ curl -X PUT localhost:8083/connectors/file-sink/topics/reset
```

If you check the topic list again, you can see that it's now empty:

```
$ curl localhost:8083/connectors/file-sink/topics
{
  "file-sink": {
    "topics": []
  }
}
```

> This topic tracking feature was added in Kafka 2.5.0 as part of KIP-558 (*https://oreil.ly/EqF3w*).

The final action you are likely to need to take in a simple deployment is deleting a connector. You can do that using the following, where file-sink is the name of the connector:

```
$ curl -X DELETE localhost:8083/connectors/file-sink
```

 When a connector is deleted, all tasks underneath it are also removed. However, the offsets for the connector aren't reset; that means if a new connector is created with the same name, it will start trying to read using those offsets. To protect against this, it is best practice to reset offsets for the connector once it is deleted. This is especially important for source connectors, since those offsets are stored in a compacted topic and Kafka will never clean these up. Sink offsets will get reset eventually by Kafka, since they are normal consumer offsets, but it is best not to rely on this behavior. You can do this using the steps we described earlier in this chapter.

Now that we've looked at creating and deleting connectors, let's review the other endpoints that are available, starting with connector and task configuration.

Connector and Task Configuration

The REST API provides options to help you list and validate configuration settings for a specific plug-in, as well as view and update the configuration of a running connector.

For example, you can get a list of the configuration settings for FileStreamSink Connector like this:

```
$ curl localhost:8083/connector-plugins/org.apache.kafka.connect.file.FileStreamS
inkConnector/config
[
  {
    "name": "file", ❶
    "type": "STRING", ❷
    "required": false, ❸
    "default_value": null, ❹
    "importance": "HIGH", ❺
    "documentation": "Destination filename. If not specified, the standard output
will be used", ❻
    "group": null, ❼
    "width": "NONE", ❽
    "display_name": "file", ❾
    "dependents": [], ❿
    "order": -1 ⓫
  }
]
```

❶ Name of this configuration setting.

❷ Expected type of the configuration value, one of BOOLEAN, STRING, INT, SHORT, LONG, DOUBLE, LIST, CLASS, PASSWORD.

❸ Indicates whether this configuration value is required.

❹ The default value; if required is true, this defaults to null.

❺ The importance level of the configuration setting. One of HIGH, MEDIUM, LOW.

❻ Information about the configuration setting.

❼ Indicates which group this configuration setting belongs to. Plug-ins may introduce their own groups for their own settings.

❽ The width of the configuration setting. One of NONE, SHORT, MEDIUM, LONG.

❾ The display name for the configuration setting; this may match the name.

❿ List of other configuration settings that depend on this setting.

⓫ The integer order number of the configuration value. -1 if not set.

As you can see, there are a lot of fields for a specific setting. The values for these fields are set by the plug-in author, so not all plug-ins have all fields set. They can be very useful if set, but don't rely on them always being present.

 The ability to list configuration options for connectors was introduced in Kafka 3.2 via KIP-769 (*https://oreil.ly/hbb_4*) in April 2022. Prior to this release, the only way to list them was through a validation request.

Once you have decided what configuration to use, you can validate it using a PUT request to /connector-plugins/<CONNECTOR_PLUGIN>/config/validate. This endpoint validates the connector-specific configuration and any generic configurations like name or tasks.max that are required for all connectors. Let's see an example with FileStreamSinkConnector if we miss the connector name from the configuration:

```
$ curl -X PUT -H "Content-Type: application/json" \
  -d '{"connector.class": "org.apache.kafka.connect.file.FileStreamSinkConnector"
, "tasks.max": "1", "topics": "sink-topic"}' \
  localhost:8083/connector-plugins/org.apache.kafka.connect.file.FileStreamSinkCo
nnector/config/validate
```

```
{
  "name": "org.apache.kafka.connect.file.FileStreamSinkConnector", ❶
  "error_count": 1, ❷
  "groups": [ ❸
    "Common",
    "Transforms",
    "Predicates",
    "Error Handling"
  ],
  "configs": [
    {
      "definition": { ❹
        "name": "name",
        "type": "STRING",
        "required": true,
        "default_value": null,
        "importance": "HIGH",
        "documentation": "Globally unique name to use...",
        "group": "Common",
        "width": "MEDIUM",
        "display_name": "Connector name",
        "dependents": [],
        "order": 1
      },
      "value": {
        "name": "name", ❺
        "value": null, ❻
        "recommended_values": [], ❼
        "errors": [ ❽
          "Missing required configuration \"name\" which has no default value."
        ],
        "visible": true ❾
      }
    },
    ...
  ]
}
```

❶ Name of the class that provides the plug-in.

❷ Count of errors that were found while validating the provided configuration.

❸ Groups that are present in the configuration settings returned.

❹ The definition of this configuration setting. Matches the output from the /connector-plugins/<CONNECTOR_PLUGIN>/config endpoint.

❺ Name of this configuration setting.

❻ The value provided for the configuration setting, null if not provided.

❼ Valid values for the configuration setting, given the other configuration values provided.

❽ An empty array if no error, or an array of error messages regarding why this value was not acceptable for the configuration setting.

❾ Indicates whether this configuration value should be listed.

When validating source connectors, you must provide the `connector.class` configuration in the request body. For sink connectors, both `connector.class` and one of `topics` or `topics.regex` must be present. Currently, you can't validate converters, transformations, or predicates using this endpoint. KIP-802 (*https://oreil.ly/X9N2n*) has been proposed to address this in a future release.

 You might see examples where the `/connector-plugins` endpoint is used with a shortened class name like `FileStreamSinkConnector` or even `FileStreamSink` instead of the fully qualified class name. This is referred to as an *alias*.

We have already mentioned that you can use the `/config` endpoint to create and update the configuration for a specific connector. This endpoint can also be used to check the current configuration of an existing connector:

```
$ curl localhost:8083/connectors/file-sink/config
{
    "connector.class": "org.apache.kafka.connect.file.FileStreamSinkConnector",
    "file": "/tmp/sink.out",
    "tasks.max": "1",
    "topics": "topic-to-export",
    "name": "file-sink",
    "value.converter": "org.apache.kafka.connect.storage.StringConverter"
}
```

Whereas the configuration of a connector is fully specified both when creating and updating it, the task configuration isn't. An individual connector will take the connector configuration and generate the configuration for the individual tasks. This configuration could be identical, or it could depend on other runtime information. Because of this generation process, it can be useful to check the configuration of individual connector tasks.

You can do this using the GET `/connectors/<CONNECTOR>/tasks` endpoint:

```
$ curl localhost:8083/connectors/file-sink/tasks
[
  {
    "id": {
      "connector": "file-sink",
      "task": 0
    },
    "config": {
      "connector.class":
        "org.apache.kafka.connect.file.FileStreamSinkConnector",
      "file": "/tmp/sink.out",
      "task.class": "org.apache.kafka.connect.file.FileStreamSinkTask",
      "tasks.max": "1",
      "topics": "topic-to-export",
      "name": "file-sink",
      "value.converter": "org.apache.kafka.connect.storage.StringConverter"
    }
  }
]
```

As you can see, the configuration for this task is identical to the connector configuration. If you run, for example, one of the MirrorMaker connectors, this is not the case.

Now let's look at how you can control the lifecycle of a connector.

Controlling the Lifecycle of Connectors

In "Operating Kafka Connect Clusters" on page 183, we covered the steps to restart failed tasks and connectors. You can restart all failed tasks in a specific connector:

```
$ curl -X POST \
"localhost:8083/connectors/file-source/restart?includeTasks=true&onlyFailed=true"
```

You can also pause or stop a running connector. This is useful if you want to temporarily stop a connector from flowing data, but want to be able to resume it later from where it left off. This could be to give your external systems a break if they are getting overwhelmed, or to apply some maintenance to the external system (such as updating its configuration) and don't want any traffic during that time.

The difference between PAUSED and STOPPED is that in the STOPPED state, all tasks are shut down so they don't use resources. This means it takes less time for a connector to resume from the PAUSED state than from the STOPPED state.

To pause a running connector, use the PUT `/connectors/<CONNECTOR>/pause` endpoint. For example, for a connector called file-sink, you can pause by running:

```
$ curl -X PUT localhost:8083/connectors/file-sink/pause
```

The status endpoint now shows the connector and all tasks in a PAUSED state:

```
$ curl localhost:8083/connectors/file-sink/status
{
  "name": "file-sink",
  "connector": {
    "state": "PAUSED",
    "worker_id": "192.168.1.110:8083"
  },
  "tasks": [
    {
      "id": 0,
      "state": "PAUSED",
      "worker_id": "192.168.1.110:8083"
    }
  ],
  "type": "sink"
}
```

To resume the connector, you use a similar command, but with `resume` instead of `pause`:

```
$ curl -X PUT localhost:8083/connectors/file-sink/resume
```

The status of the connector and tasks returns to the RUNNING state.

Since Kafka 3.5.0, you can also completely stop a connector using the PUT /connec
tors/<CONNECTOR>/stop endpoint. For example, for a connector called file-sink,
you can stop it by running:

```
$ curl -X PUT localhost:8083/connectors/file-sink/stop
```

The status endpoint now shows the connector in a STOPPED state:

```
$ curl localhost:8083/connectors/file-sink/status
{
  "name": "file-sink",
  "connector": {
    "state": "STOPPED",
    "worker_id": "192.168.1.110:8083"
  },
  "tasks": [],
  "type": "sink"
}
```

Once stopped, you also use the PUT /connectors/<CONNECTOR>/resume endpoint to
return to the RUNNING state.

Listing Connector Offsets

The GET /connectors/<CONNECTOR>/offsets endpoint lists the offsets for a particular connector. This was added to Kafka in 3.5.0 under KIP-875 (*https://oreil.ly/iaHkd*).
Future versions of Kafka Connect will include endpoints to alter and reset offsets.

The format of the response from this endpoint is different for source and sink connectors. If you call the endpoint for a connector with no committed offsets, you get back an empty list:

```
$ curl localhost:8083/connectors/file-sink/offsets
{"offsets": []}
```

Let's look at the output when running a sink connector. The keys in the response are identical for all sink connectors; for example, when running the FileStreamSink connector, you might get:

```
$ curl localhost:8083/connectors/file-sink/offsets
{
  "offsets": [
    {
      "partition": {
        "kafka_partition": 0,      ❶
        "kafka_topic": "topic-to-export"      ❷
      },
      "offset": {
        "kafka_offset": 3      ❸
      }
    }
  ]
}
```

❶ In this example, the connector has a single partition, 0.

❷ The connector is consuming records from the topic-to-export topic.

❸ The connector has consumed up to offset 3.

The output for source connectors is slightly different, and varies depending on the specific connector. For example, when running the FileStreamSource connector, you might see the following:

```
$ curl localhost:8083/connectors/file-source/offsets
{
  "offsets": [
    {
      "partition": {
        "filename": "/tmp/source.txt"
      },
      "offset": {
        "position": 41
      }
    }
  ]
}
```

The `offsets`, `partition`, and `offset` keys are common to all source connectors, but the contents inside the `partition` and `offset` JSON objects are determined by the individual connector. In this case, the `FileStreamSource` connector stores its partitions as `{"filename": "/path/to/file"}` and its offsets as `{"position": <BYTES>}`, where <BYTES> is the number of bytes in the file that have been read.

Debugging Issues

When investigating and debugging issues with Kafka Connect, it's crucial to use logs from the runtime or connectors to peek into their inner workings. Kafka Connect exposes a couple of endpoints under `/admin` to enable administrators to view and update logger levels at runtime.

You can use `GET /admin/loggers` to see the current log levels:

```
$ curl localhost:8083/admin/loggers
{
  "org.apache.zookeeper": {
    "level": "ERROR"
  },
  "org.reflections": {
    "level": "ERROR"
  },
  "root": {
    "level": "INFO"
  }
}
```

Let's say we're investigating issues with one of the MirrorMaker connectors, `MirrorSourceConnector`. This connector is in the `org.apache.kafka.connect.mirror` package. With the default loggers, it uses the `root` appender and only logs at the `INFO` level, but we can switch it to a more verbose level to get more detail. To do so we can, for example, use the `PUT /admin/loggers/<LOGGER>` endpoint:

```
$ curl -X PUT -H "Content-Type: application/json" \
  -d '{"level": "DEBUG"}' \
  localhost:8083/admin/loggers/org.apache.kafka.connect.mirror
[
  "org.apache.kafka.connect.mirror",
  "org.apache.kafka.connect.mirror.MirrorCheckpointConnector",
  "org.apache.kafka.connect.mirror.MirrorSourceConnector"
]
```

From the least to the most verbose, the valid log levels are FATAL, ERROR, WARN, INFO, DEBUG, and TRACE.

If we list loggers again, we can see the new loggers we just added:

```
$ curl localhost:8083/admin/loggers
{
  "org.apache.kafka.connect.mirror": {
    "level": "DEBUG"
  },
  "org.apache.kafka.connect.mirror.MirrorCheckpointConnector": {
    "level": "DEBUG"
  },
  "org.apache.kafka.connect.mirror.MirrorSourceConnector": {
    "level": "DEBUG"
  },
  "org.apache.zookeeper": {
    "level": "ERROR"
  },
  "org.reflections": {
    "level": "ERROR"
  },
  "root": {
    "level": "INFO"
  }
}
```

Once you have finished debugging any issues, make sure you change the log levels back to INFO; otherwise, your log will be diluted with these messages and it might be difficult to diagnose problems in other connectors. You should avoid changing the root log level if possible, and instead always configure more specific loggers. That way you can see the exact log lines that will help debug your issue.

Summary

In this chapter, we introduced the core concepts that administrators need to understand to run Kafka Connect clusters in production. Kafka Connect is a runtime, and while it can run anywhere Java is installed, administrators have to carefully consider how they deploy and run it. Administrators are responsible for picking a deployment model and integrating Kafka Connect into their environments.

We also looked at the worker plug-ins that administrators can use to customize their Kafka Connect runtimes. Configuration providers are easy to use and useful in most deployments. REST extensions are typically used in more advanced use cases where specific security measures are required. Connector client configuration policies let administrators impose restrictions on the way connectors are configured.

Then we explained how administrators should size their Kafka Connect environments by describing how Kafka Connect uses resources such as CPU, memory, and network. We saw how estimating the total throughput required helps determine the number of workers to deploy and how to decide the maximum number of tasks that each connector should run.

We walked through the most common operations that administrators have to perform when maintaining a Kafka Connect cluster. Administrators typically use tools or automation to perform these, but it's important to understand how they work under the covers to effectively operate workers.

Finally, we explored all the endpoints of the REST API by highlighting some operational scenarios. In addition to managing connectors, the REST API is a powerful tool for administrators to perform day-to-day operations.

CHAPTER 8

Configuring Kafka Connect

Throughout this book, we mention configuration settings that can be used to customize Kafka Connect. All of these settings are documented on the Apache Kafka website (*https://oreil.ly/HxIEf*), where you can find their names, types, default values, and descriptions.

In this chapter, we go over all the configuration settings and provide additional context to help you identify the key settings to be aware of. We also show how some of these configurations can be combined to achieve the behaviors required for more advanced use cases.

We first look at the runtime, from its most basic configurations that are necessary to start it to more specific settings that affect the behavior of connectors. We then look at configuring connectors, again starting from the basics and then covering more advanced concepts like client overrides and error handling. Finally, we look at all the configurations available to secure Kafka Connect clusters for production use cases.

In this chapter, we refer to both "runtime configuration" and "worker configuration." Since a worker is really just a single instance of the runtime, these terms are somewhat interchangeable. However, we aim to use "runtime configuration" when talking generically about how configuration affects the Kafka Connect runtime and "worker configuration" when talking about the specific configuration that you use to start a worker.

Since we recommend using distributed mode for production clusters, we don't specifically call out the configurations that aren't used in standalone mode. As a general rule, anything that configures connections between workers doesn't apply for standalone mode. There is only one configuration that is unique to standalone mode: `offset.storage.file.filename`. This configuration specifies the file that the standalone runtime uses to store offsets of source tasks.

Configuring the Runtime

The first set of configurations you should know are those that are required by the runtime to start up:

`bootstrap.servers`
> The address of the Kafka cluster the worker connects to; this setting takes a list. You should always either set it to multiple brokers or use the hostname of a redundant load balancer, so that Kafka Connect is able to reach Kafka even if a broker is down.

`group.id`
> The ID used by a Kafka Connect worker to join the cluster. This value must not collide with existing groups (consumer or otherwise) in this Kafka cluster, otherwise it will lead to errors such as `InconsistentGroupProtocolException`.

`key.converter` *and* `value.converter`
> The default converters the runtime provides to connectors. These configurations have no default value, so you need to explicitly set them. The last converter, `header.converter`, is set to `SimpleHeaderConverter` by default. We discussed the impact of converters in more detail in Chapter 4. Whatever you set them to, make sure the runtime has both the default converters and any converters used by specific connectors installed. We explain in "Configurations for Production" on page 212 how connectors can override these values to configure their own converters.

The last set of mandatory settings are for Kafka Connect internal topics. Each Kafka Connect cluster must use different names for its internal topics. You must specify the names of the three topics using these configurations:

- `offset.storage.topic`
- `config.storage.topic`
- `status.storage.topic`

You can also specify the replication factor of each topic by configuring the following settings:

- `offset.storage.replication.factor`
- `config.storage.replication.factor`
- `status.storage.replication.factor`

By default, the replication factors are all set to 3, which is a good value for ensuring durability. In development environments with a single broker, you need to change the replication factor for all three topics to either -1, to use the broker default, or explicitly to 1 if you are running a version older than Kafka 2.4.

Finally, you can set the number of partitions for the offset and status topics with `offset.storage.partitions` and `status.storage.partitions`. Both of these have good default values (25 and 5, respectively) and you should only consider increasing them if you have a very large Kafka Connect cluster with dozens of workers. On the other hand, the config topic requires a single partition, and this is not configurable. For all three topics, you can also specify any other topic configurations (*https://oreil.ly/vmXWT*) (apart from `cleanup.policy`, which is always set to `compact`) by prefixing the configuration with `status.storage.`, `offset.storage.`, or `config.storage.`. For example, to set `min.insync.replicas` to 2 on the status topic, you can use `status.storage.min.insync.replicas=2`.

The next three configurations are not mandatory, but we recommend always using them in all environments:

`client.id`
    This setting has no functional impact, but it is useful for monitoring and debugging. You should set a unique value to each worker so you can easily match logs and metrics to each worker instance.

`plugin.path`
    You should install connector and worker plug-ins using this configuration instead of adding them directly to the JVM classpath or the `libs` directory. Using `plugin.path` provides classpath isolation and avoids conflicts between libraries loaded by different plug-ins.

`config.providers`
    Configuration providers have to be explicitly enabled in order to be used for resolving configurations at runtime. This setting takes a comma-separated list of labels. Each label needs to be associated with a class that implements the `org.apache.kafka.common.config.provider.ConfigProvider` interface by using the following syntax: `config.providers.<LABEL>.class=<CLASS>`. You need to make sure these classes are located in a path included in `plugin.path`. You can see an example of this in action in Chapter 7.

If you want to run multiple Kafka Connect clusters connected to the same Kafka cluster, you need to make sure that each Kafka Connect cluster uses unique values for the `group.id`, `offset.storage.topic`, `config.storage.topic`, and `status.storage.topic` settings.

 If you are running multiple Kafka Connect workers on the same machine (either as part of the same cluster, or different clusters), you also need to change the `listeners` setting to avoid port clashes in the REST API, as described later in this chapter.

Now that you know the configurations that are required for getting started, let's look at the configuration settings you need before deploying to production.

Configurations for Production

In this section, we go over all the settings that you should be aware of when configuring a Kafka Connect cluster for production. Most of these settings have good default values, so you don't need to configure them all. Instead, you must understand the options Kafka Connect provides and focus on the settings that matter for your specific requirements. In addition to learning about these settings, be sure to check "Configuring Kafka Connect Clusters for Security" on page 230, which details how to secure Kafka Connect clusters.

We talk about configurations in three categories:

- Clients and connector overrides
- REST configurations
- Miscellaneous configurations

Clients and connector overrides

The runtime runs a consumer for each sink task and a producer for each source task. It also runs admin clients for source tasks that require topics to be created or when exactly-once support is enabled, and for sink tasks that use dead letter queues. For exactly-once source connectors and tasks, it also runs a consumer to read their offsets. You can change the configuration of these clients by including the desired client settings with the appropriate prefix, `consumer.` for consumers, `producer.` for producers, and `admin.` for admin clients.

For example, if you want producers for source tasks to compress records with Gzip, you can add `producer.compression.type=gzip` to your runtime configuration.

Sometimes, users may want to customize individual connector clients further. Overriding client configuration at the connector level can be useful in very advanced use cases. For example, a connector could interact with a different Kafka cluster than the one configured in the Kafka Connect runtime by overriding `bootstrap.servers` in the connector configuration. As a runtime administrator, you might want to restrict the client configurations that connectors can set by using a connector client configuration override policy, which you can do by setting `connector.client.config.override.policy`. (We detail how these policies work and their defaults in Chapter 7.) The default policy, `All`, allows connectors to override all client configurations. Since some login modules may be insecure, you can prevent particular modules from being used via the `org.apache.kafka.disallowed.login.modules` system property. This property defaults to `com.sun.security.auth.module.JndiLoginModule` since Kafka 3.4.

The Kafka Connect runtime internally uses a few Kafka clients to manage its state and interact with its internal topics. The configurations of these clients can be modified by directly including producer, consumer, or admin client settings in the runtime configuration. Because of the role of these clients, the runtime prevents you from overriding some fields, such as the serializers and deserializers. For most production use cases, it only makes sense to change a few client configurations. In environments where Kafka Connect is deployed alongside Kafka across multiple racks or data centers, one useful client configuration to change is `client.rack`. By setting this, you allow internal consumers to fetch from a broker located in the same rack if there is one available.

REST configurations

The next set of configurations for production are for the REST API. By default, the `listeners` configuration is set to `http://:8083`. This means the REST API is accessible via HTTP on the default network interface (typically `localhost`) at port 8083. This setting accepts a list of values so that Kafka Connect can be configured to listen on multiple interfaces and ports. Kafka Connect can be configured to also accept HTTPS traffic; this is described in the last section of this chapter, "Securing the REST API" on page 239.

The REST API has a subset of endpoints that are all under `/admin`. These endpoints are only meant to be used by site reliability engineers (SREs), in contrast to the other endpoints that are typically used by both SREs and data engineers when building pipelines. By default, the `/admin` endpoints are exposed on the same listeners as all other endpoints. Kafka Connect allows you to separate them to dedicated listeners so you can easily provide finer-grained access controls to these endpoints. This is done using the `admin.listeners` setting, which if set to an empty string disables these endpoints.

For both `listeners` and `admin.listeners`, when the hostname is omitted (like in the `listeners` default value), Kafka Connect listens on the default network interface. To listen on a specific interface, you need to use its IP address, or you can use `0.0.0.0` to listen on all interfaces.

As we explain in Chapter 7, workers communicate with each other using the REST API—for example, using the `PUT /<CONNECTOR>/tasks` endpoint. To do this, they advertise their REST API hostname, port, and protocol to other workers when they join the cluster. By default, this advertised listener is the first listener in the `listeners` list. However, in many network environments, the interface a worker listens on is not directly accessible to other workers; this is the case when running on infrastructure such as containers or Kubernetes. In this scenario, the worker must advertise a listener that is different from the one they are listening on. You can customize the advertised hostname, port, and protocol using `rest.advertised.host.name`, `rest.advertised.port`, and `rest.advertised.listener`, respectively. The `admin.listeners` configuration does not have a matching advertised configuration because it is not used for inter-worker communication.

Combining all of these REST configurations, a worker might have runtime configuration containing the following:

```
listeners=http://:8093 ❶
admin.listeners=http://:9093 ❷
rest.advertised.host.name=connect-worker-1 ❸
rest.advertised.port=18093 ❸
rest.advertised.listener=https ❸
```

❶ For all non-admin endpoints, the worker listens on its default interface on port 8093.

❷ The `/admin` endpoints are served on port 9093, also on the default interface.

❸ The worker advertises `https://connect-worker-1:18093` to other workers. For this configuration to work in practice, you would need another network component listening on 18093, terminating TLS and forwarding the requests to the 8093 port. In a Kubernetes environment, you typically achieve this with a sidecar container or a service mesh.

To further customize the REST API, you can use `rest.extension.classes` to enable REST extensions. This setting accepts a comma-separated list of fully qualified class names that implement the `org.apache.kafka.connect.rest.ConnectRestExtension` interface. These classes must be located in a path included in `plugin.path`. We discuss typical use cases for REST extensions in Chapter 7.

Miscellaneous configuration

The following settings don't fall under client overrides or REST configurations, but they are still important to consider when you start running Kafka Connect in production:

`metric.reporters`
Whenever you are running Kafka Connect, you should set up a system to collect its metrics so that you can monitor it. Like all the other Kafka clients, Kafka Connect can use metric reporters to expose its metrics to monitoring systems such as Prometheus or Graphite. This setting takes a comma-separated list of classes that implement the `org.apache.kafka.common.metrics.MetricsReporter` interface to let you specify reporters. By default, Kafka Connect always exposes its metrics via the Java Management Extensions (JMX) API, even if this configuration is empty.

`auto.include.jmx.reporter`
Since Kafka 3.3, it is possible to disable the JMX metrics reporter by setting this configuration to `false` (the default is `true`). This setting has been deprecated, and as of Kafka 4.0, only reporters listed in `metric.reporters` are enabled.

`scheduled.rebalance.max.delay.ms`
The maximum duration a worker can leave the cluster before a rebalance is triggered and its tasks are moved to other workers (defaults to `300000`, which is five minutes). You should time how long you take to restart a worker in production and set this to a slightly longer duration than that. That way, doing a rolling restart of your Kafka Connect cluster will not trigger unnecessary task reassignments. Note that this setting is only applied when incremental cooperative rebalancing is enabled by setting `connect.protocol` to either `compatible` or `sessioned`. Incremental cooperative rebalancing is enabled by default since 2.3.

`exactly.once.source.support`
Whether exactly-once semantics support for source connectors is enabled or not. The default value for this configuration is `disabled`. If you have existing workers with the default configuration of `disabled`, you can't switch them straight to `enabled`. First, you must change each worker to have `exactly.once.source.support` set to `preparing`. Then you can go back through each worker in the cluster and update the configuration to `enabled`.

Kafka Connect exposes a lot of configurations. Fortunately, for most use cases many of them can be left untouched and keep their default values. However, there are cases where you might set them, so we discuss them for the sake of completeness.

Fine-Tuning Configurations

The following configurations are very situational, and administrators typically only set them for very specific reasons, such as performance or compatibility. If you want to use any of these, review the documentation to make sure you are using it correctly. We have grouped these into five categories:

- Connection configurations
- Inter-worker and rebalance configurations
- Topic tracking configurations
- Metrics configurations
- Offset flush configurations

Connection configurations

There are a number of configurations to fine-tune the connections between Kafka Connect and Kafka. These are the same configurations you find on other Kafka clients, such as the consumer or producer. They apply to the internal Kafka clients used by Kafka Connect, and you configure them using the `producer.`, `consumer.`, or `admin.` prefixes:

`client.dns.lookup`
  How Kafka Connect uses DNS records returned when looking up hostnames in `bootstrap.servers`. The default since 2.6 is `use_all_dns_ips`, so if a hostname resolves to multiple IP addresses, Kafka Connect tries using them, one at a time, until it connects to the Kafka cluster.

`connections.max.idle.ms`
  The duration Kafka Connect keeps a connection to the Kafka cluster alive if there is no traffic.

`request.timeout.ms`
  The duration Kafka Connect waits for a response from the Kafka cluster after it has sent a request. Once the limit is reached, Kafka Connect retries sending the request.

`retry.backoff.ms`
  The duration Kafka Connect waits before retrying sending a request.

`metadata.max.age.ms`
  How often Kafka Connect refreshes its metadata. For example, if partitions are added to a topic, Kafka Connect detects them no more than `metadata.max.age.ms` later.

`reconnect.backoff.ms` *and* `reconnect.backoff.max.ms`
> These two settings control the initial duration and maximum duration Kafka Connect waits before reconnecting if the connection to the Kafka cluster has dropped.

`socket.connection.setup.timeout.ms` *and* `socket.connection.setup.time`
`out.max.ms`
> These two settings control the initial duration and maximum duration Kafka Connect can take setting up its connection to the Kafka cluster before it gives up.

`receive.buffer.bytes` *and* `send.buffer.bytes`
> The sizes of the TCP receive (SO_RCVBUF) and send (SO_SNDBUF) buffers.

Inter-worker and rebalance configurations

There are a few settings that configure how workers cooperate to form the Kafka Connect cluster:

`connect.protocol`
> The protocol workers use to cooperate and spread the workload among themselves. Since Kafka 2.4, this defaults to `sessioned`, which provides incremental cooperative rebalancing and inter-worker security.

`heartbeat.interval.ms`
> Workers, like consumers in a group, have to heartbeat regularly to the coordinator to notify it that they are part of the Kafka Connect cluster. This controls how often each worker sends its heartbeats.

`rebalance.timeout.ms`
> The maximum duration allowed for workers to rejoin the cluster when a rebalance happens.

`session.timeout.ms`
> The maximum duration allowed between two heartbeats from a worker. If the coordinator does not receive a heartbeat within this limit, it kicks the worker out of the Kafka Connect cluster and starts a rebalance.

`worker.sync.timeout.ms`
> The duration a broker spends trying to resynchronize with other workers if it gets out of sync before leaving the cluster.

`worker.unsync.backoff.ms`
> The duration a worker waits before attempting to rejoin the cluster when it is out of sync and has already failed rejoining the cluster within `worker.sync.time`
> `out.ms`.

`task.shutdown.graceful.timeout.ms`

This setting controls how long tasks can take to gracefully shut down before the worker terminates them. This configuration can be useful to change when running a connector that is known to be slow to perform task shutdown actions. You should take this setting into account when configuring `scheduled.reba lance.max.delay.ms`.

 Changing the `heartbeat.interval.ms`, `rebalance.timeout.ms`, and `session.timeout.ms` configurations to shorter durations reduces the time it takes to detect worker failures. However, this comes at the cost of extra heartbeat traffic and potentially detecting false positives (and triggering unnecessary rebalances) if a worker is just a bit slow. On the other hand, when they are set to longer durations, it takes longer to detect failures. The default values offer a good trade-off between these two options.

The following settings control the security configuration of inter-worker communications when `connect.protocol` is set to `sessioned`:

- `inter.worker.key.generation.algorithm` is the algorithm used to generate keys.

- `inter.worker.key.size` is the size of generated keys.

- `inter.worker.key.ttl.ms` is the time to live (TTL) of generated keys.

- `inter.worker.signature.algorithm` is the algorithm used to sign requests.

- `inter.worker.verification.algorithms` is the list of permitted algorithms used to verify requests. This can contain multiple algorithms to facilitate a zero-downtime rolling upgrade if the key signature algorithm needs to be changed.

Topic tracking configurations

Since Kafka 2.5, Connect tracks the topics that connectors interact with and exposes this information via the REST API. Since sink connectors can subscribe to topics via a regular expression and source connectors can use arbitrary topics, this feature helps SREs get some visibility about the topics actively used by each connector. This feature is enabled by default, but there's a configuration, `topic.tracking.enable`, that can be set to `false` to allow administrators to disable it.

The REST API also allows users to reset the list of active topics for a connector. This is especially useful if you reconfigure a connector to use a different set of topics. By default, resetting the list is allowed, but administrators can decide to prevent this by setting `topic.tracking.allow.reset` to `false`.

Metrics configurations

Connect, like all Kafka clients, exposes some configurations to tune how metrics are recorded.

Several types of metrics, including averages, maximums, minimums, percentiles, and more, are measured over multiple samples. A sample can be bound by the number of events or a duration. You can configure the number of samples used for measurements by using `metrics.num.samples` (it defaults to 2). Once this number of samples is reached, the oldest sample is dropped when a new one is created. You can also set the duration each sample is computed over by using `metrics.sample.window.ms` (it defaults to 30000).

Similar to application logs, each metric is associated with a recording level, which determines how fine-grained it is. The setting `metrics.recording.level` allows you to specify the minimum level a metric must be in order to be recorded. It can be set to `INFO`, which is the default, or `DEBUG`, which causes all metrics at both `INFO` and `DEBUG` to be recorded. As of Kafka 3.5, all Connect metrics use the `INFO` level, so in practice this setting currently does not allow you to enable recording additional metrics.

Offset flush configurations

There are two settings that allow you to tune how Kafka Connect saves offsets for tasks. You can configure how often offsets are committed (i.e., saved to the internal offset topic for source tasks or committed to the consumer group for sink tasks) using `offset.flush.interval.ms`, and you can set the timeout for that operation using `offset.flush.timeout.ms`. Since Kafka 3.0.1, you very rarely have to tune these settings, and you may only need to change `offset.flush.timeout.ms` if Kafka Connect is geographically far from the Kafka cluster and therefore has a high latency.

Flush Timeouts in Kafka 3.0.0 and Earlier

With Kafka Connect versions older than 3.0.1, you may see, from time to time, the following messages in your logs:

```
INFO WorkerSourceTask{id=MyConnector-0} flushing 1000 outstanding messages
    for offset commit
ERROR WorkerSourceTask{id=MyConnector-0} Failed to flush, timed out while
    waiting for producer to flush outstanding 510 messages
```

A search on the internet quickly points you to the `offset.flush.interval.ms` and `offset.flush.timeout.ms` settings. Instead of bumping the values of these two configurations, it's important to understand the scenarios that lead to this error.

When a source connector starts, in many cases it has a sizable backlog of data to flow through Kafka Connect. So the connector provides a lot of `ConnectRecord` objects to the runtime to send to Kafka. By default, the producer builds batches of 16 KB

(batch.size) and can send requests up to 1 MB (max.request.size). But if you're only sending records to a few partitions, the internal producer is not able to use up the 1 MB request size, and is limited by the relatively small batch size. Before Kafka Connect 3.0.1, the flush timeout counted the time the producer took to send records, so when the producer was overwhelmed and took a few seconds to send many batches, the offset flush timeout could expire and cause this issue.

When working with Kafka Connect 3.0.0 or earlier versions, if you see this error, instead of increasing offset.flush.timeout.ms, we recommend that you first check the producer average request size and, if it is low (just a few batches), increase the producer batch.size configuration to increase the throughput.

The best solution is to upgrade to a newer Kafka Connect release.

Now that you know how to configure the runtime, let's discuss configuring connectors.

Configuring Connectors

When configuring connectors, there are two different groups of configurations you must consider. First, there is a set of configurations that the runtime uses to start the connector and build the pipeline. These are configuration settings such as the connector class, converters, and client overrides.

Second, each connector also has its own specific configurations that it uses to interact with the external system and emit records. For example, for a file connector, you might specify a filename. There aren't any naming conventions or requirements for the connector-specific configurations. This means the only way to discover and understand these configuration settings is to either read the connector documentation or use the GET /connector-plugins/<CONNECTOR_PLUGIN>/config endpoint. We discuss some common connectors in Chapter 5, so you can also refer to that chapter. In this section, we only discuss in detail the first group of configuration settings: the ones that the runtime requires for all connectors, no matter the external system they interact with. Some of these configurations apply to both source and sink connectors, whereas some are specific to one or the other.

Both source and sink connectors have the following required configurations:

name
  The name the runtime should use for this connector

connector.class
  The class name or alias for this connector

In addition, sink connectors require either `topics` or `topics.regex` to be specified. We discuss what to set these to and other configurations for topics in more detail later in this chapter.

You need to use the connector `name` in many REST API requests, such as making configuration updates or checking status. For that reason, we recommend using a name that describes the connector and avoid using completely random names, such as generated identifiers. If there is already an existing connector within your Kafka Connect cluster with the same name, then a request to create your connector using the `POST` endpoint will fail. However, the `PUT` endpoint will accept your request and update the existing connector with your configuration. Make sure the name you have chosen is unique across the Kafka Connect cluster before making the request, to avoid accidentally updating an existing connector rather than creating a new one.

> In most cases, the names of sink connectors actually need to be globally unique across not only your Kafka Connect cluster, but any Kafka Connect clusters that are connected to the same Kafka cluster. This is because the name is used to generate the default consumer group ID that sink connectors use when consuming. If two separate Kafka Connect clusters have connectors with the same name connecting to the same topic, records are split between the connectors, rather than each of them seeing every record. If you are not able to provide a globally unique name, from Kafka 2.3 onward you can use client overrides to configure the `group.id` for the consumer group used by sink connectors. See "Client Overrides" on page 225 for more details.

The `connector.class` configuration can be either a full class name or an alias. For example, to configure the `FileStreamSink` connector, you can provide any of `File StreamSink`, `FileStreamSinkConnector`, or `org.apache.kafka.connect.file.File StreamSinkConnector`. If Kafka Connect has multiple connector plug-ins installed with the same alias, you get an error when creating the connector:

```
{
    "error_code":500,
    "message":"More than one connector matches alias FileStreamSourceConnector.
Please use full package and class name instead. Classes found: ..."
}
```

The following configurations are optional and can be supplied for both source and sink connectors:

`tasks.max`
    The maximum number of tasks for the connector to start (default is 1).

`key.converter`
>   The converter class for record keys.

`value.converter`
>   The converter class for record values.

`header.converter`
>   The converter class for record headers.

`transforms`
>   A comma-separated list of labels for the transformations that are applied to records.

`predicates`
>   A comma-separated list of labels for predicates that are used with the transformations.

`config.action.reload`
>   The action the Kafka Connect runtime takes when changes in external configuration providers result in a change to the connector configuration. The default is `restart`, and the valid values are `none` and `restart`.

The `tasks.max` configuration is passed to the connector, and the connector uses it to determine the actual number of tasks to run. This is an important configuration setting to get right because it impacts throughput and ordering. We discuss how to decide on the value in Chapter 7.

Each of the converter configuration settings (`key.converter`, `value.converter`, `header.converter`) is optional. If these aren't provided, the connector instead uses the values specified in the Kafka Connect runtime configuration. These are important settings because they define the format of the data as it goes into and out of Kafka. It is good practice to always override `key.converter` and `value.converter` at the connector level, as the correct converters to use are likely to be dependent on the specific connector that is running and the use case it satisfies.

The `transforms` and `predicates` configurations are only needed if you want to apply a transformation to your data as part of the flow. We cover how to configure these in detail in Chapter 3.

The `config.action.reload` configuration is used in conjunction with configuration provider plug-ins. When a configuration provider returns a configuration value to the Kafka Connect runtime, it has the option to include a time to live. This indicates how long this configuration value is valid for. When the runtime receives this information, it can plan to restart the connector once the amount of time specified in the time to live has passed. Kafka Connect only schedules a restart if the `config.action.reload` configuration is set to `restart`, which is the default value. It does nothing if this is set to none. Kafka Connect also only restarts the connector, not the running tasks, so the tasks don't automatically pick up this new value when the time to live is hit. Instead, the next time the task reloads the configuration, for example after a restart or during a rebalance, it picks up the new value. If you take a look at the Javadoc (*https://oreil.ly/0qygC*) for ConfigProvider, you will see that it also includes the subscribe(), unsubscribe(), and unsubscribeAll() methods. However, as of Kafka 3.5, these are not called by the Connect runtime, so Config Provider authors don't need to implement them.

Here is an example of a connector configuration with both the required and optional configuration values set:

```
{
  "name": "file-sink",
  "config": {
    "connector.class":"org.apache.kafka.connect.file.FileStreamSinkConnector",
    "tasks.max": "1",
    "key.converter": "org.apache.kafka.connect.storage.StringConverter",
    "value.converter": "org.apache.kafka.connect.storage.StringConverter",
    "header.converter": "org.apache.kafka.connect.storage.SimpleHeaderConverter",
    "transforms": "filterTombstones",
    "transforms.filterTombstones.type":
      "org.apache.kafka.connect.transforms.Filter",
    "transforms.filterTombstones.predicate": "isTombstone",
    "predicates": "isTombstone",
    "predicates.isTombstone.type":
      "org.apache.kafka.connect.transforms.predicates.RecordIsTombstone",
    "config.action.reload": "none"
  }
}
```

In addition to these common configurations, the source and sink connectors each have their own configuration settings for the topics they use.

Topic Configurations

The topic configuration settings for sink and source connectors are different. We cover each setting and discuss how topic creation works for both source and sink connectors. The topic configurations are:

- Sink connectors: topics, topics.regex
- Source connectors: topic.creation.groups

Let's start with sink connectors. Sink connectors must be configured with either a topics or topics.regex field. The topics setting is a comma-separated list of topics in Kafka that the runtime consumes from, for example topics=mytopic1,mytopic2. If the broker setting auto.create.topics.enable is set to true (the default), the topics listed are created by the broker when the connector is started. If `auto.create.top ics.enable` is `false`, you need to create the topics manually.

The `topics.regex` setting is a regular expression describing the topics to consume from. For example, `topics.regex=mytopic-(.*)` would match the topics `mytopic-a`, `mytopic-second`, and `mytopic-1`. When the connector starts, it subscribes to all topics that match the regex. If you do create additional topics later, the connector detects them automatically, but only when it refreshes its metadata after the duration set by `metadata.max.age.ms`.

Source connectors need topics to produce records to, and these topics can be created in one of three ways:

- Auto-created by the broker when the first record is sent
- Created by the Kafka Connect runtime
- Manually created ahead of time

The first option is the simplest because it doesn't require any additional configuration. Make sure the broker configuration `auto.create.topics.enable` is still using the default value of `true`; then topics are created using the broker defaults.

In many production environments, automatic topic creation is disabled to prevent applications from inadvertently creating topics. In these environments, Kafka Connect can use its admin client to explicitly create topics. This feature was added by KIP-158 (*https://oreil.ly/8XM3L*) in Kafka 2.6. To use this option, all Kafka Connect workers must have `topic.creation.enable` set to the default value of `true` in their runtime configuration. Then a connector can opt in to topic creation by configuring various settings that are prefixed with `topic.creation.`. Let's look at how this works.

You first have to specify a group of topics that will be known by a label. There is a predefined group with the label `default`, which applies to all topics. You can define additional groups using `topic.creation.groups`. For example, `topic .creation.groups=ordered,single` results in three groups; `default`, `ordered`, and `single`.

You define the specific topics to include in each group using `topic.cre ation.<LABEL>.include` and `topic.creation.<LABEL>.exclude`, where `<LABEL>` is the group name. These are both comma-separated lists of topic names or topic regex values, and the exclude list takes precedence. To define topic-level configurations (*https://oreil.ly/ZGmKC*) for a specific group, you use the following syntax, where `<CONFIG>` is any topic-level configuration:

```
topic.creation.<LABEL>.<CONFIG>
```

When you set topic-level configurations, make sure you are choosing values that are supported by your Kafka brokers. For example, from Kafka 2.4 onward, admin clients can use -1 for the replication factor and partitions to use the broker defaults, so setting the `topic.creation.<LABEL>.partitions` to -1 only works if your brokers and Kafka Connect workers are from Kafka 2.4 or newer, and therefore support this feature.

So, for example, the following connector configuration results in all topics having a replication factor of 3. Then the topic called `status` and any topics beginning with `single.` have one partition, while the rest have five partitions.

```
{
    ...
    "topic.creation.groups": "ordered",
    "topic.creation.default.replication.factor": "3",
    "topic.creation.default.partitions": "5",

    "topic.creation.ordered.include": "status,single.*",
    "topic.creation.ordered.partitions": "1",
    ...
}
```

 Kafka Connect only creates topics using the admin client if the default group has both the `replication.factor` and `partitions` set. If you specify one but not the other, the connector will fail to start.

The final option is to manually create topics. For this approach, you don't need to worry about giving Kafka Connect the permissions to create topics. However, be aware that if the topics aren't created before connectors are started, your Kafka Connect logs will fill up with warning messages:

```
WARN [file-source|task-0] [Producer clientId=connector-producer-file-source-0]
    Error while fetching metadata with correlation id 570 :
    {topic-from-source=UNKNOWN_TOPIC_OR_PARTITION}
```

We have seen how you can override the topic configurations for the topics that connectors use; now let's look at how you can override the client configurations.

Client Overrides

As discussed in "Clients and connector overrides" on page 212, the Kafka Connect runtime can specify configurations for clients that are used for source and sink tasks. You can also configure these settings at the connector level to give you even more control over the producer, consumer, and admin clients used by tasks.

To provide connector-level client overrides, first make sure the runtime configuration `connector.client.config.override.policy` allows you to set the configurations you want to change. Then add these client configurations to your connector configuration with the prefix `producer.override.`, `consumer.override.`, or `admin.override.`, depending on the client you want to override.

The advantage of providing overrides at the connector level is you can choose configuration settings that suit the particular connector and workload you are dealing with. As a general rule, you should set at the connector level any configuration that needs to be a specific value for a specific connector instance. Following this rule means you can be sure about the configuration values that your connector is using, and it protects you if the runtime-level configuration gets updated.

If you are configuring a source connector, you should specifically think about what producer client overrides you might want. Consider settings that affect how the data is batched and buffered before being sent to Kafka, such as `batch.size`, `linger.ms` and `buffer.memory`. If you know the connector will be reading large amounts of data from the external system in one go, you might increase the batch size. For source connectors, you can also override the `partitioner.class` configuration to influence how data is partitioned when it is sent to Kafka. Remember, if you want to use a custom partitioner, it has to be present in the runtime.

Configuration for a source connector could, for example, include:

```
{
    ...
    "producer.override.batch.size": "32768",
    "producer.override.partitioner.class":
      "org.apache.Kafka.clients.producer.UniformStickyPartitioner",
    ...
}
```

For sink connectors, you override consumer configuration settings. Consider where you want new connectors to start processing from and make sure you set `auto.offset.reset` appropriately. If the topic your connector is reading from has records that are sent as part of transactions, you should also consider changing the `isolation.level` configuration to `read_committed` so your connector only gets records that are part of committed transactions. It's also common to tune settings such as `fetch.max.bytes`, `fetch.min.bytes`, `max.partition.fetch.bytes`, or `max.poll.records` to adjust the capacity and performance of your connectors. For example, you might have sink connector configuration with:

```
{
    ...
    "consumer.override.auto.offset.reset": "latest",
    "consumer.override.isolation.level": "read_committed",
    "consumer.override.max.partition.fetch.bytes": "2097152",
```

```
    ...
}
```

As well as being able to override any client configurations, there are also some connector-specific configurations related to exactly-once semantics.

Configurations for Exactly-Once

We have already discussed the options you have around processing semantics in Chapter 4. In that chapter, we explain the different ways that at-most-once, at-least-once and exactly-once semantics can be achieved between external systems and Kafka. The only specific configurations that Kafka Connect provides for exactly-once semantics are for data being processed by source connectors. That is what we discuss in this section.

Exactly-once support for source connectors is a pretty recent addition to Kafka Connect. It was added in Kafka 3.3 as part of KIP-618 (*https://oreil.ly/j8Atg*). If you want to make use of this feature, first make sure the connector you are using supports it and every worker in the Kafka Connect cluster has the `exactly.once.source` `.support` configuration set to `enabled`. Then you need to specify some connector-level configurations. There are four connector-level configurations you can set:

- `exactly.once.support`
- `transaction.boundary`
- `transaction.boundary.interval.ms`
- `offsets.storage.topic`

The `exactly.once.support` configuration specifies whether the connector is required to support exactly-once semantics. If `exactly.once.source.support` is enabled at the worker level, the runtime queries new connectors during create and validate requests to see if they support it. The default value for `exactly.once.sup port` is `requested`, and this means the connector isn't required to support exactly-once semantics. This doesn't necessarily mean that it won't provide exactly-once semantics, though, and if you use this default value, you should carefully read the connector documentation to understand the behavior you will get. The other value for the `exactly.once.support` configuration is `required`, and this means any validate and create requests only succeed if the connector reports that it does support exactly-once semantics.

Exactly-once support is done using transactions that span the two actions of sending the data to Kafka and committing offsets to the offsets storage topic. The `transac tion.boundary` configuration lets you specify when these transactions should be created and committed. The allowed values are:

poll

    A new transaction is used for every batch of records that a task in the connector passes to the Kafka Connect runtime. This is the default value.

interval

    Transactions are committed after a user-defined interval. You set this interval using either the `transaction.boundary.interval.ms` configuration, or the worker level `offset.flush.interval.ms` configuration if the former isn't set.

connector

    The connector should provide the transaction boundaries. Not all connectors are able to do this. If the connector doesn't support this feature, attempts to create the connector with the configuration set to this value will fail.

Since this feature uses transactions, whatever `transaction.boundary` you configure, you need to make sure that Kafka Connect has the right permissions to participate in transactions. The Kafka documentation includes the exact permissions that are needed. Also, to prevent downstream applications consuming records from Kafka that aren't part of committed transactions, they need to have their `isolation.level` configuration set to `read_committed`.

Finally, you can use `offset.storage.topic` to configure the topic the connector uses to commit offsets and keep track of what data it has processed in the external system. This topic must be in the same Kafka cluster as the topic the connector is writing to, since transactions cannot span different Kafka clusters. By default, this configuration uses the global worker-level offset storage topic; however, it is useful to explicitly set this, for several reasons. Firstly, source connectors running with exactly-once enabled require the ACL `WRITE` for the offset topic (without exactly-once, the runtime writes to the topic instead). It is better to only grant the connector access to the topic with its own offsets, rather than a global topic containing all source connector offsets. Secondly, it reduces the impact of hanging transactions from tasks on the other connectors in the cluster.

Finally, for connector configurations, let's look at how you can influence error handling.

Configurations for Error Handling

The default configuration of Kafka Connect means that if a task encounters an error, it stops processing data and is moved into the `FAILED` state. This is true for both source and sink connectors, and requires you to restart the failed task using the REST API. However, Kafka Connect does include configurations to let you alter this behavior. First, we look at the common error configurations that can be used for both source and sink connectors, and then discuss dead letter queue configurations for sink connectors.

The set of common error configurations are:

- `errors.retry.timeout`
- `errors.retry.delay.max.ms`
- `errors.tolerance`
- `errors.log.enable`
- `errors.log.include.messages`

The first two configurations handle the behavior of Kafka Connect when an operation fails. The configuration `errors.retry.timeout` indicates how long, in milliseconds, Kafka Connect should spend retrying a failed operation. If you don't specify this configuration, it uses the default value of 0, which means no retries occur. To use infinite retries, you can set this to -1. Remember, even if you enable retries, Kafka Connect only retries certain operations that are viewed as "retriable," such as invoking converters and transformations. If you have enabled retries, you can then use `errors.retry.delay.max.ms` to control the maximum time in milliseconds Kafka Connect should wait between consecutive retries. The default value for `errors.retry.delay.max.ms` is 60000 (one minute).

The `errors.tolerance` configuration lets you configure what the connector should do if it encounters an error when processing a record. By default, this is set to none, which means the connector task stops processing records and moves into the FAILED state. If you instead want the connector to skip over the record that caused the error and keep processing, you can set this to all. Until Kafka 3.2, this setting did not apply to source tasks that failed while producing records. So, connectors with older versions of Kafka would fail in this scenario even if `errors.tolerance` was set to all. From 3.2 onward, Kafka Connect takes the value of the `errors.tolerance` property into account if it encounters this kind of error in a source flow.

The final two configurations handle how errors are logged. The first, `errors.log.enable`, configures whether Kafka Connect should log tolerated errors. If you haven't changed the `errors.tolerance` to all, you can keep this as the default value of false, since Kafka Connect will always log errors that fail a task. If you have enabled connectors to skip records, then you can change `errors.log.enable` to true so you can see when records are being skipped.

Finally, you can set `errors.log.include.messages` to true (default is false) so that Kafka Connect logs the contents of records that resulted in a failure. For sink connectors, this logs the topic, partition, offset, and timestamp of the Kafka record. For source connectors, it logs the key, value, key schema, value schema, headers, timestamp, Kafka topic, Kafka partition, source partition, and source offset. This configuration is useful when developing your pipeline to understand why certain records are causing failures.

In production, you should be cautious about changing `errors.log.enable` to `true`. Record contents, such as the key, value, and headers might contain sensitive information, which would then be leaked to the log files. Moreover, if a lot of records are causing problems, or the records are very large, this could result in a lot of additional log lines, which could make it harder to spot and diagnose other problems.

In addition to the error configurations we have already mentioned, sink connectors have three configurations for dead letter queues (DLQs). We discuss why and how you might use dead letter queues in Chapter 4. The configurations for DLQs are:

`errors.deadletterqueue.topic.name`
> The name of the topic to use as the DLQ. You must set it if you want records to be sent to a DLQ.

`errors.deadletterqueue.topic.replication.factor`
> The replication factor Kafka Connect should use for the DLQ topic if it needs to be created. The default value is 3.

`errors.deadletterqueue.context.headers.enable`
> Whether Kafka Connect should add headers containing error context to the records sent to the DLQ. The default value is `false`. If you set this to `true`, Kafka Connect creates error context headers prefixed with `__connect.errors.` to prevent header clashes.

By default, Kafka Connect is not secured, and any user can access pretty much everything. While this is practical for getting started and for development environments, this is often not suitable for production. In these environments, with real data flowing, you typically want to tighten security and police access to all resources, and there are numerous configurations that enable you to do this.

Configuring Kafka Connect Clusters for Security

Security is often looked at via these three pillars:

Confidentiality
> Controlling who has access to each piece of data

Integrity
> Controlling who can alter data and ensuring data stays intact and can't be corrupted

Availability
> Ensuring data stays available and ready to use

Kafka Connect supports a number of security standards, providing encryption, authentication, and authorization, that you can combine to obtain the required security for your use cases. By *encryption*, we mean encrypting the data as it is sent between Kafka Connect, the data sources and sinks, Kafka, and users of the REST API. *Authentication* is the process of identifying the originator of a request, while *authorization* describes whether a permission is associated with this identity.

In this section, we look at the options that Kafka Connect provides for security between itself and Kafka. You should also be securing the connection between Kafka Connect and your source and sink systems, but the way you do that is dependent on the system and the connector. Instead, we discuss options for assigning permissions to connectors, both for Kafka and the external system. We also give recommendations around vetting connectors from a security perspective. Finally, we discuss how to secure connections to the Kafka Connect REST API.

First, let's look at securing the connection to Kafka.

Securing the Connection to Kafka

Remember that Kafka Connect uses multiple different clients when talking to Kafka. You need to provide security configurations for each client using the `producer.`, `consumer.`, and `admin.` prefixes.

The first aspect to consider when securing a Kafka Connect cluster is identifying how it is going to connect to Kafka. By default, Kafka Connect interacts with Kafka via a plain-text connection, so all the data is exchanged in the clear, and Kafka Connect does not obtain a specific identity or any associated permissions in Kafka.

Using `security.protocol`, you can change the connection to use encryption via TLS and authentication via SASL. The valid values for `security.protocol` are:

PLAINTEXT
> The default; provides no encryption or authentication.

SSL
> Provides encryption and can also be used for authentication using client certificates. To use this, you need to configure some of the settings listed in "TLS configurations" on page 232.

SASL_PLAINTEXT
> Provides authentication but no encryption. To use this, you need to configure some of the settings listed in "SASL configurations" on page 234.

SASL_SSL
> This provides encryption and authentication. To use this, you need to configure some of the settings listed in both "TLS configurations" on page 232 and "SASL configurations" on page 234.

The `security.protocol` you choose has to match one of the listeners the Kafka cluster is configured with. If Kafka only exposes a `PLAINTEXT` listener, Kafka Connect cannot use encryption or authentication.

Now let's look at what configurations you can use for an encrypted connection.

TLS configurations

If the Kafka cluster exposes a `SASL_SSL` or an `SSL` listener, you can configure how the connection is encrypted using TLS configurations.

In most cases, you do not need to configure all of the settings. In many instances, such as when connecting to some public Kafka-as-a-service offerings, you don't need to set any of them, as the default values are sufficient.

If the Kafka cluster certificates are signed by a public certificate authority (CA) like Let's Encrypt (*https://letsencrypt.org*), then by default, the JVM trusts them. Otherwise—if, for example, you are using your own CA—you need to load the server certificate into a *truststore* and provide that to Kafka Connect.

By default, Kafka Connect supports two types of truststore files, `JKS` (Java KeyStore, the default) and `PEM` (Privacy-Enhanced Mail). You can configure the type you want to use with `ssl.truststore.type`. You specify where the file is in the filesystem, using the `ssl.truststore.location` setting. If your JKS truststore is password protected, you can specify the password using `ssl.truststore.password`. For PEM certificates, if you don't want to put a file in the Kafka Connect runtime containing the certificates, you can provide them directly inline by using `ssl.truststore.certificates`.

By default, Kafka Connect also validates that the server name matches the name specified in the certificate. This is done to prevent man-in-the-middle attacks. We recommend leaving this enabled, but if you need to disable this feature, you can do it by setting `ssl.endpoint.identification.algorithm` to an empty string.

Now that we've looked at validating the identity of the Kafka brokers, the next set of TLS configurations is about providing an identity to Kafka Connect. This allows you to use mutual TLS (mTLS) and ensure that both peers, the Kafka brokers and Kafka Connect, are who they claim to be. The identity provided can then be used by Kafka to perform authentication and enforce permissions. This is done via a *keystore*.

Similarly to truststores, Kafka Connect works out of the box with JKS (the default) or PEM keystores, and it's configured using ssl.keystore.type. You specify the location of the keystore on the filesystem using the ssl.keystore.location setting. If your JKS keystore is password protected, you can specify the password using ssl.keystore.password. The key in a JKS keystore can also be password protected. If that is the case, you can provide its password using ssl.key.password. For PEM keystores, if you don't want to put a file in the Kafka Connect runtime containing the keystore, you can provide them directly inline in the configuration by using ssl.keystore.certificate.chain.

There are also settings to configure the TLS version and ciphers to use when establishing a connection. When running with Java 11 or higher, ssl.protocol defaults to TLSv1.3; otherwise it defaults to TLSv1.2. Kafka Connect tries to use the chosen version when connecting to Kafka. If the Kafka cluster does not support it, Kafka Connect tries the other versions specified in ssl.enabled.protocols; this defaults to TLSv1.2,TLSv1.3. You should not use TLS versions older than those in this list, as they all have security issues. Alongside the version, ciphers determine how data is encrypted and can be configured using ssl.cipher.suites. By default, this is set to null, which allows all ciphers that are enabled in the JVM to be used.

Finally, there are advanced TLS configurations to customize how TLS is handled by the JVM running Kafka Connect. You can change the security provider used by the JVM using ssl.provider. By default, this setting is null and the JVM uses its default security provider, but you can change this setting to load your own implementation of java.security.Provider. A custom security provider allows you to deeply alter how the JVM handles TLS. If you only need to customize the SSLEngine, you can use ssl.engine.factory.class to provide your own SSLEngine factory that implements org.apache.kafka.common.security.auth.SslEngineFactory. A custom SslEngineFactory can be used to load custom keystores and truststores, or finely configure the SSLEngine and SSLContext used to encrypt data. You can also tweak various TLS components, such as the algorithm used by the Trust Manager, using ssl.trustmanager.algorithm (the default is PKIX); the algorithm used by the Key Manager, using ssl.keymanager.algorithm (the default is SunX509); and the pseudo-random number generator (PRNG) implementation, using ssl.secure.random.implementation (the default is null, which uses the default PRNG implementation of the JVM).

Now that we have discussed the configurations for encrypted connections, we look at the configurations for connections that require SASL authentication.

SASL configurations

Simple Authentication and Security Layer (SASL) is a framework for providing authentication. The framework does not specify how authentication is done; this part is defined by SASL mechanisms. Kafka supports five SASL mechanisms:

GSSAPI
> The default mechanism. This provides ticket-based authentication. The main implementation of this mechanism is Kerberos.

PLAIN
> Simple username and password authentication.

SCRAM-SHA-256
> This works with a username and password, but instead of exchanging credentials directly like in PLAIN, credentials are cryptographically hashed to 256 bits before being exchanged.

SCRAM-SHA-512
> The same as SCRAM-SHA-256, but it uses a 512-bit hash instead.

OAUTHBEARER
> OAuth 2.0 bearer token authentication.

You set the mechanism for Kafka Connect to use with the sasl.mechanism setting.

Once the mechanism is selected, SASL is configured via the Java Authentication and Authorization Service (JAAS). There are two ways to provide a JAAS configuration, using the sasl.jaas.config configuration setting or using a JAAS file.

The recommended method is to use sasl.jaas.config. The value for that setting must be in the following format: loginModuleClass controlFlag (option Name=optionValue)*;. Each mechanism has its own set of valid optionName values.

For example:

```
sasl.jaas.config="org.apache.kafka.common.security.plain.PlainLoginModule require
d username=\"alice\" password=\"alice-secret\";"
```

You can also use a JAAS file and pass it to the JVM using the -Djava.security .auth.login.config system property. The file must have the following format:

```
KafkaClient {
    loginModuleClass controlFlag
    (optionName=optionValue)*;
};
```

For example:

```
KafkaClient {
    org.apache.kafka.common.security.plain.PlainLoginModule required
```

```
        username="alice"
        password="alice-secret";
};
```

 The format of the JAAS configuration is very finicky and can fail for many reasons, including invalid spacing! Be sure to review it first when investigating authentication issues.

When using a JAAS file, all Kafka clients created in the JVM share the same credentials so you should avoid this method with Kafka Connect. Also, if you use both methods, the credentials provided via sasl.jaas.config take precedence.

Depending on your use case, in production environments, you may have to provide custom callback handlers to securely retrieve credentials at runtime. To do so, you can use:

sasl.client.callback.handler.class
: Takes a class that implements the AuthenticateCallbackHandler interface. It serves as the interface between the SASL client and the login module loaded in the JVM. When using PLAIN, this lets you retrieve credentials from an external source.

sasl.login.callback.handler.class
: Takes a class that implements the AuthenticateCallbackHandler interface. It's used by the login module loaded by the JVM to retrieve credentials from an identity provider. For example, it can be used with OAUTHBEARER to obtain and refresh tokens.

If you need to further customize the SASL login flow, you can also provide your own implementation of the org.apache.kafka.common.security.auth.Login interface by using sasl.login.class.

Let's now look at SASL configurations that apply to specific mechanisms, starting with OAUTHBEARER.

SASL OAUTHBEARER configurations

This mechanism was added in Kafka 2.0 via KIP-255 (*https://oreil.ly/CdzhE*), but it originally only provided a framework to integrate with OAuth 2.0 providers. Later, in Kafka 3.1, via KIP-768 (*https://oreil.ly/g5Kfe*), a production-ready OAuth/OpenID Connect (OIDC) implementation was added. In order to customize it, Kafka Connect exposes the following settings:

sasl.oauthbearer.token.endpoint.url
: The URL for the OAuth/OIDC identity provider.

`sasl.oauthbearer.clock.skew.seconds`
> The maximum time difference allowed between the OAuth/OIDC identity provider and Kafka Connect clocks. If a large difference is detected, the token is rejected and a new one is retrieved.

`sasl.oauthbearer.expected.audience` *and* `sasl.oauthbearer.expected.issuer`
> These two settings are used to perform sanity checks on the token retrieved and ensure that the token `aud` (for audience) and `iss` (for issuer) fields match these settings.

`sasl.oauthbearer.scope.claim.name`
> Allows you to override the name of the scope claim to allow compatibility with different providers. It defaults to `scope`.

`sasl.oauthbearer.sub.claim.name`
> Allows you to override the name of the sub claim to allow compatibility with different providers. It defaults to `sub`.

Since Kafka 2.2 and KIP-368 (*https://oreil.ly/IaOqM*), this mechanism supports reauthentications. This means brokers can force clients to reauthenticate periodically for added security. There are a few settings to configure this behavior:

`sasl.login.refresh.buffer.seconds`
> The minimum time allowed before authentication expires to trigger a reauthentication. It defaults to 300 seconds.

`sasl.login.refresh.min.period.seconds`
> The minimum time between two reauthentications. This defaults to 60 seconds.

`sasl.login.refresh.window.factor`
> When authenticating, the client is told the lifetime of its credentials. This controls at what ratio of that lifetime the client should reauthenticate. It defaults to 0.8, which means once 80% of the lifetime of the credentials has passed, the client reauthenticates.

`sasl.login.refresh.window.jitter`
> This delays by a random amount of time when reauthentication happens. This ensures reauthentication requests don't all happen at the exact same time. It defaults to 0.05, which means reauthentication can be delayed by up to 5%.

`sasl.login.connect.timeout.ms`
> The maximum duration a connection to the authentication provider can take to be established before failing. By default, this is not set and the request does not time out.

`sasl.login.read.timeout.ms`
> The maximum duration to wait when expecting a response from the authentication provider before failing. By default, this is not set and the request does not time out.

`sasl.login.retry.backoff.max.ms`
> After a failure, this specifies the maximum duration to wait before retrying. This defaults to 10 seconds (`10000`).

`sasl.login.retry.backoff.ms`
> After a failure, this specifies the minimum duration to wait. Retries are then done using an exponential backoff up to `sasl.login.retry.backoff.max.ms`. This defaults to `100` milliseconds.

SASL GSSAPI configurations

Kafka also exposes a few settings to configure GSSAPI authentication:

`sasl.kerberos.service.name`
> This must match the Kerberos name that the Kafka cluster is using.

`sasl.kerberos.kinit.cmd`
> In Kerberos, `kinit` is the command that retrieves tickets for authentication. This setting specifies the path to the command on the filesystem. This defaults to `/usr/bin/kinit`.

`sasl.kerberos.min.time.before.relogin`
> The minimum duration to wait before refreshing tickets. This defaults to `60` seconds.

`sasl.kerberos.ticket.renew.jitter`
> This delays by a random amount of time the ticket refresh. This defaults to `0.05`, which means refresh can be delayed by up to 5%.

`sasl.kerberos.ticket.renew.window.factor`
> When retrieving a ticket, the client is given a refresh time. This controls the ratio of the ticket validity time after which the client should refresh its ticket. This defaults to `0.8`, which means once 80% of the ticket validity time has passed, the client refreshes it.

Now that we have discussed specific configurations for securing the connection between Kafka Connect and Kafka, we talk about the general considerations you should make when configuring permissions in Kafka Connect, Kafka, and external systems.

Configuring Permissions

In the previous section we talked about how to configure Kafka Connect to be able to communicate with a secured Kafka cluster, but we didn't discuss how to decide on the permissions to grant Kafka Connect. As a rule of thumb, you should only give Kafka Connect the minimum set of permissions it needs to connect both to Kafka and to the external system you are flowing data to/from.

In Chapter 7, we highlight the full list of ACLs that Kafka Connect needs, both for the runtime and the individual connectors, to talk to Kafka. At a minimum, the Kafka Connect runtime needs to be able to interact with its configuration, status and offsets topics, and the group that is used for worker coordination. Each connector then needs read or write permissions to the topics it is interacting with. When you are configuring the Kafka ACLs for Kafka Connect, you have a choice between having a single principal or multiple principals for the runtime and connectors, respectively.

The simplest configuration is to have one principal that is granted all the ACLs for the Kafka Connect runtime and any connector you are going to run. With this approach, you don't need to configure any overrides for security configurations when you start connectors, because the connectors inherit their identity from the runtime. The downside of this approach is that all connectors can access any topic that the runtime has access to, meaning that a connector could potentially read or write to a topic it shouldn't.

In reality, you likely have some topics in your Kafka cluster that contain sensitive data and need to be locked down to restrict which clients can access them. If you need to run a connector to interact with such a topic, you should configure a client override in the connector configuration, so it uses its own principal. Then you only need to grant access to that specific topic to the connector principal, not to the runtime principal that is also used by other connectors.

For connections to external systems, configure your connectors to use the authentication, authorization, and encryption options they provide. Make sure you have chosen a connector that supports authentication and authorization and that you configure your external system to require authenticated connections. Security in a pipeline has to happen end to end, and like a chain, it is only as strong as its weakest link.

You should carefully vet any connectors that you plan to install into the runtime. Remember that Kafka Connect does not provide an out-of-the-box mechanism to restrict who can start which type of connector. Anyone with permissions for the REST API can start a connector using any of the installed connector plug-ins. Make sure you understand what permissions and actions the connectors in your runtime are capable of, and decide whether there are any security risks from these connectors.

If you are running Kafka 3.1 or older, you should also remove the `connect-file-<VERSION>.jar` file, which contains the `FileStreamSource` and `FileStreamSink` connector, from the `libs` directory of your Kafka Connect runtime. This is because they can read and write from/to the file system, and they can be used by bad actors to scrape sensitive information from Kafka Connect workers. They have been removed from the default classpath in Kafka 3.1.1 onward.

The final part in securing Kafka Connect is to secure the REST API. The REST API exposes a lot of features, so it shares the same security concerns we've described at the start of this section. If needed, data can be encrypted, and access to REST endpoints can be protected via authentication and authorization.

Securing the REST API

To encrypt data sent via the REST API, you need to expose it over HTTPS. The HTTPS configuration reuses all the `ssl.*` configurations detailed earlier in this chapter. However, note that in this case, Kafka Connect is the server, as opposed to previously, where Kafka Connect was the client connecting to Kafka. Being the server, we can also make Kafka Connect validate the identity of clients connecting and authenticate them by using mutual TLS. To do so, you can set `ssl.client.auth` to `required` to only allow clients that have a trusted certificate. You can also set it to `requested` to optionally authenticate clients if they provide a certificate. By default, this is set to `none`, which disables this feature.

In order to change TLS settings, you need to prefix them with `listeners.https.`. For example, you might have the following runtime configuration:

```
listeners=https://:8443  ❶
listeners.https.ssl.keystore.location=/my/path/keystore.jks  ❷
listeners.https.ssl.keystore.password=${file:/tmp/ssl.properties:password}  ❸
ssl.client.auth=required  ❹
```

❶ This exposes an HTTPS listener on the default interface on port 8443.

❷ The configuration overrides `ssl.keystore.location` to point to a specific keystore on the filesystem.

❸ Always use a configuration provider to protect sensitive settings.

❹ This enables mandatory mutual TLS for all clients.

The REST API also supports cross-origin resource sharing (CORS). This allows requests to be made to the REST API from a different domain. This is disabled by default, but you can allow specific domains by adding them to `access.control.allow.origin` as a comma-separated list, or allow all domains by setting this configuration to `*`. The `access.control.allow.methods` setting also lets you restrict the HTTP methods (GET, POST, PUT, etc.) allowed from cross-origin requests. The default value, an empty string, allows the following methods: GET, POST, and HEAD.

In order to protect REST API endpoints, it's sometimes necessary to have headers included in responses, and many enterprise security scanners report issues in cases where headers like X-XSS-Protection or Content-Security-Policy are missing. In order to address that, as of Kafka 2.6 (KIP-577 (*https://oreil.ly/_uxUn*)) you can configure Kafka Connect to include HTTP response headers by using the response.http.headers.config setting. This takes a comma-separated list of header rules, where each rule has the following format: [<ACTION>] [<HEADER_NAME>]: [<HEADER_VALUE>]. The <ACTION> field can be:

set
:   To set, or create if it does not exist, a header with a value.

add
:   To add a value to a header. Headers can have multiple values.

setDate
:   To set, or create if it does not exist, a header with the number of milliseconds since the epoch.

addDate
:   To add the number of milliseconds since the epoch to a header. Headers can have multiple values.

For example, you can set it to the following:

```
response.http.headers.config=add X-XSS-Protection: 1; mode=block, add Strict-Trans
port-Security: max-age=31536000; includeSubDomains, add X-Content-Type-Options: no
sniff
```

In that case, a response contains:

```
HTTP/1.1 200 OK
Date: Wed, 18 May 2022 11:10:56 GMT
Strict-Transport-Security: max-age=31536000;includeSubDomains
X-XSS-Protection: 1; mode=block
X-Content-Type-Options: nosniff
Content-Type: application/json
```

The last approach to secure the REST API is to use REST extensions by setting rest.extension.classes. We cover REST extensions in Chapter 7, and explain how the built-in BasicAuthSecurityRestExtension can be used to authenticate requests to the API. In a similar manner, you can build REST extensions that perform authorizations, and only allow some users to access specific endpoints. You can also use this plug-in to perform validation on requests. For example, you can ensure a connector always overrides SASL settings and provides its own identity, instead of relying on the identity of the Kafka Connect runtime. REST extensions are a very powerful mechanism that you can use to deeply customize the REST API to satisfy your requirements.

Summary

In this chapter, we looked at all the configuration settings Kafka Connect exposes, and provided some background and context to help you decide when to tune them. While most settings have good default values, it's important to understand what each setting is doing, to be able to adapt Kafka Connect to your specific use case.

We first looked at the runtime configurations and explained the main settings that are required to start Kafka Connect. On top of the basic required configurations, we also recommended that you always set the `client.id`, `plugin.path`, and `config.providers` configurations. When setting up the runtime for your use cases, you can also set some more fine-grained configurations that may be useful in particular scenarios.

In the second section, we walked through the configurations for connectors. Source and sink connectors share many configurations, but they work differently when it comes to topics. We recommend you make conscious decisions about how topics are created and configured. You can also make use of more specific settings like client overrides, exactly-once semantics and error handling configurations.

The last section was dedicated to configurations that are used to secure Kafka Connect clusters. Kafka supports the use of encrypted connections using TLS, and has multiple options for authentication, from mutual TLS to various SASL mechanisms. You also have a choice of how to split permissions, and can use a single principal or connector-specific principals. Finally, we finished with an overview of the protections administrators can put in place to secure the REST API. The REST API is sometimes overlooked when it comes to security, but since this is how you start and stop connectors, it is essential that it is properly secured.

CHAPTER 9

Monitoring Kafka Connect

As an administrator or SRE of a Kafka Connect pipeline, it is your job to make sure that it is running correctly. To do this, you need to set up monitoring so you can easily check the state of the system and quickly diagnose problems. Along with identifying and fixing existing problems, monitoring can allow you to spot potential future problems and make changes before they have an impact.

If you have other users or systems that are relying on your pipeline, you should have an understanding with them about the guarantees you can offer in terms of uptime, availability, latency etc. These guarantees are referred to as service-level objectives (SLOs) or service-level agreements (SLAs). Having a good monitoring setup lets you not only spot and resolve problems more quickly, but also makes it easier to provide an accurate SLO or SLA.

In this chapter, we look at the different mechanisms you can use to monitor Kafka Connect and give some guidance on how best to use them. There are three ways for you to get insights into Kafka Connect clusters:

- Analyzing metrics
- Using the REST API
- Processing log messages

Each of these resources provides a slightly different view of the system, and together they allow you to fully monitor Kafka Connect.

The most reliable way to quickly identify problems in your system is by tracking metrics. Even a small Kafka Connect pipeline produces thousands of metrics, so you should use monitoring tools to do this. These tools can be configured with alerts that contact administrators or SREs if a particular metric is reporting an unexpected value. Make sure you understand the key metrics that indicate the current state of the system and have a process in place to respond if they flag a problem.

As well as triggering alerts, these metrics can also be used to diagnose specific problems and to identify trends. In order to spot these kinds of trends, you need to not only collect the metrics, but also graph them using some kind of dashboard. Since there are so many metrics, you should be selective about which metrics you alert on, which you use for dashboards, and which you simply collect to refer to during an outage.

Once you know about a problem, you need to have the correct tooling in place to let you diagnose it. The first step for diagnosing Kafka Connect problems is usually to check the status endpoints of the REST API. We show how to do this in detail in Chapter 7, but as a reminder, the following endpoints provide status information:

- GET /connectors?expand=status
- GET /connectors/<CONNECTOR>/status
- GET /connectors/<CONNECTOR>/tasks/<TASK_ID>/status

This information should help you narrow down where the problem is occurring. For example, is it affecting a single connector or task, or all of them? You can also use the REST API as a quick way to check the status of your system during development, startup, or maintenance.

The final resource you can use to monitor your clusters is logs. You should be familiar with the structure of the Kafka Connect logs and understand the key messages that are written out. Logs are useful to identify key actions that have been taken by Kafka Connect and to pinpoint when a problem occurred and why.

Now that we have looked at the high-level processes needed for monitoring, let's look at logging and metrics in more detail. We start with logging.

Monitoring Logs

The logging code in Kafka Connect uses the SLF4J (*https://www.slf4j.org*) facade and, as of the time of writing, reload4j (*https://reload4j.qos.ch*) as the logger implementation. The SLF4J facade is an API for writing Java log lines that hides the implementation. This means developers can use it to write their logging code once, and the implementation can be changed or updated without the code needing to be rewritten.

Kafka originally used Log4j (*https://oreil.ly/C63dl*) as the logger implementation, but this library has reached end of life and is not receiving updates anymore. With KIP-653 (*https://oreil.ly/rHKvR*), Kafka will move to Log4j2 (*https://oreil.ly/M5Pqs*), but only in Kafka 4.0, as the community only breaks compatibility in major releases. So in the meantime, since 3.1.1, Kafka has switched to reload4j, which is a fork of Log4j that still receives updates, including fixes for security vulnerabilities. That is why the default properties file refers to Log4j in the configuration, even though the implementation being used is reload4j.

In this section, we first discuss how to configure logs and why you might change this configuration. Then we look at specific log lines that are written, and how to use them to diagnose problems and review the health of your system.

Logging Configuration

Kafka Connect uses a properties file to configure the specific types of logs that should be included, and where those logs should be stored. The Kafka distribution includes a file, *config/connect-log4j.properties,* with an example configuration to get started. Let's take a look at it.

Log4j Levels and Appenders

If you haven't used a logging system like Log4j before, there are two key concepts you need to know to understand the logs and the configuration: *levels* and *appenders*.

Each log line is associated with a specific level, and then the application (in our case Kafka Connect) can easily be configured and reconfigured to specify which level of log entries should be logged. The levels are FATAL, ERROR, WARN, INFO, DEBUG, and TRACE. These are ordered by severity, so if the log level is set to FATAL, only FATAL log entries are written out. If the level is INFO, log entries that are FATAL, ERROR, WARN and INFO are written, and a log level of TRACE means all entries are written. A default level for all classes is set using a rootLogger; that way you can specify a custom level for a class or all classes in a package using a specific logger. Log level overrides are specified using the format log4j.logger.<PACKAGE_OR_CLASS_NAME>=<LEVEL>.

The locations that logs are written to are configured using appenders, and each appender is given a unique label. First you must specify the class that should be used for the appender, then you can provide specific configuration for that appender. For example, to use the DailyRollingFileAppender and specify the layout configuration, you would use:

```
log4j.appender.<LABEL>=org.apache.log4j.DailyRollingFileAppender
log4j.appender.<LABEL>.layout=org.apache.log4j.PatternLayout
```

> The configuration required varies depending on the specific appender you are using. You can also use different appenders for different packages. You provide the appender after the log level when you define the logger; for example, `log4j.logger.<PACKAGE_OR_CLASS_NAME>=<LEVEL>, <NAME>`.

In Kafka 3.5.0, the file contains the following:

```
log4j.rootLogger=INFO, stdout, connectAppender ❶

log4j.appender.stdout=org.apache.log4j.ConsoleAppender ❷
log4j.appender.stdout.layout=org.apache.log4j.PatternLayout

log4j.appender.connectAppender=org.apache.log4j.DailyRollingFileAppender ❸
log4j.appender.connectAppender.DatePattern='.'yyyy-MM-dd-HH
log4j.appender.connectAppender.File=${kafka.logs.dir}/connect.log
log4j.appender.connectAppender.layout=org.apache.log4j.PatternLayout

connect.log.pattern=[%d] %p %X{connector.context}%m (%c:%L)%n ❹

log4j.appender.stdout.layout.ConversionPattern=${connect.log.pattern} ❺
log4j.appender.connectAppender.layout.ConversionPattern=${connect.log.pattern}

log4j.logger.org.apache.zookeeper=ERROR ❻
log4j.logger.org.reflections=ERROR
```

❶ The `rootLogger` sets the default logging level of all classes and which appenders should be used for writing out the logs.

❷ An appender determines where the logs are sent, and `ConsoleAppender` writes to the console.

❸ By default, Kafka Connect also writes to a log file in the directory specified by the value of the `kafka.logs.dir` JVM argument. Kafka Connect creates a new file each day, renaming the old one to have the date in the name as specified by `log4j.appender.connectAppender.DatePattern`.

❹ The log pattern specifies what is included in log messages. The various characters with the % prefix all map to specific values, such as the date or line number. This pattern includes a custom variable `connector.context`. Kafka Connect uses this variable to include additional information if a log line has come from a particular connector or task. This makes it easier to separate out the runtime and connector-level logs later.

❺ Both the configured appenders use the same custom log pattern.

❻ In addition to the root logger, you can customize the logging levels of individual classes. By default, any logs from classes in the `org.apache.zookeeper` or `org.reflections` packages only log at the ERROR level, not INFO.

Kafka Connect is given the location of the logging configuration file as part of the JVM arguments. You can see the location that it's using by checking the logs for Kafka Connect, which prints out the JVM arguments when it starts up. For example, if you start up Kafka Connect on your local machine, you see the following:

```
INFO WorkerInfo values: jvm.args = -Xms256M, -Xmx2G, ...,
  -Dkafka.logs.dir=/kafka/kafka_2.13-3.5.0/bin/../logs,
  -Dlog4j.configuration=file:./bin/../config/connect-log4j.properties
```

The argument `log4j.configuration` provides the location of the logging configuration file, while `kafka.logs.dir` is used by that configuration file. You can configure these arguments using environment variables. Before you start Kafka Connect, you can set `KAFKA_LOG4J_OPTS` to configure the properties file location and `LOG_DIR` to set the value of the `kafka.logs.dir` argument. For example, to use a properties file in */tmp/custom-config/connect-log4j.properties* and a logs directory of `/tmp/connect/my-logs`, you would run:

```
$ export KAFKA_LOG4J_OPTS="-Dlog4j.configuration=file:/tmp/custom-config/connect-log4j.properties"
$ export LOG_DIR=/tmp/connect/my-logs
```

For production systems, we recommend that you tune the logging configuration rather than use the default properties file. The default configuration uses the `DailyRollingFileAppender`, so a new log file is created every day, meaning that the size of the data in the log directory will be ever increasing. Instead, you should configure Kafka Connect so that the logs are written in a way that your logging analysis tools can handle and such that you can manage their size appropriately. For example, appenders like the `RollingFileAppender` let you configure an upper bound for the number and size of log files.

 No matter what appenders you use, it's often useful to configure the console appender. That way you can easily see the current logs for the running workers without needing to consult your logging tool.

You should also think carefully about the log levels you specify. The default configuration for Kafka Connect sets the `rootLogger` level to INFO, meaning that by default you don't see any DEBUG or TRACE level logs. The default levels you choose should give you enough information to see what is happening in the cluster, but not so much that sifting through the logs becomes tricky. Changing the level to get more log lines can also impact the performance of the Kafka Connect workers. If you want to see some

DEBUG or TRACE level logs, you should set these for a specific package or class, rather than changing the rootLogger. This is because the DEBUG and TRACE levels can be very noisy, use a lot of resources, and quickly fill up your disk.

If something goes wrong with Kafka Connect or a connector, you can use the logs to help with diagnosing the problem. Sometimes you can do this with the default levels, but often it's useful to increase the logging level in the area where the problem is happening. Rather than stopping Kafka Connect, changing the configuration file and restarting it, it is better to change the levels dynamically while Kafka Connect is still running.

As we explain in Chapter 7, you use the REST API to change the logging levels dynamically. You use the PUT /admin/loggers/<LOGGER> endpoint, where the <LOGGER> is the package or class you want to set the level for. You can check the current levels using the GET /admin/loggers endpoint. You should use the configuration file option to specify the default logging levels and appenders that you want to use during normal operation.

Using a logging tool to store, aggregate and analyze logs makes it much easier to examine historical logs and diagnose problems. Kibana (*https://github.com/elastic/ kibana*) is a popular tool choice, as it is open source and is designed to be used as part of an ELK monitoring stack (using Elasticsearch (*https://oreil.ly/t3HGZ*), Logstash (*https://oreil.ly/dVnQY*) and Kibana together). Other popular tools include Splunk (*https://www.splunk.com*) and Datadog (*https://www.datadoghq.com*). Some of these tools provide Log4j appenders that send the logs directly to them, while others read the logs from a file. It is also very common for logging tools to be able to read logs directly from standard out, meaning you can just use the console appender.

Now that we know how to configure the logging, let's look at some of the actual log messages that are written out.

Understanding Startup Logs

There are many different log entries that are written out by a Kafka Connect cluster. You don't need to be familiar with every single one, but it is useful to understand the general structure of the logs and the kind of things that you should look out for. Let's begin by looking at the logs that are written out while Kafka Connect is starting up. These are important because you can use them to verify your cluster setup.

 For all of the log snippets, we have omitted some of the lines and the date and time that precedes the log message to make it more readable.

The first thing that Kafka Connect logs out when it starts up is information about the JVM and operating system that is running the worker. This includes the JVM arguments, the specific JVM that is running, and the classpath:

```
INFO WorkerInfo values:
    jvm.args = -Xms256M, -Xmx2G, ..., -Dkafka.logs.dir=/kafka/kafka_2.13-3.5.0/bi
n/../logs, -Dlog4j.configuration=file:./bin/../config/connect-log4j.properties
    jvm.spec = Homebrew, OpenJDK 64-Bit Server VM, 11.0.14.1, 11.0.14.1+0
    jvm.classpath = /kafka/kafka_2.13-3.5.0/bin/../libs/activation-1.1.1.jar:/kaf
ka/kafka_2.13-3.5.0/bin/../libs/...
    os.spec = Mac OS X, x86_64, 11.6.8
    os.vcpus = 12
(org.apache.kafka.connect.runtime.WorkerInfo:71)
```

This is very useful to verify things like the logging configuration and Java version.

Secondly, Kafka Connect prints out the plug-ins and aliases that it finds and loads. Any plug-ins you have added using the plug-in path are loaded first by the Plugin ClassLoader:

```
INFO Scanning for plugin classes. This might take a moment ...
INFO Registered loader: PluginClassLoader{pluginLocation=file:/kafka/kafka_2.13-3
.5.0/connectors/connect-file-3.5.0.jar}
INFO Added plugin 'org.apache.kafka.connect.file.FileStreamSinkConnector'
```

Then, Kafka Connect uses the AppClassLoader to load plug-ins from the classpath:

```
INFO Registered loader: jdk.internal.loader.ClassLoaders$AppClassLoader@6a6824be
...
INFO Added plugin 'org.apache.kafka.connect.mirror.MirrorSourceConnector'
```

This is a quick way to check that Kafka Connect has loaded the connectors, transformations, predicates, and configuration providers that you want to use.

Kafka Connect also logs out each alias that has been added for the different plug-ins.

```
INFO Added aliases 'MirrorSourceConnector' and 'MirrorSource' to plugin
'org.apache.kafka.connect.mirror.MirrorSourceConnector'
```

Next, Kafka Connect logs out the different configurations that it is using. The first of these is the DistributedConfig:

```
INFO DistributedConfig values:
    ...
    bootstrap.servers = [localhost:9092]
    config.storage.replication.factor = 1
    config.storage.topic = connect-configs
    connect.protocol = sessioned
    connector.client.config.override.policy = All
    group.id = connect-cluster
    header.converter = class org.apache.kafka.connect.storage.SimpleHeaderConverter
    key.converter = class org.apache.kafka.connect.json.JsonConverter
    listeners = [http://:8083]
```

```
offset.storage.partitions = 25
offset.storage.replication.factor = 1
offset.storage.topic = connect-offsets
security.protocol = PLAINTEXT
ssl.enabled.protocols = [TLSv1.2, TLSv1.3]
status.storage.partitions = 5
status.storage.replication.factor = 1
status.storage.topic = connect-status
value.converter = class org.apache.kafka.connect.json.JsonConverter
...
    (org.apache.kafka.connect.runtime.distributed.DistributedConfig:376)
```

This includes all of the worker configurations and means you can verify any custom configurations you have set. Some other values you might want to check when you are starting Kafka Connect for the very first time are:

- Kafka Connect internal topic configurations
- Bootstrap servers configuration
- Security configurations
- Client override policy
- Default converters

Every time Kafka Connect starts a Kafka client, it logs out the configuration for that client. So both during startup and once the worker is running, you can use this to check the configuration for the admin, producer, or consumer clients that are used. This is particularly important if you have set client overrides in your Kafka Connect configuration.

After each of the configuration log lines, you might see warnings similar to the following:

```
WARN The configuration 'config.storage.topic' was
supplied but isn't a known config.
```

The configuration provided to the Kafka Connect worker can be worker specific or it can be for one of the clients. Every configuration is read by every client; however, some configurations are only recognized by one of them. So when a client reads a configuration it doesn't recognize, it prints out this warning. This means you are likely to see this warning even if your configuration is valid. This doesn't affect the running of Kafka Connect, as each client ignores the unknown configurations.

The first worker to start in a Kafka Connect cluster creates three internal topics, if they have not already been created. Subsequent workers, and any workers that are restarted later, will then have to reprocess the data on these topics when they start up.

This can be a very chatty process and produce a lot of log lines. You can spot when this is happening by looking out for log lines that reference the internal topic names. For example:

```
INFO [Consumer clientId=consumer-connect-cluster-3, groupId=connect-cluster]
  Subscribed to partition(s): connect-configs-0
```

When the worker has finished starting and it is ready to receive requests via the REST API and run connectors, you see some messages similar to the following:

```
INFO REST resources initialized; server is started and ready to handle requests
INFO Kafka Connect started
```

Now we have looked at the logs that are printed during startup, let's discuss the logs that are written out at runtime and how you can use them.

Analyzing Logs

You can use the Kafka Connect logs in two different ways: to see what is currently happening in your cluster, and to identify and diagnose past issues. As we mentioned earlier, you should collect and store your logs in a log analysis tool to make this process easier.

Log contexts

There are many components that make up Kafka Connect, which can make it tricky to determine which component the log line is from. To solve this, many log lines use a context to indicate the worker, client, or connector that the log is related to. Not all lines contain a context; for example, most of the logs during startup omit it. Most log analysis tools let you filter logs for a keyword. If you are diagnosing a bug with a particular connector, you can increase the logging level for that connector and then use the context as the keyword to view all the logs related to this connector.

The following log lines show example lines, the first one with no context, then with a worker context, and finally with a connector context:

```
INFO Kafka Connect started
INFO [Worker clientId=connect-1, groupId=connect-cluster]
  Finished starting connectors and tasks
INFO [file-sink|task-0] Instantiated task file-sink-0 with version 3.5.0 of type
  org.apache.kafka.connect.file.FileStreamSinkTask
```

The context is included straight after the log level and is surrounded by square brackets. Some log lines include multiple contexts, for example with the task and the client. The client contexts state what kind of client it is, then include further metadata in a comma-separated list to identify the client, such as the clientId, and for consumers, the groupId.

A connector context always has the connector name, then a pipe symbol and the task ID.

Key events

If you are investigating a problem, or want to verify that Kafka Connect is working as you expected, you can use the logs to identify key actions that it has taken. This is useful to confirm when a connector was created, updated or deleted. Here are a few examples of the log messages that Kafka Connect writes for significant events:

```
INFO [file-sink|worker] Creating connector file-sink of type
    org.apache.kafka.connect.file.FileStreamSinkConnector ❶
INFO [file-sink|worker] Finished creating connector file-sink ❷

INFO [Worker clientId=connect-1, groupId=connect-cluster]
    Connector file-sink config updated ❸

INFO [file-sink|task-0] Creating task file-sink-0 ❹
INFO [file-sink|task-0] WorkerSinkTask{id=file-sink-0} Executing sink task ❺

INFO Successfully processed removal of connector 'file-sink' ❻
```

❶ A new connector is being created.

❷ A new connector has finished being created.

❸ The configuration of a connector has been updated.

❹ A new task is being created for a connector; notice the context with the connector and task name included.

❺ The task is starting up.

❻ A connector is deleted.

Whenever Kafka Connect finishes making updates to the running connectors and tasks, it prints out the following:

```
INFO [Worker clientId=connect-1, groupId=connect-cluster]
    Finished starting connectors and tasks
```

Errors

The Kafka Connect logs are very useful for spotting problems with the system and diagnosing bugs. When a problem occurs in Kafka Connect, it writes a message to the log indicating what happened and often giving a cause. Log messages that have been written out as a result of a problem are given the log level WARNING, ERROR, or FATAL.

If you know there was a problem with Kafka Connect, it is often useful to search the logs for these log levels to quickly find useful information.

For example, if Kafka Connect cannot reach Kafka, you see the following log line:

```
WARN [AdminClient clientId=adminclient-1]
    Connection to node -1 (localhost/127.0.0.1:9092) could not be established.
    Broker may not be available.
```

You should also look out for stack traces in the logs, as this indicates that something went wrong. A stack trace includes the Java classes and line numbers involved, so you can start investigating the problem to determine the cause. Many logging tools have features that let you find stack traces automatically.

If someone makes an invalid request to the REST API, you get an ERROR line that includes a stack trace in the logs. For example, when trying to access a nonexistent endpoint:

```
ERROR Uncaught exception in REST call to /invalid
javax.ws.rs.NotFoundException: HTTP 404 Not Found
    at org.glassfish.jersey.server.ServerRuntime$1.run(ServerRuntime.java:252)
    at org.glassfish.jersey.internal.Errors$1.call(Errors.java:248)
    ...
```

Now that we know how to use the logs, let's move on to look at the metrics.

Monitoring Metrics

In this section we describe how you can expose Kafka Connect metrics to your monitoring systems, and we share some best practices for setting up effective dashboards and alerts. We also demonstrate how you can browse metrics manually, as this is useful when getting started and when working in development environments.

In order to quickly find the metrics that are relevant to you, it's important to understand how they are categorized and named.

A metric name is composed of three parts:

- A *group*, sometimes also called a *domain*
- A set of *keys* and *values* called *tags*
- An *attribute*

For example, a metric might have a group of kafka.connect, with tags type=app-info and an attribute called commit-id.

The Kafka Connect runtime emits metrics, then each Kafka client it uses internally also emits its own metrics. Each type of client has its own group for easy identification:

- `kafka.admin.client` for admin clients
- `kafka.consumer` for consumers
- `kafka.producer` for producers
- `kafka.connect` for the Kafka Connect runtime

 Connectors can also emit their own metrics. For example, the Debezium connector we explore in Chapter 5 does. For these metrics, each connector typically has its own group.

To further identify what a metric is related to, Kafka uses the `type` tag to specify which internal component or category each metric comes from. The example metric we used previously had a tag of `type=app-info`, meaning the type is `app-info`. This category contains metrics that provide metadata about the instance.

Each metric is associated with a value, which is typically, but not necessarily, a number. The behavior of Kafka Connect, as well as the kind of metric, determines how its value evolves over time. In order to track a variety of things, there are different kinds of metrics, including the following:

Counters
    Counters track quantities that keep increasing, for example the number of errors that have happened. Such metrics often have the `-total` or `-count` suffix in their attribute.

Gauges
    Gauges measure amounts that can have arbitrary values, for example the rate of errors per second. Such metrics often have the `-rate`, `-ratio`, or `-avg` suffix in their attributes

Maximum and minimum
    Maximum and minimum track the extreme values recorded for a measurement, for example the maximum and minimum latency observed when producing records to Kafka. Such metrics have the `-max` and `-min` suffix, respectively, in their attributes.

There are also a few configurations you can set on the runtime to alter the behavior of metrics. These are detailed in in "Metrics configurations" on page 219.

Now that you understand how metrics are named and the different kinds that are emitted, let's look at how Kafka Connect exposes them.

Metrics Reporters

Like all components of Apache Kafka, Connect uses metrics reporters to expose its metrics. A metrics reporter is a class that implements the org.apache.kafka .common.metrics.MetricsReporter interface. Kafka provides a built-in implementation, org.apache.kafka.common.metrics.JmxReporter, that exposes metrics via the Java Management Extensions (JMX) API by registering a managed bean (MBean) for each metric. You can write your own implementation of this interface to expose metrics with your desired mechanism, or reuse one of the implementations the community has already built. You configure the metrics reporters that you want to use via the metric.reporters configuration, which is a comma-separated list of metrics reporters.

> Notice that the configuration for metrics reporters is called met ric.reporters, with no "s" on the end of the word metric. Make sure you specify this correctly and don't accidentally add an "s"!

If you choose to use the JmxReporter, there are a couple of configurations you can use to filter the metrics it exposes; metrics.jmx.include and metrics.jmx.exclude. As Kafka components emit a lot of metrics, if you know the metrics you want to monitor, you can use these configurations to reduce the amount of metrics collected and sent to your monitoring system.

Up to Kafka 4.0, JmxReporter is enabled by default, even if not specified via metric.reporters. From Kafka 3.4.0, if you are not using JmxReporter, you can disable it by setting auto.include.jmx.reporter to false. From Kafka 4.0, only reporters listed in metric.reporters will be enabled.

In most cases, as many tools support interacting with JMX, you can rely on JmxRe porter. Otherwise, you have the choice of using or building a metrics reporter especially designed for your monitoring tools.

Exposing metrics via a reporter lets you get them into a monitoring system, observe them, and set alerts for detecting issues.

Analyzing Metrics

Due to the large number of metrics available, you should use a monitoring system to process them. Metrics come from all components running on the many hosts of your pipelines, so a monitoring system allows you to collate and query them efficiently. You can then generate graphs and charts to visualize them. There are many tools available; for example, if you want to use open source software, you can pick Prometheus (*https://prometheus.io*) for storing and querying, and Grafana (*https://grafana.com*) for rendering dashboards. The Prometheus project has a tool called JMX Exporter (*https://oreil.ly/LXgQc*) that can retrieve metrics from JMX and make them accessible to Prometheus.

Out of the hundreds of metrics emitted at runtime by a Kafka Connect environment, you typically only want to collect a subset, create graphs for an even smaller subset, and have alerts for the few most important ones. This is illustrated in Figure 9-1.

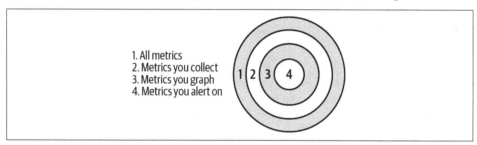

1. All metrics
2. Metrics you collect
3. Metrics you graph
4. Metrics you alert on

Figure 9-1. Euler diagram showing the different sets of metrics you use for collecting, graphing, and alerting on, respectively

For all the metrics that you decide to graph, you should consider how to organize and display them. Tools like Grafana allow you to build dashboards that group multiple graphs together. It's common to have one dashboard that is designed to show high-level indicators of whether everything is working as expected, and then use separate dashboards for finer-grained metrics. For example, for Kafka Connect, you might have a dashboard that shows the number of connectors in different states, then a separate dashboard with representations of the network traffic.

There are a number of different types of graphs you can use to visualize your metrics, so consider the kind of metric you are dealing with when choosing the graph. For example, you will likely want a time series for metrics you want to observe over time, such as the incoming byte rate from Kafka. In comparison, some Kafka Connect metrics, like the number of failed connectors, might be better represented with a gauge so you can quickly see the current value. Other graph types you can use include bar charts, pie charts, histograms, and heatmaps. It's worth spending time designing dashboards that quickly and effectively convey the state of the environments you monitor.

As mentioned earlier in this chapter, metrics are often the main source for raising alerts that either trigger automated recovery processes or call engineers when an issue is detected. Prometheus lets you set alerts that are integrated with incident management systems such as PagerDuty (*https://www.pagerduty.com*). The main thing to consider when setting up alerts is the action that is expected when the alert triggers. For example, a common alert for Kafka Connect pipelines is one that triggers when a task from a connector enters the FAILED state. When this triggers, the correct action is to restart the task. Rather than relying on people to remember the actions, alerts are typically linked with a description of the issue and instructions to address it. These instructions are often called a runbook, playbook, or standard operating procedure (SOP).

You should avoid creating alerts that fire and auto-resolve immediately. For example, if you set alerts based on latency metrics, a short network blip can significantly increase the latency for a few seconds before returning to normal. Instead, you should configure the alert so it only fires when the latency metric has been above the normal value for a minimum duration.

Now that we understand how to monitor metrics, let's see how to manually access metrics via the command line.

Exploring Metrics

A good way to get a feel for the various metrics available is to access them manually, so, in this section, we explore them using the command-line tools jconsole and JmxTool.

By default, most JVMs make their JMX API accessible for other local processes to attach to. So if you start Kafka Connect via the connect-distributed.sh script, you can normally use a tool like jconsole, which is included in your JDK, to access the metrics of your Kafka Connect instance. This is very useful for debugging, especially in development environments.

To see this in action, start jconsole from your command line, select the Kafka Connect process, org.apache.kafka.connect.cli.ConnectDistributed, and click on the Connect button, as shown in Figure 9-2.

```
$ jconsole
```

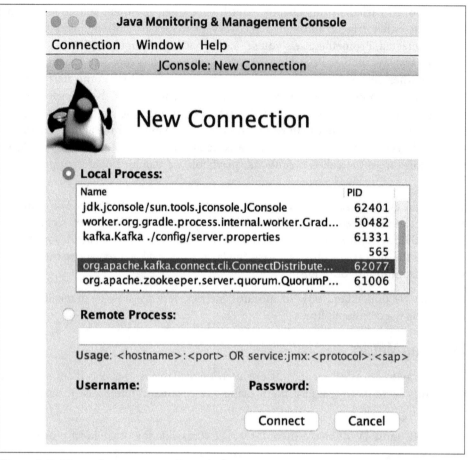

Figure 9-2. JConsole new connection window

When connecting without TLS, jconsole asks for confirmation before making an insecure connection. Go to the MBeans tab and you can then browse all metrics from this instance.

> In jconsole, you can double-click on a metric value to switch the display to a graph instead of the instant value. While we recommend using dedicated monitoring tools to graph metrics in production, it can be useful to quickly graph a specific value in jconsole during development.

You may need to expose JMX over the network to access it; if so, you need to set a port for JMX to listen to. Using the connect-distributed.sh script, you can do this by setting the JMX_PORT environment variable. For example:

```
$ JMX_PORT=9998 \
    ./bin/connect-distributed.sh ./config/connect-distributed.properties
```

Then you can also use `jconsole` by providing a host and port to connect to the Connect process:

```
$ jconsole localhost:9998
```

Then, go to the MBeans tab again to browse the metrics.

Exposing JMX in this way may be necessary to make it accessible to your monitoring systems, but you should consider the security implications.

 You need to be careful when exposing JMX over the network. Because JMX can load arbitrary classes, a malicious user could gain access to your workers. If you need remote JMX access, configure the JVM to use TLS and authentication to strictly control who can remotely interact with JMX. Check the JMX security configurations available in your JVM. You can provide them by setting the `KAFKA_JMX_OPTS` environment variable when starting Kafka Connect.

Kafka also comes with a tool, `JmxTool`, to retrieve metrics from the terminal. This can be useful if `jconsole` is not available in your environment. For example, if Kafka Connect is exposing JMX on port 9998, and TLS and authentication have not been enabled, you can use the following command to dump some metrics:

```
$ ./bin/kafka-run-class.sh org.apache.kafka.tools.JmxTool \  ❶
    --jmx-url service:jmx:rmi:///jndi/rmi://:9998/jmxrmi \  ❷
    --one-time=true \  ❸
    --object-name kafka.connect:type=app-info  ❹
Trying to connect to JMX url: service:jmx:rmi:///jndi/rmi://:1234/jmxrmi.
"time","kafka.connect:type=app-info:commit-id","kafka.connect:type=app-info:start
-time-ms","kafka.connect:type=app-info:version"
1660146910127,38103ffaa962ef50,1660146350598,3.5.0
```

❶ This tool does not have a dedicated script, so you need to start it via the `kafka-run-class.sh` script.

❷ The host and port to connect to are provided via the `--jmx-url` argument. In this case, the hostname is omitted, so it's `localhost` on port 9998.

❸ The tool can collect metrics periodically; in this case, we only want it to run once.

❹ By default, the tool dumps all metrics. In this case, we specify that we only want the `kafka.connect:type=app-info` metric, which contains some metadata about the instance.

The output is composed of three lines. The first line can be ignored; it only indicates that the tool is establishing a connection. The second line describes the attributes of the metrics retrieved. The line starts with `time`, which is inserted by `JmxTool` to indicate when it collected the metrics; this is not an attribute. This metric has three attributes, `commit-id`, `start-time-ms`, and `version`.

The third line provides the actual values for the `time` and for each attribute. So, the previous output has given us the following information:

`time: 1660146910127`
> The Unix timestamp in milliseconds when the command ran

`commit-id: 38103ffaa962ef50`
> The hash of the Git commit Kafka Connect is running

`start-time-ms: 1660146350598`
> The Unix timestamp in milliseconds when Kafka Connect started

`version: 3.5.0`
> The version of Kafka Connect

`JmxTool` supports TLS and authentication as well as several options to retrieve specific metrics or attributes by name, change the output format, and control whether it runs periodically or not.

It's now time to look at the actual metrics from the various components in a Kafka Connect pipeline that you should monitor.

Key Metrics

We are going to look at the metrics in the format in which they are exposed via `JmxReporter`, which is MBean. If you use a different reporter, their exact name may vary slightly, but the types and attributes should be the same.

As a reminder of the format, if we take the following MBean, `kafka.con nect:type=app-info:commit-id`, then `kafka.connect` is the group, it has a single tag (`type`) that is set to `app-info`, and `commit-id` is the attribute.

Let's start by looking at the metrics emitted by the Kafka Connect runtime.

Kafka Connect Runtime Metrics

The Kafka Connect runtime metrics are the ones that are emitted by each of the Kafka Connect workers. These metrics all have the `kafka.connect` group. To make it a bit easier to explore them all, we have grouped them into five categories:

- Metadata metrics
- Network metrics
- Group protocol metrics
- Connector-level metrics
- Task-level metrics

Metadata metrics

The metrics that provide metadata about the Kafka Connect runtime all have the `type` tag set to `app-info`.

Under `kafka.connect:type=app-info`, the most important metrics you should collect are:

`start-time-ms`
> The Unix timestamp in milliseconds of when the runtime started. It is helpful to track when the current runtime was last restarted.

`version`
> The Kafka Connect version. It allows you to track the version each runtime is running and, for example, follow the progress of upgrades.

Network metrics

There are a number of metrics that track the connectivity between the Kafka Connect runtime and brokers in the Kafka cluster. They have the `type` tag set to `connect-node-metrics` and they are grouped based on the Kafka broker connection they are related to. This is done using the `node-id` tag that specifies their corresponding broker ID. These metrics give a good overview of the activity over each connection. The most important ones you should collect and graph are:

`incoming-byte-rate, outgoing-byte-rate`
> The read and write rate, respectively, in bytes per second, of the Kafka Connect runtime from and to the specified Kafka broker. These are useful to validate that data is flowing between Kafka Connect and Kafka.

`request-latency-avg`
> The average latency in milliseconds for requests Kafka Connect is sending to the specified broker. This allows you to compare latency between the different brokers and Kafka Connect workers so you can identify if a particular instance is overloaded.

The node-id tag has some special values that represent specific connections to Kafka. If it is a negative number, the metric is for a connection to one of the brokers that was specified as a bootstrap server. On the other hand, if it is a very large number (near 2^{31}), the metric is for the dedicated connection to the coordinator.

Group protocol metrics

As we describe in Chapter 4, Kafka Connect workers cooperate by using the group membership protocol. In order to do so, they communicate with one of the brokers in the Kafka cluster that acts as their group coordinator. Metrics in this category track how well workers are cooperating in their group. They have the `type` tag set to `connect-worker-rebalance-metrics` or `connect-coordinator-metrics`.

For a high-level overview of rebalances across the Kafka Connect cluster, there are the `kafka.connect:type=connect-worker-rebalance-metrics` metrics. The most important ones that you should collect and graph are:

`rebalancing`
> Set to 1 if a rebalance is currently happening; otherwise, it is set to 0. While a rebalance is ongoing, some endpoints of the REST API return HTTP 409 (conflict) and some tasks may not be running.

`rebalance-avg-time-ms, time-since-last-rebalance-ms`
> The average duration of rebalances in milliseconds and the number of milliseconds since the last rebalance, respectively. It can be useful to track the trends of these metrics to ensure that the health of the environment is not slowly degrading.

There are also a few other attributes that are typically less useful on a daily basis, but still interesting to collect:

`completed-rebalances-total`
> The total number of rebalances this worker has done.

`leader-name`
> One of the workers in the Kafka Connect cluster is given the leader role as part of the group. This metric reports the protocol, host, and port of the leader's REST API, for example, `http://worker1:8083/`.

`connect-protocol`
> The worker's rebalance protocol. If you are changing the current protocol, for example upgrading from `eager` to `sessioned`, you can use it to track the protocol used by each worker.

Under `kafka.connect:type=connect-coordinator-metrics` you can find metrics covering details of the group protocol. Most of these metrics are very fine grained and only useful when debugging group protocol issues. However, there are a couple of metrics you should collect and graph:

assigned-connectors, assigned-tasks
> Tracks how many connectors and tasks have been assigned to this worker, respectively. You want to ensure each worker has a similar number of connectors and tasks. As described in Chapter 7, these metrics can be useful for capacity planning and detecting if you need to scale your Kafka Connect cluster up or down.

Finally, under `kafka.connect:type=connect-metrics`, there are some even finer-grained network metrics for the connection to the coordinator. These can be useful when investigating specific network issues but are not important for day-to-day operations.

Connector-level metrics

All of these metrics track details about a specific connector. Each worker only reports metrics for the connectors it runs. The associated connector is specified via the connector tag. For example, `kafka.connect:type=connector-metrics,connector=s3sink` has the metrics for the connector named s3sink. These metrics have the type tag set to `connector-metrics` or `connect-worker-metrics`.

First, under `kafka.connect:type=connector-metrics`, you can find details about each running connector. The most important metric you should collect and graph is:

status
> The current state of the connector. This can be either unassigned, running, paused, stopped, failed, or destroyed. The meaning of each of these states are described in Chapter 4. This metric is also a good candidate for setting up an alert so you notice a connector moving into the failed state.

There are also a few other attributes that can be interesting to collect to get an inventory of what connectors are deployed:

connector-class
> The same value as the connector.class field in the connector configuration.

connector-version
> The version of the connector.

connector-type
> This can be either sink or source.

Then, under `kafka.connect:type=connect-worker-metrics`, you can find the current state of the tasks of each connector. The most important metrics to collect and graph are:

`connector-failed-task-count`
> The number of failed tasks for the specified connector. This is a good candidate for an alert, as failed tasks don't process data, so they need to be explicitly restarted via the REST API.

`connector-unassigned-task-count`
> Unassigned tasks have not been assigned to a worker, so they are not yet processing data. If this stays at a non-zero value, it indicates an issue with the Kafka Connect cluster. This is also a good candidate for an alert.

There are also attributes for the number of tasks in each state. It can be useful to collect one or more of them, depending on how you want to display the state of your tasks:

- `connector-paused-task-count`
- `connector-restarting-task-count`
- `connector-running-task-count`
- `connector-destroyed-task-count`
- `connector-total-task-count`

The `connect-worker-metrics` type also has metrics without the `connector` tag that track connector and task startup successes and failures. In practice, it's often enough to monitor the state of connectors and tasks directly, rather than rely on these high-level metrics.

Task-level metrics

These metrics are all tagged with both the connector and task ID, for example: `kafka.connect:type=task-error-metrics,connector=s3sink,task=0`. They have the `type` tag set to one of `connector-task-metrics`, `sink-task-metrics`, `source-task-metrics`, or `task-error-metrics`.

A lot of the metrics in this category can be useful when fine-tuning your connectors and tasks, to see, for example, how the connector is handling things like offset commits or batches. You can review these metrics before and after configuration changes to understand how these affect your connector.

Under `kafka.connect:type=connector-task-metrics`, the most important metric you need to collect and graph is:

status

> The current state of the task. Tasks in the `failed` state need to be explicitly restarted via the REST API. If you are running a Kafka Connect version older than 3.0, this is a good candidate for an alert, because failed tasks have to be restarted individually. If you are using a newer version, you can instead use the connector-level metric that just gives a total count of failed tasks.

Under `kafka.connect:type=sink-task-metrics`, there are metrics specific to sink connectors. The most important metrics to collect and graph are:

partition-count

> The number of partitions this task is subscribed to in Kafka. Ideally, each task should handle a similar number of partitions, and if tasks are handling too many or too few partitions, you should consider tuning the number of tasks appropriately.

sink-record-send-rate

> The number of records given to this task per second by the Kafka Connect runtime after the converter and transformations have been applied. If you have transformations potentially dropping records, you can also use `sink-record-read-rate` for the rate before transformations are run.

Similarly, `kafka.connect:type=source-task-metrics` contains metrics for source connectors. The most important metrics to collect and graph are:

source-record-write-rate

> The number of records per second given to the Kafka Connect runtime by this task after transformations have been applied. If you have transformations potentially dropping records, you can also use `source-record-poll-rate` for the rate before transformations run.

poll-batch-avg-time-ms

> The average duration in milliseconds the connector takes to retrieve records from the external system when polled by the Kafka Connect runtime.

transaction-size-avg

> The average transaction size in number of records. This only applies when exactly-once support is enabled on the worker.

The last category, `kafka.connect:type=task-error-metrics`, has metrics related to errors encountered by tasks. These metrics depend on the various error handling configurations, described in "Configurations for Error Handling" on page 228. The important metrics to collect and monitor are:

`deadletterqueue-produce-failures`, `deadletterqueue-produce-requests`
> Counts the number of times the runtime failed to produce records and the number of times it attempted to produce records to the dead letter queue. They only apply to sink connectors that have been configured with a dead letter queue.

`last-error-timestamp`
> The Unix timestamp in milliseconds of the last error. This can be useful to identify when errors first started happening and locate the matching error messages in logs. If no errors have occurred, this defaults to 0.

`total-errors-logged`
> If `errors.log.enable` is set to `true`, this reports how many errors the task has logged.

`total-records-errors`
> Tracks the number of errors this task encountered if `errors.tolerance` is set to `none`.

`total-records-failures`
> Tracks the number of errors this task encountered regardless of whether or not they could be retried or ignored.

`total-records-skipped`
> If `errors.tolerance` is set to `all`, tasks skip records they fail to process. This metric tracks the number of records that have been skipped by this task.

Other System Metrics

In addition to the metrics from the runtime, in order to assert that your pipelines are working correctly, you need to monitor all of the other components. This starts with the consumers, producers, and admin clients used by the runtime and connectors. It also includes metrics from your workers' hosts and from all the systems Kafka Connect interacts with, including Kafka!

As mentioned in Chapter 7, the capacity of a Kafka Connect cluster depends on the CPU, memory, and network resources allocated to each worker, so it's critical to monitor these closely to ensure that workers can perform as expected. In environments like Kubernetes, host metrics can easily be collected from all nodes and sent to a tool like Prometheus. On the other hand, if you run your own bare metal servers, you need to install and configure a tool like Collectd (*https://collectd.org*) to collect these system metrics.

Alongside host metrics, the health of the JVM is also crucial, as it further impacts how well workers run. The most important metrics from the JVM are about garbage collection and memory usage. The names of the metrics depend on the JVM you are using. For example, with OpenJDK, the memory metrics you should always collect and graph are:

- `java.lang:type=Memory:HeapMemoryUsage`
- `java.lang:type=Memory:NonHeapMemoryUsage`

These are, respectively, the current size of the Java heap and the amount of native memory allocated. You should ensure these stay stable over time and don't slowly creep up.

For the garbage collection, again with OpenJDK, you should collect and graph:

- `java.lang:name=G1   Old   Generation,type=GarbageCollector:Collection Count`
- `java.lang:name=G1   Old   Generation,type=GarbageCollector:Collection Time`
- `java.lang:name=G1   Young  Generation,type=GarbageCollector:Collection Count`
- `java.lang:name=G1   Young  Generation,type=GarbageCollector:Collection Time`

These indicate how many times garbage collection has happened and how long it has taken, in milliseconds, since the JVM started.

Internal Kafka client metrics

Each Kafka client emits hundreds of metrics that cover its behavior extensively. While you may need to dive into very arcane network metrics to diagnose a specific issue, there are a few metrics that you should always monitor.

For sink connectors, it's important to track their lag. Lag indicates how far from the end of the input topics they are, so it lets you estimate the gap between the data in Kafka and in the target system. Also, if the lag grows too large, records being processed by the connector could be deleted by the topic retention policies. Ideally, you want the lag to be small and stable.

The metric you should monitor for sink connector lag is `kafka.consumer:type=consumer-fetch-manager-metrics,client-id=connector-consumer-<CONNECTOR_NAME>-<TASK_ID>,topic=<TOPIC>,partition=<PARTITION>`. It has a few attributes, but the most important ones are:

- `records-lag` is the current lag in number of records.

- `records-lag-avg` is the average lag in number of records since the consumer started. This can help you see trends and, for example, find out if adding tasks to a connector helped reduce lag.

For source connectors, you need to monitor how well producers used by the runtime are working. The most important metrics are their throughput and whether they are hitting errors producing to the Kafka cluster.

The metric you should monitor is `kafka.producer:type=producer-topic-metrics, client-id=connector-producer-<CONNECTOR_NAME>.<TASK_ID>,topic=<TOPIC>`. It has a few attributes, but the most important ones are:

`byte-rate`
> The throughput of the producer in bytes per second. This is often a useful metric on its own, but in order to make decisions it has to be compared to the expected amount of data in the source external system. If the connector has processed all data, and no new data is available, the byte rate could be 0 while everything is fine.

`record-error-rate`
> The number of errors per second encountered by the producer while sending records to the Kafka topic. Under normal circumstances, there should be no errors. If this metric spikes while the byte rate drops, that indicates a probable issue.

The admin client also has metrics, but due to the nature of its usage in Kafka Connect, it is usually not very important to actively monitor them.

Kafka and external system metrics

In order to investigate and debug some issues, it may be useful to get logs and metrics from Kafka and whichever systems your connectors interact with. However, as the person running Kafka Connect, you may not have access to metrics from these systems. If that's the case, you should proactively reach out to the other teams managing them to set up lines of communication and status reporting, so you can quickly engage with them if needed.

On the Kafka side, at a very high level, the most important metrics related to Kafka Connect are about the overall cluster health and the throughput of the topics Kafka Connect uses.

The following metrics are usually a good start to quickly assess cluster health:

`kafka.server:type=ReplicaManager,name=UnderMinIsrPartitionCount:Value`
    Indicates the current number of partitions that have fewer in-sync replicas (ISR) than the configured `min.insync.replicas` value. Partitions in this state are not fully available and reject produce requests with `acks=all`, which is what Kafka Connect uses for source tasks.

`kafka.controller:type=KafkaController,name=ActiveControllerCount:Value`
    Indicates the number of controllers in the cluster. This should be 1 at all times. If it is not, operations such as creating topics may not work, and the cluster metadata could be invalid.

`kafka.server:type=KafkaRequestHandlerPool,name=RequestHandlerAvgIdlePer`
`cent:FifteenMinuteRate`
    Tracks the percentage of time request handling threads are idle. Values below `0.3` (30%) often indicate a serious performance problem, which would typically cause timeouts and retries in Kafka Connect.

To track throughput for the Kafka Connect topics, you can use:

`kafka.server:type=BrokerTopicMetrics,name=BytesInPer`
`Sec,topic=<TOPIC>:FifteenMinuteRate`
    The incoming byte rate (in bytes per second) to the topic over the last fifteen minutes.

`kafka.server:type=BrokerTopicMetrics,name=BytesOutPer`
`Sec,topic=<TOPIC>:FifteenMinuteRate`
    The outgoing byte rate (in bytes per second) from the topic over the last fifteen minutes.

In both metrics, `<TOPIC>` is the name of the topic associated with the metric. There are also metrics across all topics in the cluster; they have the same names and attributes, just without the `topic` tag.

The host and JVM metrics we covered for Kafka Connect are also important to Kafka, so should be tracked in the same way.

For a more thorough look at monitoring Kafka, refer to Chapter 13, "Monitoring Kafka," of *Kafka: The Definitive Guide* (O'Reilly).

Finally, each of the external systems that Kafka Connect interacts with has its own metrics. You should check the documentation of your external systems to identify the key metrics you need to collect and the various tools and techniques that are recommended to monitor them effectively.

Summary

In this chapter, we covered why logs and metrics are critical for monitoring Kafka Connect clusters. Logs and metrics enable administrators to assert that their pipelines work as expected, and they also provide clues to help debug in case failures happen. This is true whether a Kafka Connect environment is run once (to copy a bounded set of data from one place to another) or whether it's long-lived and consistently streams data between Kafka and other systems.

We first took a look into logs by highlighting key log lines Kafka Connect emits at startup and at runtime to indicate its state. As an administrator, you should be aware of the most common log lines, as this also helps identify unexpected messages that could be linked to issues. We also introduced basic concepts from Log4j that you should be familiar with, as this is what Kafka Connect uses to configure its logging behavior.

Then we explained how metrics work in Kafka Connect and how metrics reporters are used to expose metrics to monitoring systems. You can use the built-in reporter (JmxReporter) or provide your own. It is very important to understand the common tools and techniques for turning metrics into graphs and dashboards; you can use these to efficiently track the health of clusters and automatically raise alerts when incidents are detected.

Finally, we took a deep dive into the actual Kafka Connect runtime metrics you should know. You can use these as a starting point for which metrics to graph and use for alerts, and to refer to later. However, you should also take the time to explore the metrics yourself and review them with your pipeline in mind. You should also monitor the other components in your pipeline. Don't overlook these, as they can be essential for spotting and fixing problems.

CHAPTER 10

Administering Kafka Connect on Kubernetes

Kubernetes has become a popular deployment environment for many workloads. According to the Cloud Native Computing Foundation (*https://www.cncf.io*) (CNCF), record numbers of companies are now using Kubernetes and containers as their foundation for deploying workloads. In 2021, they found that 96% (*https://oreil.ly/B0tIv*) of organizations were evaluating or using these technologies.

In this chapter, we look at why Kubernetes is so popular and review the considerations required for running Kafka Connect on Kubernetes. We also discuss some of the benefits that a Kubernetes operator provides, such as automating the deployment of resources, and letting you manage your workloads declaratively. Finally, we introduce the Strimzi operator as an example of one that provides support for Kafka Connect.

Introduction to Kubernetes

To understand why you might be interested in deploying Kafka Connect to Kubernetes, it is important that you understand the benefits that containers and Kubernetes provide, and some fundamentals of how these technologies work. If you are already familiar with Kubernetes, then you can skip this section.

Virtualization Technologies

Before diving into Kubernetes, let's look at containers. A container is a self-contained virtual environment used to run an application. They allow you to run multiple different workloads on the same underlying infrastructure in an isolated way. Individual containers can have reserved CPU and memory, meaning that the applications running in them do not interfere with other applications running in other containers. They also have their own internal local network, providing further isolation.

Containers are not the first technology to provide this sort of isolation. Virtual machines (VMs) also provide similar features. The key difference between a container and a VM is that a container does not contain an operating system (OS); instead, it relies on the OS of the host system. This means they are much smaller and more lightweight in terms of resource usage than VMs. They are also quicker to start up and shut down, as the OS doesn't need to be started or stopped. A container allows repeatable deployment by including all the libraries and dependencies needed to run an application. This means that if you have multiple environments, you don't have the overhead of having to install the correct dependencies in each of them. It removes the "works on my machine" problem and, instead, you simply run your container platform of choice.

Containers are very popular for use alongside other practices such as cloud computing and continuous integration and deployment (CI/CD). Across many industries, companies have adopted containers and use them for their applications in production. Companies often have hundreds, if not thousands, of containers running their workloads and need tools to be able to easily deploy, manage, and monitor them. This is where Kubernetes comes in.

Kubernetes (also known as K8s) is a CNCF project that provides an open source container orchestration platform. Its features include:

Self-healing
Restarting containers that have failed.

Rollouts and rollbacks
Managing updates to containers while maintaining container health.

Horizontal scaling
Scaling up and down the number of instances of a container.

Automatic bin packing
Calculating best placement of containers to optimize resource use.

Application configuration
Mechanisms to support application configuration without the need to restart the containers running those applications.

Batch execution
Running batch processes.

Storage orchestration
Abstractions over the underlying storage.

Networking
> Abstractions over the underlying network and mechanisms to facilitate discovery and load balancing over applications.

In addition to these features, Kubernetes is designed to be extensible. So, as we see later, you can further customize it to suit your workloads. You can run Kubernetes yourself on your own infrastructure, or make use of one of the various Kubernetes distributions that are offered by technology vendors. These vendors often add additional features and provide commercial support.

> The Cloud Native Computing Foundation (CNCF) (*https://www.cncf.io*) is a Linux foundation project that helps to bring together and promote many open source projects that focus on cloud native computing. To be a part of CNCF, projects must fulfill a set of criteria. This includes adopting the CNCF Code of Conduct, regular contributions from multiple organizations, and a certain number of adopters. CNCF has three different maturity levels for projects to help them develop and become eligible for full project status. They first enter as sandbox projects, then move to incubating, and finally become graduated projects.

Let's take a brief look at how Kubernetes works, and some of the key terms and concepts you should be familiar with.

Kubernetes Fundamentals

Kubernetes takes a declarative approach to managing workloads. This means that you describe the shape of your desired system, and Kubernetes performs the tasks needed to get the system into that shape.

To achieve this, Kubernetes is split into two main parts; the *worker nodes* and the *control plane*. The worker nodes are a set of machines where containers are provisioned. These containers are deployed in groups called *Pods*. The control plane is responsible for managing the worker nodes and the Pods running on those nodes.

The control plane is made up of a number of components, including:

The API server
> Provides the Kubernetes API which is used to make requests to the control plane. This is the declarative endpoint that you use to request your workload to be deployed.

Etcd
> Used to store the cluster data.

The kube-scheduler
> Responsible for determining which Pods to run on which nodes, taking into account the resources available.

The kube-controller-manager
> Runs the processes that manage the workload. These processes monitor the cluster and make sure it matches the required state; they are commonly called *controllers*.

The worker nodes include the following components:

Kubelet
> An agent that ensures the containers in Pods are running.

Kube-proxy
> A network proxy to allow communication between Pods.

Container runtime
> Responsible for running the containers.

Figure 10-1 shows these components.

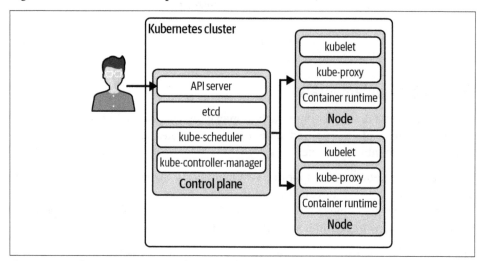

Figure 10-1. Components in a Kubernetes cluster

The most common way to get workloads deployed onto a running Kubernetes cluster is to use the kubectl command line tool and provide the configuration of your objects as YAML files. The kubectl CLI converts the YAML into JSON and sends requests to the Kubernetes API to create, update, or delete objects. As an example, let's look at the YAML required to define a Pod. Each Pod consists of one or more containers deployed together, sharing a local network and storage. For each container we want included in the Pod, we can specify a name, container image,

and an array of ports. So to create a Pod running a single container with the image
my-container:latest, you can create a file with the following contents:

```
apiVersion: v1
kind: Pod
metadata:
  name: my-pod
spec:
  containers:
  - name: my-container
    image: my-container:latest
    ports:
    - containerPort: 80
```

If you save the YAML into a file called *pod.yaml*, you can then create the object in
Kubernetes using the command:

```
$ kubectl create -f pod.yaml -n my-project
pod/my-pod created
```

This creates the Pod in the my-project *namespace*. Kubernetes uses namespaces to
provide some level of isolation between workloads. An object must have a unique
name within a specific namespace, rather than within the whole cluster.

The containers, image, and ports fields in the YAML file are needed to create a
Pod object. However, there are some common fields that usually appear in all object
YAML files. A YAML file for Kubernetes normally looks like this:

```
apiVersion: v1   ❶
kind: Pod   ❷
metadata:   ❸
  name: my-pod
  namespace: my-project   ❹
spec:   ❺
  ...
status:   ❻
  conditions:   ❼
    - type: Ready
      status: "True"
      lastTransitionTime: 2023-01-01T00:00:00Z
    ...
```

❶ The version of the Kubernetes API you are using to create the object.

❷ The kind indicates the type of object you want to create. This example is creating
a Pod.

❸ The metadata to identify the object. Here we only specified a name and name
space, but objects can also have labels added that further help to identify them.

❹ The `namespace` the object is placed into.

❺ The `spec` contains the information about what the object should look like. The contents of this field vary depending on the `kind` of object you are creating.

❻ The `status` is automatically populated to reflect the current state of the object. You do not write this yourself; instead Kubernetes adds it. It doesn't have a set structure, so the contents vary depending on the `kind` of object.

❼ Many Kubernetes objects contain `conditions` in their `status`. The most common is the `Ready` condition that indicates whether the object is ready to be used or not.

Although a Kubernetes Pod is the most common resource used, normally, as an administrator you don't create Pods directly. Instead, you interact with objects that manage a set of Pods, for example a *Deployment* or a *StatefulSet*. Both these objects represent a set of one or more similar Pods. The advantage of using these objects instead of a Pod directly is that Kubernetes takes actions to manage the lifecycles of the Pods.

The easiest way to understand this is by looking at an example. Let's start with a Deployment. The basic YAML for a Deployment looks something like:

```
apiVersion: apps/v1
kind: Deployment
metadata:
  name: my-deployment
  labels:
    app: my-app-deploy
spec:
  replicas: 3 ❶
  selector: ❷
    matchLabels:
      app: my-app
  template: ❸
    metadata:
      labels:
        app: my-app
    spec:
      containers:
      - name: my-container
        image: my-container:latest
        ports:
        - containerPort: 9092
```

❶ The number of `replicas` is the number of Pods you want to have as part of your Deployment. To add or remove Pods, you can simply change this field; you don't have to create the new Pod YAML yourself.

❷ The `selector` is used to identify the Pods that are in the Deployment.

❸ The `template` defines how you want the Pods in the Deployment to be configured. Notice that as well as the normal `spec` you find in a Pod, it includes a field
called `labels`. These `labels` are applied to the Pods and used by the `selector`
that you configured higher up to find the Pods associated with this Deployment.

Deployments are managed by a controller that is run as part of the kube-controller-
manager in the Kubernetes control plane. This is basically a process that is watching
for objects with `kind: Deployment`. When one is created, the controller creates the
required Pods. It also reacts to changes in the Deployment—for example, adding or
removing Pods based on the `replicas` configuration, or reconfiguring the Pods if the
`template` is updated. As well as creating the Pods, the controller also monitors them
and makes sure there is always the correct number of Pods present in the cluster.
StatefulSets are similar to Deployments in that they also manage a group of Pods.
We delve into the differences between a Deployment and a StatefulSet later on in this
chapter.

 In practice, a Deployment does not manage the Pods directly; it
actually creates something called a *ReplicaSet*. A ReplicaSet has its
own controller that is responsible for making sure the right number
of Pods is currently running. You are unlikely to need to interact
with a ReplicaSet directly, so you can treat this as a sort of internal
Kubernetes object. This is because the ReplicaSet controller doesn't
contain any logic to roll out updates to the Pods. When you update
the configuration in a Deployment, the Deployment controller
actually creates a new ReplicaSet with the new configuration. It
then scales down the old ReplicaSet and scales up the new one,
ensuring that only a certain number of Pods are down at any one
time. If you wanted to use a ReplicaSet directly, you would have to
handle these updates yourself.

The other object kind you should be familiar with is a *Service*. Services are usually
used alongside Deployments and StatefulSets, and define a known endpoint that can
be used to discover and connect to one of the Pods in the group. Here's an example:

```
apiVersion: v1
kind: Service
metadata:
  name: my-service
spec:
  selector:
    app: my-app
  ports:
    - protocol: TCP
```

```
    port: 80
    targetPort: 9092
```

This Service can be addressed by other applications in the Kubernetes cluster using the hostname my-service and port 80. It routes requests to any Pods that have the label app: my-app to port 9092 of that Pod. We go into more detail about why Services are important when we discuss how to deploy Kafka Connect to Kubernetes.

If you want to learn more, the Kubernetes documentation (*https://oreil.ly/j4w5y*) contains details about all the different objects, including tutorials for how to use them. Now let's look at how to get a Kafka Connect cluster and connectors running on Kubernetes.

Running Kafka Connect on Kubernetes

There are multiple ways that you can deploy Kafka Connect to a Kubernetes cluster. Instead of trying to list all of the options, we discuss the key decisions you need to make and discuss the artifacts you need to find or create. The things you need to consider are:

- Container image
- Deploying workers
- Networking and monitoring
- Configuration

Container Image

The Kafka project doesn't provide a ready-made container image for Kafka Connect. Instead, you can either create one yourself or use a third-party image that has been created by the Kafka community. For example, a basic image may have the following definition:

```
FROM eclipse-temurin:17

RUN mkdir -p /opt/kafka/bin /opt/kafka/libs /opt/kafka/config /opt/kafka/logs
COPY ./kafka/bin /opt/kafka/bin/
COPY ./kafka/libs /opt/kafka/libs/
COPY ./kafka/config/connect-distributed.properties /opt/kafka/config/
COPY ./kafka/config/connect-log4j.properties /opt/kafka/config/
RUN mkdir -p /opt/kafka/connectors
COPY <CONNECTOR_JARS> /opt/kafka/connectors/
WORKDIR /opt/kafka
EXPOSE 8083

ENTRYPOINT ["./bin/connect-distributed.sh",
  "./config/connect-distributed.properties"]
```

Remember that for any connector plug-ins you copy into the image, you need to tell Kafka Connect about them. So, for the previous image, you would need to update *connect-distributed.properties* so that the `plugin.path` configuration includes /opt/ kafka/connectors. Consider the order of commands when you write your container definition. A container image is built in layers, so the container platform executes each line and caches the resulting image as a layer. The connectors you are adding are the most likely thing to change in between builds, since you will need to update to new versions. By having the `COPY` line to copy in the connector JAR files last, you will find that later builds are quicker, which is because the container platform can reuse the cache and only rebuild the layer that includes these files.

The container definition provided earlier includes specific connectors. Ideally, you should build a custom image for each Kafka Connect cluster that only includes the specific plug-ins it needs; this prevents your Kafka Connect image from becoming bloated, and also makes it easier to manage from a security perspective. For every plug-in you add to your container image, you need to make sure it is up to date and that the version doesn't have any known security problems. You also need to check what actions the plug-in takes—for example, does it need access to files on disk?—and assess them to understand the security impact.

To make it easier to maintain different images with different plug-ins, you can create a base image. To do this, you would start with a container definition similar to the one just shown, but without the line `COPY <CONNECTOR_JARS> /opt/kafka/connec tors`. Then you can build an image with the tag `connect-base` and have custom cluster image definitions like this:

```
FROM connect-base

COPY <CONNECTOR_JARS> /opt/kafka/connectors/
WORKDIR /opt/kafka
EXPOSE 8083
ENTRYPOINT ["./bin/connect-distributed.sh",
  "./config/connect-distributed.properties"]
```

That way, you don't have to duplicate the setup of the Kafka Connect worker in each Kafka Connect cluster image definition file you need.

Once you have defined your container image definition(s), you need to build them and push them to a registry that is accessible from your Kubernetes cluster. There are many different registries to choose from; the default registry when using the docker command line is DockerHub (*https://hub.docker.com*). Make sure you have secured the registry location for your images so that you know who has permissions to push new images. If you are using the docker command line, you can build the image by running:

```
$ docker build -t kafka-connect:0.0.1 .
```

The build command takes a tag to name and version the image; in this case, kafka-connect is the name and 0.0.1 is the version. Many container runtimes use the version to identify whether an image has been updated and needs to be pulled fresh. You can log into your container registry and push the image using the docker commands:

```
$ docker login <REGISTRY_ADDRESS>
$ docker tag kafka-connect:0.0.1 <REGISTRY_ADDRESS>/kafka-connect:0.0.1
$ docker push <REGISTRY_ADDRESS>/kafka-connect:0.0.1
```

There are a lot of steps involved in creating and maintaining a container image. For each plug-in, you not only have to find the JAR(s) for the plug-in, but also update the Kafka Connect container image to use it, build the new image, push it to the registry, and update the worker Pods to use the new image version. If you are building the deployment pipeline yourself, keep this in mind; put mechanisms in place that automate these steps and let you identify which connectors and versions are installed.

Once you have a container image, you can then consider how to manage the Pods that make up your cluster.

Deploying Workers

To deploy Kafka Connect on Kubernetes, you need to decide how to represent the Kafka Connect workers as Pods and how to manage those Pods. Note that here we are talking about the Kafka Connect workers that make up a Kafka Connect cluster, not the Kubernetes worker nodes that the Pods run on. Before we look at what kind of Kubernetes objects you can choose to manage your Kafka Connect workers, let's first discuss the Kafka Connect worker to Pod ratio. When running in Kubernetes, you should still run Kafka Connect in distributed mode rather than standalone. This makes it easier to scale your Kafka Connect cluster. With this in mind, it makes sense to have a single Pod and single container within that Pod for each Kafka Connect worker. This is because workers are the way that Kafka Connect can be scaled. If you need to add more workers, you can add more Pods.

Now let's look at those worker Pods and how we should define and scale them. You should use the same container image for all of the workers in a Kafka Connect cluster. This is because each worker in a particular cluster needs to be able to run the same types of connectors. However, each worker Pod in the cluster needs to have a unique REST API endpoint; although users can call the REST API on any worker, the workers themselves need to be able to call a specific member of the cluster for intra-cluster communication and actions like forwarding a request.

To get the best out of Kafka Connect when running on Kubernetes, you need to choose an object kind that rolls out updates by taking down the existing Pod before creating a new one. This is due to the way that Kafka Connect rebalances are triggered. When using incremental cooperative rebalancing, if a Kafka Connect worker becomes unresponsive, its connectors and tasks are not reassigned immediately. Instead, there is a delay of five minutes by default, which is controlled by the configuration `scheduled.rebalance.max.delay.ms`. If the worker comes back, after the delay expires a rebalance is triggered, and the tasks and connectors are reassigned to the worker. During this time, if a new worker joins, it does not immediately receive assignments and instead has to wait for the rebalance to trigger.

However, if a new worker joins the cluster when no workers have left, then Kafka Connect immediately triggers a rebalance and redistributes some of the connectors and tasks to the new worker. This means that if an update creates new Pods first, you always see at least two rebalances, whereas if it takes down the old Pods first, you only see one. In general, you want to reduce the number of rebalances and connector/task reassignments that happen in Kafka Connect because they add additional strain and pause the data flow.

Now that we've identified the main requirement for the object managing our workers, let's look at the specific features of Deployments and StatefulSets. There are two ways to address a Pod in Kubernetes: via a Service, or directly using the Pod IP address. A Service provides a fixed endpoint that can be used to route requests to a set of Pods. When you define the Service, you specify a selector that determines which Pods it can route to.

In a Deployment, all Pods are identical, so there is no way for a Service to distinguish between Pods. This means that for Kafka Connect, the only option when using a Deployment is to provide the Pod IP as the `rest.advertised.host.name`. This Pod IP is unique to each Pod, but it is not stable through updates. When a Pod is deleted and recreated, the Pod IP changes. Kubernetes does not provide a mechanism to easily discover the Pod IP, so you must write your own mechanism to make it available to the Pod. If you use a Deployment, the configured update strategy can also cause unnecessary connector and task reassignment. By default, a Deployment uses an update strategy called `RollingUpdate`. In this mode, Kubernetes ensures that only a certain number of Pods are down and only a certain number of Pods exist beyond the required number. With the default configuration, an update results in a new Pod being created before the old one is removed. In Kafka Connect, this means a rebalance is triggered immediately, which is not optimal.

To solve this, you have two options; configure the `maxSurge` or change the rollout strategy. If you set the `maxSurge` configuration in the Deployment to 0, Kubernetes always deletes a Pod before creating new ones. To do this, you also need to have `maxUnavailable` set to greater than 0 (the default value of 25% is acceptable). Alternatively, you can change the rollout strategy to `Recreate`. When using `Recreate`, Kubernetes removes all existing Pods before creating the new ones. This solves the rebalance problem, but if the new Pods don't come up successfully, your pipeline is down until you can successfully start the new Pods.

A StatefulSet is designed for use with stateful applications, and has some features that make it a better fit for Kafka Connect workers. The key difference from Deployments is that StatefulSets provide a stable identity for each of the Pods they manage, and graceful, ordered deployment and scaling. Pods in a StatefulSet have a fixed name that is kept between updates. This stable identity also means that with a StatefulSet, each Pod has a stable endpoint you can call. This stable endpoint has the form of `<POD_NAME>.<SERVICE_NAME>`. This is ideal for Kafka Connect, because this stable endpoint can be more easily discovered by the Pod than the Pod IP that you need in a Deployment. When Kubernetes updates a StatefulSet using the default update strategy, it deletes a single Pod, starts a new one to replace it, and then only moves onto the next Pod when the first one is back running. This means for Kafka Connect, you don't get an immediate task and connector assignment triggered.

When configuring your Kafka Connect workers, think carefully about the value of `scheduled.rebalance.max.delay.ms`. If this value is shorter than the time taken to roll out an update across the whole cluster, you might see a rebalance triggered while you are still making updates. However, the higher you set the value, the longer it takes Kafka Connect to notice if a worker has left permanently. You should at minimum set it to a value greater than the time it takes for a single Pod to be updated.

Networking and Monitoring

When running Kafka Connect in Kubernetes, you need to make sure the REST API is accessible for the workers to collaborate, and so that you can manage your Kafka Connect cluster and connectors. Later in this chapter, we discuss ways to manage Kafka Connect in a more "Kubernetes-native" way, but even with this approach the REST API still needs to be accessible.

There are three options for how administrators can connect to endpoints in Kubernetes:

- From within the Pod
- From inside the Kubernetes cluster using a Service or Pod IP
- From outside the Kubernetes cluster

Kubernetes allows users with certain permissions to run commands directly inside Pods. Any user that has accessed a Pod in this way is able to call the endpoints exposed by the containers in the Pod. However, this is not a recommended approach, because as well as accessing endpoints, this user is able to see any files on disk and make other changes to the running application. For production systems, you should severely limit the number of users that can access Pods in this way and instead set up alternative ways to perform administrative tasks.

To make the REST API accessible within the Kubernetes cluster, you can use the same mechanisms described in the previous section: the Pod IP for workers in a Deployment, and the stable Pod endpoint for workers in a StatefulSet.

In Kubernetes, the *Ingress* object is designed to define external access to the cluster via HTTP or HTTPS. However, although the object is part of the Kubernetes API, there isn't a controller for Ingress started in the control plane by default. To use this kind, you need to either deploy an Ingress controller yourself, or run your workload on a Kubernetes installation that provides a controller for this type. The Kubernetes project supports a few different controllers, and there are many available from the wider Kubernetes community.

In Kafka Connect, you can choose whether to expose the entire REST API through a single listener, or use the `admin.listeners` configuration to expose the API via two different listeners. If you choose a single listener, you can use Ingress to expose separate routes for specific REST API endpoints—for example, you can use it to have a different route for the `/admin` endpoints to control how they can be accessed. On the other hand, if you have two listeners, each can have its own Service and, optionally, its own Ingress. The method you choose depends on the way you want users to access the different endpoints.

> No matter which option you choose, make sure the REST API is secured. You can use the same steps as described in Chapter 8 to secure it or use features of your Ingress controller.

In addition to managing the running connectors, you need to manage the workers and monitor the system. If you deploy a single worker as a Pod, then you can easily manage the number and configuration of your workers by updating the object that you've chosen to manage the Pods.

For monitoring, you should use Kubernetes tools to collect both logs and metrics from the workers, and forward them to your monitoring systems. Exactly how you do this depends on the Kubernetes platform you are using and what tools you want to use. Most Kubernetes platforms are able to collect logs from running containers and make them available elsewhere. For metrics, you need to put in place a mechanism to expose them. A popular tool for monitoring in Kubernetes is Prometheus (*https:// prometheus.io*), which is also a CNCF project. If you choose to use Prometheus, you can use a library like the JMX Exporter (*https://oreil.ly/LXgQc*) to provide an endpoint for Prometheus to scrape. This runs as a Java agent, so you need to add it to your Kafka Connect worker image. Once you have made the metrics accessible, you can monitor them in the same way we describe in Chapter 9.

Configuration

When you are running Kafka Connect on Kubernetes, the simplest way to provide configuration to your Kafka Connect workers is to add the configuration file, *connect-distributed.properties*, directly to the worker image when you build it. Although this is easy to set up, anytime you want to update a setting, you need to rebuild the image. In addition, your image becomes specifically configured for a particular environment, with hardcoded connection details to a Kafka cluster, so you can't easily reuse it. This can also add a lot of overhead, especially during development, when settings may be tuned frequently.

To avoid having to hardcode configurations into your container images, you can use a *ConfigMap*. A ConfigMap is a Kubernetes object for storing key/value pairs of configuration. You can specify individual key/value pairs, or have a key where the value represents the contents of a file. Kubernetes provides a few different options for making the configuration available to a Pod. These include making the keys and values available as environment variables, and mounting the values as files in the Pod. If you choose to mount the value as a file, you can run the Kafka Connect worker as though it has the configuration file on disk, without needing to build an image with the file included. When you need to change the configuration, just update the ConfigMap and restart the worker Pods to pick up the change.

> Normally, applications that store configuration in a ConfigMap do not need to be restarted every time the configuration changes. This is because the contents of the environment variables or file contents are updated by Kubernetes immediately. However, Kafka Connect workers only read their configuration at start-up, hence the need for a restart.

For example, you might have a ConfigMap that looks like this:

```
apiVersion: v1
kind: ConfigMap
metadata:
  name: connect-configuration
data:
  connect-config.properties: |
    bootstrap.servers=my-kafka:9092
    group.id=connect-cluster-1
  ...
```

You can make it available to the Pods using a volume mount in the Deployment or StatefulSet:

```
...
containers:
  - name: kafka
    image: kafka:latest
    volumeMounts:
    - name: connect-config
      mountPath: "/opt/config"
      readOnly: true
volumes:
  - name: connect-config
    configMap:
      name: connect-configuration
```

This results in the file *opt/config/connect-config.properties* being available in the Pod.

While most configurations match across all workers, there are some, like the `client.id`, that should be unique to the worker. If you want some configurations to be worker specific, you shouldn't use the ConfigMap to set them. The easiest way to set these types of configurations is when the container starts up. Rather than using a simple command as the entrypoint for the container, you can use a script and set them in the script before starting the worker. This script can use any environment variables that are set in the Pod. For example, if you are using a StatefulSet, you can add the Pod name as an environment variable that is unique. You do this using the Kubernetes downward API (*https://oreil.ly/4cUKy*):

```
...
env:
  - name: POD_NAME
    valueFrom:
      fieldRef:
        fieldPath: metadata.name
```

If the StatefulSet set was called `connect-cluster` with three replicas, then you would have Pods called `connect-cluster-0`, `connect-cluster-1`, and `connect-cluster-2`. Each Pod would have the environment variable `POD_NAME` set to a different value; you could then use this environment variable in a startup script in your container to alter the worker configuration file you are using. In a StatefulSet, the Pod name can also be used to determine the value needed for `rest.advertised.host.name`.

The final thing to consider for configuring the worker is any sensitive configuration values, such as authentication passwords or certificate files. Kubernetes provides the *Secret* object to store small amounts of sensitive data. It provides the same options as a ConfigMap, where the data can be simple key/value pairs or a key with a file-like value. They are slightly more complex to create, as the value is base64 encoded. A Secret object is better than a ConfigMap for storing sensitive data, because Kubernetes provides additional restrictions on how the data can be used. For example, the Secret is only made available on nodes that have existing Pods that require access to it. Also, only containers that are explicitly declared to have access can see the Secret once it is mounted. You can also configure role-based access controls (RBAC) so that Secrets are only accessible to administrators of the Kubernetes cluster.

Although Secrets are advertised as the way to store sensitive data, you should be very careful with how you use them, in order to make sure that your sensitive data is secure. For example, by default, they are stored unencrypted. If you do want to use a Secret to store information like authentication credentials or certificates, make sure you understand how to use them in a secure way. The Kubernetes documentation provides details on best practices for using Secrets (*https://oreil.ly/5nTgA*).

There are other Kubernetes tools for storing and providing access to confidential information. Vault (*https://www.vaultproject.io*) is becoming a popular choice, as it is designed for managing secrets and sensitive data.

As you can see, choosing exactly how to configure your Kafka Connect workers in Kubernetes isn't straightforward. For each configuration option, you need to decide four things:

- Where the value will be stored
- The process for updating the value
- How the value will be exposed to the Kafka Connect worker
- If the configuration is being stored in a way that respects the sensitivity of the data

It is worth considering each of these upfront so that you have a fully defined approach for configuration management. It's likely that the final solution will include a script to start the worker that pulls configurations from a combination of Config-Maps, Secrets, environment variables, and other configuration stores.

Once you have considered how to configure the Kafka Connect workers, you need to consider the connectors. Most connector configurations are sent as part of the REST API request. However, for sensitive credentials, you might want to use configuration providers. We explain how configuration providers work in detail in Chapter 7. If you want to store sensitive credentials in a Kubernetes Secret, you can use the same process we described earlier to mount the Secret into the Pod as a volume. Then, you can use `FileConfigProvider` or `DirectoryConfigProvider` to specify the location of the configuration. If you choose this method, make sure the resulting file that is mounted into the Pod is formatted as a properties file.

The drawback of using a Kubernetes Secret combined with the `FileConfigProvider` for connector configuration is that every time you want to update the value of the configuration for one connector, you have to restart your Kafka Connect worker as well as your connector. A better solution is to have the configuration provider fetch the latest value from the Secret when it configures the connector. The Strimzi project has created a configuration provider that does this for both ConfigMaps and Secrets; you can find it on GitHub (*https://oreil.ly/vAR-1*). It can be used with any Kafka Connect that runs on Kubernetes, so it is a great tool to use.

Using a Kubernetes Operator to Deploy Kafka Connect

As described earlier, it is perfectly possible to deploy Kafka Connect to Kubernetes yourself. However, there is a lot of overhead involved, and even with all these steps, your final deployment won't necessarily feel "Kubernetes-native." Normally, workloads in Kubernetes are managed using an "infrastructure-as-code" approach. This means you have a file (in this case, a YAML file), ideally checked into source control, that describes the state of the system. When you need to change something, you update this file and have automation that applies it to your cluster. This flow works well for managing workers because you can change the configuration of the StatefulSet or other object you are using to influence the number and configuration of your workers. However, it doesn't work well for connectors, which are managed using the REST API. This means that unless you create your own abstraction over the REST API, you are forced to coordinate two different management mechanisms.

Kubernetes operators are designed to reduce the overhead for running workloads on Kubernetes and make them accessible in a more Kubernetes-native way. They provide a controller application with domain-specific knowledge for how to manage a particular workload. Let's look at how a Kubernetes operator works, and then see an example of one that has been created for Kafka Connect.

Introduction to Kubernetes Operators

A Kubernetes operator provides an extension to Kubernetes to add one or more custom Kubernetes API objects. You do this by installing a *custom controller* and a new object definition, called a *Custom Resource Definition* (CRD), into your Kubernetes cluster. The CRD defines the API for the workload you are deploying. So in the same way that for a Deployment there is a set of configurations you can provide (like number of Pods, image, etc.), a CRD defines the specific configuration for the workload the operator manages. In the CRD for a Kafka Connect operator, you would expect to see options like being able to specify the number of workers you need, the configuration of those workers, and the connector plug-ins that should be made available. The custom controller watches for new instances of the CRD, called *Custom Resources* (CRs), and creates the underlying Kubernetes objects that you need. If the contents of an existing CR are updated, the controller notices the change and updates the objects.

There are other tools, like Helm (*https://helm.sh*), that you can use to deploy and update Kubernetes objects. However, the key benefit of an operator is that it is always running in the Kubernetes cluster, so it goes beyond the initial deployment of the objects and can provide features to help day-two operations. This means it can automate complex and error-prone administrative operations that are required during the lifespan of the workload. The exact behavior and features of an operator depend on the workload it is managing and the specific operator. Some operators only deploy and update workloads, while others have complicated logic around upgrades, can intervene when something goes wrong, or even scale the workload automatically. Some potential benefits of using a Kubernetes operator to manage Kubernetes workloads are:

- Deployment, upgrades, and removal of the workload is automated.

- The operator can use workload-specific knowledge to roll out updates correctly.

- As a user, you only have to interact with the CR and not the complicated set of Kubernetes objects actually running the workload.

Kubernetes Operators for Kafka Connect

There are a few different Kubernetes operators for Kafka Connect available in the community. They each work slightly differently and manage Kafka Connect in their own way. Although they might not all provide the same features, the kind of management tasks you can expect them to handle are:

- Deploying the Kafka Connect workers as Kubernetes objects

- Deploying networking objects to enable connectivity between workers and access to the REST API

- Building Kafka Connect worker images with custom plug-ins

- Exposing a Kubernetes API to managing running connectors

- Managing updates to Kafka Connect workers, for example by only rolling a worker if a rebalance is not in progress

- Automatically restarting failed connectors and tasks

- Providing a mechanism to expose metrics

Many Kafka Connect operators can also manage Kafka clusters, so you can have a single operator for both types of cluster. In this chapter, we look at an open source operator called Strimzi as an example.

Strimzi

Strimzi (*https://strimzi.io*) is an open source CNCF sandbox project that provides tools for deploying the Kafka platform to Kubernetes. These tools include Kubernetes Custom Resource Definitions (CRDs) to represent different Kafka components, and a set of operators to manage any deployed Custom Resources (CRs). Strimzi can deploy Kafka clusters, Kafka Connect clusters, and MirrorMaker, and can also handle the creation and management of Kafka topics and users. Strimzi also provides tools to help you with ongoing management of your Kafka cluster; for example, the drain cleaner tool can drain Kafka Pods from Kubernetes nodes without disrupting the cluster. Strimzi also has integration with Cruise Control to rebalance Kafka clusters.

In this section, we look at the features provided by Strimzi for managing Kafka Connect and MirrorMaker, and see an example of these in action.

Strimzi provides the following CRDs:

- KafkaConnect to deploy and manage Kafka Connect clusters
- KafkaConnector to manage connectors
- KafkaMirrorMaker2 to deploy and manage Kafka Connect clusters running the MirrorMaker connectors

Instances of each of these CRDs are managed by the Strimzi cluster operator, which means that if you are already using Strimzi to manage your Kafka clusters, you don't need to install an additional operator to use these types. However, they are all designed to connect to any Kafka cluster, which means you can also use them alongside your pre-existing Kafka clusters.

> There is also a CRD in Strimzi called KafkaMirrorMaker, which was created to deploy and manage instances of the old Mirror-Maker tool. When Kafka created the new MirrorMaker feature that uses Kafka Connect, Strimzi created the KafkaMirrorMaker2 CRD. In this section, when we talk about support for Mirror-Maker, we are referring to the KafkaMirrorMaker2 CRD, since the KafkaMirrorMaker CRD has been deprecated and will be removed when Strimzi moves to Kafka version 4.0.0.

Getting a Kubernetes Environment

To run Strimzi, you need a Kubernetes environment and the `kubectl` CLI installed. Strimzi works with any Kubernetes cluster, so if you have one already, you can use that. If not, there are a few different tools available:

- minikube (*https://oreil.ly/-3KEl*) runs a single-node Kubernetes cluster on your local machine. Requires a container or virtual machine manager such as Docker, HyperKit, or VirtualBox.

- kind (*https://oreil.ly/xSI9k*) uses Docker and Go to run a Kubernetes test environment. Originally created to test Kubernetes itself.

- Docker Desktop (*https://oreil.ly/reeeA*) lets you enable a local Kubernetes cluster as part of your existing Docker Desktop installation.

Whatever tool you choose, make sure you provide enough memory to the tool to start the components. For a basic Strimzi install, 4 GB is a good starting point. If you are using `minikube`, the default is 2 GB, so you can use the following command to start it with higher memory:

```
$ minikube start --memory=4096
```

Starting the Operator

Before creating the CRs for Kafka Connect or MirrorMaker, you need to have the Strimzi cluster operator up and running in your Kubernetes cluster. All of the Kubernetes YAML files you need to install the Strimzi operator, the CRDs, and the permission files are available from GitHub (*https://oreil.ly/rac0Y*) and OperatorHub (*https://oreil.ly/akuXL*). You can also use Helm charts (*https://oreil.ly/Axp0b*) to deploy the operator.

If this is your first time using Strimzi, the easiest way to get started is to follow the steps in the Strimzi quick start guide (*https://oreil.ly/Q7VEd*). This downloads the latest version of the Strimzi deployment files from the website.

First, create a Kubernetes namespace named `connect` for your operator:

```
$ kubectl create namespace connect
```

Then run the following command to install the operator into the namespace:

```
$ kubectl create -f 'https://strimzi.io/install/latest?namespace=connect'
```

This creates a Deployment with the latest version of the Strimzi cluster operator:

```
$ kubectl get deployment -n connect
NAME                      READY   UP-TO-DATE   AVAILABLE   AGE
strimzi-cluster-operator  1/1     1            1           80s
```

You can also optionally use Strimzi to create a Kafka cluster to connect to. If you already have a Kafka cluster running somewhere accessible to your Kubernetes environment (i.e., not running using the scripts in the Kafka distribution locally), then you can skip this step.

```
$ kubectl apply \
  -f https://strimzi.io/examples/latest/kafka/kafka-persistent-single.yaml \
  -n connect
kafka.kafka.strimzi.io/my-cluster created
```

If you are using Strimzi to also install Kafka, you should wait for the cluster to be
ready before moving on to install Kafka Connect or MirrorMaker:

```
$ kubectl wait kafka/my-cluster --for=condition=Ready --timeout=300s -n connect
kafka.kafka.strimzi.io/my-cluster condition met
```

Now you are ready to install a Kafka Connect cluster using Strimzi.

Kafka Connect CRDs

There are two CRDs that Strimzi provides to help you deploy and manage a Kafka
Connect cluster: KafkaConnect and KafkaConnector. We introduce the most commonly used fields in the CRDs and then look at an example of how to use them. We
don't cover every single field in the CRDs, just those needed to get started. The full
specifications can be found in the Strimzi documentation (*https://oreil.ly/TRFmd*).

The first CRD is called KafkaConnect and it defines a Kafka Connect cluster. For
example:

```
apiVersion: kafka.strimzi.io/v1beta2
kind: KafkaConnect
metadata:
  name: my-connect-cluster
  annotations:
    strimzi.io/use-connector-resources: "true"  ❶
spec:
  version: 3.4.0
  replicas: 1  ❷
  bootstrapServers: my-cluster-kafka-bootstrap:9093  ❸
  authentication:  ❸
    type: tls
    certificateAndKey:
      certificate: source.crt
      key: source.key
      secretName: my-user-source
  tls:  ❸
    trustedCertificates:
      - secretName: my-cluster-cluster-ca-cert
        certificate: ca.crt
  config:  ❹
    group.id: connect-cluster
    ...
  build:  ❺
    output:  ❻
      type: docker
      image: <REGISTRY_ADDRESS>/my-connect-cluster:latest
      pushSecret: my-registry-credentials
```

```
    plugins:  ❼
      - name: kafka-connect-file
        artifacts:
          - type: maven
            group: org.apache.kafka
            artifact: connect-file
            version: 3.4.0
```

❶ If you add this annotation to your CR, you can then use the KafkaConnector CRD to manage your running connectors. This is optional, so if you don't add it you will need to use the REST API.

❷ The `replicas` configuration determines how many Kafka Connect workers to deploy.

❸ The `bootstrapServers`, `authentication`, and `tls` configurations give Strimzi the information about where the Kafka cluster that Kafka Connect will talk to is located and how to securely connect to it. Both `authentication` and `tls` expect the actual credentials or certificates to be stored in a Kubernetes Secret.

❹ The `config` section allows you to further customize the configuration of your Kafka Connect workers.

❺ The `build` section is optional, and when it is configured, Strimzi builds a new Kafka Connect worker container image before starting the cluster. This is a handy way to add plug-ins to the worker.

❻ The `output` determines where the new Kafka Connect worker image is stored. The type options are `docker` or `imagestream`. The `docker` type is for pushing to a Docker-compatible container registry, and `imagestream` is for pushing to an OpenShift ImageStream.

❼ The `plugins` configuration takes an array of connector plug-ins. These are available to use in the Kafka Connect cluster. You can specify artifacts from Maven Central (*https://search.maven.org*), as shown in the example, or provide a URL to a `jar`, `zip`, or `tgz` file for Strimzi to download.

The second CRD that Strimzi provides is for managing a connector:

```
apiVersion: kafka.strimzi.io/v1beta2
kind: KafkaConnector
metadata:
  name: my-source-connector
  labels:
    strimzi.io/cluster: my-connect-cluster  ❶
spec:
  class: org.apache.kafka.connect.file.FileStreamSourceConnector  ❷
```

```
    tasksMax: 2   ❸
    config:   ❹
      file: "/opt/kafka/LICENSE"
      topic: my-topic
```

❶ Strimzi needs to know which Kafka Connect cluster you want it to create
this connector in. The `strimzi.io/cluster` label indicates the name of the
KafkaConnect CR for that cluster. Remember that the KafkaConnect CR must
have the `strimzi.io/use-connector-resources` annotation set to `true`. The
KafkaConnector CR must be in the same namespace as your KafkaConnect CR.

❷ The `class` name or alias of the connector to create.

❸ The `tasksMax` configuration to provide to the connector.

❹ The `config` is where you provide the custom configuration for the specific
connector you are running. In this example, the `FileStreamSourceConnector`
has two configurations: `file` and `topic`.

Now that we have looked at the two CRDs that Strimzi provides for deploying a
Kafka Connect cluster and connectors, let's try using them.

Deploying a Kafka Connect Cluster and Connectors

First, make sure you have the Strimzi cluster operator running and a Kafka cluster to
connect to.

Create a file called *kafka-connect-build.yaml* with the following contents:

```
apiVersion: kafka.strimzi.io/v1beta2
kind: KafkaConnect
metadata:
  name: my-connect-cluster
  annotations:
    strimzi.io/use-connector-resources: "true"
spec:
  version: 3.4.0
  replicas: 1
  bootstrapServers: my-cluster-kafka-bootstrap:9092
  config:
    group.id: connect-cluster
    offset.storage.topic: connect-cluster-offsets
    config.storage.topic: connect-cluster-configs
    status.storage.topic: connect-cluster-status
    # -1 means it will use the default replication factor
    # configured in the broker
    offset.storage.replication.factor: -1
    config.storage.replication.factor: -1
    status.storage.replication.factor: -1
```

```
build:
  output:
    type: docker
    image: ttl.sh/strimzi-connect-example-3.4.0:24h
  plugins:
    - name: kafka-connect-file
      artifacts:
        - type: maven
          group: org.apache.kafka
          artifact: connect-file
          version: 3.4.0
```

This is based on the *kafka-connect-build.yaml* file in the Strimzi repository (*https:// oreil.ly/jXuf_*) in the `examples/connect` folder. It assumes that you are running Kafka using Strimzi with a non-secured listener available on port 9092. Customize the file to include your specific Kafka connection details. You should also check the Kafka version, as newer versions of Strimzi might use a newer Kafka than 3.4.0.

When you create this CR in your Kubernetes cluster, Strimzi pulls the `connect-file` JAR file containing `FileStreamSourceConnector` from Maven Central, builds a new Kafka Connect worker image, and pushes it to an anonymous container registry named *ttl.sh*. You can change the location to point to your own container directory instead, but make sure that you create and configure a Secret to store the credentials to push and pull images from this registry.

Apply the file:

```
$ kubectl apply -f kafka-connect-build.yaml -n connect
kafkaconnect.kafka.strimzi.io/my-connect-cluster created
```

The operator runs a Pod to build the image in:

```
$ kubectl get pods -n connect
NAME                                  READY   STATUS    RESTARTS   AGE
...
my-connect-cluster-connect-build      1/1     Running   0          98s
```

Then it creates the Pod(s) for the Kafka Connect workers (in this case, there is just one because we set replicas to 1):

```
$ kubectl get pods -n connect
NAME                                         READY   STATUS    RESTARTS   AGE
...
my-connect-cluster-connect-59956c6dc7-ktr7b  1/1     Running   0          5m31s
```

The Strimzi operator also updates the status field of the KafkaConnect CR to say that the cluster is ready, and it lists all available connector plug-ins along with their versions:

```
$ kubectl get kafkaconnect my-connect-cluster -n connect -o yaml
```

```
apiVersion: kafka.strimzi.io/v1beta2
kind: KafkaConnect
metadata:
  name: my-connect-cluster
  namespace: connect
  ...
spec:
  ...
status:
  conditions:
  - lastTransitionTime: "2023-01-01T00:00:01"
    status: "True"
    type: Ready
  connectorPlugins:
  - class: org.apache.kafka.connect.file.FileStreamSinkConnector
    type: sink
    version: 3.4.0
  - class: org.apache.kafka.connect.file.FileStreamSourceConnector
    type: source
    version: 3.4.0
  - ...
```

Strimzi also creates a Service with access to the REST API:

```
$ kubectl get service -n connect
NAME                            TYPE        CLUSTER-IP     EXTERNAL-IP   PORT(S)
...
my-connect-cluster-connect-api  ClusterIP   10.96.98.44    <none>        8083/TCP
```

You can call the REST API from within the Kubernetes cluster using a temporary Pod:

```
$ kubectl -n connect run connect-api \
  -ti --image=quay.io/strimzi/kafka:0.35.1-kafka-3.4.0 \
  --rm=true --restart=Never \
  -- curl http://my-connect-cluster-connect-api:8083/connector-plugins
```

Now that the Kafka Connect cluster is ready, we can start a connector. For this example, we run the FileStreamSourceConnector and have it read the contents of the Kafka license file on disk and write that to a topic. We use a KafkaConnector CR rather than calling the REST API ourselves.

Create a file called *source-connector.yaml* with the following contents:

```
apiVersion: kafka.strimzi.io/v1beta2
kind: KafkaConnector
metadata:
  name: my-source-connector
  labels:
    strimzi.io/cluster: my-connect-cluster
spec:
  class: org.apache.kafka.connect.file.FileStreamSourceConnector
  tasksMax: 1
```

```
config:
  file: "/opt/kafka/LICENSE"
  topic: my-topic
```

 If you have set auto.create.topics.enable to false in your
Kafka cluster, you will need to create the my-topic topic before
applying the preceding file.

Now apply the file to your Kubernetes namespace:

```
$ kubectl apply -f source-connector.yaml -n connect
kafkaconnector.kafka.strimzi.io/my-source-connector created
```

When Strimzi has started the connector, it updates the status field of the
KafkaConnector CR to show that the connector is ready:

```
$ kubectl get KafkaConnector my-source-connector -n connect -o yaml
apiVersion: kafka.strimzi.io/v1beta2
kind: KafkaConnector
metadata:
  name: my-source-connector
  namespace: kafka
  ...
spec:
  ...
status:
  conditions:
  - lastTransitionTime: "2023-01-01T00:00:01"
    status: "True"
    type: Ready
  connectorStatus:
    connector:
      state: RUNNING
      worker_id: 172.0.0.1:8083
    name: my-source-connector
    tasks:
    - id: 0
      state: RUNNING
      worker_id: 172.0.0.1:8083
    type: source
  ...
```

Notice that Strimzi also adds the status of the connector and all tasks that are
running. If the connector or tasks fail at any time, Strimzi marks the KafkaConnector
CR as not ready.

You can run a consumer against the my-topic topic to see the records that the
connector sent to Kafka. If you are running your Kafka cluster with Strimzi, you can
run a temporary Pod in your Kubernetes cluster to do this:

```
$ kubectl -n connect run kafka-consumer \
  -ti --image=quay.io/strimzi/kafka:0.35.1-kafka-3.4.0 \
  --rm=true --restart=Never \
  -- bin/kafka-console-consumer.sh \
  --bootstrap-server my-cluster-kafka-bootstrap:9092 \
  --topic my-topic --from-beginning
```

MirrorMaker CRD

There are two ways to deploy MirrorMaker with Strimzi:

- Use the KafkaConnect and KafkaConnector CRDs
- Use the KafkaMirrorMaker2 CRD

The benefit of the KafkaMirrorMaker2 CRD is that it is designed to allow you to configure multiple mirroring routes using a single CR. This means you likely end up with a simpler set of Kubernetes objects to manage if you use KafkaMirrorMaker2 CRDs rather than using the individual KafkaConnect and KafkaConnector CRs.

No matter which approach you take, it is important that you understand the fundamentals for how MirrorMaker works. As we explain in Chapter 6, MirrorMaker is a toolbox of connectors that can be combined in many different ways to address different use cases. So, whichever CRD you choose to use, you need to understand the topology you want to deploy before you can write your CRs.

 In this section, we don't show an example of how to use the KafkaConnect and KafkaConnector CRs for deploying MirrorMaker. However, you can use the examples from Chapter 6 and the previous section in this chapter to create your MirrorMaker topology. You need a separate KafkaConnector CR for each MirrorMaker connector you want to deploy and a separate KafkaConnect CR for each Kafka Connect cluster. Alternatively, you can use the KafkaConnect CR only, and reuse the REST API commands from Chapter 6 to manage the connectors.

The KafkaMirrorMaker2 CR is used to deploy a Kafka Connect cluster in distributed mode that is running one or more MirrorMaker connectors. There is a one-to-one mapping between a KafkaMirrorMaker2 CR and a Kafka Connect cluster. In the CR, you specify the Kafka cluster you want the Kafka Connect cluster to use to store its state. Then, you define a set of mirroring routes and the connectors you want to run as part of those mirroring routes. Since a single CR deploys a single Kafka Connect cluster, every mirroring route must use the same target cluster in order to use this object. This target is also the one you provide as the Kafka cluster for Kafka Connect to store state in.

Let's look at an example. Start by creating two Kafka clusters called east-kafka and west-kafka. We want to copy data from the east-kafka cluster to the west-kafka cluster. As we discuss in Chapter 6, you would normally want the Kafka Connect cluster deployed close to the target, so we want Kafka Connect to use the west-kafka cluster to store state. In this example, we run both MirrorSourceConnector and MirrorCheckpointConnector, but not MirrorHeartbeatConnector, because it would require starting a second Kafka Connect cluster.

A KafkaMirrorMaker2 CR for this setup looks like this:

```
apiVersion: kafka.strimzi.io/v1beta2
kind: KafkaMirrorMaker2
metadata:
  name: west-connect
spec:
  replicas: 1   ❶
  version: 3.4.0   ❷
  connectCluster: "west-kafka"   ❸
  clusters:   ❹
  - alias: "east-kafka"
    bootstrapServers: east-kafka-kafka-bootstrap:9092
  - alias: "west-kafka"
    bootstrapServers: west-kafka-kafka-bootstrap:9092
    config:
      config.storage.replication.factor: -1
      offset.storage.replication.factor: -1
      status.storage.replication.factor: -1
  mirrors:   ❺
  - sourceCluster: "east-kafka"
    targetCluster: "west-kafka"
    sourceConnector:   ❻
      tasksMax: 10
      config:
        replication.factor: -1
        offset-syncs.topic.replication.factor: -1
        refresh.topics.interval.seconds: 10
        sync.topic.configs.interval.seconds: 10
        sync.topic.acls.enabled: "false"
        topics: ".*"
    checkpointConnector:
      tasksMax: 10
      config:
        checkpoints.topic.replication.factor: -1
        refresh.groups.interval.seconds: 10
        groups: ".*"
        sync.group.offsets.enabled: "true"
```

❶ The replicas field indicates the number of Kafka Connect workers in the Kafka Connect cluster.

❷ The version is the Kafka Connect version to use.

❸ The connectCluster is the alias for the Kafka cluster you want the Kafka Connect cluster to use for its state. This must match one of the alias values provided in the clusters array.

❹ The Kafka clusters MirrorMaker connects to. This includes the cluster that Kafka Connect uses for state, as well as any clusters that data is mirrored to or from. Here, you configure the alias to use elsewhere in the CR, as well as connection details such as bootstrap servers and authentication details.

❺ The mirrors field contains mirroring routes and the associated connectors. If you omit a connector name, the connector isn't created. This example only starts MirrorSourceConnector and MirrorCheckpointConnector, not MirrorHeartbeatConnector. You can only specify one connector of each type for each mirroring route.

❻ You can override the configuration for the individual connectors. Here, we choose similar settings to the example shown in Chapter 6. These shorter intervals are good for testing purposes, but in production you would choose minutes, not seconds. We also disable the mirroring of ACLs to make the example simpler to use.

If you deploy this CR, you get a KafkaMirrorMaker2 resource called west-connect created. This represents a Kafka Connect cluster called west-connect. You can list the MirrorMaker clusters using:

```
$ kubectl get kafkamirrormaker2 -n connect
NAME            DESIRED REPLICAS    READY
west-connect    1
```

In your Kafka clusters, you see the following topics:

- In east-kafka cluster:

    mm2-offset-syncs.west-kafka.internal

- In west-kafka cluster:

    east-kafka.checkpoints.internal
    mirrormaker2-cluster-configs
    mirrormaker2-cluster-offsets
    mirrormaker2-cluster-status

If you query the GET /connectors endpoint in the Kafka Connect cluster, you see two connectors running: east-kafka->west-kafka.MirrorSourceConnector and east-kafka->west-kafka.MirrorCheckpointConnector. Notice that Strimzi has chosen sensible names for the connectors to help you identify the direction the data is flowing and the type of connector that is running.

Now let's look at how `MirrorHeartbeatConnector` works in the KafkaMirrorMaker2 CR. Since a KafkaMirrorMaker2 CR maps to a single Kafka Connect cluster, you wouldn't use the same CR to run `MirrorHeartbeatConnector` for this mirroring route. Instead, you need a separate CR that uses the `east-kafka` cluster as its `connectCluster`. This is because the aim of the `heartbeats` topic is to allow you to measure how long it takes to mirror data. So, you want heartbeats to be sent to the `east-kafka` cluster, and then `MirrorSourceConnector` mirrors them to the `west-kafka` cluster.

To configure `MirrorHeartbeatConnector`, you might have a CR that looks like this:

```
apiVersion: kafka.strimzi.io/v1beta2
kind: KafkaMirrorMaker2
metadata:
  name: east-connect
spec:
  version: 3.4.0
  replicas: 1
  connectCluster: "east-kafka"       ❶
  clusters:
  - alias: "east-kafka"
    bootstrapServers: east-kafka-kafka-bootstrap:9092
    config:  ❷
      config.storage.replication.factor: -1
      offset.storage.replication.factor: -1
      status.storage.replication.factor: -1
      config.storage.topic: mirrormaker2-cluster-configs.internal
      offset.storage.topic: mirrormaker2-cluster-offsets.internal
      status.storage.topic: mirrormaker2-cluster-status.internal
  - alias: "west-kafka"
    bootstrapServers: west-kafka-kafka-bootstrap:9092
  mirrors:
  - sourceCluster: "east-kafka"
    targetCluster: "west-kafka"
    heartbeatConnector:
      config:
        heartbeats.topic.replication.factor: -1
        target.cluster.bootstrap.servers: "east-kafka-bootstrap:9092"  ❸
```

❶ The `connectCluster` is set to `east-kafka`, as this is where we want the new Kafka Connect cluster to store its state.

❷ Since `MirrorSourceConnector` is already mirroring topics from `east-kafka` to `west-kafka`, we need to rename the internal topics so they won't be mirrored. Here, we choose to add `.internal` suffix, which by default means MirrorMaker will ignore them. We provide the configuration under the alias for east-kafka, since that is the one configured as the connectCluster.

❸ Since we want the heartbeats topic to appear in east-kafka first, we override the target.cluster.bootstrap.servers configuration for MirrorHeartbeatConnector.

Once you deploy this new KafkaMirrorMaker2 CR, you have a new Kafka Connect cluster with a single running connector called east-kafka->west-kafka.MirrorHeartbeatConnector. You also now have a heartbeats topic in east-kafka and an east-kafka.heartbeats topic in west-kafka. The records being sent to the heartbeats topic look like:

```
Heartbeat{sourceClusterAlias=east-kafka, targetClusterAlias=west-kafka,
timestamp=1666896771382}
```

 Remember, to view the heartbeats topic records in a readable format, you need to deserialize them using the provided formatter—for example, by specifying --formatter org.apache.kafka.connect.mirror.formatters.HeartbeatFormatter when using the console consumer.

The KafkaMirrorMaker2 CR does make it easier to deploy the Kafka Connect cluster and connectors for your mirroring use cases, but you still need to decide exactly what connectors you want to run, which Kafka clusters to use for Kafka Connect, and the source and target Kafka clusters.

Summary

In this chapter, we looked at the requirements for running Kafka Connect on Kubernetes. If you want to deploy Kafka Connect on Kubernetes from scratch, then you need a good understanding of both Kafka Connect and Kubernetes.

We covered some of the requirements you need to fulfill, such as:

- Creating a container image for the workers
- Defining Kubernetes objects to deploy and manage the workers effectively
- Defining Kubernetes objects to configure the networking between workers
- Configuring monitoring tools to collect logs and metrics
- Specifying worker configuration so it can be updated easily

Although it is possible to deploy Kafka Connect yourself, it does require a lot of setup just to get a basic Kafka Connect cluster up and running. We introduced Kubernetes operators as an alternative way to deploy Kafka Connect without having to start from scratch. If you can find an operator that works for you, this makes it much quicker to get started on Kubernetes. You can also take advantage of the expertise of the contributors to that operator and all of its pre-existing users.

Finally, we showed an example of running the Strimzi operator. The Strimzi project offers a mature Kafka operator and provides many other tools that you can use to better manage both Kafka Connect and Kafka clusters on Kubernetes.

PART IV

Building Custom Connectors and Plug-Ins

The last part of this book describes how to use the Kafka Connect API to build connector and worker plug-ins. It is aimed at developers who need specific functionalities that don't already exist in the plug-ins developed by the community.

For each type of plug-in, it covers all the methods of the API, the best practices to follow when implementing them, and how the various components interact with each other.

CHAPTER 11

Building Source and Sink Connectors

As mentioned in previous chapters, the Apache Kafka project does not include any connectors apart from MirrorMaker and the example FileStream connectors. Instead, the Kafka community and many vendors build connectors. There are now hundreds of them available for the most popular databases, data processing tools, storage tools, and protocols.

However, if there are no connectors for the systems you use, or if the existing connectors are not suitable for your use cases, you can build your own source and sink connectors. In this chapter, we describe the process of implementing a connector from scratch. We cover the classes in the Kafka Connect public API that you need to implement and explain the main steps, best practices, and decisions you need to make in order to build a connector that satisfies your requirements.

Source and sink connectors share a lot of the same building blocks, so many pieces of work and decision points are the same when building your own. Before diving into the specifics of each type of connector, we look at the concepts that apply to both types, such as how to build the connector and the common APIs.

Common Concepts and APIs

As explained in previous chapters, a connector consists of two parts: the connector and the tasks. The initial entry point is the connector, which then configures one or more tasks that actually do the work. These parts map to the Connector and Task classes that you need to implement in the Kafka Connect API. (For example, a source connector must implement SourceConnector and SourceTask, while a sink connector must implement SinkConnector and SinkTask.) At runtime, you have one instance of your SourceConnector or SinkConnector class and one or more instances of your SourceTask or SinkTask class.

In addition to the `Connector` and `Task` classes, the Kafka Connect API contains a set of context classes, which enable connectors and tasks to interact with the runtime and either get insights into what it is doing or impact how it behaves.

Before delving into these APIs, let's look at how you can access the classes you need and set up your build environment.

Building a Custom Connector

All the classes you need access to when building your connector are part of the Kafka Connect public API, which is written in Java. This means you must implement connectors in Java or in a language that is compatible, such as Scala. In the source code, the classes are in the `org.apache.kafka.connect` package, then all these classes are made available as part of the `connect-api` package; when creating your connector project, you need to add this dependency to access these classes. You should not depend on any of the other Kafka Connect or Kafka JARs in your connector, as these are not part of the public API and may change without notice. In practice, `connect-api` also brings `kafka-clients` as a transitive dependency, which contains a lot of useful classes for defining configurations and metrics, and many utilities.

There are a couple of different ways you can get hold of the `connect-api` JAR file. Firstly, the file is included in the Kafka distribution package under the `libs` directory. Secondly, you can pull it from an artifact repository, such as the Maven Central Repository, using a build tool like Maven or Gradle.

Implementing a connector

When building connectors, you should follow the same best practices as for any applications. This includes adding logging and metrics where appropriate, so that users can efficiently run the connector and debug it if it encounters issues. Kafka Connect already provides the SLF4J logging facade, so it's not necessary to explicitly include it with your connector. Also, you should not include a logging backend in your JAR package and instead rely on the backend provided by Kafka Connect. That way, users can utilize the `/admin/loggers` endpoints from the REST API to manage the log levels of your connector.

Connectors can be tricky to properly test due to their interactions with external systems and the complexity of the interactions with the runtime. There are many ways the connector can influence or react to the behavior of the runtime, so ideally you need to verify the connector in an end-to-end pipeline. This means that although you can write unit tests for individual methods, in many cases you also need to build some integration and system tests to fully validate how your connector works in different scenarios. This requires a relatively complex environment, as you first need to start a Kafka cluster, the external system, and a Kafka Connect cluster with the connector.

In addition to testing the connector in a full pipeline, you also need to understand how it behaves with different data and when combined with different converters and transformations. Since Kafka Connect is pluggable, you can't assume the user will always choose the same plug-ins that you are testing with. Kafka Connect does not expose a framework to test plug-ins, so it's something you need to set up yourself. A common approach is to use a framework like Testcontainers (*https://testcontain ers.com*) to orchestrate the deployment of all the components so that you can focus on the actual scenarios you want to test.

Packaging a connector

Once you have implemented your connector classes, you need to package them into a JAR file that users can then add to their Kafka Connect runtime. You also need to include any dependencies that your connector needs at runtime. There are two ways to do this:

- Create an "uber" JAR that contains both your connector classes and any dependencies.
- Provide several JAR files that, together, contain everything. It's common to put them in an archive such as a ZIP file so that they're easier to distribute.

Whichever mechanism you choose, make sure not to include the `connect-api` or any other Kafka JAR files. The Kafka Connect runtime provides these dependencies to the connector when it starts, so omit them from your package.

The exact build setup you have depends on your specific project, but we have included examples in Maven and Gradle to get you started.

A Maven *pom.xml* for a connector might include the following dependencies and packaging steps:

```
<project>
  ...
  <dependencies>
    <dependency>
      <groupId>org.apache.kafka</groupId>
      <artifactId>connect-api</artifactId>
      <version>3.5.0</version>
      <scope>provided</scope> ❶
    </dependency>
  <dependency>
  ...
  <build>
    ...
    <plugins>
      <plugin>
        <artifactId>maven-assembly-plugin</artifactId>
        <version>3.6.0</version>
```

```
      <configuration>
        <descriptorRefs>
          <descriptorRef>jar-with-dependencies</descriptorRef> ❷
        </descriptorRefs>
      </configuration>
      <executions>
        <execution>
          <id>make-assembly</id>
          <phase>package</phase>
          <goals>
            <goal>single</goal>
          </goals>
        </execution>
      </executions>
    </plugin>
    ...
  </build>
  ...
</project>
```

❶ By specifying the scope of the `connect-api` dependency as `provided`, you are instructing Maven not to include it in the resulting JAR file. Any dependencies that are given the `compile` scope (which is the default if not specified) are included in the resulting JAR.

❷ This build creates two JAR files; make sure you use the one that has `jar-with-dependencies` as a suffix, as that is the uber JAR containing all your compile dependencies.

Use the command `mvn package` to build a JAR file for your connector using this *pom.xml*.

If you are using Gradle, a *build.gradle* file may contain the following:

```
plugins {
    id 'java'
}

repositories {
    mavenCentral()
}

dependencies {
    implementation 'org.apache.kafka:connect-api:3.5.0' ❶
}
```

❶ The `connect-api` dependency is loaded with the `implementation` configuration, so it's used to compile the code.

Then, you can execute `gradle jar` to build a JAR file for your connector. Note that if you add other dependencies to the `dependencies` section, you need included in the JAR file, you need to update your *build.gradle* file to explicitly include them. The default Gradle build creates a JAR file with just the classes from your project.

 As of Kafka 3.5.0, there is a KIP in progress, KIP-898 (*https:// oreil.ly/4m2q9*), which aims at updating the way plug-ins are loaded by the runtime. To speed up plug-in discovery and improve the reporting of loading errors, the runtime will use the Java Service Provider to load connector plug-ins in future versions. This mechanism requires adding a service provider configuration file in your plug-in package. We describe how this works in Chapter 12, as this is already used by worker plug-ins.

The next sections go over the main classes you need to use to create connectors. We explore the methods that the `Connector`, `Task`, and `ConnectorContext` APIs provide. We also look at the classes you use to define configuration, and examine the `ConnectRecord` class, which you use to pass records to the runtime. The Kafka project publishes the Javadoc (*https://oreil.ly/BfNOA*) for its public APIs and we recommend that developers implementing connectors consult it for the full API reference.

The Connector API

The entry point for a connector is via the `SourceConnector` or `SinkConnector` class. Both of these classes extend the `Connector` abstract class, and it's this class that brings most of the methods you need to implement. The public methods from the `Connector` interface are:

- `String version()`
- `ConfigDef config()`
- `void initialize(ConnectorContext ctx)`
- `void start(Map<String, String> props)`
- `Class<? extends Task> taskClass()`
- `List<Map<String, String>> taskConfigs(int maxTasks)`
- `void stop()`

For advanced use cases, you can also override this default method from `Connector`:

```
Config validate(Map<String, String> connectorConfigs)
```

The `Connector` interface also has a `context()` method that returns a `ConnectorContext`. This is overridden by the `SourceConnector` and `SinkConnector` classes. We cover all three of these methods here, as they work the same.

 Note that the `Connector` API also exposes two other methods:

- `initialize(ConnectorContext ctx,`
  `    List<Map<String, String>> taskConfigs)`
- `void reconfigure(Map<String, String> props)`

These methods are not used by the runtime, so you should not implement them.

Let's look at the role of all these methods and see how Kafka Connect uses them.

The version() method

The `version()` method should return the version of the connector as a `String` object. The only functional impact of the version is that if multiple versions of a connector are found, Kafka Connect uses the plug-in with the latest version. It should be defined with care so it is also useful to users. For example, the version should be unique for each release of a connector so that users can easily identify what code they are running. Also, even though its format is free, in most cases it is preferable to use semantic versioning with the `major.minor.patch` format (for example, 1.0.2), so users can infer whether subsequent versions may be backward compatible.

This method is called at two different moments in the lifecycle of a connector. First, when the Kafka Connect runtime starts up, it scans the plug-in paths to discover plug-ins and for each connector it finds, it calls the `version()` method. This is done so the `GET /connector-plugins` endpoint can expose the available connectors and their versions. Second, this method is called when the connector starts and the returned version is then used in log lines and metrics.

The config() method

This method returns the configuration definitions for the connector as a `ConfigDef` object. This object contains the details of all the configurations the connector accepts and is used to check if the configuration provided by users is valid or not. We explain how to populate and use `ConfigDef` objects in "Configurations" on page 314.

The `config()` method is called when a connector is created via the REST API and when the `PUT /connector-plugins/<CONNECTOR_PLUGIN>/config/validate` endpoint is called to make sure the requested configuration is valid.

The initialize() method

This method has a default implementation, and in most cases connectors don't need to override it. It allows running some code before a connector is started. The argument of this method is the ConnectorContext class associated with the connector. If you override this method, you should always invoke the default implementation, as it saves the ConnectorContext in the context field of the connector.

This method is called just before the runtime starts a connector. It is not called when a connector is restarted after being paused.

The start() method

The start() method is used to start the connector. The Map<String, String> props argument contains the configuration provided by the user. The runtime should have already checked this configuration against the ConfigDef returned from the config() method, so you can assume that it should be valid. In the body of this method, the Map should be saved, as it is typically needed for the taskConfigs() method.

This method can also be used for other logic you need to run in your connector. For example, MirrorSourceConnector launches logic that periodically retrieves the list of topics from the source cluster. If new topics appear, it can then trigger a reconfiguration via the ConnectorContext. See the following sections for more details about this mechanism.

The start() method is called when the connector is first created, but also when it is resumed after being paused (via the REST API), or when it is reconfigured (also via the REST API).

The taskClass() method

This method returns the Class object for the Task of this connector. For a Sink Connector, it should return a class that extends SinkTask (and SourceTask for a SourceConnector). In order for the runtime to run custom connectors and tasks, it needs to know the classes to run. The Connector class is specified in the connector configuration via the connector.class field, but the configuration does not include the class for tasks. Instead, the runtime uses this method.

A typical implementation just returns the class. For example, FileStreamSource Connector uses this:

```
public Class<? extends Task> taskClass() {
    return FileStreamSourceTask.class;
}
```

This method is only called when the runtime requests task configurations, which can be when the connector is started or when it is reconfigured.

The taskConfigs() method

The `taskConfigs()` method is used to request the configuration of tasks for the connector. It returns a `List` object whose size indicates the number of tasks the connector wants to create. An empty list indicates that no tasks should be created. Each entry in the `List` is a `Map<String, String>` object containing the configuration for that task. The `maxTasks` argument is the value of the `tasks.max` field in the configuration that the user provided for the connector, so this method should not return a `List` with more entries than this number.

In many cases, all tasks share the same configurations, so each entry in the list can be set to the `Map` that was provided to the `start()` method. However, the connector can also generate unique configurations for each task and inject additional configurations that are not settable by users. For example `MirrorSourceConnector` uses this feature to split the work among all tasks, and each task gets a different list of partitions to mirror.

In order to split a list of resources across a specific number of tasks, you can use the `ConnectorUtils.groupPartitions(List<T> elements, int numGroups)` method. Its first argument is the `List` of resources to split, and the second argument is the number of tasks. For example, if a connector interacts with five tables in a database and wants to spread them across three tasks, it can use:

```
List<String> tables = Arrays.asList(
    "users", "orders", "offers", "customers", "billing");
List<List<String>> lists =
    ConnectorUtils.groupPartitions(tables, 3);
System.out.println(lists);
```

This prints:

```
[[users, orders], [offers, customers], [billing]]
```

Be aware that if the size of `elements` is less than the integer `numGroups`, the method still returns a `List` of size `numGroups`, so one or more of the inner lists will be empty.

It is up to you to decide how to use the `maxTasks` argument in your connector. Some connectors, such as the `FileStreamSource` connector, only ever create a single task and ignore this value. Others choose a value based on a combination of the `maxTasks` argument and some other configuration or information from the external system. For example, `MirrorSourceConnector` computes the number of tasks by selecting the smallest value between the number of partitions from the source cluster to mirror, and the `maxTasks` argument.

This method is only called when the runtime needs to create tasks, which can be when the connector is started or when it is reconfigured.

The stop() method

The `stop()` method is used to stop the connector. It provides an opportunity to release resources that were created in `start()`, such as connections to the external system or schedulers.

This method is called when the connector is deleted, but also when it is paused or reconfigured via the REST API.

The validate() method

This method is for running additional validations against the configuration provided. It can be used to check things that can't be specified via the `ConfigDef`. For example, it can validate the connectivity to the external system, or it can check whether a combination of multiple settings is valid.

The `validate()` method has a default implementation, so you don't necessarily need to override it. If you override it, the method needs to return a `Config` object containing a `ConfigValue` entry for each setting. In most cases, you can still use the default method, by calling `super.validate(connectorConfigs)`, and for each setting with an invalid value, add error messages via the `addErrorMessage()` method.

This method is called via two code paths. The first one is when the `PUT /connector-plugins/<CONNECTOR_NAME>/config/validate` endpoint is called. It is also called when connectors are created or reconfigured via the REST API to validate the configuration before accepting the request.

The context() methods

The `Connector`, `SourceConnector` and `SinkConnector` classes each have a `context()` method to retrieve the context associated with the connector. These methods return a `ConnectorContext`, `SourceConnectorContext`, and a `SinkConnectorContext` instance. The details of each context are described in the sections "The ConnectorContext API" on page 327, "The SourceConnectorContext and SourceTaskContext APIs" on page 332, and "The SinkConnectorContext and SinkTaskContext APIs" on page 341.

Contrary to other methods, `context()` methods are not invoked by the Kafka Connect runtime but instead are meant to be used by connectors to retrieve their context.

Connector API lifecycle

Putting it all together, Figure 11-1 shows how the various methods on the Connector API are called.

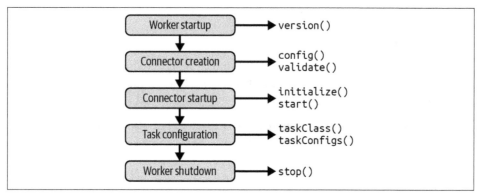

Figure 11-1. The order that methods in the Connector API are called during the normal lifecycle of a connector

When a worker starts, it discovers all plug-ins installed and retrieves their version by calling the version() method. Then, other methods on a Connector are only invoked when the connector is used. First, the config() and validate() methods are called when a user creates the connector via the REST API. These two methods are also called whenever the connector is reconfigured. If the configuration is valid, the runtime proceeds to start the connector and calls the initialize() method, followed by start(). If the connector started successfully, the runtime then starts tasks. To do so, it retrieves the class to run with the taskClass() method, and then the configuration for each task by calling the taskConfigs() method.

A large part of writing a Connector class is deciding what configuration settings you provide to users. In the next section, we delve into this in more detail.

Configurations

Another important feature of connectors is the ability to configure them. We've seen that connectors have the config() method to expose their configurations. This method returns a ConfigDef object that represents the available settings. In this section, we explain how you construct this ConfigDef object and then how you can use it in your connector and task.

In order to create a new instance of ConfigDef, you use the default constructor:

```
ConfigDef configDef = new ConfigDef();
```

If you want to extend an existing `ConfigDef` object, you can also use the `public ConfigDef(ConfigDef base)` constructor.

Once you have a `ConfigDef` instance, you can add individual settings via one of the `define()` methods. This is a fluent API, so you can chain `define()` calls to create multiple configurations. The many overloaded `define()` methods allow you to specify a different number of attributes for each setting. At a minimum, each setting needs a name, a type, an importance, and a documentation. The most commonly used attributes are the following:

Name
The name of the setting as a `String`.

Type
The type of the configuration. The types are described in the next section.

Importance
Indicates whether this is an important setting that users must configure. It uses the `Importance` enum, which has three possible values: `LOW`, `MEDIUM`, and `HIGH`. This is just an indicator, and is not used as part of the configuration validation.

Documentation
The associated documentation, with the setting as a `String`. You should provide clear and detailed documentation so users understand how to effectively configure their connectors.

Default value
The default value the setting has if users don't explicitly set it.

Validator
This allows you to provide logic to validate the value users set. It must implement the `Validator` interface. You can implement your own validators or use one of the built-in validators. We explain how validators work in more detail and list the built-in validators later in this section.

Dependents
Allows you to list other settings that depend on this setting. It is provided as a `List<String>` where each entry is the name of the other settings.

Recommender
Allows you to provide logic to recommend valid values for settings that depend on other settings. It must implement the `Recommender` interface. We explain how to implement a recommender later in this section.

Let's look at an example. `FileStreamSourceConnector` has the following configuration definition with three settings, `topic`, `file`, and `batch.size`:

```java
public static final String TOPIC_CONFIG = "topic"; ❶
public static final String FILE_CONFIG = "file";
public static final String TASK_BATCH_SIZE_CONFIG = "batch.size";
public static final int DEFAULT_TASK_BATCH_SIZE = 2000;

static final ConfigDef CONFIG_DEF = new ConfigDef() ❷
        .define(FILE_CONFIG,
                Type.STRING,
                null,
                Importance.HIGH,
                "Source filename. If not specified, the standard " +
                    "input will be used")
        .define(TOPIC_CONFIG,
                Type.STRING,
                ConfigDef.NO_DEFAULT_VALUE,
                new ConfigDef.NonEmptyString(),
                Importance.HIGH,
                "The topic to publish data to")
        .define(TASK_BATCH_SIZE_CONFIG,
                Type.INT,
                DEFAULT_TASK_BATCH_SIZE,
                Importance.LOW,
                "The maximum number of records the source task can " +
                    "read from the file each time it is polled");
```

❶ Constants are defined for the names of all three settings and for the default batch size. These are public, so they can be accessed from the `FileStreamSourceTask` class too.

❷ A new `ConfigDef` object is created, and calls to `define()` are chained to add the settings. You should not mutate the `ConfigDef` instance you return in the `configs()` methods.

There are also a few other attributes that are less commonly specified and have no functional use in Kafka Connect. They are intended to be used by tools that display configurations, and you can use them to make it easier for users to explore configurations, especially with connectors that have many settings.

Group
Allows related settings to be grouped together, and it is specified as a `String`.

Order in group
If you use groups, you can provide an order for the settings within the group. The order is an `int`.

Display name

Can be used to provide an alternative name, as a String, more suitable for display. For example, command-line tools might use this when displaying information about a connector.

Width

Can be used to specify the width required to display this setting. It uses the Width enum that has the following values: NONE, SHORT, MEDIUM, and LONG.

The ConfigDef class also exposes a few methods to generate documentation for the configurations. You can use the toHtml() and toRst() methods to produce HTML and reStructuredText content, respectively, for the configurations defined on the ConfigDef instance.

Configuration types

Settings specify their type using the Type enum, which has the following values:

- BOOLEAN
- STRING
- INT
- SHORT
- LONG
- DOUBLE
- LIST
- CLASS
- PASSWORD

Each type maps to the matching Java type and has an associated getter method in the AbstractConfig class. For example, BOOLEAN maps to the Java Boolean type, and settings of this type should be retrieved using the getBoolean() method. The PASSWORD type maps to the org.apache.kafka.common.config.types.Password type.

The CLASS and PASSWORD types have some specificities. The PASSWORD type is similar to STRING, but when it's printed, it returns a placeholder, [hidden], to avoid leaking sensitive values. You should use this type for any setting that contains credentials such as passwords or keys. The CLASS type allows users to provide custom implementations for some logic. When using a configuration with this type, the runtime can automatically create the instance of the provided class and, if it implements the Configurable interface, it automatically calls the configure() method with the connector configuration.

Validators and recommenders

Validators and recommenders are pluggable and allow you to customize the validation of configurations. They are both called when the connector is created or when its configuration is updated. They are also called when users query the validate endpoint.

The Validator interface is used to dynamically determine if a setting has an acceptable value. It has a single method: void ensureValid(String name, Object value). It receives the setting's name as the first argument and the value set by the user as the second argument. In order to indicate a value is not valid, it should throw a ConfigException with a descriptive message that the runtime returns to the user.

You can implement your own Validator or reuse one of the built-in implementations:

- CompositeValidator allows combining multiple validators. It takes a List of Validator objects.

- LambdaValidator allows providing a lambda to validate the value. The lambda must have the following type: BiConsumer<String, Object>.

- ListSize ensures a LIST setting has at most the specified number of elements.

- NonEmptyString ensures a STRING setting is not null and not empty.

- NonEmptyStringWithoutControlChars works like NonEmptyString but also ensures the value does not contain any ISO control characters.

- NonNullValidator ensures the value is not null.

- Range ensures a numeric setting (SHORT, INT, LONG, DOUBLE) is within the specified range.

- ValidList ensures a LIST setting only contains the specified strings.

- ValidString ensures a STRING setting is equal to a value in the specified list of strings.

- CaseInsensitiveValidString works like ValidString but ignores case when doing the comparison.

The Recommender interface is used to dynamically compute valid values for settings that depend on other settings. A recommender can also conditionally mark settings as not visible when they are not active anymore based on the rest of the configuration. The visible flag has no functional effects in Kafka Connect, but it can be used by tools interacting with the validate endpoint to build interfaces.

For example, a recommender can be used if a connector has two options for providing credentials: either a username and password, or a private key. The connector configuration could use a recommender to mark the private key setting as not visible if both the username and password have been set.

The Recommender interface has two methods:

- `List<Object> validValues(String name, Map<String, Object> parsed Config)`
- `boolean visible(String name, Map<String, Object> parsedConfig)`

The `validValues()` method returns a `List` of allowed values for this setting. To compute them, the recommender receives the setting name as the first argument and the rest of the configuration as the second argument. At this stage, the configuration is partially parsed, so each entry in the `Map` should have the correct type.

The `visible()` method returns a `boolean` indicating if this configuration should be marked as visible or not. By default, all settings are marked as visible. This method takes the exact same arguments as `validValues()`.

There are no built-in Recommender implementations.

Now that we have discussed how to build a `ConfigDef` object, let's discuss some best practices for interacting with configurations at runtime.

Interacting with configurations at runtime

When the connector and tasks start, the configuration from the user is passed via the `start()` method as a `Map<String, String>` object. You should not directly use this `Map`, as this does not take into account the different types and attributes set via the `ConfigDef` object. Instead, you can use the `AbstractConfig` class that has specific getters to retrieve configurations based on their types.

For example, a connector can use the following logic to retrieve its configurations:

```
ConfigDef CONFIG_DEF = new ConfigDef()  ❶
            .define("timeout",
                ConfigDef.Type.LONG,
                ConfigDef.Importance.HIGH,
                "Documentation for this setting");

public void start(Map<String, String> props) {
    AbstractConfig config = new AbstractConfig(CONFIG_DEF, props);  ❷
    Long timeout = config.getLong("timeout");  ❸
}
```

❶ We have a `ConfigDef` with a single setting called `timeout` of type `LONG`.

❷ We first create an `AbstractConfig` object using the configuration definition, as well as the configuration provided by the user.

❸ We use the appropriate getter for the configuration to retrieve its value with the correct type.

The AbstractConfig class has getters for all the configuration types. For CLASS settings, it can return the raw class object or directly create an instance. When creating an instance, if the class implements the Configurable interface, its configure() method is automatically invoked with the connector configuration.

There are also a few other interesting methods in AbstractConfig. For example, unused() returns configurations provided by the user that do not match any defined configurations. Also, the methods originalsWithPrefix(), valuesWithPre fixAllOrNothing(), and valuesWithPrefixOverride() are useful for handling configurations with prefixes. These three methods allow connectors to retrieve configurations that have been grouped with a specific prefix. For example, MirrorSource Connector accepts configurations with the producer. or consumer. prefixes to tune different clients, so it uses these methods to handle these configurations together.

In many cases, you can also extend the AbstractConfig class and have a dedicated class for the connector configuration. This is useful if the connector has many configurations, or if you want to retrieve more than just the raw configurations. If both the Connector and Task classes interact with the configuration, a custom configuration class also allows mutualizing common logic. For example, MirrorMaker connectors have their own configuration classes (MirrorSourceConfig, MirrorCheck pointConfig and MirrorHeartbeatConfig) that encapsulate the ConfigDef object for the connectors, and provide high-level specialized methods. For instance, Mirror SourceConfig has the following method:

```
Duration syncTopicAclsInterval() {
    if (getBoolean(SYNC_TOPIC_ACLS_ENABLED)) {
        return Duration.ofSeconds(getLong(SYNC_TOPIC_ACLS_INTERVAL_SECONDS));
    } else {
        // negative interval to disable
        return Duration.ofMillis(-1);
    }
}
```

This method encapsulates configuration logic because the sync interval depends on the value of two settings. It prevents this type of logic from leaking into MirrorSource Connector.

Once you have implemented a Connector class, you need to write a Task class using the Task API.

The Task API

The `SourceTask` and `SinkTask` abstract classes represent Kafka Connect tasks. They both extend the `Task` interface and each have a few specific methods. In this section, we only discuss the common methods that are used by both `SourceTask` and `Sink Task`.

The `Task` interface has the following public methods:

- `String version()`
- `void start(Map<String, String> props)`
- `void stop()`

The `version()` method should return the same value as the `version()` method of the Connector. This value has no functional uses; it is only used in log lines.

Both `SourceTask` and `SinkTask` have `initialize()` methods that work the same, so although they're not part of the `Task` interface, we also cover these methods in this section.

The initialize() methods

Like in the `Connector` API, the `initialize()` methods in the `SourceTask` and `SinkTask` APIs allow running logic before tasks start. These methods have default implementations which are suitable for most use cases, so you don't need to override them. The argument of this method is the context associated with the task, a `Source TaskContext` object for source tasks, and a `SinkTaskContext` object for sink tasks. If you override them, you should always invoke the default implementation, as it saves the context in the `context` field of the task.

These methods are called just before the `start()` method when the runtime starts the task.

The start() method

The role of the `start()` method is to get the task ready to handle records. This typically means retrieving details from the configuration and establishing connections to the external system. The `props` argument in this method is a `Map` that contains the configuration generated for this task by the `taskConfigs()` method from the connector. Tasks should not use the `Map` directly to retrieve specific configuration. Instead, they should build an `AbstractConfig` object using the `ConfigDef` of the connector and use the appropriate getters for each type.

The `FileStreamSinkTask` has a good example of a typical `start()` method:

```
private String filename;
private PrintStream outputStream;

public void start(Map<String, String> props) {
    AbstractConfig config = new AbstractConfig(
        FileStreamSinkConnector.CONFIG_DEF, props); ❶
    filename = config.getString(FileStreamSinkConnector.FILE_CONFIG);
    ❷
    if (filename == null || filename.isEmpty()) {
        outputStream = System.out;
    } else {
        try {
            outputStream = new PrintStream(
                Files.newOutputStream(Paths.get(filename),
                                    StandardOpenOption.CREATE,
                                    StandardOpenOption.APPEND),
                false,
                StandardCharsets.UTF_8.name());
        } catch (IOException e) {
            throw new ConnectException("Couldn't find or create file '" +
                filename + "' for FileStreamSinkTask", e); ❸
        }
    }
}
```

❶ It first builds an AbstractConfig object from the user configuration and Config
Def, and then retrieves the specified filename.

❷ It then has some logic to open a PrintStream on the file or on standard output,
so it's ready to export records.

❸ If it can't interact with the specified file, it immediately throws an exception, so
the task never enters the RUNNING state.

This method is called when the runtime starts the task. The runtime waits for the
start() method to complete before moving the task status into the RUNNING state.

The stop() method

This method allows resources allocated by the task to be released, such as connections
to the target system.

Again, taking FileStreamSinkTask as an example, its stop() method has the following logic:

```
public void stop() {
    if (outputStream != null && outputStream != System.out)
        outputStream.close(); ❶
}
```

❶ It closes the PrintStream that was created in the start() method.

This method is called when the runtime wants the task to stop. It is not guaranteed to be the last method the runtime calls when it is stopping a connector; for that reason, if other methods rely on resources that are closed in this method, you should add logic to make sure these calls don't result in an exception. For example, you can use this method to set a variable indicating that stop() has been called. Then other methods in the task can return immediately if stopping is in progress instead of hitting exceptions.

Task API lifecycle

Figure 11-2 shows how the various methods on the Task API are called. This picks up where Figure 11-1 in the Connector API lifecycle section left off, so the runtime has retrieved the configuration for each task from the connector and has created an instance of the Task class.

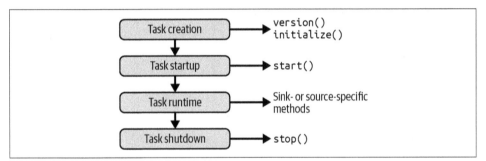

Figure 11-2. The order that methods in the Task API are called during the normal lifecycle of a task

When the runtime is starting a connector, after calling the taskClass() and taskCon figs() methods from the Connector API, it begins starting tasks. For each task, it creates an instance of the class retrieved via taskClass() and calls the version() and initialize() methods to set it up. Then it actually starts the task via the start() method and proceeds to call the methods to exchange data with the external system. These methods are provided by the SourceTask and SinkTask abstract classes, which we describe in detail later. If the connector is reconfigured, existing tasks are first stopped using the stop() method, before calling start() on new tasks with the new configuration. Finally, if the task must be shut down, for example when the worker is shutting down, the runtime calls stop() to let the task end.

Within Kafka Connect, data is exchanged between the runtime and the tasks as ConnectRecord objects. Although the records do vary between source and sink, they share a lot of common parts that we cover in the next section.

Kafka Connect Records

The `ConnectRecord` is an abstract class that specifies the common aspects of records exchanged between tasks and the Kafka Connect runtime. There are two concrete classes that extend it: `SourceRecord` and `SinkRecord`. Each one adds some specific fields that are used by source and sink tasks, respectively.

Regardless of the type of connector you are building, it's important to understand the information that is encapsulated in `ConnectRecord` objects. If you are writing a source connector, you need to create `SourceRecord` objects in your `SourceTask`. On the other hand, when writing a sink connector, you need to decide how to map `SinkRecords` to resources in your external system.

`ConnectRecord` has the following fields:

`topic`
> The Kafka topic the record should be sent to (for source connectors) or that it originates from (for sink connectors).

`value`
> The value for the record.

`valueSchema`
> The schema for the record value.

`key`
> The key for the record.

`keySchema`
> The schema for the record key.

`headers`
> The set of headers for the record.

`kafkaPartition`
> The partition the record should be sent to (for source connectors) or originates from (for sink connectors).

`timestamp`
> The timestamp of the record.

Both the `value` and the `key`, if specified, have a related schema object that can be provided.

Schemas

One of the most important parts of the `ConnectRecord` is the schema for the value, and—if you are using it—the key. In both source and sink pipelines, the schema can be used by transformations to manipulate the record, and the converter to either serialize or deserialize the data when it is sent to or from Kafka. So, the schema that gets used in the ConnectRecord can heavily influence the format of the data downstream in your pipeline.

The Kafka Connect runtime provides a Schema class that supports the following types:

- Int8
- Int16
- Int32
- Int64
- Float32
- Float64
- Boolean
- String
- Bytes
- Array
- Map
- Struct

> The number in the numeric types (Int8, Int16, ...) indicates the number of bits used to store the value. This directly maps to the range of values a type covers. For example, Int8 allows 2^8 (256) values from –128 to 127. All the Int types are signed, and Float types use IEEE 754 representation.

The types range from primitive ones, like integers, booleans, strings, and bytes, to more complex types like arrays, maps and structs. A *struct* is a structured record containing a set of named fields, where each field has its own schema that can be one of the schema types.

The Kafka Connect runtime provides a SchemaBuilder class to make it easier for you to build your schemas. This is a fluent API, so, for example, to construct a basic String schema, you can use the following:

```
Schema myStringSchema = SchemaBuilder.string()
  .name("com.example.CalendarDate")
  .version(1)
  .doc("A calendar date including month, day and year")
```

```
   .defaultValue("January 1st 2023")
   .optional()
   .build();
```

The SchemaBuilder class lets you provide additional information about your schema, such as giving it a name, version, and default value, and defining whether this value is optional.

If you want to build a more complex schema, you need to use the struct() method to define multiple fields:

```
Schema myStructSchema = SchemaBuilder.struct()
   .name("com.example.CalendarDate")
   .version(2)
   .doc("A calendar date including month, day, and year.")
   .field("month", Schema.STRING_SCHEMA)
   .field("day", Schema.INT8_SCHEMA)
   .field("year", Schema.INT16_SCHEMA)
   .build();
```

The preceding example uses static variables, Schema.STRING_SCHEMA, Schema .INT8_SCHEMA, and Schema.INT16_SCHEMA, to specify the Schema for each field. However, these are just shortcuts that could be replaced by explicit calls to Schema Builder to specify additional information like the default value. For example, the Schema.STRING_SCHEMA static variable executes SchemaBuilder.string().build() under the covers.

If you are using a struct schema, you can then use the Struct class to create the actual value you want to pass along with this schema:

```
Struct struct = new Struct(myStructSchema)
   .put("month", "July")
   .put("day", 15)
   .put("year", 2023);
```

The Schema class contains a set of methods that let you examine a Schema instance. For example, if you wanted to find the type, name, and fields in a Struct schema, you could use:

```
String name = mySchema.name();
Type type = mySchema.type();
if (Type.STRUCT.equals(type)) {
    List<Field> fields = mySchema.fields();
}
```

This is particularly useful in sink connectors, where you might need to examine the schema to understand how to interpret the data you received.

The ConnectorContext API

In Kafka Connect, context objects enable `Connector` and `Task` instances to interact with the runtime. There are different context objects for connectors and tasks, and for the type of connector (source or sink). In this section, we only cover the `Con nectorContext` API that both `SourceConnectorContext` and `SinkConnectorContext` extend. The source- and sink-specific contexts are covered in later sections.

The `ConnectorContext` API exposes two methods:

- `void requestTaskReconfiguration()`
- `void raiseError(Exception e)`

Both `SourceTaskContext` and `SinkTaskContext` have `configs()` methods that work the same, so although it's not part of the `ConnectorContext` interface, we also cover these methods in this section.

The requestTaskReconfiguration() method

Connectors can call this method to notify the runtime that it should recreate all tasks. When it is called, the runtime calls the `taskConfigs()` method on the `Connector` to regenerate task configurations, before stopping all existing tasks and then finally creating new tasks. This allows connectors to change the number of tasks and their configuration at runtime without any user input. This is useful if the `Connector` class has logic that makes decisions by interacting with the external system. For example, `MirrorSourceConnector` regularly fetches metadata from the source cluster to detect new topics or partitions. When they appear, it calls `requestTaskReconfiguration()` to create or update existing tasks.

This is an expensive operation, as this effectively fully restarts all tasks and thus halts processing for a short period, so keep this in mind when calling this method.

The raiseError() method

If a connector encounters an unrecoverable error, it can use this method to report the exception back to the runtime and set its state to `FAILED`. The runtime emits an `ERROR` log line with the exception, and it is also visible via the REST API.

The configs() method

The `configs()` method returns the latest configuration of the task as a `Map<String, String>`, which could be different from the one that was passed in on the `start()` method. This method is useful for tasks where the configuration is using one or more `ConfigProvider` instances. For example, if the `ConfigProvider` uses an external secret to populate the configuration and that secret has changed, the task can use this method to get the latest value.

Now that we've looked at the common considerations for writing a connector, let's look at what is required to write a source connector.

Implementing Source Connectors

Source connectors pull data from external systems and then send it to Kafka. In practice, that means the connector has to construct and pass SourceRecord objects to the runtime.

In this section, we focus on the requirements that are unique to source connectors. If you are writing your own source connector, you should make sure you also understand everything we discussed in the previous section.

The first class you need for a source connector is one that implements the SourceConnector abstract class. On top of the common methods that are inherited from the Connector interface, there are two public methods you can implement that relate to exactly-once support. Later in this section, we describe how to implement exactly-once support in your source connector.

The second class you need to implement is the SourceTask class.

The SourceTask API

The SourceTask class is likely where the bulk of your code will go, as this is the class that actually takes data from your external system and passes it to the Kafka Connect runtime. In addition to the methods that are inherited from the Task interface, SourceTask adds the following public methods:

- List<SourceRecord> poll()
- void commit()
- void commitRecord(SourceRecord record, RecordMetadata metadata)

Of these three methods, the poll() method is the only one that you are required to implement.

The poll() method

The poll() method is used to pass new records to the runtime to be sent to Kafka. It returns a List of SourceRecord objects, or null if there is no new data. We go into more details about the considerations for constructing SourceRecords later in this chapter.

Most source connectors use the poll() method to trigger a request to the external system to fetch the latest data. Then, if there is no new data, the method returns immediately with a null value. However, depending on your system, you might decide to pre-fetch data and just return it immediately when called. Determining the best approach can be tricky, and you should consider how you would normally interact with your external system and the duration it takes to fetch records. Then you can see which option works best for your connector.

Once the task has been started, the runtime starts calling the poll() method to retrieve records to send to Kafka. While records are being sent asynchronously to Kafka, it calls poll() again. It is important that you don't block this method indefinitely. If a connector is paused or stopped, the runtime does not make any new calls to poll(), but it won't interrupt the thread that is calling poll(), either. The runtime waits for the amount of time specified by the worker configuration task.shutdown.graceful.timeout.ms (which defaults to 5000), then goes ahead and shuts down the producer client it is using to send records to Kafka. This means if you block in this method for longer than the configured timeout, you will likely see error messages when poll() returns, and any records returned won't be sent to Kafka.

In previous versions of Kafka Connect, the poll() and stop() methods were called on different threads. This made it possible to have a long running process in the poll() method and set a flag in the stop() method to interrupt that process. However, from Kafka 2.8.0 onward stop() is called on the same thread as poll() preventing this behavior. There is an open Jira (KAFKA-15090 (*https://oreil.ly/49OOR*)) in Kafka to address the problem, so the threading behavior might be updated in a future version.

The commit() and commitRecord() methods

The commit() and commitRecord() methods provide hooks for tasks to track the sending of records. The commitRecord() method has two arguments: a SourceRecord object and a RecordMetadata object. The SourceRecord class is the same as the one returned by the poll() method. This contains the record that was given to the Kafka Connect runtime to send to Kafka. The RecordMetadata class represents the metadata of a Kafka record after it has been sent to Kafka. This is the same type that is returned in the producer client when you call send(). The RecordMetadata contains information like the topic and partition that the record was sent to, and the offset that it was given by Kafka.

Both of these methods are optional to implement and are provided to allow connectors to track when records have been sent and, optionally, store offsets in an external system.

Many source connectors use the built-in offset support that the runtime offers, rather than these methods. The benefit of using the built-in support is that Kafka Connect can be configured to enable exactly-once semantics, which uses transactions to send records and commit offsets atomically. For some external systems, it isn't possible to directly retrieve information about where you have read to, but they sometimes provide their own mechanisms to save that information. In this case, you can use the commit() and commitRecord() methods to drive these calls to the external system.

As an example, MirrorCheckpointTask lets the runtime handle offsets, but overrides the commitRecord method to compute metrics about latency:

```
public void commitRecord(SourceRecord record, RecordMetadata metadata) {
    metrics.checkpointLatency(
        MirrorUtils.unwrapPartition(record.sourcePartition()),
        Checkpoint.unwrapGroup(record.sourcePartition()),
        System.currentTimeMillis() - record.timestamp()
    );
}
```

The runtime calls the commitRecord() method each time it has successfully sent an individual record to Kafka. If your pipeline has transformations configured, the runtime still calls commitRecord() for any records that have been filtered, and are therefore not actually sent to Kafka. The runtime calls the commit() method whenever offsets have been committed to the source offsets topic. It performs an offset commit on an interval which is configured using offset.flush.interval.ms. There is no alignment between the calls to poll() and commit(), so it is not possible for the connector to determine which records were committed when commit() is invoked. The commit() and commitRecord() methods may be called on different threads to the poll() method, so keep this in mind when implementing them.

SourceTask API lifecycle

When you are deciding how to implement the methods in the SourceTask API, make sure you consider all of the methods together and how they relate to what the runtime is doing. Figure 11-3 shows the calls between Kafka, the Kafka Connect runtime, and the SourceTask class.

The Kafka Connect runtime calls the poll() method to get a batch of records, and then passes these to its producer to send on to Kafka. Then it starts the loop again by calling poll(). Once the runtime producer has successfully sent the records, it calls commitRecord() for each record with the record and the RecordMetadata object that it received back from Kafka. Each time the runtime commits offsets to Kafka, it also calls the commit() method. Remember, unless exactly-once is enabled, the runtime doesn't commit offsets to Kafka every time it has successfully sent a batch of records

to Kafka. Instead, it only performs an offset commit when the offset.flush.inter
val.ms has passed.

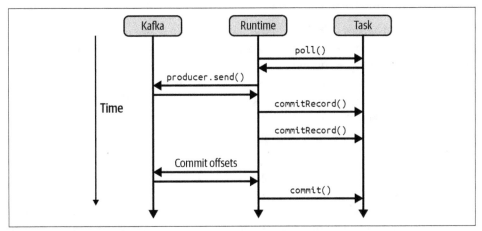

Figure 11-3. Interactions between Kafka, the Kafka Connect runtime and the
SourceTask class

Source Records

In the poll() method of your task, you need to construct SourceRecord objects
from the data fetched from your external system. A SourceRecord inherits all fields
from the ConnectRecord class, but when you are constructing an instance, the only
required fields from the ConnectRecord are topic and value.

There are two additional fields that are specific to SourceRecord: sourcePartition
and sourceOffset.

The topic field allows you to specify the topic the runtime should send this record to,
so the value you use depends on your use case. As an example, the FileStreamSource
connector directly exposes a topic configuration option to the user and then uses
that. In contrast, the Debezium MySQL source connector constructs the topic name
using a combination of the names of the database and table the data is from, and
some user configurations.

Both the value and the key, if specified, have a related schema object that can be
provided. These are not required; however, in many cases it is best to explicitly
declare the schema you intend Kafka Connect to use. That way, you can be sure
that your transformations, converters, and downstream consumers (including sink
connectors) are handling records as expected.

When you are creating your connector, it is very important to consider how the
schema impacts your users. Using a more complex schema makes it easier for

transformations to manipulate the data before it is sent to Kafka. However, if you want your connector to be more performant, you can use a simpler schema like the Bytes type and avoid parsing the data you receive to determine the correct schema.

Both the key and headers fields are optional because these are not required by Kafka. It's up to you as the connector author to decide whether to populate these. Some connectors allow these to be configured by the user, while others infer the information from metadata contained in the source system. Remember that, depending on the configuration of the runtime, the key you use may impact how the data is partitioned in Kafka, and is required for compacted topics. If records from your external system are ordered, they may need to be sent with the same key to guarantee that ordering is maintained.

The kafkaPartition and timestamp are also both optional fields. If they have not been set, the Kafka Connect runtime sets them automatically. For kafkaPartition, the runtime uses the partitioner that has been configured for its producer clients to determine the correct partition to use. If the timestamp is omitted, the Kafka Connect runtime adds the current timestamp as it sends the record.

In many source systems, you can re-read the same piece of data multiple times. If this is the case for your source system, then your connector needs to be able to find its position after a restart. You can either store the offsets and partitions yourself by using the commit() and commitRecord() methods, or let the runtime take care of it by making use of the sourceOffset and sourcePartition fields. When you construct a SourceRecord, if you specify a sourceOffset and sourcePartition, the runtime stores that information in its offsets topic after it sends the record to Kafka. Although the runtime handles these objects, it is only the connector that actually uses them. This means they can have whatever structure is suitable for your use case. The only restrictions are to use a Map with strings for the keys, and primitive types for the values of the sourceOffset argument.

The sourcePartition represents a location in the source system where a particular record has come from, such as a file name for a file connector or a table name for a database connector. The sourceOffset then represents the offset within that location—for example, a line or row number. The connector can use these two pieces of data combined to identify where to restart collecting data from in the external system if it is restarted. We explain how to discover the latest commit offset information in the next section when we introduce the offsetStorageReader() method.

The SourceConnectorContext and SourceTaskContext APIs

The SourceConnectorContext and SourceTaskContext classes allow the connector and task to interact with the Kafka Connect runtime.

The SourceConnectorContext only has one method that is outside the ConnectorCon text class we discussed earlier: OffsetStorageReader offsetStorageReader().

The SourceTaskContext contains the following three methods:

- OffsetStorageReader offsetStorageReader()
- TransactionContext transactionContext()
- Map<String, String> configs()

We already covered configs() in "The ConnectorContext API" on page 327. Let's look at how you can use the other methods.

The offsetStorageReader() method

This method is used to fetch the latest committed offset for a partition. This uses the sourcePartition and sourceOffset fields that are in the SourceRecord, so if you want to use this method, make sure you are setting these fields in your SourceRecord. You can call the offsetStorageReader() method from either your SourceConnector or SourceTask, and it returns an OffSetStorageReader class that has the following methods:

- <T> Map<String, Object> offset(Map<String, T> partition)
- <T> Map<Map<String, T>, Map<String, Object>> offsets(Collection<Map <String, T>> partitions)

The first method takes a single partition reference, whereas the second takes a Collection of partition objects.

You can see an example of how to use this method in the FileStreamSourceTask class, where it makes use of the OffsetStorageReader:

```
Map<String, Object> offset = context.offsetStorageReader().offset(
    Collections.singletonMap("filename", filename));
```

If there is an offset present, the task doesn't read the file from the beginning, and instead starts from the provided offset. By specifying the sourcePartition and sourceOffset in the SourceRecord, and making use of the offsetStorageReader() function, you let the runtime do the heavy lifting of storing offsets, rather than having to write that logic into your connector.

The transactionContext() method

The transactionContext() method returns the TransactionContext class, which can be used by connectors to define their own producer transaction boundaries when exactly-once support is enabled. We discuss this in more detail in the next section.

Exactly-Once Support

When writing your source connector, you need to decide whether it supports exactly-once semantics. The mechanism to allow exactly-once semantics was added via KIP-618 (*https://oreil.ly/DnBHw*) in Kafka 3.3. If enabled, the runtime uses a transactional producer to send records and commit their offsets atomically to Kafka. In Chapter 8, we describe how a user can configure a source connector to enable exactly-once semantics. The Kafka Connect workers have to be configured for exactly-once semantics, and then the user can also configure the connector so that exactly-once is required.

Additionally, users can configure the connector so that transaction boundaries are set by the connector, rather than the runtime. The runtime has two ways that it can handle transactions. Either it uses a new transaction for each poll() invocation, or it commits transactions on a fixed interval. These options are likely good enough for most source connectors; however, you might want more control over when the transactions are committed or aborted. Custom transaction boundaries can be used to influence which records and offsets should be delivered as part of the same transaction, for example in systems where it isn't possible to assign a unique offset to each record. The runtime automatically starts a new transaction when it receives some records from a task and there isn't a transaction currently opened.

The methods used to implement exactly-once support are spread across two different APIs, the SourceConnector API and the TransactionContext API.

The SourceConnector API has two public methods:

- ExactlyOnceSupport exactlyOnceSupport(Map<String, String> config)
- ConnectorTransactionBoundaries canDefineTransactionBoundaries(
    Map<String, String> config)

The TransactionContext provides the following methods to manage the transaction boundaries:

- void commitTransaction()
- void commitTransaction(SourceRecord record)
- void abortTransaction()
- void abortTransaction(SourceRecord record)

To add exactly-once support to your connector, first make sure that you have implemented the exactlyOnceSupport() method in your SourceConnector class. You also need to make sure the runtime is storing offsets by making proper use of the source Partition and sourceOffset fields. Finally, your connector needs to use the stored offsets to resume when it is restarted by calling the `offsetStorageReader()` method in either the `SourceConnectorContext` or `SourceTaskContext` class. We describe how you can use these earlier in this chapter.

If you want to support connector-defined transaction boundaries, you need to implement the `canDefineTransactionBoundaries()` method in your `SourceConnector` class. Then you actually define your transaction boundaries using the `transaction Context()` method, which is available on the `SourceTaskContext` API.

If the `transaction.boundary` configuration is set to `connector`, the `transactionCon text()` method either returns an instance of the `TransactionContext` class or returns `null`. If your connector is running on an older version of Kafka Connect that doesn't support exactly-once semantics, then you get an exception from this method, so you should surround the call with a try/catch block:

```
TransactionContext transactionContext;
try {
    transactionContext = context.transactionContext();
} catch (NoSuchMethodError | NoClassDefFoundError e) {
    transactionContext = null;
}
```

When you are deciding how to use the `TransactionContext` methods, you should keep the following things in mind. First, for consumers with the isolation level set to `read_commited`, the longer you wait to commit the transaction, the bigger latency you will see in your pipeline. However, there is an overhead to starting a new transaction, so having one transaction per record isn't performant either. Secondly, if a task is restarted, the latest offset it can retrieve from Kafka is one that is part of a committed transaction. This means if you have transactions that span many records, your task will have to reprocess all those records if it is restarted.

Now that we have discussed at a high level how to implement exactly-once support, let's look at the methods in more detail.

The exactlyOnceSupport() method

This method is used to indicate whether this connector supports exactly-once semantics, given the provided configuration. For older connectors, there is a default method that returns `null`, but if you are writing a connector, you should always implement this function. The return type for the method is an enum called `ExactlyOnceSupport` with two possible values, `SUPPORTED` and `UNSUPPORTED`.

For example, the `FileStreamSource` connector only returns `SUPPORTED` if it is reading from a file and can therefore track offsets:

```
public ExactlyOnceSupport exactlyOnceSupport(Map<String, String> props) {
    AbstractConfig parsedConfig = new AbstractConfig(CONFIG_DEF, props);
    String filename = parsedConfig.getString(FILE_CONFIG);
```

```
    return filename != null && !filename.isEmpty()
            ? ExactlyOnceSupport.SUPPORTED
            : ExactlyOnceSupport.UNSUPPORTED;
}
```

You could also use this method to verify that `transaction.boundary` is set to `connec` `tor` if that is a requirement your connector has in order to provide exactly-once semantics. The runtime calls this method before it starts the connector. If this method returns `ExactlyOnceSupport.UNSUPPORTED` and the connector configuration has `exactly.once.support` set to `required`, the API request fails and the runtime does not start the connector.

The canDefineTransactionBoundaries() method

The `canDefineTransactionBoundaries()` method is used to declare whether this connector is capable of specifying its own transaction boundaries. Similar to the `exactlyOnceSupport()` method, this method returns an enum, this time called `Con` `nectorTransactionBoundaries`, with the possible values of `SUPPORTED` and `UNSUPPOR` `TED`. This method has a default implementation that returns `UNSUPPORTED`, so if your connector does not support defining its own boundaries, you don't need to implement this method. If your connector returns `ConnectorTransactionBoundaries` `.SUPPORTED`, it doesn't mean that your connector always defines its own transaction boundaries. Connector-defined transaction boundaries are only used if the user opts in by setting `transaction.boundary` to `connector` in the connector configuration.

The runtime calls this method before it starts the connector if the connector configuration has `transaction.boundary` set to `connector` and exactly-once support is also enabled. If this method returns `ConnectorTransactionBoundaries.UNSUPPORTED`, then the API request fails and the runtime does not start the connector.

The commitTransaction() methods

There are two `commitTransaction()` methods you can call in the `TransactionCon` `text`. The first one is used to tell the runtime to commit the current transaction after it has finished processing the next batch of records from the `poll()` method. The second method takes a `SourceRecord` as its argument and is used to request a transaction commit after that particular source record has been processed.

The abortTransaction() methods

There are two `abortTransaction()` methods in the `TransactionContext`. These work similarly to the `commitTransaction()` methods, but request the transaction be aborted rather than committed. The first triggers the transaction to be aborted after the next batch of records is returned from the `poll()` method. All the records in the transaction are discarded; however, the offsets for them are still committed. This means you shouldn't use this method if you want those records to be reprocessed. The second method takes a `SourceRecord` object and aborts the transaction after that record is processed, so the provided record is the last in the aborted transaction. Similar to the first method, the offsets are still committed.

Let's now do a similar deep dive into sink connectors and see what it takes to implement one.

Implementing Sink Connectors

In this section, we focus on the specificities of sink connectors. So, if you are writing your own sink connector, you should make sure you also understand everything we discussed in "Common Concepts and APIs" on page 305.

Sink connectors receive records from the Kafka Connect runtime as `SinkRecord` objects, and have to send them to an external system. They are the last step in a sink pipeline, and run after records have been converted and flowed through the transformations.

Sink connectors have to extend the `SinkConnector` abstract class. `SinkConnector` inherits all methods from the `Connector` interface and does not add any extra methods. It only adds a single field, `TOPICS_CONFIG`, that represents the `topics` field. This field can be used by connectors or tasks that need to retrieve the set of topics the user specified in the configuration.

Unlike source connectors, sink connectors don't have specific APIs for enforcing exactly-once semantics. Because sink connectors write to an external system, exactly-once semantics are only possible if that system provides certain guarantees. There are two main ways this can be achieved:

1. As described in Chapter 5, with the Confluent S3 sink connector, exactly-once semantics are possible if the target system supports idempotent writes and if the connector emits `SinkRecord` objects in a deterministic way.

2. Some systems allow you to query for the last record written. If the offset is part of the record, tasks can use their context to reset their position and carry on from the next record to send. This approach also requires a mechanism to ensure unresponsive tasks can be properly fenced out to avoid interfering when new tasks are started.

Now let's look at the specifics of writing a `SinkTask` class.

The SinkTask API

The SinkTask class is responsible for taking records from the Kafka Connect runtime and sending them to the external system. In addition to the methods inherited from Task, it has the following methods:

- void put(Collection<SinkRecord> records)
- Map<TopicPartition, OffsetAndMetadata> preCommit(Map<TopicPartition, OffsetAndMetadata> currentOffsets)
- void flush(Map<TopicPartition, OffsetAndMetadata> currentOffsets)
- void open(Collection<TopicPartition> partitions)
- void close(Collection<TopicPartition> partitions)

Of these methods, the put() method is the only one you are required to implement.

The put() method

The put() method enables the connector to receive records from the runtime to send to the external system. The records are received as a Collection of SinkRecord objects.

The runtime calls this method every time it completes a call to poll() in its internal consumer client. If there are no new records, the Collection passed to the method is empty. When a connector is stopped, the runtime waits for this method to return before trying to shut down the connector. However, it only waits for the duration of the worker configuration task.shutdown.graceful.timeout.ms (defaults to 5000), then it abandons the task without waiting any longer for it to complete shutdown.

The preCommit() method

This method lets the task take some action before offsets are committed to Kafka, and influence what offsets are committed. Its argument is a Map<TopicPartition, Offset Metadata> that represents the latest offset that has been passed to the put() method. The preCommit() method returns a Map<TopicPartition, OffsetMetadata> for the runtime to commit.

For example, the Confluent S3 sink connector uses this method to tell the runtime which records it has successfully written to S3 so that only those offsets are committed. This helps ensure that records aren't lost if the task is restarted.

The runtime calls preCommit() just before it commits offsets to Kafka. Remember that only the offsets returned by this method are committed to Kafka—so if you implement this method to always return an empty Map, the runtime does not store any offsets in Kafka. The preCommit() method is called on the same thread as put(). Before each call to put(), the runtime checks how long it has been since the last commit. If this time is longer than the offset.flush.interval.ms worker configuration (which defaults to 60 seconds), it triggers an offset commit. If the latest offset has not changed since the last time the runtime committed offsets, it still calls preCommit() with that latest offset.

If an exception is thrown from this method, the runtime aborts the offset commit and resets its consumer to the latest successfully committed offset. The runtime then reconsumes the failed record, along with any previous records whose associated offsets it hadn't committed yet, and passes them to the connector.

The default implementation of this method calls flush() with the Map it has been passed, and then returns the Map unchanged.

The flush() method

This method is used to make sure that batches of records have been flushed to the external system before offsets are committed. The method is called with Map<Topic Partition, OffsetAndMetadata>, which represents the offset state at the time of the last call to put().

The runtime actually only calls this method in the default implementation of the preCommit() method. So, if you provide your own implementation for preCommit() that does not call flush(), this method will never be called. Depending on your use case, you might find this method useful to drive the coordination with the external system. For example, the FileStreamSinkTask doesn't override preCommit(), and it uses this method to call flush() on the output stream.

The open() and close() methods

The open() and close() methods give the sink task an opportunity to open or close clients or connections to the external system for specific partitions when a rebalance happens. Both methods have a single argument of Collection<TopicPartition>. The runtime calls these methods when it has changed the Kafka partitions that are allocated to this task.

For example, imagine a Kafka topic with two partitions and a connector that always configures the number of tasks as equal to tasks.max. If the connector is started with tasks.max set to 1, when the task starts, the runtime calls open() with a Collection containing both partitions. If the connector is then reconfigured to set tasks.max to 2, the existing task then sees close() called with both partitions and then open() called with a single partition. A new task is also started, and it also sees open() called with the other partition.

The runtime calls the open() method after it has finished re-assigning partitions and before it starts fetching data. The runtime calls the close() method after it has stopped fetching new data, but before it starts rebalancing the partitions.

The SinkTask API lifecycle

The SinkTask API only has one required method: put(). However, it includes several other methods that give the task insights into what the runtime is doing. When you are implementing these methods, make sure you understand how they relate to the interactions between the runtime and Kafka. Figure 11-4 shows the interactions between Kafka, the Kafka Connect runtime, and the SinkTask class.

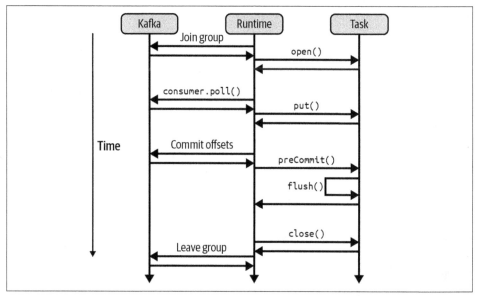

Figure 11-4. Interactions between Kafka, the Kafka Connect runtime, and the SinkTask class

The runtime calls poll() from its internal consumer client to get new records and passes them to the task using the put() method. The runtime then calls the preCommit() method before it commits offsets to Kafka. It only commits those offsets that are returned by this method. Once the offsets are committed, it starts the loop again. The runtime doesn't commit offsets every time it fetches new records. Instead, it only does this if the offset.flush.interval.ms has been reached.

Remember that the runtime only makes calls to open() and close() when a rebalance happens and it needs to change the partitions that are assigned to the task. This happens when the task starts and stops, but can also be triggered by other group members (tasks) being added and removed.

Now that we have looked at the `SinkTask` API, let's look in more detail at the `SinkRecord` objects that the `SinkTask` receives.

Sink Records

When the runtime calls the `put()` method on a sink task, it provides a collection of `SinkRecord` objects. A `SinkRecord` inherits all fields from the `ConnectRecord` class and is constructed by the runtime from a Kafka record.

There are two additional fields that are specific to `SinkRecord`: `kafkaOffset` and `timestampType`.

The `topic`, `key`, `value`, `headers`, `kafkaPartition`, `kafkaOffset`, `timestamp`, and `timestampType` fields come directly from the Kafka record.

The `keySchema` and `valueSchema` fields depend on the `Converter` used. For example, `ByteArrayConverter` always sets the schema with the `Bytes` type and just passes the raw bytes from Kafka, whereas converters that work with complex types such as JSON or Avro attempt to build schemas matching the payload.

Whether to use structured or raw schemas depends on the use cases, logic, and configuration options of the connector. A structured schema allows connectors and transformations to selectively pick inner fields of Kafka records and alter payloads before sending them to the target system. It also allows for the creation of some types of resources in the external system. For example, a sink connector for a database might create the columns in the table based on the schema from the Kafka record. Like for source connectors, this flexibility has a performance cost, as all records have to be parsed. If your connector requires a structured schema, you should document it so users can select the appropriate converters for both the sink connector itself and all upstream data sources (including source connectors).

The SinkConnectorContext and SinkTaskContext APIs

The `SinkConnectorContext` and `SinkTaskContext` interfaces allow interacting with the Kafka Connect runtime.

The `SinkConnectorContext` interface does not add any new methods. On the other hand, `SinkTaskContext` has nine methods:

- `void offset(Map<TopicPartition, Long> offsets)`
- `void offset(TopicPartition tp, long offset)`
- `void timeout(long timeoutMs)`
- `Set<TopicPartition> assignment()`
- `void pause(TopicPartition... partitions)`

- void resume(TopicPartition... partitions)
- void requestCommit()
- ErrantRecordReporter errantRecordReporter()
- Map<String, String> configs()

We cover configs() in "The ConnectorContext API" on page 327 earlier in this chapter. Let's look at how you can use the other methods.

The offset() methods

Sink connectors that store their offsets in the external system can use the two offset() methods to reset their positions when they start up. To reset the offset of a single partition, you use void offset(TopicPartition tp, long offset); otherwise use the void offset(Map<TopicPartition, Long> offsets) method to reset multiple partitions in a single call.

Connectors that rely on Kafka Connect's built-in offset tracking typically don't need to use these methods.

The timeout() method

The timeout() method allows setting the timeout the runtime uses the next time it polls data from Kafka. You provide the desired timeout in milliseconds; this is only a hint, and the runtime picks the shortest duration between this and the time before the next offset commit takes place. The timeout defaults to -1 and is ignored by the runtime if the value is negative. Between each poll, the runtime resets the timeout value to -1 so tasks wanting to consistently change the timeout have to call this method each time their put() method is called.

The assignment() method

This method returns the current set of partitions assigned to this task as a Set<Topic Partition> collection. The set of assigned partitions can change for several reasons; for example, new partitions being added to a topic, a new topic being created (when topics.regex is used), or a working being added or removed from the cluster. The assignment() method can be useful if you are controlling the flow of records using the pause() and resume() methods.

The pause() and resume() methods

The pause() and resume() methods allow sink tasks to control the flow of records for each partition. This is useful to prevent the external system becoming overwhelmed. Both methods accept a Collection of TopicPartition objects. After calling pause() on a partition, the task does not receive records, via its put() method, from this partition anymore, until it calls `resume()`. When tasks are started, all partitions are automatically resumed.

Tasks that want to finely control the flow of records for each partition should keep track of the partitions they have paused, as the context does not provide a way to retrieve this information. In order to resume all partitions, you can also call `resume()` with the result of the `assignment()` method.

The requestCommit() method

The `requestCommit()` method allows sink tasks to ask the runtime to commit offsets. As explained in "The Task API" on page 321, the runtime commits offsets periodically. Using this method, tasks can hint to the runtime when it's best to commit instead of waiting for the configured interval. However, this is only a hint, and the runtime does not immediately commit offsets whenever this is called. In fact, the API provides no guarantees over how calling this method will impact the time until the next call to commit offsets.

The errantRecordReporter() method

This method is related to dead letter queue support in sink connectors. As explained in Chapter 4, a dead letter queue allows saving records that are not processable so they are not lost. The `errantRecordReporter()` method either returns an `Errant RecordReporter` instance or `null` if the dead letter queue is not enabled on the runtime. See "Configurations for Error Handling" on page 228 for details on how to enable dead letter queues. This method can also throw `NoSuchMethodError` or `NoClassDefFoundError` if the connector runs on a version of Kafka Connect older than 2.6.0 that doesn't support the dead letter queue feature. For this reason, it's sensible to surround calls to this method with a try/catch:

```
ErrantRecordReporter errantRecordReporter;
try {
    errantRecordReporter = context.errantRecordReporter();
} catch (NoSuchMethodError | NoClassDefFoundError e) {
    errantRecordReporter = null;
}
```

The `ErrantRecordReporter` class has a single method, `report(SinkRecord record, Throwable error)` that allows tasks to send records to the dead letter queue. It takes the `SinkRecord` to send and a `Throwable` object for the associated error. For example:

```
public void put(Collection<SinkRecord> records) {
    for (SinkRecord record : records) {
        try {
            processRecord(record);
        } catch (Exception e) {
            errantRecordReporter.report(record, e);
        }
```

```
        }
    }
```

The `report()` method is asynchronous. This means it returns immediately with a `Future<Void>` object before the record is sent to the dead letter queue topic. The `Future<Void>` object completes once the send is successful, or if it fails. The runtime only calls the `preCommit()` method once the returned future is resolved. If you want to determine if the record was successfully sent to the dead letter queue, you can use the `get()` method on the `Future` object:

```
Future<Void> future = errantRecordReporter.report(record, e);
try {
    future.get(10, TimeUnit.SECONDS);
    // Record successfully sent to dead letter queue
} catch (Exception ex) {
    // Record failed
}
```

The `Future` interface has two `get()` methods. The method without arguments blocks until the `Future` completes. In practice, it's often better to use the overloaded method that takes a timeout, using `long` and `TimeUnit` arguments to avoid blocking for too long.

If the record is successfully sent to the dead letter queue, the `Future` returns nothing (`Void`). In case it fails, it throws an `Execu tionException`, and you need to use the `getCause()` method to retrieve the reason for the failure. If you use the `get()` method with a timeout, it throws a `TimeoutException` if the timeout is reached. It can also throw an `InterruptedException` if the thread is interrupted while it's waiting.

Summary

In this chapter, we have seen what it takes to build custom source and sink connectors. Starting with creating a Java project, you need to use the `connect-api` dependency to access the public interfaces and classes from the Kafka Connect API. We also saw how you should package the connector classes as a JAR file so you can then install it in a Kafka Connect environment.

We explored the common concepts between the two types of connectors. They share a lot of commonalities via the `Connector`, `Task`, context, and record classes. This also demonstrated how to create effective configurations via the `ConfigDef` class and its many options.

Then we looked in detail at source connectors and highlighted the specificities in their classes. We covered the `SourceConnector`, `SourceTask`, `SourceConnector Context`, and `SourceTaskContext`, as well as the best practices when building

SourceRecord objects. In practice, the bulk of your logic is likely going to be in the poll() method in your SourceTask. However, there are plenty of ways you can impact the flow of data to optimize for your use case. We also detailed the methods that source connectors can implement to offer exactly-once semantics.

Finally, we showed how to implement sink connectors. When you are writing a sink connector, the put() method in the SinkTask receives new records from Kafka and is responsible for sending them to the target system. The SinkTask and SinkTask Context expose a few methods to finely control the flow of data from Kafka so that your connector and your downstream system are not overwhelmed.

Ultimately, how you implement your connector comes down to your specific use case. The best way to interact with the Kafka Connect runtime depends on what is important for the external system you are integrating with. Since many connectors are open source, it can be beneficial to look at other connectors and see how they are implemented. Don't be afraid to iterate over time, as it's unlikely you will find the best implementation the first time. Make sure you have good levels of logs and metrics, then run your final connector in a test environment to see how it handles failures in both Kafka and your external system.

CHAPTER 12

Extending Kafka Connect with Connector and Worker Plug-Ins

Kafka Connect has two different kinds of plug-ins that you can use to extend its functionality:

Connector plug-ins
Used to influence the behavior of a particular pipeline

Worker plug-ins
Used to customize the Kafka Connect runtime

Kafka Connect comes with a few built-in plug-ins, and the Kafka community has also built many more. In this chapter, we explain how to implement your own connector and worker plug-ins. In "Implementing Connector Plug-Ins" on page 348, we omit connectors because we explain how to implement those in Chapter 11. Before considering writing your own plug-in, check to see if there is already one available for your use case.

There are a few common considerations that apply no matter which type of plug-in you are implementing. First, the building and packaging process for connector and worker plug-ins is the same as for connectors. We describe the steps in "Building a Custom Connector" on page 306. Secondly, there are some `Exception` classes included in the `connect-api` and `clients` packages that you can use in your plug-in when you need to throw an `Exception`. Two such classes are `DataException` and `ConfigException`. You can either use these directly or subclass them. Finally, as for any piece of software, it's important to test the plug-ins you implement to ensure that they work as expected.

Connector and worker plug-ins tend to be easier to test than connectors because they have much simpler lifecycles. After being instantiated, the `configure()` method is called, followed by calls to the main method of the plug-in—`apply()` for transformations, `test()` for predicates, etc.—and then `close()`. Plug-ins also have fewer methods with important logic so you can focus your tests on these key methods and rely almost exclusively on unit tests to validate their logic.

In many cases, you can obtain good coverage and confidence in your logic by simply using unit tests. If you plan on combining multiple plug-ins in a pipeline, we recommend having some integration tests to validate that they work together. When writing unit tests, make sure you pay attention to the different combinations of arguments that the runtime might use to call the method. In particular, note which arguments might be `null`. For example, in the `Converter` API, the headers object passed to `fromConnectData()` is always non-`null`, while the value can be `null`.

Let's look at what is required to implement the different connector plug-ins.

Implementing Connector Plug-Ins

Apart from connectors, there are four other kinds of connector plug-ins that are used to extend Kafka Connect:

- `Transformation`
- `Predicate`
- `Converter`
- `HeaderConverter`

 By default, the `GET /connector-plugins` endpoint only lists connectors. If you want to see all the connector plug-ins that are currently installed in your Kafka Connect runtime, from Kafka 3.2 onward you can set the `connectorsOnly` flag to `false`:

```
curl localhost:8083/connector-plugins?connectorsOnly=false
```

Each connector plug-in type has its own class or classes that form the API that you need to implement; however, there is some overlap in the kinds of methods these classes include. We include every method for completeness; however, there are some common best practices for how to implement the `config()` and `configure()` methods, and what kinds of `Exception` you can throw.

To provide specific configuration settings for your connector plug-in, you construct a `ConfigDef` object. This is the same type that is returned by the `config()` method in the Connector API. In the configure() method of your connector plug-in, you receive a Map containing the configuration. Instead of using this Map directly, you should construct an AbstractConfig using your ConfigDef object. This allows you to use getters to parse and access the configuration values with the correct type. For a deeper dive into the ConfigDef object and how to instantiate both ConfigDef and AbstractConfig, see "Configurations" on page 314.

When encountering errors, each of the main methods in the connector plug-ins can tell the runtime how to react by throwing specific exceptions. These main methods are:

- apply() for Transformation
- test() for Predicate
- fromConnectData() and toConnectData() from Converter
- fromConnectHeader() and toConnectHeader() from HeaderConverter

If you throw a RetriableException (or a subclass) from these methods, the runtime attempts to rerun the method after a short interval if errors.retry.timeout is set to a value larger than 0 (default is 0 milliseconds). If this timeout expires while the method is still throwing a RetriableException, the record is skipped. Otherwise, if the method returns any other RuntimeException, such as DataException, the runtime decides what to do based on the value of errors.tolerance. If errors.tolerance is set to none (the default), it fails the related task, and if it is set to all, it skips the record.

Now let's look at each of the four kinds of connector plug-ins in more detail.

The Transformation API

The transformation plug-in is the one you are most likely to have to implement. This is because although Kafka Connect has a number of built-in transformations, their logic depends very much on the data being processed.

Transformations allow you to make lightweight transformations to records as they flow through Kafka Connect. A transformation is a class that implements the Transformation interface. This interface has two methods:

- R apply(R record)
- ConfigDef config()

In addition, the Transformation interface implements the Configurable and Closeable interfaces, which contain the following two methods:

- void configure(Map<String, ?> configs)

- void close()

You are required to implement all of these methods.

The runtime creates one instance of the transformation for each task of the connector. New instances are created if tasks are stopped and restarted.

The apply() method

The apply() method is the main method, as it performs the transformation. This method takes a single argument, which is a record to transform. The argument has the R extends ConnectRecord<R> type, so transformations can accept both SourceRecord and SinkRecord objects and run in source or sink data pipelines. The method returns the transformed record with the same type.

The apply() method can return the original record if no transformations are necessary, null if the record should be dropped, or a new, transformed record. When transforming a record, you should not modify the incoming record, but instead always create a new instance. You can do that by calling the newRecord() method on the incoming ConnectRecord.

For example, a transformation that overrides the topic field and always sets it to newtopic could use the following logic:

```
@Override
public R apply(R record) {
    return record.newRecord("newtopic",
                            record.kafkaPartition(),
                            record.keySchema(),
                            record.key(),
                            record.valueSchema(),
                            record.value(),
                            record.timestamp());
}
```

The runtime calls this method once for each record. In a source pipeline, it receives records returned by the source connector. In a sink pipeline, it receives records once they have been converted by the converter.

The config() method

As for other connector plug-ins, the config() method allows defining configuration for the transformation. This method returns the configuration settings for the transformation as a ConfigDef object.

This method has no default implementation, so if your transformation has no config-uration settings, you still need to return an empty ConfigDef instance. For example:

```
public static final ConfigDef CONFIG_DEF = new ConfigDef();

@Override
public ConfigDef config() {
    return CONFIG_DEF;
}
```

The runtime calls this method when users retrieve the transformation's config-uration using the GET /connector-plugins/<TRANSFORMATION>/config endpoint, where <TRANSFORMATION> is your transformation class. It is also called when creating a connector with the transformation.

The configure() method

The configure() method configures the transformation so that it is ready to be used. The argument is a Map<String, ?> that contains only the configuration settings that were provided with the prefix for that transformation; for example, if the transforma-tion alias is addSuffix, the prefix is transform.addSuffix..

The method is called by the runtime when the transformation is created.

The close() method

The close() method allows releasing resources that the transformation is using. The runtime calls it just after it calls stop() on the sink or source task that is using the transformation.

The Predicate API

As explained in Chapter 3, the role of predicates is to determine if a transformation should be applied. A predicate is a class that implements the Predicate interface. This interface has two methods:

- boolean test(R record)
- ConfigDef config()

In addition, the Predicate interface implements the Configurable and AutoClose able interfaces, with the following two methods:

- void configure(Map<String, ?> configs)
- void close()

You must implement all these methods.

The test() method

The `test()` method is the main method for the plug-in and determines if the associated transformation should run or not. The transformation runs if this method returns `true` and the `negate` flag has not been set, or if it returns `false` and `negate` is set to `true`. This method takes a single argument, which is a record. This argument has the `R extends ConnectRecord<R>` type, so predicates can accept both `SourceRecord` and `SinkRecord` objects and run in source or sink data pipelines.

For example, the `RecordIsTombstone` predicate has the following logic that returns `true` if the record is a tombstone, i.e. its value is `null`:

```
@Override
public boolean test(R record) {
    return record.value() == null;
}
```

The runtime calls this method once for each record. In a source pipeline, it receives records returned by the source connector. In a sink pipeline, it receives records once they have been returned by the converter.

The config() method

The `config()` method allows defining configuration for the predicate. This method returns the configuration settings for the predicate as a `ConfigDef` object.

This method has no default implementation, so if your predicate has no configuration settings, you still need to return an empty `ConfigDef` instance. For example:

```
public static final ConfigDef CONFIG_DEF = new ConfigDef();

@Override
public ConfigDef config() {
    return CONFIG_DEF;
}
```

The runtime calls this method when users retrieve the predicate configuration using the `GET /connector-plugins/<PREDICATE>/config` endpoint where `<PREDICATE>` is your predicate class and when creating a connector with the predicate.

The configure() method

The `configure()` method configures the predicate such that it is ready for it to be used. The argument is a `Map<String, ?>` that contains only the configuration settings that have the predicate's prefix; for example, a predicate with alias `topicMatch` receives the configuration settings that have been prefixed with `predicates.topicMatch.`. This method is called by the runtime when the predicate is created.

The close() method

This method allows releasing resources that the predicate used. The runtime calls it just after it calls stop() on the sink or source task that is using the predicate.

The Converter and HeaderConverter APIs

Converters are used to serialize and deserialize data before it is sent to or from Kafka. There are two interfaces that you can implement if you want to write your own converter. For converting record keys and values, you implement Converter, and for converting headers you implement HeaderConverter. Some converters, such as the StringConverter, implement both interfaces.

Converters should be specifically focused on serializing and deserializing data between the Kafka Connect internal record format and byte arrays. If you need to manipulate the data in some way rather than just convert it between formats, you should use a transformation for the manipulation part.

The Converter interface has the following methods:

- byte[] fromConnectData(String topic, Schema schema, Object value)
- byte[] fromConnectData(String topic, Headers headers, Schema schema, Object value)
- SchemaAndValue toConnectData(String topic, byte[] value)
- SchemaAndValue toConnectData(String topic, Headers headers, byte[] value)
- ConfigDef config()
- void configure(Map<String, ?> configs, boolean isKey)

The methods you are required to implement are configure() and the fromConnect Data(), and toConnectData() methods that don't take a Headers argument.

The HeaderConverter interface has the following methods:

- byte[] fromConnectHeader(String topic, String headerKey, Schema schema, Object value)
- SchemaAndValue toConnectHeader(String topic, String headerKey, byte[] value)
- ConfigDef config()

In addition, the HeaderConverter interface implements the Configurable and Close able interfaces, which add the following two methods:

- void configure(Map<String, ?> configs)
- void close()

You are required to implement all of these methods.

Each connector that is running on the worker gets its own instance of the configured key, value, and header converters. Even if they all use the same class, the runtime uses separate instances for each type of conversion it needs to do.

The fromConnectData() methods

There are two fromConnectData() methods. Both have the arguments topic, schema, and value, and one additionally has a headers argument. The topic is the name of the topic the record is being sent to as a Java String. The value is passed as a generic Java Object and represents either the record key or value, depending on what this converter is being used for. The schema is the schema for the key or value; it is of type Schema and can be null. The headers argument is of type Headers and contains the headers for the record, if there are any. The method returns a byte[], which the runtime uses as either the key or value for the record when it sends it to Kafka.

The runtime only interacts directly with the method that includes record headers. This was added in Kafka 2.4. To enable backward compatibility, this method has a default implementation that calls the other fromConnectData() method, ignoring the headers. Unless you need your connector to work with older versions of Kafka, we recommend implementing the method that includes headers so that you have the option to influence them. In that case, you can simply throw an Exception from the other method, since the runtime never calls it.

The schema passed in can be null, but the value can also be null if the SourceRecord has a null key or value. You can return a null byte[] from this method if you want the subsequent Kafka record to have a null key or value. If your converter is unable to serialize the data, you should throw an Exception.

For example, the StringConverter returns null if the passed-in value was null, and it throws a DataException if it can't serialize the value:

```
public byte[] fromConnectData(String topic, Schema schema, Object value) {
    try {
        return serializer.serialize(topic,
                                    value == null ? null : value.toString());
    } catch (SerializationException e) {
        throw new DataException("Failed to serialize to a string: ", e);
    }
}

public byte[] serialize(String topic, String data) {
```

```
    try {
        if (data == null)
            return null;
        else
            return data.getBytes(encoding);
    } catch (UnsupportedEncodingException e) {
        throw new SerializationException(
            "Error when serializing string to byte[] due to unsupported " +
            "encoding " + encoding);
    }
}
```

The `headers` argument that is passed in is a reference to the `RecordHeaders` object for the record. This means that any changes you make to the headers are included in the resulting record that is sent on to Kafka. For example, the schema registry from Apicurio has converters that add the ID of the schema as a header for downstream applications to use. The `headers` argument is always non-`null`, so you can safely add additional headers without constructing a new `Headers` object. For example, to always add a header called `headerKey`, you could implement this method in the following way:

```
public byte[] fromConnectData(String topic, Headers headers,
                              Schema schema, Object value) {
    headers.add("headerKey", "headerValue".getBytes(StandardCharsets.UTF_8));
    if (value == null) {
        return null;
    } else {
        return value.toString().getBytes(StandardCharsets.UTF_8);
    }
}
```

The runtime runs the header converter before the key or value converters, so any changes you make here are not seen by the header converter.

The runtime calls the `fromConnectData()` method every time it processes a record in a source pipeline. It calls the method after it has called the connector and any configured transformations, but before it sends the record to Kafka.

The toConnectData() methods

There are two `toConnectData()` methods. Both receive the topic name as a `String` and the record key or value as a `byte[]`. One method also has a `headers` argument that is of type `Headers`, containing any headers that were included in the Kafka record. The return type of the method is a `SchemaAndValue` object. This is used by the runtime to construct the `ConnectRecord` that is passed downstream.

Similar to `fromConnectData()`, the runtime only interacts directly with the method that includes record headers. To enable backward compatibility, this method has a default implementation that calls the other `toConnectData()` method, ignoring headers. Unless you need your connector to work with Kafka versions older than 2.4, you should implement the method that includes the headers and throw an Exception from the other method, since it is never called.

The runtime calls this method on the key and value converters even if the record from Kafka has a null key or value. This means the value argument can be null. If you want the subsequent SinkRecord to have a null key or value, you still need to return a SchemaAndValue object. You can either construct one with an optional schema and null value, or use the NULL static variable in the SchemaAndValue class.

Unlike the fromConnectData() method, you can't influence the headers that are added to the resulting SinkRecord. If your converter cannot deserialize the data, you can throw an Exception. For example, the StringConverter has the following logic to convert key and value byte arrays to SchemaAndValue objects:

```
public SchemaAndValue toConnectData(String topic, Headers headers,
                                    byte[] value) {
    try {
        return new SchemaAndValue(Schema.OPTIONAL_STRING_SCHEMA,
                                  deserializer.deserialize(topic, value));
    } catch (SerializationException e) {
        throw new DataException("Failed to deserialize string: ", e);
    }
}

public String deserialize(String topic, byte[] data) {
    try {
        if (data == null)
            return null;
        else
            return new String(data, encoding);
    } catch (UnsupportedEncodingException e) {
        throw new SerializationException("Error when deserializing byte[]" +
            " to string due to unsupported encoding " + encoding);
    }
}
```

The runtime calls the toConnectData() method when it receives a new record from Kafka in a sink pipeline.

The fromConnectHeader() method

This method has four arguments:

topic
> The name of the topic where the record containing the header is being sent. It has type String.

headerKey
> The key of the header as a String.

schema
> The schema for the header value. It has type Schema and may be null.

value
> The value of the header as a Java Object and may be null.

The method returns a byte[] representing the value of the header. The runtime uses this value when it constructs the record to send to Kafka. Similar to fromCon nectData(), you can return null from this method or throw an Exception if the serialization fails. For example, the SimpleHeaderConverter has the following logic:

```
public byte[] fromConnectHeader(String topic, String headerKey,
                                Schema schema, Object value) {
    if (value == null) {
        return null;
    }
    return Values.convertToString(schema, value).getBytes(UTF_8);
}
```

The runtime calls this method for every header in the records it processes as part of a source pipeline. This happens after the connector and any configured transformations have run, but before it sends the record to Kafka. The runtime does header conversion first, so the headers that are passed to key and value converters have already been through a header converter.

The toConnectHeader() method

The toConnectHeader() method has the arguments topic, headerKey, and value. The topic is a Java String of the name of the topic the record containing this header came from. The headerKey is a String of the header key and the value is a byte[] of the header value. The method returns a SchemaAndValue that represents the converted header value.

The value passed into this method can be null. If you want to return a header with a null value, you still need to return a SchemaAndValue. You can create a SchemaAndValue with null for both the schema and value, or use an optional schema.

For example, the SimpleHeaderConverter has logic similar to the following:

```
public SchemaAndValue toConnectHeader(String topic, String headerKey,
                                      byte[] value) {
    if (value == null) {
        return new SchemaAndValue(null, null); ❶
    }
    try {
        String str = new String(value, UTF_8);
```

```
        return Values.parseString(str); ❷
    } catch (NoSuchElementException e) {
        throw new DataException("Failed to deserialize value for header", e); ❸
    } catch (Throwable t) {
        return new SchemaAndValue(Schema.BYTES_SCHEMA, value); ❹
    }
}
```

❶ If the value is null, the converter returns a new SchemaAndValue with null for both arguments.

❷ If there's a value, the converter attempts to parse it as a String.

❸ If the parsing fails due to NoSuchElementException, the converter throws a DataException.

❹ The converter has a catch-all for other errors that sets the schema to BYTES_SCHEMA and returns the raw value.

The runtime calls this method during a sink pipeline for each header in each record it receives from Kafka. The returned SchemaAndValue is passed on to any configured transformations and the connector. Unlike in a source flow, in a sink flow the key and value converters receive the raw header value; they don't have access to the converted value.

The config() methods

Both the Converter and HeaderConverter interfaces have an identical config() method. This method returns the configuration settings for the converter as a Config Def object. The Converter interface includes a default implementation for config() that returns an empty ConfigDef object. This is not the case for HeaderConverter, so you must implement it for this plug-in type.

The runtime calls this method when the GET /connector-plugins/<CONVERTER>/ config endpoint is called, where <CONVERTER> is your converter class.

The configure() methods

The Converter and HeaderConverter interfaces both have a configure() method. Both methods are used to configure the converter, but they have slightly different arguments. They both have a Map<String, ?> argument that contains only the configuration settings that were provided with the relevant prefix. For a Converter, these are the configurations that have either the converter.key. or converter.value. prefix, and for a HeaderConverter, the configurations with the converter.header. prefix. The method from the Converter interface also takes a boolean value that is true if the converter has been configured as a key converter, or `false` if it is a value converter.

The runtime calls this method when it creates the task for the connector that is using this converter.

The close() method

This method is only present in the `HeaderConverter` interface. It gives the converter an opportunity to close any open streams or release resources it is using. The runtime calls it just after it calls `stop()` on the sink or source task that is using the `Header Converter`.

Now that we have covered connector plug-ins, let's look at worker plug-ins.

Implementing Worker Plug-Ins

There are three different kinds of worker plug-ins you can implement to customize the Kafka Connect runtime:

- `ConfigProvider`
- `ConnectorClientConfigOverridePolicy`
- `ConnectRestExtension`

In Chapter 7, we explain the roles of these plug-ins and show examples of how to configure and use them. In this section we look at their APIs and explain what you need to do to implement your own worker plug-ins.

Unlike connector plug-ins, there is no way to list the different worker plug-ins that are installed in your Kafka Connect cluster. There is also no way for worker plug-ins to advertise the custom configuration settings they accept, so make sure you clearly document any configuration options that your worker plug-in has.

The Kafka Connect runtime uses the Java Service Provider mechanism to load worker plug-ins. This means, in addition to implementing the required methods, you must include a service provider configuration file in your plug-in package. If you don't include this file, Kafka Connect is not able to load the plug-in from a plug-ins directory.

You need to create a file called `META-INF/service/<PLUGIN_INTERFACE>` where `<PLUGIN_INTERFACE>` is the Java interface your plug-in implements; for example, `org.apache.kafka.common.config.provider.ConfigProvider` for a ConfigProvider plug-in. The contents of this file must be a single line that specifies the package and class name of your plug-in. For example, given a custom configuration provider in package `com.example` with class name `CustomConfigProvider`, the file would contain:

```
com.example.CustomConfigProvider
```

The ConfigProvider API

A configuration provider is a worker plug-in that implements the `ConfigProvider` interface. Configuration providers are generally used for either adding sensitive credentials to connector plug-in configuration, or to allow connectors in different environments to have environment-specific configurations.

When using a configuration provider, you need to use the format `${<ALIAS>:<PATH>:<KEY>}` for configuration values, where `<ALIAS>` is the alias for the configuration provider, the `<PATH>` is an optional path for the configuration, and `<KEY>` is the configuration key.

The `ConfigProvider` interface contains the following methods:

- `ConfigData get(String path)`
- `ConfigData get(String path, Set<String> keys)`
- `void subscribe(String path, Set<String> keys, ConfigChangeCallback callback)`
- `void unsubscribe(String path, Set<String> keys, ConfigChangeCallback callback)`
- `void unsubscribeAll()`

In addition, the `ConfigProvider` interface implements the `Configurable` and `Closeable` interfaces, which add the following two methods:

- `void configure(Map<String, ?> configs)`
- `void close()`

You are only required to implement the `get()`, `configure()` and `close()` methods.

As described in Chapter 7, you must enable configuration providers in the Kafka Connect runtime configuration in order to use them.

The get() methods

There are two different `get()` methods in the `ConfigProvider` interface. Both have a `String` argument, which represents the path of the configuration being retrieved. One also has a `Set<String>` of keys at the given path. Both methods return a `ConfigData` object, which has two fields: a `Map<String, String>` of the requested configurations, and a Long indicating the time to live (TTL) in milliseconds. (This is an optional indicator that the ConfigProvider can set to tell the runtime when a particular configuration is due to expire.)

The runtime only interacts with the get() method that has both the path and keys as arguments. This is the main method for the ConfigProvider. If the path has been omitted from the configuration, the runtime calls this method with an empty string for the path. Although you are required to implement the other method that only has the keys as the argument, you can throw an exception from this method, since the runtime never calls it. The runtime expects the returned ConfigData to contain a Map<String, String>, where the keys match the keys that were passed into the method. If it cannot find a particular key in the Map, it just instantiates the component with the raw configuration, i.e. with ${<ALIAS>:<PATH>:<KEY>} as the configuration value.

The runtime uses the TTL value differently depending on how it has been configured. If the config.reload.action configuration is set to restart (the default), it schedules a restart of the connector after the time indicated. If the configuration is set to none, the runtime ignores the TTL value.

When the TTL expires for a particular configuration, the runtime restarts the related connector, but not the specific plug-in that is using the configuration. This means if you use a configuration provider with, for example, a converter configuration, only the connector using that converter is restarted. However, because the converter has not been restarted, it does not use the latest configuration value. For this reason, we recommend only using configuration providers that include a TTL in their ConfigData with connectors, not other kinds of plug-ins.

For example, the FileConfigProvider has the following get() method:

```
public ConfigData get(String path, Set<String> keys) {
    Map<String, String> data = new HashMap<>();
    if (path == null || path.isEmpty()) {
        return new ConfigData(data);   ❶
    }
    try (Reader reader = Files.newBufferedReader(Paths.get(path))) {   ❷
        Properties properties = new Properties();
        properties.load(reader);
        for (String key : keys) {   ❸
            String value = properties.getProperty(key);
            if (value != null) {
                data.put(key, value);
            }
        }
    }
```

```
        return new ConfigData(data);
    } catch (IOException e) {
        log.error("Could not read properties from file {}", path, e);
        throw new ConfigException(
            "Could not read properties from file " + path); ❹
    }
}
```

❶ The `FileConfigProvider` implicitly requires a path. Otherwise it returns a `ConfigData` object containing an empty map, which results in the raw configuration being used.

❷ Each time it is called, this configuration provider re-reads the entire file at the specified path so that it's able to see new values if the file changes.

❸ The `ConfigData` object that is returned has an entry for each key that was passed in, given that it is present in the file.

❹ If the file cannot be read for some reason, it throws a `ConfigException`, which fails the operation; for example, it prevents a connector using this configuration provider from starting, since the configuration cannot be loaded.

The runtime calls the `get()` method that takes a path and keys each time it needs to retrieve a configuration from the `ConfigProvider`. This happens when it is creating a plug-in or client that is configured using a `ConfigProvider`.

The configure() method

This method is used to configure the configuration provider. It has a single argument, which is a `Map<String, ?>` of the configuration keys and values set in the Kafka Connect runtime configuration. Users specify these settings using the format `config.providers.<ALIAS>.param.<KEY>=<VALUE>`.

The runtime calls the `configure()` method when it creates an instance of the configuration provider.

The close() method

The `close()` method allows the configuration provider to release resources. If the configuration provider is used by a client or plug-in, the runtime only calls this method when the worker is shutting down. If the configuration provider has been created but is not referenced in any configuration, the runtime calls `close()` immediately after calling `configure()`.

The subscribe(), unsubscribe(), and unsubscribeAll() methods

The runtime does not call these methods, so we recommend you do not implement them. They are all optional and have default implementations that throw an Unsuppor tedOperationException.

The ConnectorClientConfigOverridePolicy API

This plug-in allows administrators to police the client configurations that can be overridden by connectors. The policy applies to the clients (producers, consumers, and admin clients) that are used by the runtime to run tasks. Source tasks create producers and can also use admin clients if automatic topic creation is enabled, as well as consumers if configured with a per-connector offsets topic. Sink tasks create consumers, but also producers and admin clients if a dead letter queue is enabled.

The ConnectorClientConfigOverridePolicy interface has a single method:

- List<ConfigValue> validate(ConnectorClientConfigRequest request)

It also implements the Configurable and AutoCloseable interfaces, so it has the following two methods:

- void configure(Map<String, ?> configs)
- void close()

You must implement these three methods.

There is a single instance of ConnectorClientConfigOverridePolicy for each worker that is created when the worker starts.

The validate() method

This method is the main method and validates whether client overrides defined in the connector configuration are valid or not. Its only argument, ConnectorClient ConfigRequest, contains details about the connector configuration. It exposes the following methods to access the values:

Map<String, Object> clientProps()
    The the configuration overrides specified in the connector configuration for the client being created.

ClientType clientType()
    The type of client being created. ClientType is an enum with three possible values: PRODUCER, CONSUMER and ADMIN.

```
String connectorName()
```
The name of the connector.

```
ConnectorType connectorType()
```
The type of the connector, the ConnectorType enum has three possible values: SOURCE, SINK, and UNKNOWN. UNKNOWN is not used.

```
Class<? extends Connector> connectorClass()
```
The class of the connector.

The validate() method returns a List<ConfigValue> collection. The list should contain a ConfigValue object for each configuration that is returned by clientProps(). You can create an instance using the ConfigValue(String name, Object value, List<Object> recommendedValues, List<String> error Messages) constructor.

For configurations that are valid, you should set the recommendedValues and error Messages to empty List. Otherwise, you should insert at least one error message so users know why the configuration was rejected. If no error messages are specified, the configuration is treated as valid. This method should never return null.

For example, the PrincipalConnectorClientConfigOverridePolicy has a validate() method similar to this:

```
public final List<ConfigValue> validate(ConnectorClientConfigRequest request) {
    Map<String, Object> inputConfig = request.clientProps(); ❶
    return inputConfig.entrySet() ❷
        .stream()
        .map(this::configValue)
        .collect(Collectors.toList());
}

protected ConfigValue configValue(Map.Entry<String, Object> configEntry) {
    ConfigValue configValue = new ConfigValue(
            configEntry.getKey(),
            configEntry.getValue(),
            new ArrayList<>(),
            new ArrayList<>()
    );
    if (!ALLOWED_CONFIG.contains(configValue.name())) { ❸
        configValue.addErrorMessage(
            "The '" + policyName() + "' policy does not allow '" +
            configValue.name() + "' to be overridden in the " +
            "connector configuration.");
    }
    return configValue;
}
```

① The plug-in first grabs the client overrides provided by the user in the connector configuration.

② For each entry in the input configuration, it constructs a `ConfigValue` to return.

③ If the configuration is not allowed to be overridden, it adds an error message to the `ConfigValue` object. This policy only checks the configuration key against a list of allowed keys. Other policies could additionally validate if the configuration value is allowed, or evaluate other configuration metadata, such as the client type.

This method is called when the runtime creates clients when it starts tasks.

The configure() method

The `configure()` method configures the plug-in such that it is ready for it to be used. The argument is a `Map<String, ?>` that contains every runtime configuration.

The method is called when the plug-in is created.

The close() method

This method allows closing resources that were used, and it is called by the runtime during worker shutdown. Before Kafka version 3.5.0, this method was not called.

The ConnectRestExtension APIs

REST extensions allow customizing the Kafka Connect REST API by injecting JAX-RS components. You inject *Filters* to access and modify request and response headers, or *Interceptors* to access and modify request and response bodies.

> Implementing JAX-RS Filters and Interceptors is outside the scope of this book. If you want to implement your own `ConnectRestEx tension` with a custom Filter or Interceptor, make sure that you understand these components. We recommend taking a look at Chapter 12, Filters and Interceptors, of Bill Burke's *RESTful Java with JAX-RS 2.0* (O'Reilly).

These plug-ins implement the `ConnectRestExtension` interface, which has a single method:

- `void register(ConnectRestExtensionContext restPluginContext)`

The interface also implements the `Configurable`, `Closeable`, and `Versioned` interfaces, so you must also implement the following methods:

- `void configure(Map<String, ?> configs)`
- `void close()`
- `String version()`

There is a single instance of each `ConnectRestExtension` plug-in for each worker that is created when the worker starts.

The register() method

The `register()` method is the main method and allows injecting JAX-RS components. It has a single argument, a `ConnectRestExtensionContext` object that has two methods:

- `Configurable<? extends Configurable<?>> configurable()`
- `ConnectClusterState clusterState()`

The `configurable()` method returns a `javax.ws.rs.core.Configurable` object (not to be confused with the `org.apache.kafka.common.Configurable` interface with the `configure()` method). This JAX-RS `Configurable` object has a few `register()` methods to inject Filters and Interceptors.

The `clusterState()` method returns an instance of a class that implements the `ConnectClusterState` interface. This interface has a few methods to describe the connectors (including their state and configuration) currently running in the Kafka Connect cluster.

For example, the built-in `BasicAuthSecurityRestExtension` REST extension has the following logic:

```
public void register(ConnectRestExtensionContext restPluginContext) {
    log.trace("Registering JAAS basic auth filter");
    restPluginContext.configurable().register(
        new JaasBasicAuthFilter(configuration.get()));
    log.trace("Finished registering JAAS basic auth filter");
}
```

It registers `JaasBasicAuthFilter`, which is a class that implements `Container RequestFilter` to interact with request headers. This class then uses the `Authoriza tion` header to perform the basic authorization.

The `register()` method is called when the plug-in is created, but after the `config ure()` method.

The configure() method

The configure() method configures the ConnectRestExtension so that it is ready to be used. The argument is a Map<String, ?> that contains every runtime configuration. The method is called when the plug-in is created.

The close() method

This method allows closing resources that were used by the plug-in. It is called when the worker shuts down.

The version() method

This method works like the version() method in the Connector and Task APIs. It returns the version of the REST extension as a String. This method is currently not used by the runtime.

Summary

In this chapter we looked at the APIs you need to implement to build your own connector and worker plug-ins for Connect.

The four types of connector plug-ins are Transformation, Predicate, Converter, and HeaderConverter. These interfaces all have config() and configure() methods to manage their configurations. You should implement these methods in a similar way to the corresponding methods in connectors and tasks.

In the Transformation interface, apply() is the method that performs the transformation and returns the transformed record. It can also return null to filter the record, or the original record if no transformations are required. A Predicate determines if transformations should run and must implement the test() method that returns a boolean. Converters often implement both the Converter and Header Converter interfaces. The main methods in these interfaces are fromConnectData(), fromConnectHeader(), toConnectData(), and toConnectHeader(). These are all used to convert records between their Kafka and Kafka Connect formats.

The second part of the chapter detailed the worker plug-ins ConfigProvider, Connec torClientConfigOverridePolicy, and ConnectRestExtension. Unlike connector plug-ins, there is no way for worker plug-ins to advertise the configuration they accept. This means it's very important to properly document your worker plug-ins.

Both ConnectorClientConfigOverridePolicy and ConnectRestExtension plug-ins are given access to all of the runtime configurations in their configure() method. However, ConfigProvider plug-ins are only given access to the specific parameters that have been set for them. Configuration providers supply values via their get()

method and can include a time to live for values that should be regularly refreshed. The runtime determines if particular client overrides are allowed by calling `vali date()` on the configured `ConnectorClientConfigOverridePolicy` plug-ins. They can also provide error messages for invalid configurations. Finally, `ConnectRest Extension` plug-ins can inject JAX-RS components to customize the REST API by implementing the `register()` method.

Once you have written your custom plug-in, you need to build and test it. Refer back to Chapter 11 for details on building plug-ins. When testing plug-ins, focus on the main methods that do the work and make sure your integration tests include all the combinations of plug-ins you need to support.

Index

About the Authors

Mickael Maison is a committer and the chair of the Project Management Committee (PMC) for Apache Kafka. He has been contributing to Apache Kafka and its wider ecosystem since 2015.

Mickael currently works as a principal software engineer in the Kafka team at Red Hat. He has over 10 years of software development experience. Previously, he was part of the Event Streams team at IBM that runs hundreds of Kafka clusters for customers.

He also has deep expertise in Kafka Connect's internals. He has made a number of code contributions to Kafka Connect itself and regularly reviews pull requests and KIPs from the community on this component.

Finally, Mickael really enjoys sharing expertise and teaching. He has been writing monthly Kafka digests since 2018 and enjoys presenting at conferences.

Kate Stanley is a software engineer, technical speaker, and Java Champion. She has experience running Apache Kafka on Kubernetes, developing enterprise Kafka applications, and writing connectors for Kafka Connect.

Kate currently works as a principal software engineer in the Red Hat Kafka team. She also contributes to multiple projects in the Kafka ecosystem, including the open source Kafka operator, Strimzi. Kate started her journey with Kafka as part of the Event Streams team at IBM in 2018, quickly becoming well known in the community.

Alongside development, Kate has a passion for presenting and sharing knowledge. She is a regular speaker at technical conferences around the world, including events such as Kafka Summit, Jfokus, Devoxx UK, and JavaOne. She has authored two LinkedIn Learning courses on MicroProfile and Apache Kafka and written an eBook on writing microservices with Java.

Colophon

The animal on the cover of *Kafka Connect* is an Argentine horned frog (*Ceratophrys ornata*), more affectionately known as the Pac-Man frog.

Argentine horned frogs earned their Pac-Man nickname due to the size of their mouth. They have extremely powerful jaws that are approximately one-third to one-half the length of their bodies, which gives them the appearance of being only a head with legs attached. Their jaw is lined with tooth-like protrusions that help them grip their prey. Their typical body color is bright green with red markings, though they can also be found in other shades of reddish-brown, yellow, black, white, and green. The upper eyelids of an Argentine horned frog have fleshy projectiles that are called horns.

These frogs are native to South America and are primarily found in Brazil, Uruguay, and Argentina. They live in rainforests and tropical swamplands, and can also be found in grasslands near water, ditches, and irrigated cropland. They are carnivorous ambush predators that enjoy feasting on worms, roaches, small rodents, snakes, lizards, and a variety of other insects.

Argentine horned frogs are currently listed as near threatened on endangered species lists. Many of the animals on O'Reilly covers are endangered; all of them are important to the world.

The cover illustration is by Karen Montgomery, based on an antique line engraving from Lydekker's *Royal Natural History*. The cover fonts are Gilroy Semibold and Guardian Sans. The text font is Adobe Minion Pro; the heading font is Adobe Myriad Condensed; and the code font is Dalton Maag's Ubuntu Mono.

O'REILLY®

Learn from experts.
Become one yourself.

Books | Live online courses
Instant answers | Virtual events
Videos | Interactive learning

Get started at oreilly.com.

Printed in the USA
CPSIA information can be obtained
at www.ICGtesting.com
JSHW061731301023
51111JS00013B/97

9 781098 126537